Christoph Gladisch

Extending KeY for the Verification of C Programs

Christoph Gladisch

Extending KeY for the Verification of C Programs

The Development of a Prototype

VDM Verlag Dr. Müller

Imprint

Bibliographic information by the German National Library: The German National Library lists this publication at the German National Bibliography; detailed bibliographic information is available on the Internet at http://dnb.d-nb.de.

Cover image: www.purestockx.com

Publisher:
VDM Verlag Dr. Müller Aktiengesellschaft & Co. KG, Dudweiler Landstr. 125 a, 66123 Saarbrücken, Germany,
Phone +49 681 9100-698, Fax +49 681 9100-988,
Email: info@vdm-verlag.de

Produced in USA and UK by:
Lightning Source Inc., La Vergne, Tennessee, USA
Lightning Source UK Ltd., Milton Keynes, UK
BookSurge LLC, 5341 Dorchester Road, Suite 16, North Charleston, SC 29418, USA

ISBN: 978-3-639-00002-3

Acknowledgement

In first place I would like to thank my supervisor Prof. Dr. Bernhard Beckert for offering me much time of fruitful discussions, for supporting my visit at the Chalmers University of Technology in Gothenburg, and for his patience during the writing of the thesis. I thank Prof. Dr. Reiner Hähnle who offered me an office in Chalmers and who integrated me into his reasearch group. Also I would like thank Prof. Dr. Bernhard Beckert and Prof. Dr. Furbach for offering me an office at the University of Koblenz-Landau and allowing me to participate in the artificial intelligence working group AGKI. My special thanks is to Dr. Richard Bubel who explained to me the implementation of the KeY-System during my visit at the University of Karlsruhe. I also specially thank Celina Jelonek for proof-reading over 200 pages of the thesis. Finally I thank my parents and grand parents for their great support.

Table of contents

List of tables xi

List of figures and diagrams 1

1 Preliminaries 1

1.1 Overview 2
1.2 Related Work 3
1.3 Notation 5

2 C and Java 5

2.1 Representation of Integers 6
2.2 ANSI C 10
2.3 MISRA C 12
2.4 C0 13
2.4.1 Types 14
2.4.2 Operators 14
2.4.3 BNF-Syntax 16
2.4.4 Program Variables 21
2.5 C++ 21
2.6 JAVA 22
2.7 JAVA CARD 25

3 Formal Basis for Verification 25

3.1 Dynamic Logic 26
3.1.1 Syntax 28
3.1.2 Semantic 35
3.1.3 Satisfaction, Validity, and Consequence 36
3.1.4 Application to Software Verification 36
3.1.4.1 Functional Correctness 37
3.1.4.2 Program States 38
3.1.4.3 Partial and Total Correctness 39
3.2 Substitution and Term rewriting 40

3.3 Sequent Calculus . . . 41
3.3.1 First-order Calculus . . . 42
3.3.2 Integration of Rewrite Rules . . . 43
3.3.3 Generalisations for Dynamic Logic . . . 44

4 KeY Concepts . . . 45

4.1 The KeY-System . . . 45
4.1.1 Taclets . . . 48
4.2 Updates . . . 49
4.2.1 Syntax . . . 49
4.2.2 Semantic . . . 53
4.2.3 Substitution and Rewriting Revised . . . 54
4.2.4 Update Calculus . . . 55
4.3 Datatype Refinement for Integer Arithmetic . . . 57
4.3.1 Motivation . . . 58
4.3.2 Syntax . . . 61
4.3.3 Semantic . . . 64
4.3.4 Properties of S_{KeY} . . . 65
4.3.5 Calculus . . . 69

5 Handling of Special Concepts in C: Program Variables, Pointer Operators and Assignments . . . 69

5.1 Preliminaries . . . 69
5.1.1 Notation . . . 70
5.1.2 Motivation . . . 72
5.1.3 Lambda Calculus . . . 72
5.1.3.1 Syntax . . . 72
5.1.3.2 α-conversion . . . 72
5.1.3.3 β-reduction . . . 73
5.2 Representation of Program Variables as Terms . . . 73
5.2.1 Motivation . . . 73
5.2.2 Representation of Simple Program Variables . . . 73
5.2.2.1 Mono Representation . . . 74
5.2.2.2 Dual Representation . . . 74
5.2.2.3 Accessor Path Representation . . . 74
5.2.3 Program Variables and Substructures . . . 75
5.2.4 Representation of Program Variables . . . 76
5.2.5 Syntax . . . 76
5.2.6 Calculus . . . 77
5.3 Unfolding . . . 78
5.4 Deep copy updates . . . 78
5.4.1 Syntax . . . 79

5.4.2 Semantic . . . 81
5.4.2.1 Valuation Examples . . . 83
5.4.3 Calculus . . . 83
5.4.4 Discussion . . . 85
5.4.4.1 Semantic . . . 86
5.4.4.2 Calculus . . . 86
5.5 Experiments . . . 87
5.5.1 List of Experiments . . . 87
5.5.2 Apply Update on Term . . . 100
5.5.3 Apply Update on Update . . . 106
5.5.4 Apply merged Updates on Term . . . 106
5.5.4.1 Apply on simple program variable . . . 114
5.5.4.2 Apply Update on Sub-Structure . . . 120
5.5.4.3 Apply Update on dereferenced Variable . . . 123
5.5.4.4 Apply Update on dereferenced Sub-Structure . . . 133

6 CDL . . . 133

6.0.5 Notation . . . 133
6.1 Syntax . . . 133
6.2 Semantic . . . 134
6.2.1 Operators . . . 134
6.2.1.1 Arithmetic operators . . . 134
6.2.1.2 Type conversion . . . 135
6.2.1.3 Comparison operators . . . 135
6.2.1.4 Logical Operators . . . 135
6.2.1.5 Bit-wise operators . . . 137
6.2.2 Semantic of statements 1 . . . 137
6.2.2.1 Definition . . . 139
6.2.2.2 Rules and soundness . . . 141
6.2.2.3 Discussion . . . 142
6.2.3 Semantic of statements 2 . . . 142
6.2.3.1 Definition . . . 145
6.2.3.2 Rules and soundness . . . 149

7 Adaption of Program Rules from KeY Calculi for CDL . . . 149

7.1 Notation . . . 150
7.2 Included rules . . . 150
7.3 Statements . . . 155
7.4 Derived Rules from DLJ . . . 155
7.4.1 Derivation of Rule 6.4.2 . . . 161
7.4.2 Rules for Simplifying Compound Expressions . . . 164
7.4.3 Rules for Handling Simple Expressions . . . 168

7.4.4 Rules for Handling Unary Operators 170
7.4.5 Rules for Handling Increment and Decrement Expressions . 172
7.4.6 Rules for Handling Type Casts 175
7.4.7 Rules for Conditional Expression and Numeric Comparison Operators 177
7.4.8 Rules for Handling Boolean Logical Operator 179

8 Implementation 179

8.1 Overview 180
8.2 Notation 182
8.3 `.key`-Files 182
8.3.1 javaC.key 186
8.3.2 Problem Files 187
8.3.3 Syntax of Terms and Formulas in KeY 187
8.4 Classes of the KeY prover 189
8.4.1 Main application classes 190
8.4.2 *SourceElements* 194
8.4.3 *Types* and *Sorts* 198
8.4.4 *Terms* and *Operators* 202
8.4.5 Conversion from *ProgramElements* to *Terms* 206
8.4.6 Updates 207
8.4.7 Program variables 214
8.4.8 Meta Constructs 216
8.4.8.1 AbstractMetaOperator 217
8.4.8.2 ProgramMetaConstruct 218
8.5 Implementation of the Prototype 219
8.5.1 JavaC 219
8.5.1.1 Type system 221
8.5.1.2 Statements 221
8.5.1.3 Expressions 222
8.5.1.4 Declarations 222
8.5.2 *ProgramSVSorts* for JavaC operators 223
8.5.3 Moving *ProgramVariables* and *AccessOps* to the logic part . 223
8.5.3.1 Modification of the classes `ProgramVariable` and `AccessOp` 224
8.5.3.2 Class `NonRigidFunctionVarySort` 225
8.5.3.3 Conversion by a meta construct 225
8.5.3.4 Conversion by the *TypeConverter* 226
8.5.3.5 Taclets 227
8.5.3.6 Updates 228
8.5.4 Unfolding 229
8.5.4.1 Traversing attributes of *ClassDeclarations* 229
8.5.4.2 Unfolding assignments in the program part 231

8.5.4.3 Unfolding of Terms 234
8.5.4.4 Unfolding of assignments in the logic part 235
8.5.4.5 Unfolding of comparisons 236
8.5.5 Guidelines for the implementation of deep copy updates . . 236
8.5.6 Reference and dereference operators 236
8.5.6.1 Implementation by meta constructs 239
8.5.6.2 Implementation by the *TypeConverter* 239
8.5.6.3 Handling of type informations 241
8.5.7 Dynamic creation and deletion 242
8.5.7.1 SubStruct 243
8.5.7.2 isDynamic 244
8.5.7.3 Dynamic creation 244
8.5.7.4 Dynamic deletion 245
8.5.7.5 Other related extensions 246
8.6 Examples 251

9 Summary and Conclusions 253

Appendix A List of modifications and extensions 255

Bibliography 255

List of tables

C0 operator precedence 15
Signature of C0 operators 16
Symbols 17
C0 syntax: global definitions and declarations 18
C0 syntax: components of declarations 19
C0 syntax: statements and expressions 20
C0 syntax: lexpression, basic_rexpr, type_specifier, elementary_type, var_declaration(s) 20
Propositional Inference Rules 42
First-Order Inference Rules. 43
Rewrite rule application 43
Global inference rules 45
Conditional Term 55
Term Rewrite Rules. 56
Quantified update application 56
Derived Inference Rules 57
Dereferenciation Rules 83
Referenciation Rules 84
Update Application Rules 84
Program Variable Rules 85
Utility Rules 85
Application of deep copy updates on terms 88
Application of deep copy updates on deep copy updates 88
Application of merged deep copy updates on simple program variables 88
Application of merged deep copy updates on sub-structures 89
Application of deep copy updates on dereferenced program variables 89
Application of deep copy updates on dereferenced sub-structures 89
Included Rules 150
Deep Copy Update Rules 151
KeY Update Rules 151
Derived Inference Rules 151
Syntax of terms and meta constructs generating terms. 188
Syntax of formulas and meta constructs which create formulas. 189

List of figures and diagrams

Logics overview 26
KeY's architecture 46
Main application classes 193
Source elements 196
Typecasts, Declarations, Types, and Sorts 199
Terms and Operators 204
Term example 205
Updates 208
Representation of a quantified update by a `Term`. 209
The method `mayBeAliased` 211
Update Simplifier 212
Super classes and interfaces of program variables. 213
Meta constructs of the program part 215
Traversing attributes of class declarations 230

Chapter 1

Preliminaries

1.1 Overview

This thesis has been carried out as part of the KeY-project [4] in order to investigate how the KeY-system can be extended for the verification of programs written in C; especially the C dialects C0 and MISRA C. The KeY-system is a CASE-tool with an integrated (interactive and automatic) theorem prover for (first order) dynamic logic [22] which has been developed primarily for the formal specification and verification of JAVA CARD programs. The result of the investigation provides answers to the following questions which will be discussed subsequently:

1. What are the major differences or extensions between C and JAVA CARD?

2. How can the differences or extensions be expressed in a dynamic logic and handled by a calculus?

3. How can the proposed solutions be implemented into the KeY-system?

The differences between C and JAVA CARD are regarded relatively to the capabilities of the KeY-system. Taking the specifications of both languages and comparing them can be done arbitrarily precisely. One way to reduce the complexity of this task is first to concentrate on the C dialect C0 [25] instead of MISRA C and then make some important extensions for MISRA C. C0 is used for verification by the Verisoft project and has been designed for this purpose. It is simpler than MISRA C and has a precise specification. Therefore a verification system for C0 is a suitable step in-between before the development of a verification system for MISRA C.

We have developed a dynamic logic called CDL and a calculus for the verification of C0 programs. CDL is based on the dynamic logics JavaCardDL and its extention DLJ which are used for the verification of JAVA CARD programs and the dynamic logic ODL. This basis is extended in two ways according to the two issues which we regard as major differences between JAVA CARD on the one hand and C0 and MISRA C on the other hand. Classifying these issues as extensions from JAVA CARD to C0 is not trivial. C0 and JAVA CARD have both the expressibility of a Turing machine. A C0 program could be verified by first translating it into a JAVA CARD program and then verifying the obtained JAVA CARD program. The approach of the thesis follows KeY's philosophy which is "that formal verification should be accessible to software engineers without years of training in formal methods" [27]. In order to achieve this, *customized* concepts are developed for handling features of the programming language that deserve special treatment. These are

1. Handling of program variables in the presence of the reference `&` and dereference `*` operators
2. Assignments of nested structures and arrays.

For ANSI C the third issue would be the explicit deallocation of "objects" but C0 and MISRA C do not support this feature.

Along the thesis we go through different stages in the development of CDL while we extend syntax, semantics and the calculus. In this way we realize a modular approach. On the one hand we describe distinct concepts in separate sections and on the other hand we adapt definitions for the purpose of CDL. The advantage of this approach is that sections concentrate on the main ideas of these concepts and complexity is reduced; giving syntax, semantic and calculus in three chapters would be infeasible.

Finally, a prototype of the KeY prover is implemented for handling of the special concepts of C. The goal of the implementation is to find out how the KeY system can be extended for the verification of C. This amounts on the one hand to the documentation of certain parts of the KeY system which is otherwise not available and the documentation of the actual implementation.

1.2 Related Work

The most related work to the thesis is [38] where also a dynamic logic for C0 is developed. Similarly as in this thesis questions arise how to handle pointers and how to represent data structures. However, because of the solutions reused from JavaCardDL and ODL for handling pointers and objects, our investigation concentrates on the continuation and improvement of the existing methods.

For the theorem prover Nqthm the C semantic has been specified. The work is documented in the technical reports [28] and [15]. For the development of a verification system for MISRA C certainly the formal specification of the ANSI C language is of great importance which has been carried out as a Phd thesis [31]. A derivation of verification rules for C from operational definitions in [29] is a similar approach to our work.

1.3 Notation

We use the following abbreviations:

Abbreviation	Meaning
wrt.	"with respecto to"
$:\Leftrightarrow$	"is defined as"
$\Longleftrightarrow$	"is equivalent with"
iff	"if and only if'
def.	"definition"

We use the bold written words "**For**", "**Exist**", "**and**", "**or**", "**not**", and "**implies**" as abbreviations of natural language phrases with the intuitive meaning of the logic symbols $\forall$, $\exists$, $\wedge$, $\vee$, $\neg$, $\rightarrow$ of predicate logic in the text. With "**For**" we mean that a statement is true for all elements of some domain which should be understood from the context of the statement. Analogically, with "**Exist**" we mean that there is at least one element in the respective context for which we claim that the statement is correct. "**And**" and "**or**" are understood in a logical sense with respect to our statement in contrast to "and" and "or" which are used outside of statements, e.g., referring to a list of items by "and" or considering different thoughts using "or". With "**not**" we mean that it is not the case that the following statement holds true in the respective context; in other words the statement is wrong in the context. With "**implies**" we mean that if it is the case that the preceding statement is true, then we claim that the following statement is true as well; we claim that the following statement is true only in the case where the preceding statement is true. Thus, if the preceding statement of "**implies**" is false, we make no statement about the conclusion. Furthermore, we use parentheses in the text to prevent ambiguous interpretations of the abbreviated statements in the natural language (with abbreviations).

The definitions of sets are implicitly assumed to be the definitions of the minimal sets which means that the sets contain only those elements which are explicitly mentioned in the definitions.

Chapter 2
C and Java

2.1 Representation of Integers

An integer is represented on a computer by a bit vector consisting of $\{0,1\}$. Since the mathematical set of integers $\mathbb{Z}$ is infinite, only a finite subset of $\mathbb{Z}$ can be represented by a bit vector. Program variables which are intended to represent a subset of $\mathbb{Z}$ are declared to have a basic type of the category integral type. The integral types of an implemented compiler of a programing language determine the size of the bit vector and thus the potential range of integers which can be represented by the type. The sizes of the bit vectors for each type are *usually*[2.1] multiplicities of a unit called byte.

Furthermore, there are several possibilities of how integers can be represented by bit-vectors. Some representations are for instance *sign-and-magnitude*, *one's complement*, *two's complement*, and *excess-N*. Since the two's complement representation is most widely used in computer systems and is the computational model of C0, we describe only this representation.

An important distinction in the two's complement representation is whether a type represents only positive integers or positive and negative integers. The respective types are called *signed* types and *unsigned* types. In two's complement representation the bit vectors of signed types are interpreted differently from unsigned types. For signed types the highest order bit is called the *sign bit,* and it determines the signedness of the value.

The two's complement representation can be defined by the functions $from\_bv_T$ and to_bv_T which map between bit vectors in two's complement representation and $\mathbb{Z}$.

Definition 2.1. **($from\_bv_T$)**[2.2] *The function $from\_bv_T$ maps a bit-vector b of type T to an integer in $\mathbb{Z}$. Let $b[i]$ be the i-th bit of the bit vector b and let n be the number of bits of the bit vector determined by type T. Then $from\_bv_T$ computes the value of b as:*

$$from\_bv_T(b) = \begin{cases} \sum_{i=0}^{n-1} b[i] * 2^i & \text{if } T \text{ is unsigned} \\ -b[n-1] * 2^{n-1} + \sum_{i=0}^{n-1} b[i] * 2^i & \text{if } T \text{ is signed} \end{cases}$$

2.1. A bit field in MISRA C may consist of 2 bits for example.

2.2. According to [14]

Definition 2.2. (to_bv_T)[2.2] *The function* to_bv_T *computes for a number* x *the bit vector* b *of matching bit-width such that the following equations hold:*

$$\begin{aligned} to\_bv_t(from\_bv_t(b)) &= b \\ from\_bv_t(to\_bv_t(x)) &= x \end{aligned}$$

In order for a number x to be representable by a bit vector of size n the following inequation must hold:

$$n \geqslant 1 + ld(abs(n))$$

If this inequality cannot be satisfied for some number x then the usual treatment in case of unsigned types is that the result is calculated *modulu* the biggest representable value increased by one of the type. For signed types the value is usually undefined. If such a case happens because of the execution of an operator, then an overflow occurs.

Definition 2.3. (Overflow) *An Overflow occurs if the computation of an operator yields a value that is bigger than the biggest value of the range of the type of the operator.*

2.2 ANSI C

C was invented and first implemented by Dennis Ritchie. In the 70'ies and 80'ies, the version of C described in *The C Programming Language* by Brian Kernighan and Dennis Ritchie (Englewood Cliffs, N.J.: Prentice-Hall, 1978) was the only reference of "existing practice" and is often referred to by K&R C. In the summer of 1983 a committee was established to create an ANSI (American National Standards Institute) Standard for C [5]. The Standard was finalized in December 1989 and adopted by ANSI and ISO (International Standard Organization) in 1990 [7]. This version of C is commonly called C89. The *Rational* [6] contains much of the Standard's text and discusses thoughts and intentions of the standardization committee as well differences to K&R C. C89 was then subject to two technical corrections and amendments until 1996 [8] resulting in the Standard called C96. The work on the standardization has continued and resulted 1999 in the Standard called C99 [35]. Also for C99 a Rationale [9] has been written which retains much of the text of the Rationale for C89. The Rational summarizes the Standards and gives interpretations of the Standards which are informally specified in natural language. ([35] and [9])

Definition 2.4. (A strictly conforming program) *A* strictly conforming program *is another term for a maximally portable program.* [9]

Definition 2.5. (Conforming program) *A* Conforming program *is thus the most tolerant of all categories, since only one conforming implementation needs to accept it.* [9]

In specifying the Standards the committees of the Standard C89 used several principles which were used also for the development of C99. In the following the term "implementation" refers to the interpretation of the Standard by the implementation of a compiler.

- "**Existing code is important, existing implementations are not.** A large body of C code exists of considerable commercial value. Every attempt has been made to ensure that the bulk of this code will be acceptable to any implementation conforming to the Standard.[...]" [9]
- "**C code can be portable.**[...] The C89 committee attempted to specify the language and the library to be as widely implementable as possible, while recognizing that a system must meet certain minimum criteria to be considered a viable host or target for the language." [9]
- "**C code can be non-portable.** [...] the C89 committee did not want to *force* programmers into writing portably, to preclude the use of C as a 'high-level assembler': the ability to write machine specific code is one of the strengths of C. It is this principle which largely motivates drawing the distinction between *strictly conforming program* and *conforming program*." [9]
- "**Avoid 'quiet changes'.** [...] the C89 committee avoided changes that quietly alter one valid program to another with different semantics, that cause a working program to work differently without notice. In important places where this principle is violated, both the C89 Rationiale and (C99) Rationale point out a QUIET CHANGE" [9]
- "**A Standard is a treaty between implementor and programmer.** Some numerical limits were added to [...] give both implementors and programmers a better understanding of what must be provided by an implementation, of what can be expected and depended upon to exist [...] with the understanding that any implementor is at liberty to provide higher limits than the Standard mandates." [9] This concerns in particular ranges and bit-representations of data types.
- "**Keep the spirit of C.** [...] Some of the facets of the spirit of C can be summarized in phrases like:

  [...]

  - Don't prevent the programmer from doing what needs to be done.

[...]

- Make it fast, even if it is not guaranteed to be portable.

The last proverb needs a little explanation. The potential for efficient code generation is one of the most important strengths of C. [..] many operations are defined to be how the target machine's hardware does it rather than by a general abstract rule. An example of this willingness to live with *what the machine does* can be seen in the rules that govern the widening of `char` objects for use in expression: whether the values of `char` objects widen to signed or unsigned quantities typically depends on which byte operation is more efficient on the target machine." [9]

- "**Minimize incompatibilities with C90.** [...]" [9]

The Standards intentionally leave some issues *unspecified*, *undefined*, and *implementation-defined*.

- "*Unspecified behavior* gives the implementor some latitude in translating programs. This latitude does not extend as far as failing to translate the program, however, because all possible behaviors are 'correct' in the sense that they don't cause undefined behavior in any implementation." [9]
- "*Undefined behavior* gives the implementor license not to catch certain program errors that are difficult to diagnose. It also identifies areas of possible conforming language extension: the implementor may augment the language by providing a definition of the officially undefined behavior." [9]
- "*Implementation-defined behavior* gives an implementor the freedom to choose the appropriate approach, but requires that this choice be explained to the user [...]" [9]

The semantics of the C dialects are informally defined using natural language...

> "...This causes a number of ambiguities and problems of interpretation, clearly manifested in numerous discussions taking place in the newsgroup `comp.std.c`. It is worthwhile noticing that members of the standardization committee and other distinguished researchers participating in the discussions often give contradictory answers when asked about the intended semantics of surprisingly small programs, and that their answers are usually based on different possible interpretations of the Standard." (*A case study in specifying the denotational semantics of C* by N.Papaspyrou [32]).

Remark 2.6. We use the terms C90 or ANSI C to refer to any of the versions from C89 to C99 as it is done in [26], [31], and other literature. This simplification of notation is justified by the great compatibility between the dialects of C.

A formal specification of ANSI C is given in the PhD thesis [31] by N.Papaspyrou. The specified language "differs slightly from ANSI C" [31]. Because of what has been said above, the specification must leave some space for further instantiation of the specification or leave some aspects unspecified.

The *important message* of this section are the statements that:

1. the specification of the C language is hard to understand in detail, and
2. the specification of the C language gives room for interpretations and customization of a C implementation

The second statement is clear from what has been said above. We support the first statement by another observation. Looking at the book titles *C:The complete Reference* [35] and *The Annotated ANSI C Standard* both by Herbert Schildt one might assume that the author does understand the ANSI C specification and that using the books as a basis for either the development of a formal semantic or for a comparison with other languages is a good choice. In [37] we read however:

> "C: The Complete Reference is a popular programming book, marred only by the fact that it is largely tripe. Herbert Schildt has a knack for clear, readable text, describing a language subtly but quite definitely different from C. [...] Don't bother contacting the publisher; they apparently don't feel these errors are significant.
>
> The following is a partial list of the errors I am aware of [...] I am not including everything; just many of them. I am missing several hundred errors." [37]

A similar review of the book is given by ACCU (Association of C & C++ Users) in [21]. C.D.W. Feather, who is a member of the standardization committee gives similar critique for the secondly mentioned book in [16]. ACCU provides, however, a list with even more books about C which are not recommended written by other authors. This gives rise to the assumption that there are *many* programmers which make wrong assumptions about ANSI C. In [14] we read "one can transform C programs into C0 programs with a simple preprocessor". Even for a certain implementation/instance of ANSI C (some suitable size and bit representation of data types, order of evaluation of operators, etc...) which resembles the abstract machine defined in [14] a converter from ANSI C to C0 cannot be called simple, e.g. C0 does not mimic the integer promotion rules of ANSI C, there are no bit-fields and unions in C0, arbitrary casting is not possible, etc.. .

Yet, "the C programming language is growing in importance and use for real-time embedded applications within the automotive industry..." [26] Specific reasons for its use include:

- "For many of the microprocessors in use, if there is any other language available besides assembly language then it is usually C. In many cases other languages are simply not available for the hardware." [26]
- "C gives good support for the high-speed, low-level, input/output operation, which are essential to many automotive embedded systems." [26]
- "Increased complexity of applications makes the use of a high-level language more appropriate than assembly language." [26]
- "C can generate smaller and less RAM-intensive code than many other high-level languages." [26]
- "A growth in portability requirements cause by competitive pressures to reduce hardware costs by porting software to new, and/or lower cost, processors at any stage in a project life cycle." [26]
- "A growth in the use of auto-generated C code from modeling packages." [26]
- "Increasing interest in open systems and hosted environments." [26]

2.3 MISRA C

From what has been said in the previous section it seems to be hard to write safe software in C. "If, for *practical reasons*, it is necessary to use C on a safety-related system, then the use of the language must be constrained to avoid, as far as is *practicable*, those aspects of the language which do give rise to concerns." [26] s.1.3. The MISRA C (Motor Industry Software Reliability Association) manual [26] developed by the MISRA consortium provides one such set of constrains resulting in a *subset* of C96 called MISRA C. "The MISRA consortium is not intending to promote the use of C in the automotive industry. Rather it recognizes the already widespread use of C, and this document seeks only to promote the safest possible use of the language." [26]

The MISRA C manual consists of 141 rules which restrict the use of C96.

Remark 2.7. We will use the letter 'r' when we refer to a rule followed by the number of the id-number of the rule. The word 'shall' in the MISRA manual means 'it is required that'.

Here we list a some important restrictions of MISRA C with respect to C96:

- Limited dependence should be placed on C's operator precedence rules in expressions and the value of an expression shall be the same under any order of evaluation that the ANSI C Standard permits. r.12.1 and r.12.2
- Directly or indirectly recursive functions are not allowed (r.16.2) and functions may only have a single point of exit which is at the end of the function. r.14.7
- Dynamic heap memory allocation (and deallocation) shall not be used r.20.4
- Pointer arithmetic is restricted to pointers that address elements of the same array. r.17.1
- Use of `goto` (r.14.4), `continue` (r.14.5) and the comma-operator (r.12.10) is prohibited
- Unions shall not be used. r.18.4
- The way expressions may be constructed is restricted regarding the types of the arguments by the rules r.10.1 and r.10.2
- Broadly, type casts between pointers are restricted to be independent from the memory representation. r.11.1 to r.11.5
- The increment and decrement operators should not be mixed with other operators in an expression. r.12.13
- Switch-statements are restricted in their form regarding labels and `break` statements. r.15.1-r.15.5 and iteration statement may have at most one `break` statement used for loop termination. r.14.6
- Functions have a constant number of arguments r.16.1, and have a single point of exist at the end of the function declaration r.14.7 via `return` r.16.8
- The functions `abort` and `exit` (r.20.11), the error indicator `errno` (r.20.5) and the signal handling facilities (r.20.8) shall not be used.

The usage of MISRA C in the production of safety-critical software like for automotive embedded systems makes MISRA C an interesting real world programming language for verification. The MISRA C manual explicitly states that some static checker and validation tools have to be used. In addition, where a checker tool has capabilities to perform check beyond those required by the MISRA rules it is recommended that the extra checks are used. [26] s.4.2.3

A precise specification of the semantic of a programming language is a fundamental basis for verification. Due to the fact that the specification of ANSI C [31] is a PhD thesis with over 260 pages in size and that the ANSI C specification is the underlying specification for MISRA C, it is obvious that the specification of the semantic, the development of a verification calculus and the implementation of a verification system for MISRA C cannot be done in a diploma thesis. The thesis focuses therefore rather on the C-like language C0, which is introduced in section 2.4.

2.4 C0

C0 is a C-like language which is used in the Verisoft project[2.3] for the implementation of an operating system and basic applications which are completely verified from the bottom up using Isabel/HOL[2.4]. This proves C0 to be a suitable programming language for verification. The main restrictions compared with C concern the side effects and the nondeterminism allowed:

- no side effects in expressions (e.g. operators like `i++`, `i--`),
- no functions as sub expressions,
- size of arrays is statically fixed at compile time,
- exactly one return statement in each function as last statement,
- only one scope for variables inside a function,
- evaluation of expressions in the standard order defined by post order traversal of syntax trees,
- no pointers to local memories or to functions,
- pointers are strictly typed. [14]
- two's complement representation of integral types.

C0 has a deterministic semantic that is formally specified using an abstract machine. When instantiating the ANSI C specification for a specific suitable hardware C0 can be seen as a subset of ANSI C. A feature of C0 not present in ANSI C is that array types are treated as proper types, which makes the assignment between arrays possible and changes the semantic of passing arguments of array types to functions. One oversimplification of C0 with respect to ANSI C is that it does not mimic the integer promotion rules of ANSI C, rather all operations are done in the type of the operands.

2.3. `www.verisoft.de`

2.4. `http://www.cl.cam.ac.uk/Research/HVG/Isabelle/`

If we don't instantiate the ANSI C specification suitably, then C0 cannot be seen as a subset of every ANSI C implementation because for instance, the basic data types of C0 outrange the limits of the data-types of ANSI C and an ANSI C implementation may use one's complement representation for data-types.

In a broader sense, however, C0 can be viewed as a subset of ANSI C. It cannot be viewed, however, as a subset of MISRA C because the latter does not allow recursive functions and dynamic memory allocation. On the other hand, when ignoring dynamic memory allocation MISRA C and C0 are more similar to eachother than C96 and C0.

The definition of the syntax is given in [25] and the semantic is defined in [14] and [39]. In the following subsection we define the syntax of C0 as defined in [25] and [14] but adjusted for the purpose of our notation. Additionally, the ranges of elementary types are defined here as well because they are a static property of every program. The following sections shall be understood as a sequence of definitions.

2.4.1 Types

The type system of C0 consists of four classes of types, namely elementary types, pointer types, array types and structure types.

Definition 2.8. (Integral types) *The set* $\mathrm{TYP}_{\mathrm{int}}^{C0}$ *of integral types with the ranges* $\{\mathrm{MIN\_}T, ..., \mathrm{MAX\_}T\}$ *and number of bits for each integral type* T *consists of:*

Type name (T)	MIN_T	MAX_T	*bits*
`char`	*0*	2^8-1	*8*
`int`	-2^{31}	$2^{31}-1$	*32*
`unsigned int`	*0*	$2^{32}-1$	*32*

Definition 2.9. (Elementary types) *The set* $\mathrm{TYP}_{\mathrm{el}}^{C0}$ *of elementary types is defined as:*

$$\mathrm{TYP}_{\mathrm{el}}^{C0} = \mathrm{TYP}_{\mathrm{int}}^{C0} \cup \texttt{bool}$$

where the range of the type `bool` *consists of* $\{\mathrm{true}, \mathrm{false}\}$.

Definition 2.10. (Types of C0) *The set* $\mathrm{TYP}_{\mathrm{el}}^{C0}$ *of types of C0 is the union of* TYP_{i}^{C0} *where:*

- $\mathrm{TYP}_0^{C0} \supset \mathrm{TYP}_{\mathrm{el}}^{C0}$
- $\mathrm{TYP}_i^{C0} \subset \mathrm{TYP}_{i+1}^{C0}$
- *arrays: if* $n \in \mathbb{N}$ *and* $t \in \mathrm{TYP}_i^{C0}$ *then* $t[n] \in \mathrm{TYP}_{i+1}^{C0}$
- *structs: if* $s \in \mathbb{N}$ *and* $n_1, ..., n_s$ *are names and* $t_1, ..., t_s \in \mathrm{TYP}_i^{C0}$, *then* $\mathit{struct}\{n_1, t_1; ...; n_s, t_s\} \in \mathrm{TYP}_{i+1}^{C0}$

- *if t is a name, then* $ptr(t) \in \mathrm{TYP}_0^{C0}$.

Definition 2.11. (Signature) *In the context of programming languages the* signature *of a function, method, operator, etc. is the type definition of the respective construct. If we refer to the signature of one of these constructs, we don't only mean the 'return' type of the resulting value but also the types of the parameters.*

2.4.2 Operators

Table 2.1 contains C0 operators from which expressions may be constructed. Rows of the table which are not separated by a line consist of operators which have an equal binding force. Operators separated by a horizontal line have a different binding force and are listed in the table according to the strength of their binding from top to bottom. Furthermore, binary operators are left associative and unary operators are right associative. The binding of the type cast operator allows no ambiguities even if it was not contained in the table, but it is listed for a complete reference of available operators in C0.

Arity	Operator	Meaning
2	||	logical or
2	&&	logical and
2	|	bit-wise or
2	^	bit-wise xor
2	&	bit-wise and
2	==	equality
2	!=	inequality
2	<	lest than
2	>	greater than
2	<=	less or equal
2	>=	greater or equal
2	<<	bit-wise shift left
2	>>	bit-wise shift right
2	+	addition
2	-	substraction
2	*	multiplication
2	/	division
1	!	logical negation
1	-	unary minus
1	&	reference operator
1	*	dereference operator
1	~	bitwise negation
1	$T()$	type cast

Table 2.1. C0 operator precedence

The signature of the operators restricts the way in which they can be composed to build expressions.

Operator	Signature	Abbreviations
`+, -, *, /,&,|,^`	$T \times T \rightarrow T$	$T \in \mathrm{TYP}^{C0}_{\mathrm{int}}$
`||, &&`	`bool` $\times$ `bool` $\rightarrow$ `bool`	
`>,<,>=,<=,==`	$T \times T \rightarrow$ `bool`	$T \in \mathrm{TYP}^{C0}_{\mathrm{int}}$
`==`	$ptr(T) \times ptr(T) \rightarrow$ `bool`	$T \in \mathrm{TYP}^{C0}_{\mathrm{int}}$
`<<, >>`	$T_1 \times T_2 \rightarrow T_1$	$T_1 \in \mathrm{TYP}^{C0}_{\mathrm{int}}, T_2 \in \mathrm{TYP}^{C0}_{\mathrm{int}}$
`~`	$T \rightarrow T$	$T \in \mathrm{TYP}^{C0}_{\mathrm{int}}$
`-`	`unsigned int` $\rightarrow$ `unsigned int`	
`[]`	$T_2[\in \mathbb{N}] \times T_1 \rightarrow T_2$	$T_1 \in \mathrm{TYP}^{C0}_{\mathrm{int}}, T_2 \in \mathrm{TYP}^{C0}$
`.`	$struct\{T_0 n_0, ..., T_s n_s\} \rightarrow T_i$	$0 \leqslant i \leqslant s \; T_i \in \mathrm{TYP}^{C0}$
`*`	$ptr(T) \rightarrow T$	$T \in \mathrm{TYP}^{C0}$
`&`	$T \rightarrow ptr(T)$	$T \in \mathrm{TYP}^{C0}$
`int()`	$T \rightarrow$ `int`	$T \in \{$`char, unsigend int`$\}$
`unsigned()`	$T \rightarrow$ `unsigned int`	$T \in \{$`int, char`$\}$
`char()`	$T \rightarrow$ `char`	$T \in \{$`int, unsigend int`$\}$

Table 2.2. Signature of C0 operators

The reference operator may be applied only to global variables. The types of variables and constants are as they are declared in the program.

Given the rules of operator binding and their signatures we can define the syntax of C0 in BNF-form.

2.4.3 BNF-Syntax

int	INT
unsigned	UNSIGNED
char	CHAR
bool	BOOL
typedef	TYPEDEF
struct	STRUCT
NULL	NULL
if	IF
else	ELSE
while	WHILE
true	TRUE
false	FALSE
return	RETURN
new	NEW
extern	EXTERN
->	ARROW
<=	LE
>=	GE
==	EQUALS
!=	NOTEQUALS
&&	LOGICALAND
||	LOGICALOR
<<	SHIFTLEFT
>>	SHIFTRIGHT
[a-zA-Z][a-zA-Z0-9]*	ID
(0|([1-9][0-9]*))	NUMERIC_CONSTANT
(0|([1-9][0-9]*))u	UNSIGNED_NUMERIC_CONSTANT
'.'	CHAR_CONSTANT
'[0-7]{3}'	CHAR_CONSTANT

Table 2.3 Symbols

```
translation_unit:
  external_declaration
  | translation_unit external_declaration

external_declaration:
  function_definition
  | function_declaration
  | EXTERN function_declaration
  | declaration

declaration:
  var_declaration
  | EXTERN var_declaration
  | type_definition
  | struct_id_definition

function_definition:
  type_specifier function_name '(' parameter_list ')' function_body
  | type_specifier function_name '(' ')' function_body

function_declaration:
  type_specifier function_name '(' parameter_list ')' ';'
  | type_specifier function_name '(' ')' ';'

function_name:
  ID
  | '*' ID

function_body:
  '{' '}'
  | '{' statement_list '}'
  | '{' var_declaration_list '}'
  | '{' var_declaration_list statement_list '}'

compound_statement:
  '{' '}'
  | '{' statement_list '}'

var_declaration_list:
  var_declaration
  | var_declaration_list var_declaration

statement_list:
  statement
  | statement_list statement
```

Table 2.4 C0 syntax: global definitions and declarations

```
type_definition:
  TYPEDEF type_specifier identifier ';'type_definition:
  TYPEDEF type_specifier identifier ';'

struct_id_definition:
  STRUCT ID '{} var_declarations '}' ';'
  | STRUCT ID ';'

struct_type:
  STRUCT ID

identifier_list:
  identifier
  |identifier_list ',' identifier

identifier:
  identifier2
  | '*' identifier

idenfifier2:
  ID
  | identifier2 '[' NUMERIC_CONSTANT ']'
  | identifier2 '[' UNSIGNED_NUMERIC_CONSTANT ']'
  | identifier2 '[' CHAR_CONSTANT ']'

parameter_spec:
  type_specifier identifier

parameter_list:
  parameter_spec
  | parameter_list ',' parameter_spec

type_declaration:
  type_specifier identifier_list ';'

constant:
  TRUE
  | FALSE
  | NIL
  | NUMERIC_CONSTANT
  | UNSIGNED_NUMERIC_CONSTANT
  | CHAR_CONSTANT
```

Table 2.5 C0 syntax: components of declarations

```
statement:
  lexpression '=' rexpression ';'
  | lexpression '=' NEW '(' type_specifier ')' ';'
  | lexpression '=' ID '(' rexpre_list ')' ';'
  | lexpression '=' ID '(' ')' ';'
  | ID '(' rexpr_list ')' ';'
  | ID '(' ')' ';'
  | WHILE '(' rexpression ')' compound_statement
  | RETURN rexpression ';'
  | IF '(' rexpression ')' compound_statement
  | IF '(' rexpression ')' compound_statement ELSE compound_statement
  | ';'

rexpr_list:
  rexpression
  | rexpre_list ',' rexpression

rexpression:
  basic_rexpr %prec BASICREXPR
  | constant
  | rexpression '|' rexpression
  | rexpression '&' rexpression
  | BITWISENEGATION rexpression
  | rexpression SHIFTLEFT rexpression
  | rexpression SHIFTRIGHT rexpression
  | rexpression XOR rexpression
  | rexpression LOGICALAND rexpression
  | rexpression LOGICALOR rexpression
  | rexpression EQUALS rexpression
  | rexpression NOTEQUALS rexpression
  | rexpression '<' rexpression
  | rexpression '>' rexpression
  | rexpression LE rexpression
  | rexpression GE rexpression
  | rexpression '+' rexpression
  | rexpression '-' rexpression
  | rexpression '*' rexpression
  | rexpression '/' rexpression
  | '-' rexpression %prec UNARY_MINUS
  | '!' rexpression
  | '&' lexpression %prec ADDRESSOF
  | INT '(' rexpression ')'
  | UNSIGNED '(' rexpression ')'
  | CHAR '('
```

Table 2.6 C0 syntax: statements and expressions

```
lexpression:
  ID
  | '*' lexpression %prec DEREFERENCE
  | lexpression '[' rexpression ']'
  | lexpression '.' ID
  | lexpression ARROW ID
  | '(' lexpression ')'

basic_rexpr:
  ID
  | '*' lexpression %prec DEREFERENCE
  | basic_rexpr '[' rexpression ']'
  | basic_rexpr '.' ID
  | basic_rexpr ARROW ID
  | '(' rexpression ')'

type_specifier:
  elementary_type
  | struct_type
  | ID

elementary_type:
  INT
  | BOOL
  | UNSIGNED INT
  | CHAR

var_declarations:
  var_declaration
  | var_declaration var_declarations

var_declaration:
  type_declaration
```

Table 2.7 C0 syntax: lexpression, basic_rexpr, type_specifier, elementary_type, var_declaration(s)

2.4.4 Program Variables

Definition 2.12. (Direct Sub-variable) *We call x a direct sub-variable of y if x is an expression and:*

- *y is of type array and it holds $x = y[e]$ for some e,*
- *or y is of type struct and it holds $x = y.n_j$ for some i.*

Definition 2.13. (Implicit program variables) *We define the set of implicit declared program variables by induction:*

- *All "simple" program variables are in* $impl_0$
- $impl_{i+1} := \{a \mid \text{there is } x \in impl_i \text{ such that } a \text{ is direct sub-variable of } x\}$

The set of implicit declared program variables is defined as $impl(m) := \bigcup_i impl_i(m)$.

For the rest of the thesis we use the term *program variable* to refer to implicit program variables and the terms *simple program variable* or *elementary program variable* to refer to program variables which are not of an array type or structure type.

Definition 2.14. (Substructure) *A substructure is an element of an array object or a member (attribute, field) of a structure object.*

2.5 C++

C++ is an object oriented and imperative programming language based on C96 except for some details. It is important to be aware of the following:

> "C++ is a different language to C [...]. C++ is not simply a super-set of C (i.e. C plus extra feature). There are a few specific construct which have different interpretations in C and C++. [...] code written in C and conforming to the ISO C Standard will not necessarily compile under a C++ compiler with the same results as under a true C compiler." [26]

We will not dwell further on the properties of the language as it does not belong to the scope of the thesis.

2.6 JAVA

JAVA is an object oriented and imperative programming language. An excellent book on JAVA written in German is [24]. The syntax of the language is similar to that of C++. The motivation in designing JAVA was to create a similar language to C and C++, but without the flaws like unspecified, undefined or implementation-defined behaviors as described in section 2.2. In particular elementary data-types are fully specified as well as the semantic and evaluation order of expressions. Therefore JAVA is portable; it is not necessary to recompile a JAVA program for different platforms in contrast to C and C++. In contrast to C and C++ it is not possible in JAVA to write purely procedural programs. JAVA is simpler to learn than C and C++ and there is less space for pitfalls. [24]

Object oriented features of JAVA are interfaces, inheritance, virtual methods, overloading, dynamic object creation and scoping. JAVA allows single- but not multiple inheritance of implementations (in contrast to C++). Multiple inheritance of non-implementations is possible via Interfaces. Furthermore, JAVA has a structured exception handling. [24]

2.7 JAVA CARD

JAVA CARD [40] is a language derived from JAVA and is designed for programming smart cards[2.5]. JavaCard can be viewed as a subset of JAVA. Applications running in a JAVA CARD environment are called applets. A JAVA program has a main method which is invoked by the system. An applet implements the methods `install` and `process` which are invoked by the system. JAVA CARD is designed to depend only on minimal hardware capabilities. In contrast to JAVA, JAVA CARD contains only the basic datatypes `byte`, `short`, and `boolean`. Large primitive data types like `int`, `long`, `double`, `float`, `char` (and Strings; they are part of the API) are not part of the language because of very limited computing resources of smart cards. JAVA CARD does not support multidimensional arrays, dynamic class loading, threads (concurrency)[2.6] and garbage collection. Furthermore, it contains all object oriented features of JAVA. One difference to JAVA is that the values of instance variables are preserved between the sessions of an applet. This is because the values are stored in EEPROM memory which keep its state without power supply. Every change of the value of a variable or object field is atomic. By hardware means, e.g. when plugging out a smart card from a card reader, an applet may be terminated in an invalid temporary state. To allow termination only in valid states, the JAVA CARD API provides transactions. A transaction can compose several state changes into one atomic state change.[27]

JAVA CARD is interesting for verification because applications written in JAVA CARD often have to be safe and secure. For instance, they are used for authentification tasks or as electronic cash on smart cards. Smart cards are usually distributed in large amounts so that errors may be very costly, especialy if they have to be exchanged. Some application areas even require the use of formal methods like digital signature. A practical reason for the interest in the verification of JAVA CARD programs is the relative simplicity of the language and because applets are usually small. For these reasons the KeY system has been developed for the verification of JAVA CARD programs. [27]

2.5. Generally speaking JAVA CARD is the whole technology for programming smart cards, but we will refer by JAVA CARD to the language.

2.6. There can be more than one applets existing on a single Java Card, but only one can be active at a time.

Chapter 3

Formal Basis for Verification

3.1 Dynamic Logic

A logic is a formal language for expressing statements about a domain or about properties of objects of a domain. The statements are called formulas and may consist of different *ingredients* from which different logics result. How formulas may be build is determined by the syntax of the logic. The definition of the meaning of the formulas and its parts is called the semantic of the logic and is done by mapping the syntactic symbols into a relational structure using an interpretation function[3.1].

Definition 3.1. (Relational Structure)*A relational structure is a tuple* $[\mathfrak{F}]$ *whose first component is a nonempty set* $[W]$ *called the universe (or domain) of* $[\mathfrak{F}]$*, and whose remaining components are relations on* $[W]$*. We assume that every relational structure contains at least one relation.*[3.2]* [13]

*We augment the definition to allow the relations on $[W]$ to be collected in a set which is the second component of $[\mathfrak{F}]$.

For formulas the interpretation function specifies the truth (logical) value of each formula. Formulas can play the roles of premises (assumptions) and conclusions. Usually a logic is associated with a calculus which is a set of rules of inference for the derivation of proofs. Systems of derivation or proofs "model the construction of inferences from premises to conclusion". [18] Due to the close connection between a logic and an associated calculus with the logic, authors sometimes refer by "logic" just to the formal language and sometimes to the formal language and a calculus.

3.1. The mapping of compound symbols is usually done by a valuation function which is indexed by an interpretation and continued by the interpretation function for elementary symbols..

3.2. The brackets [] indicate that the contained symbols may be different in special contexts.

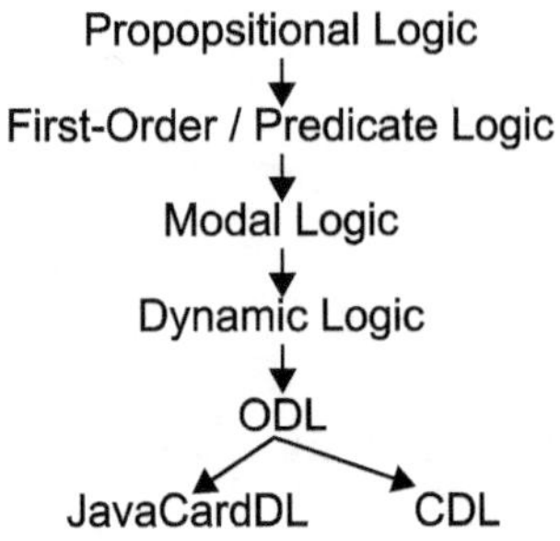

Figure 3.1 Logics overview

3.1.1 Syntax

Dynamic logic is designed for expressing statements about programs. Therefore programs are part of the logic. They are integrated in the form of *modal operators* which extend some other logic like *propositional logic* or *first-order logic*. The resulting logics are therefore special multi-modal logics and in the mentioned cases called *propositional dynamic logic* (PDL) and *first-order dynamic logic* respectively. The logics JavaCardDL [10], DLJ [36], and ODL [33] which are used in KeY are extensions of first-order dynamic logic. The major extension which is common to the KeY-logics is a special modal operator called *update* which is introduced in section 4.2. Figure 3.1 illustrates how the logics are related to each other, where the arrows point to the further derived logics[3.3]. In this thesis we define the syntax and semantic of CDL and give a calculus for the verification of C0 Programs. CDL is based on the ideas from JavaCardDL, DLJ and ODL which are adapted to C0 and extended for the treatement of special features of C0. As we describe the syntax and semantic of dynamic logic these descriptions are implicitly meant for CDL.

The syntax of first-order dynamic logic consists of the syntactical elements of first-order logic which are *function symbols*, *predicate symbols*, *variables*, *quantors*, and *logical connectives*. Function symbols and predicate symbols may be adapted to certain domains for which the logic may be used and are collected in the set Σ, the *signature*.[3.4] The signature may be further divided into Σ^f the set of function symbols and Σ^r the set of predicate symbols. The set with all variables is denoted by V. Compositions of function symbols and variables according to the syntax definition

3.3. Historically JavaCardDL was developed before ODL.

3.4. The word signature is used with two meanings in this thesis. In the context of programs the signature is the specification of the type of a function. In the context of logic the signature is a set of symbols.

of the logic are called *terms* and are collected in the set Trm. Formulas are collected in the set Fml and consist of compositions of terms, predicate symbols, quantors and logical connectives. In a *typed logic* a term belongs to a *type* or *sort* which restricts the composition of terms and predicates with terms. The types are collected in the set TYP. The sets Trm and Fml can in this case be annotated with the type to which the elements of the set belong. Dynamic logic extends this syntax by the modal operators box $[p]$ and diamond $\langle p\rangle$ for each program p. The set of programs is denoted by Prg or π. The modal operators may prepend formulas and terms so that $\langle p\rangle\varphi$ and $[p]\varphi$ are formulas iff φ is a formula and $\langle p\rangle t$ and $[p]t$ are terms iff t is a term. The intuitive meaning of $\langle p\rangle\varphi$ is that φ holds after the execution of p.

In order to express statements about values of program variables or expressions there must be a way to use them as terms in the construction of predicates. If the programming language uses logical terms as its program variables and expressions[3.5] no extensions have to be made to the syntax. In case of JAVA or C, either the set of terms is extended with program variables, numeric- and string-literals, and expressions from the programming language like array access and comparison operators[3.6] or a mapping from the program elements to terms is added. Because the programs in the modal operators and first-order elements of dynamic logic have often similar concepts like variables, boolean values, terms and expressions, we will use the terms *program-part* and the *logic-part* for a clearer distinction. The syntax of the programming language may be extended as well. The purpose of the extension is not to change the means of programming with the programming language, but rather to suite the calculus, e.g. to handle method invocation by replacing a method call by the method body.

Definition 3.2. (Types) *The set* TYP *of types of CDL consists of*

- $\mathrm{nat} \subset \mathrm{TYP}$ *natural number*
- $\mathrm{nat} \subset \mathrm{INT} \subset \mathrm{TYP}$ *mathematical integers*
- $\mathrm{TYP}^{C0} \subset \mathrm{TYP}$ *types of C0*

Definition 3.3. (Signature) *The set signature* Σ *of CDL consists of*

- $0, 1$ *of type* nat *(but we write just decimal numbers instead of* $(((0+1)+1)+1)\ldots$*)*
- *The function symbols* $+, -, *, /, \mathrm{mod}$ *of type* $\mathrm{INT} \times \mathrm{INT} \rightarrow \mathrm{INT}$
- *The function unary minus* $-$ *of type* $\mathrm{INT} \rightarrow \mathrm{INT}$

3.5. This is the case for ODL.

3.6. The comparison operator of the programming language may be treated as a function in order to be used as a term. In this case the boolean value of the operator is not of the same kind as the boolean values of formulas, because the operator is not a formula. However the boolean values of the programming languages can be easily mapped to true or false in the logic-part by a predicate.

- *The equality predicate* $\doteq$ *for any type*
- *Comparison predicates* $<, \leqslant, \geqslant, >$ *of type* $\mathrm{INT} \times \mathrm{INT} \rightarrow \{true, false\}$
- *The unary function symbol* obj_T *of type* $\mathrm{nat} \rightarrow T$ *for every* $T \in \mathrm{TYP}^{C0}$
- *The (non-rigid) constant* next_T *of type* nat *for every* $T \in \mathrm{TYP}$

Definition 3.4. (Terms) Trm_τ *is the set of terms of CDL of type* τ *with variables in* V *over the signature* Σ. *It is defined as the minimal set such that*

- *Every variables* $x \in V$ *of type* τ Trm_τ.
- *If* $f \in \Sigma$ *is a function symbol of type* $\sigma_1 \times \ldots \times \sigma_n \rightarrow \tau$ *and* $t_1 \in \mathrm{Trm}_{\sigma_1}, \ldots, t_n \in \mathrm{Trm}_{\sigma_n}$ *then* $f(t_1, \ldots, t_n) \in \mathrm{Trm}_\tau$.

The set Trm *is the union of* Trm_τ *for all types* $\tau \in \mathrm{TYP}$

Definition 3.5. (Formulas) Fml *is the set of formulas of CDL with variables in* V *over the signature* Σ. *It is minimal with the following properties.*

- *If* $p \in \Sigma$ *is a predicate symbol of type* $(\sigma_1 \times \ldots \times \sigma_n)$ *and* $t_1 \in \mathrm{Trm}_{\sigma_1}, \ldots, t_n \in \mathrm{Trm}_{\sigma_n}$ *then* $p(t_1, \ldots, t_n) \in \mathrm{Fml}$.
- *If* $\phi, \psi \in \mathrm{Fml}$ *then* $\neg\phi, (\phi \vee \psi), (\phi \wedge \psi), (\phi \rightarrow \psi), (\phi \leftrightarrow \psi) \in \mathrm{Fml}$.
- *If* $\phi \in \mathrm{Fml}$ *and* $x \in V$ *is a variable then* $\forall x \phi, \exists x \phi \in \mathrm{Fml}$.
- *If* $\phi \in \mathrm{Fml}$ *and* $P \in \mathrm{Prg}$ *is a C0* `statement_list` $\langle\!\{P\}\!\rangle \phi \in \mathrm{Fml}(\Sigma \cup V)$ *and* $[\!\{P\}\!]\phi \in \mathrm{Fml}(\Sigma \cup V)$

Remark 3.6. Descriptions concerning the modal operators $\langle\rangle$ and $[]$ apply implicitly to the modal operators $\langle\!\{\}\!\rangle$ and $[\!\{\}\!]$. The reason why the two notations are used is that in a later chapter the modality update denoted by $\{\}$ will be introduced and for which the concepts described here apply as well. Thus we abstract from variants of modal operators and distinguish only between box operators and diamond operators.

3.1.2 Semantic

After defining which symbols are part of the logic their meaning is defined by a mapping into a relational structure; in case of dynamic logic it is called a Kripke structure. Formulas can be true or false in a certain context and are therefore mapped into the set $\{true,\ false\}$. Terms represent certain objects or entities of a domain which is partitioned according to the types of the terms. Function symbols are mapped to functions on the domain and predicate symbols are mapped to relations.[3.7] Programs are executed in one state and terminate in the same or another state if they terminate at all. The difference between the semantic of first-order logic and the semantic of modal

3.7. Note that functions and relations are usually not part of the domain.

logic and it's derivates is that in the first case formulas are evaluated with respect to one global structure and in modal logic different states or worlds are contained in a Kripke structure to which formulas can be related by the modal operators. Because the modal operators of dynamic logic consist of programs the states of the Kripke structure represent program states. These states are defined as first-order structures or mappings into a first-order structure, so that after the execution of different programs a formula can be evaluated differently. Because of this connection we will describe how the the semantic of first-order logic is defined and then the semantic of dynamic logic.

For first-order logic the relational structure is $\mathcal{A} = (U, I_\Sigma)$, where the universe U is a countably infinite set and I_Σ is a set of relations and functions[3.8] over U as required by the definition of a relational structure (def. 3.1). I_Σ is obtained by the interpretation of the symbols of the logic in Σ by the interpretation function I. I_Σ is independent from any signature; this compound notation "I_Σ" reflects the idea that these relations may have syntactical counterparts in a signature Σ which are linked by a Σ-dependent interpretation $I\colon \Sigma \rightarrow I_\Sigma$.[3.9] A first-order structure is usually written as (U, I) in other literature. This is not a relational structure according to definition 3.1, because I is not a relation over U, but a mapping from Σ to relations over U. However, since we want to define the semantic of the first-order logic relative to (U, I_Σ) *and* by using an interpretation $I\colon \Sigma \rightarrow I_\Sigma$ indexed with elements of Σ, we will write $\mathcal{M} = (U, I)$ as first-order structure for a shorter notation, which can be viewed as the Σ-dependent version of (U, I_Σ).

The interpretation of a symbol $s \in \Sigma$ is written as $I(s)$, or s^I. For an n-ary function symbol f, the interpretation of f is $f^I\colon U_1 \times \ldots \times U_n \rightarrow U \in I_\Sigma$ an n-ary function of tuples $U_1 \times \ldots \times U_n$ into the universe U [3.10]. Since a function is a special relation this doesn't contradict the definition of $\mathcal{A}$. Functions of arity 0 are constants, because they are independent of any parameters and map always[3.11] to the same element of U. For every n-ary predicate symbol p the interpretation I maps to $p^I \subset U_1 \times \ldots \times U_n \in I_\Sigma$ a relation on U [3.12]. A relation $p^I \in I_\Sigma$ can be seen as a mapping of tuples $U_1 \times \ldots \times U_n$, which are elements of the relation to *true* and of tuples which are not elements of the relation to *false*. Additionally, in case of a typed logic the interpretation of a type $t \in \text{TYP}$ is a subset of the universe for every type.

3.8. A function $f\colon U_1 \times \ldots \times U_n \rightarrow U$ can be viewed as a special relation $f\colon U_1 \times \ldots \times U_n \times U_{n+1}$.

3.9. The notation for I_Σ is motivated idea that it can be seen as *instantiated* version of I by Σ or rather by all elements of Σ.

3.10. The indices $1 \ldots n$ of $U_1 \times \ldots \times U_n$ represent only the size of the tuple; it is not a distinction between different universes.

3.11. Constants map to the same element in U in first-order logic, but in dynamic logic the interpretation of non-rigid constants may vary.

3.12. Predicates of arity 0 have the same meaning a propositional variables in propositional logic.

Variables $x \in V$ are assigned elements of the universe U by a variable assignment β. The analogous concepts in [18] and [22] are called "valuation". In [22] a valuation defines the semantic of variables and terms. In [18] a valuation is just a set of elements of U (similarly as there *would be* an I_Σ for variables or constants) and a "*valuation of an interpretation* is a [variable assignment] with respect to the domain of I" (similarly like I in contrast to I_Σ but for variables) and therefore it corresponds to β. The *denotational meaning* — the mapping into U — of terms t is written in [18] as VALUE(t, I, β). This is what *we* call a "valuation" in this thesis and we reserve the term "variable assignment" to β.

The meaning of compound symbols is defined using a valuation function $\text{val}_{\mathcal{M},\beta}$: $\text{Trm} \cup \text{Fml} \rightarrow U \cup \{true, \; false\}$[3.13] which is applied recursively on the structure of terms and formulas until symbols from the signature are "reached" and interpreted by the interpretation function I and variable assignment β as described before. The valuation of terms is a mapping into the universe and the valuation of formulas is a mapping into the boolean set $\{true, \; false\}$.

In dynamic logic symbols are interpreted relative to a Kripke structure. In the literature also the terms *frame* and *model* are used instead of Kripke structure. To provide the reader with a clearer picture on this topic we will give in addition to the definition of a Kripke structure also the definitions of a frame and a model as it is done in [13] and [18] and compare them with other definitions from [22] and [33].

Definition 3.7. (DL-Kripke Structure) *A DL-*Kripke structure $\mathcal{K}$ *is a relational structure* (S, ρ_π) *where* S *is a set of pairs* $(\mathcal{M}, \beta)$ *called* states *and* ρ_π *is a set of relations over* S *which are called* accessibility relations. $\mathcal{M}$ *is a (Σ-dependent) first-order structure* (U, I) *and* β *is a variable assignment from* V *to* U. *We will call* S *the* state-space *of* $\mathcal{K}$ *and refer by universe or domain to* U. *Each accessibility relation* $\rho(p)$ *corresponds to one or more programs* $p \in \text{Prg}$ *so that* ρ *is a mapping from programs in* π *to relations between states or set of state-transitions* $\rho\colon \pi \rightarrow (S \times S)$. S *consists only of states which can be reached by the accessibility relations.*

A state consists of the three components: U, I, and β. In the definitions of the semantic of dynamic logic usually not all of these components vary between different states. The common aspect of I and β is that they define the denotational value of symbols. I gives meaning to function symbols and predicate symbols which are both contained in Σ and β gives meaning to variables which are symbols in V. It may be suitable to distinguish further between I^f for the interpretations of functions symbols and I^r for the inter-

3.13. Because the range of val_I is $U \cup \{true, \; false\}$ the boolean values true and false may be considered to be elements of U by other authors, but not here.

pretation of predicate symbols and eventually I^c for the interpretation of constants as it is done in [18]. Symbols in Σ which have the same denotational value in all states are called *rigid* and symbols which denotational meaning may vary between different states are called *non-rigid*. The set Σ can be therefore further partitioned into the set of rigid symbols Σ_r and non-rigid symbols Σ_{nr}.[3.14] If β is constant (for a Kripke structure) then the values of (logical) variables do not vary between different states. In this case variables provide a "connection" between different states and are used for quantification. Different states are then represented by different interpretations I so that symbols in Σ_{nr} have different denotational meanings in different states, which is the case in the KeY logics. The function and predicate symbols of CDL defined in def. 3.4 are rigid except for next_T.

The universe U may vary or be constant in different states as well. In the first case we talk about *varying domain semantics* and in the second case about *constant domain semantics*. Varying domain semantics is considered to be more complicated in [33], [18] p.433; more on this topic can be found in [17]. Therefore constant domain semantics is usually chosen for dynamic logic. The interesting question in this context is how *dynamic creation of objects*[3.15] is handled because programming languages like C0 or JAVA provide this feature. We assume that there is an infinite reservoir of objects of any type of the programming language already contained in the universe which may be created during program execution. In order to distinguish objects which are already created and those which are not created, every object has an attribute or flag, which says whether the object is really created[3.16]. Alternatively every object can be associated with a numerical identifier and a global counter[3.17] keeps track of the identifier of the object which was created last. The later the approach used in [33] and CDL. Dynamicaly created objects and global program variables are identified by symbols $\mathrm{obj}_T(n)$ and the global conter for each type is next_T. In order to restrict quantification over objects which were already created an implicit premise is attached to the quantifiers semantic definition. In [33] this concept is called *relativized constant domain semantics*.

Definition 3.8. (Frame) *"A frame $\mathfrak{F}$ is a relational structures $(\mathfrak{S}, \mathfrak{R})$ where $\mathfrak{S}$ is a set of states (or worlds) called the state-space and $\mathfrak{R}$ is a relation over the state-space called accessibility relation. In case of a multi-modal logic like dynamic logic $\mathfrak{R}$ is not a single relation, but a set of relations on $\mathfrak{S}$."* [13]

3.14. We write Σ_r^f for the set of rigid function symbols, Σ_{nr}^f for non-rigid function symbols and the respective combinations for predicate symbols, i.e., $\Sigma = \Sigma_r^f \cup \Sigma_{\mathrm{nr}}^f \cup \Sigma_r^r \cup \Sigma_{\mathrm{nr}}^r$.

3.15. There are no objects in C; we refer with this term to entities which may be created dynamically. We assume that these entities are elements of the universe.

3.16. This approach was originally chosen for JavaCardDL, but may be changed in the future.

3.17. This approach is chosen in [33].

Definition 3.9. (Model) *"A model $\mathfrak{M}$ is a tuple $(\mathfrak{F}, \mathrm{Va})$ where $\mathfrak{F}$ is a frame and Va is a function called a valuation which maps formulas into a subset of the state-space of $\mathfrak{F}$."* [13]

A model can also be written as $(\mathfrak{S}, \mathfrak{R}, \mathrm{Va})$. In this context the intuitive meaning of the valuation Va is that it maps a formula to a set of states in which the formula is true. It could have also been defined such that given a state $s \in \mathfrak{S}$ and a formula $p \in \mathrm{Fml}$ the mapping would be $\mathrm{Va}(s, p) \in \{true, false\}$ depending on whether p is true or false in state s. Unfortunately there are two meanings of the term "model" which are used in literature about logic. The concept of a model according to def. 3.9 must not be confused with the concept of a model in the context of first-order logic. In first-order logic a model is an interpretation and (if free variables are allowed, which are not implicitly quantified) variables assignments (I, β) in which some formula φ is true.

When comparing the definitions of a Kripke structure $\mathcal{K}$, a frame $\mathfrak{F}$, and a model $\mathfrak{M}$, it turns out that $\mathcal{K}$ has the same properties as $\mathfrak{M}$, and $\mathfrak{F}$ has the same properties as a tuple (S_Σ, ρ_π) where ρ_π is a set of accessibility relations over S_Σ, and S_Σ consists of (Σ-independent) first-order structures (U, I_Σ)[3.18]. This becomes clear when considering that a Kripke structure or model for dynamic logic could also be written as the tuple $(S_\Sigma, \rho_\pi, (I, \beta))$ where it holds that for each $a \in \Sigma$ $I(a) \in I_\Sigma$ and $v \in V$ $\beta(v) \in U$. Thus a frame $(\mathfrak{S}, \mathfrak{R})$ or (S_Σ, ρ_π) is just an abstract set of states with relations between them and a Kripke structure or model like $(\mathfrak{F}, V)$, $(\mathfrak{S}, \mathfrak{R}, V)$, $(S_\Sigma, \rho_\pi, (I, \beta))$, or (S, ρ_π) gives concrete meaning to formulas.

In [22] however, which is currently an important source on dynamic logic in literature, a Kripke frame is *not* a frame in the sense of definition 3.8, but rather a model according to our definitions[3.19]. According to our notation a Kripke structure in [22] is written as a tuple $(U, \mathfrak{m})$ where for symbols $a \in \Sigma$ it is $\mathfrak{m}(a) = I(a)$, for programs $p \in \pi$ it is $(\mathrm{val}_{(I,\beta')} \times \mathrm{val}_{(I,\beta')}) \in \mathfrak{m}(p)$ or $\mathfrak{m}(p) \subseteq \beta' \times \beta'$ where β' stands for sets with different variable assignments, and for formulas $\varphi \in \mathrm{Fml}$ we have $\mathfrak{m}(\varphi) = \mathrm{val}_{(I,\beta)}(\varphi)$ or $\mathfrak{m}(\varphi) \subseteq \beta'$[3.20]. The *meaning function* $\mathfrak{m}$ does not evaluate variables. Variables are evaluated by varying variable assignments β'. In other words, different states result from different variable assignments or valuations with different variable assignments and all functions and relations are rigid.

3.18. Except for the difference that in first-order logic a valuation function is used for compound symbols and the interpretation for atomic symbols and the valuation V of a model evaluates only formulas in one step without intermediate steps like predicates and terms..

3.19. The reason for this is *maybe* to avoid confusion between the two meanings the word model.

3.20. We don't distinguish here between the interpretation and valuation precisely. The alternative translations for $\mathfrak{m}(p)$ and $\mathfrak{m}(\varphi)$ result from the different possibilities of a definition of a model as described earlier.

Yet another terminology is used in [33] from where some definitions and notations are used in this thesis. Instead of the terms Kripke structure or model the term "interpretation" is used which is a Kripke structure as defined in def. 3.7. The variable assignment β is "invisibly" integrated into the interpretation. The reason for this is firstly that contrary to [22] states don't result from different variable assignments — variables are rigid — , but from different interpretations of some non-rigid function symbols and secondly there are no free variables in ODL — and in the other KeY-logics as well — because free variables are implicitly quantified. Therefore the meaning of a formula is independent of any variable assignment β because, loosely speaking, it becomes overwritten by quantification anyway. In order to use the terminology from [33] we will define an interpretation as a special Kripke structure. This interpretation must not be confused with the first-order interpretations I of the state-space S. The later we call states or worlds.

Definition 3.10. (Interpretation) *An interpretation l is a DL-Kripke structure $\mathcal{K}$ as defined in def 3.7 with a typed constant domain. Variables and predicates are rigid. Different states result from different (first-order) interpretations of some non-rigid function symbols. The interpretation l contains a variable assignment β.*

We will use the notations from [33] for the definition of the semantic of CDL in this thesis. The accessibility relation is written in *infix* notation as $\rho_l(\alpha)$ where $\alpha \in \pi$. The notation for the semantic of a symbol $a \in \Sigma \cup V \cup \mathrm{Trm} \cup \mathrm{Fml}$ is $\mathrm{val}_l(s, a)$ where s is a state[3.21]. For symbols in $\Sigma \cup V$ the valuation function plays therefore the same role as the interpretation and variable assignment described for the definition of the semantic of first-order logic. A subset of the universe corresponding to a type $t \in \mathrm{TYP}$ is written as $l(t)$. The state-space of l is denoted by S^l.

Definition 3.11. (Valuation)

- *bijections* $\mathrm{val}_l(w, \mathrm{obj}_T): l(\mathrm{nat}) \rightarrow O_T$ *into disjoint sets* $O_T \subset U$ *of object of type* T
- *the set* $l(\tau) := O_T \subset U$ *objects (and numbers) of type* T.
- *an object* $\mathrm{val}_l(w, c) \in l(\tau)$ *with each individual symbol* $c \in \Sigma \cup V$ *of type* τ.
- *an object* $\mathrm{val}_l(w, f): l(\sigma_1) \times \ldots \times l(\sigma_n) \rightarrow l(\tau)$ *with each function symbol* f *of type* $\sigma_1 \times \ldots \times \sigma_n \rightarrow \tau$.

3.21. This valuation function is not only used for compound symbols as described above for the definition of the semantic of first-order logic, but for all syntactic symbols except for programs. Note that the valuation function maps to different sets, namely to U, $\{\mathrm{true}, \mathrm{false}\}$, functions on U and relations on U.

- *a relation* $\mathrm{val}_l(w,p) \subseteq l(\sigma_1) \times \ldots \times l(\sigma_n)$ *with each predicate symbol of type* $(\sigma_1 \times \ldots \times \sigma_n)$.

– $\mathbb{N} = l(\mathrm{nat}) \subset l(\mathrm{INT}) = \mathbb{Z}$

– *The interpretation of number constants, arithmetic functions and predicates has the regular meaning*

[33]

Definition 3.12. (Valuation of Terms) *Let w be a state of an interpretation l. The valuation of terms with respect of l and w is defined as follows.*

1. *if f is a function symbol of arity n an $t_1, \ldots t_n \in \mathrm{Trm}$ are terms.*

$$\mathrm{val}_l(w, f(t_1, \ldots, t_n)) := (\mathrm{val}_l(w, f))(\mathrm{val}_l(w, t_1), \ldots, \mathrm{val}_l(w, t_n))$$

[33]

We have now established a context of concepts, terminology, and notations in which we can precisely describe what the extension of first-order logic by the modal operators $\langle\alpha\rangle$ and $[\alpha]$ in front of a formula $\varphi \in \mathrm{Fml}$ with a program $\alpha \in \pi$ means. For an interpretation l and states s and s' in S^l the semantic of the formulas $\langle\alpha\rangle\varphi$ and $[\alpha]\varphi$ denoted by $\mathrm{val}_l(s, \langle\alpha\rangle\varphi)$ and $\mathrm{val}_l(s, [\alpha]\varphi)$ is defined as:

$$\mathrm{val}_l(s, \langle\alpha\rangle\varphi) \;:\Leftrightarrow\; \begin{cases} \text{true, there exists } s' \in S^l \text{ with } s\,\rho_l(\alpha)\,s' \textbf{ and } \mathrm{val}_l(s', \varphi) = \text{true} \\ \text{false, otherwise} \end{cases}$$

$$\mathrm{val}_l(s, [\alpha]\varphi) \;:\Leftrightarrow\; \begin{cases} \text{true, for all } s' \in S^l \text{ with } s\,\rho_l(\alpha)\,s' \textbf{ implies } \mathrm{val}_l(s', \varphi) = \text{true} \\ \text{false, otherwise} \end{cases}$$

This shows how, on a level of semantic definitions, programs can be separated from formulas resulting in an accessibility relation $\rho_l(\alpha)$ between states and a first-order formula whose satisfiability and validity depends on a state. The definitions of $\mathrm{val}_l(s', \varphi)$ and $\rho_l(\alpha)$ depend on the concrete logic and program semantics. For a deterministic program α the accessibility relation $\rho(\alpha)$ is a partial function from states to states. This means that for every state $s \in S$ there is at most one state $s' \in S$ such that $(s, s') \in \rho(\alpha)$. The partiality arises from the possibility that the program might not terminate; in this case $\rho(\alpha)$ is undefined [22].

Definition 3.13. (Valuation of Formulas) *Let l be an interpretation and $w \in S^l$ a state. The valuation of formulas with respect to l and w is defined as follows. Let $t, t', t_1', \ldots, t_n' \in \mathrm{Trm}$, $\phi \in \mathrm{Fml}$, $\alpha \in \mathrm{Prg}$ and $x \in V$ a variable of type τ.*

1. *if p is a predicate symbol of arity n*

$$\mathrm{val}_l(w, p(t_1, \ldots, t_n)) := (\mathrm{val}_l(w, p))(\mathrm{val}_l(w, t_1), \ldots, \mathrm{val}_l(w, t_n)$$

2. $\text{val}_l(w, t \doteq t') = \text{true} \;:\Leftrightarrow\; \text{val}_l(w, t) = \text{val}_l(w, t')$.
3. $\text{val}_l(w, \phi \wedge \psi) = \text{true} \;:\Leftrightarrow\; \text{val}_l(w, \phi) = \text{true}$ *and* $\text{val}_l(w, \psi) = \text{true}$
4. $\text{val}_l(w, \phi \vee \psi) = \text{true} \;:\Leftrightarrow$ *either* $\text{val}_l(w, \phi) = \text{true}$ *or* $\text{val}_l(w, \psi) = \text{true}$ *or both are* true.
5. $\text{val}_l(w, \neg\phi) = \text{true} \;:\Leftrightarrow\; \text{val}_l(w, \phi) = \text{false}$
6. $\text{val}_l(w, \forall x \phi) = \text{true} \;:\Leftrightarrow$ *for each* $d \in l(\tau)$ $\text{val}_{l[x \mapsto d]}(w, \phi) = \text{true}$.
7. $\text{val}_l(w, \exists x \phi) = \text{true} \;:\Leftrightarrow$ *there is* $d \in l(\tau)$ $\text{val}_{l[x \mapsto d]}(w, \phi) = \text{true}$.
8. $\text{val}_l(w, [\alpha]\,\phi) = \text{true} \;:\Leftrightarrow$ *for each* $w' \in S^l$ *if* $w \rho_l(\alpha) w'$ *then* $\text{val}_l(w', \phi) = \text{true}$.
9. $\text{val}_l(w, \langle\alpha\rangle\,\phi) = \text{true} \;:\Leftrightarrow$ *there is* $w' \in S^l$ *where* $w \rho_l(\alpha) w'$ *and* $\text{val}_l(w', \phi) = \text{true}$.

[33]

3.1.3 Satisfaction, Validity, and Consequence

When the semantic of the logic is defined it is interesting to make statements about relations between formulas. In this context we need the notion of satisfaction, validity, and consequence. The following definitions are taken from [33] where the definition of the consequence relation is again from [17].

Definition 3.14. (Satisfaction Relation) *For a state w of an interpretation l and a formula $\phi \in \text{Fml}$ we define the satisfaction relation $\models$ as*

$$\begin{aligned} l, s \models \phi \;&:\Leftrightarrow\; \text{val}_l(s, \text{Cl}_\forall \phi) = \textit{true} \\ l \models \phi \;&:\Leftrightarrow\; \text{for each } s \in S^l\, l, s \models \phi \end{aligned}$$

Where $\text{Cl}_\forall \phi := \forall x_1 ... \forall x_n \phi$ *is the* universal closure *of the formula ϕ with the free variables $\{x_1, ..., x_n\}$.*

We say that a formula ϕ is *satisfiable* in l if there is at least one state $s \in S^l$ such that the universal closure of ϕ evaluates to true. ϕ is *valid in l* if $\text{Cl}_\forall \phi$ evaluates to true for every state $s \in S^l$. A formula is *valid* if it is valid in every interpretation; in this case it is also called a *tautology*. The universal closure ensures that free variables in a formula are universally quantified when talking about its satisfiability or validity.

Definition 3.15. (Consequence Relation) *The consequence relation $\models \triangleright$ between a formula $\chi \in \text{Fml}$ and a set of local premises $\Psi \subseteq \text{Fml}$ with a set of global premises $\Phi \subseteq \text{Fml}$ is defined as*

$$\begin{aligned} \Phi \models \Psi \triangleright \chi \;:\Leftrightarrow\;& \textit{for each interpretation } l \textit{ with } l \models \Phi\text{:} \\ & \quad \textit{for each state } s \textit{ if } l, s \models \Psi \textit{ then } l, s \models \chi \end{aligned}$$

Where $l \models \Phi$ *means that* $l \models \Phi$ *for each* $\phi \in \Phi$, *and* $l, s \models \Psi$ *means that* $l, s \models \psi$ *for each* $\psi \in \Psi$. *The local consequence relation* $\models_l$ *and the global consequence relation* $\models_g$ *are defined as*

$$\Psi \models_l \chi \;:\Leftrightarrow\; \models \Psi \rhd \chi$$
$$\Phi \models_g \chi \;:\Leftrightarrow\; \Phi \models \rhd \chi$$

In the case of $\Phi = \emptyset$ *the notation* $\models_l \psi$ *shall be sufficient instead of* $\emptyset \models_l \psi$.

The previous definition is maybe easier to read by abbreviations in a similar style to first-order logic notation:

$$\Phi \models \Psi \rhd \chi \;:\Leftrightarrow\; \mathbf{All}\, l.(\mathbf{All}\, s.\, l, s \models \Phi\, \mathbf{implies}\, \mathbf{All} s.\, (l, s \models \Psi\, \mathbf{implies}\, l, s \models \chi))$$
$$\Psi \models_l \chi \;:\Leftrightarrow\; \mathbf{All}\, l.\mathbf{All}\, s.\, (l, s \models \Psi\, \mathbf{implies}\, l, s \models \chi)$$
$$\Phi \models_g \chi \;:\Leftrightarrow\; \mathbf{All}\, l.(\mathbf{All}\, s.\, l, s \models \Phi\, \mathbf{implies}\, \mathbf{All}\, s.\, l, s \models \chi)$$

Probably the most important relation between formulas is the equivalence relations which is defined as follows:

Definition 3.16. (Local Equivalence) *The local equivalence relation* $\equiv$ *between formulas* ϕ *and* ψ *is defined as*

$$\phi \equiv \psi \;:\Leftrightarrow\; \text{for each interpretation } l \text{ for each state } s$$
$$l, s \models \phi \iff l, s \models \psi$$

3.1.4 Application to Software Verification

3.1.4.1 Functional Correctness

The kind of software verification we consider here is the proving of the *functional correctness* of programs with respect to a *specification*. This means that, given a specification of "input" and "output" of a program the goal is to prove that the program produces the output when started with the specified input. Other software verification tasks which are not considered in this thesis are for example to prove that, a general specification subsumes a more specific specification, or that the execution of a program does not exceed a certain amount of time of computation, or that the allocation of memory during the execution of program does not exceed a certain limit.

The specification of input and output is done in a *general* way by formulas which can specify arbitrary sets of input and output. The *precondition* $\phi \in$ Fml specifies a state in which the execution of the program p starts and the *postcondition* $\varphi \in$ Fml specifies the state in which the execution ends. An implication $\phi \rightarrow [p]\varphi$ states therefore that if the program p is started in a state where ϕ holds, then after execution of the program the new state satisfies φ.

The implication $\phi \to [p]\varphi$ can be seen as the Hoare Triple $\{\phi\}p\{\varphi\}$. Dynamic logic is however more expressive than Hoare logic. In DL ϕ and φ are DL-formulas, because DL is closed under the logical operators, and hence ϕ and φ may contain programs in contrast to Hoare logic where ϕ and φ are pure first-order formulas. In this way programs may be used in the pre- and postconditions to specify a state or special properties of objects and data structures, e.g. that a data structure is not cyclic [10].

We will now discuss the connection between states of the program part and the logic part with a perspective on the requirements of a calculus.

3.1.4.2 Program States

A program state consists of the current position of execution in the program and a set of assignments of values to program variables. There are two approaches for handling the first issue. Dynamic logic and Hoare Logic are *exogenous*, which means that its programs are explicit in the syntax of the logic. This way (in Dynamic logic) the modal operators can be composed to new modal operators or transformed in some other way which is what makes dynamic logic a *special* modal logic. In particular this allows the analysis of the programs by structural induction which is one central paradigm of verification [22]. Another paradigm of verification resulting from the *compositionality* of the modal operators is *syntactic execution* of the program. The program is decomposed into smaller programs until atomic programs are reached and embedded in proof obligations. This technique can be suitably expressed by a set of rules of the sequent calculus which will be introduced in section 3.3. The current position of execution in the program from the perspective of a formula or term is the position after executing the whole program of the preceeding modal operator. Temporal logic is in contrast *endogenous* which means that the current position in the execution of the program is stored in a special variable, called program counter [22].

The second issue is what we *actually* mean with state, i.e., the values of program variables. A state can be viewed as a set of assignments of values to program variables. Therefore assignments play a crucial role in the program; they are the atomic programs which are responsible for state changes[3.22]. The values of program variables cannot be denoted explicitly as concrete values, because this would allow only the analysis of a single execution (or run) of the regarded program. Instead, syntactic execution of programs allows the assignment of terms to program variables[3.23]. The denotational meaning of the terms may then represent different initial states and program runs if they contain quantified variables[3.24]. The representation of values by terms allows

3.22. With assignments we mean also implicit assignments like in the case of an increment operator or method invocation.

3.23. ;or the translations of program variables to non-rigid functions.

also a richer analysis of relations between program variables. This is however only possible, because terms have no side-effects in contrast to expressions. Side-effects occur if an expression contains implicitly or explicitly assignments which have influence on the value of other sub-expression. A major task of the verification calculus which follows this paradigm is therefore to resolve side-effects and generate terms from expressions and other terms. For the treatment of assignments *updates* were developed in the KeY project which will be introduced section 4.2.

3.1.4.3 Partial and Total Correctness

When comparing the diamond operator $\langle\rangle$ with the box operator $[]$ the first impression might be that $[\alpha]\varphi$ implies $\langle\alpha\rangle\varphi$; that box is stronger than diamond. However, contrary to the box operator the diamond operator *insists* on the existence of a state s' after the execution of α. If α does not terminate then $[\alpha]\varphi$ is true, but $\langle\alpha\rangle\varphi$ is false. A *partial correctness proof* ensures therefore only that a postcondition holds in a state after the execution of a program *if* the program terminates. A *total correctness proof* ensures additionally the termination of a program. Thus a program is called *partially* or *totally* correct with respect to a specification[3.25].

The diamond operator has characteristics of the existential quantifier from first-order logic and the box operator has characteristics of the universal quantifier. In fact augmenting a logic by suitable multi-modal operators can result in a more expressive logic, e.g. propositional multi-modal logic may gain the expressibility of first-order logic when it is extend with suitable modal operators. The duality principle which states that $\forall x\varphi \equiv \neg\exists x\neg\varphi$ holds therefore analogously for the modal operators: $[\alpha]\varphi \equiv \neg\langle\alpha\rangle\neg\varphi$. By abuse of a first-order-logic-like notation as the meta-language the equivalence can be shown as follows[3.26]:

$$\begin{aligned} l,s \models \neg\langle\alpha\rangle\neg\varphi &\iff \textbf{not}\,(\textbf{Exist}\,s'.\,s\rho_l(\alpha)s'\,\textbf{and}\,l,s'\models\neg\varphi)\\ &\iff \textbf{All}\,s'.\textbf{not}\,(s\rho_l(\alpha)s'\,\textbf{and}\,l,s'\models\neg\varphi)\\ &\iff \textbf{All}\,s'.\,(\textbf{not}\,s\rho_l(\alpha)s')\,\textbf{or}\,(\textbf{not}\,l,s'\models\neg\varphi)\\ &\iff \textbf{All}\,s'.\,\textbf{not}\,s\rho_l(\alpha)s'\,\textbf{or}\,l,s'\models\varphi\\ &\iff \textbf{All}\,s'.\,s\rho_l(\alpha)s'\,\textbf{implies}\,l,s'\models\varphi\\ &\iff l,s\models[\alpha]\varphi \end{aligned}$$

3.24. In the KeY-logics free variables are not allowed; all variables are quantified. In stead of variables also skolem functions may be used. These are new function symbols which have arbitrary interpretations.

3.25. A specification is of the form $\varphi \rightarrow \langle\alpha\rangle\phi$ or $\varphi \rightarrow [\alpha]\phi$ where φ is the precondition and ϕ is the postcondition of the program α.

3.26. The transformations of the linguistic abbreviations correspond to replacements of definitions of first-order logic semantics and application of first-order logic calculus rules on a meta-level. These concepts will be defined in the second chapter.

3.2 Substitution and Term Rewriting

Definition 3.17. (Substitution) *A (uniform variable) substitution is a total endomorphism* σ: Trm $\to$ Trm *(respectively* σ: Fml $\to$ Fml *for substitutions on formulas) of finite support, i.e.*

$$\begin{aligned}
\sigma(f(t_1, ..., t_n)) &= f(\sigma t_1, ..., \sigma t_n) \\
\sigma|_\Sigma &= \text{id } \textit{except for a finite number of variables}^{3.27} \\
\sigma|_V &= \text{id } \textit{except for a finite number of variables} \\
\sigma(\phi(t_1, ..., t_n)) &= \phi(\sigma t_1, ..., \sigma t_n) \\
\sigma\forall x.\phi &= \forall x.\sigma\phi \\
\sigma\exists x.\phi &= \sigma\exists x.\phi
\end{aligned}$$

with $f(t_1, ..., t_n) \in \text{Trm}$ *and* $\phi(t_1, ..., t_n) \in \text{Fml}$

Definition 3.18. (Admissible Substituition)

1. *A substitution* σ *is* first-order admissible *or* free of collisions *for a formula* ϕ, *if no free variable* x *occurs within the scope of a quantifier binding a variable of* σx.

2. *A substitution* $[s \mapsto t]$ *is admissible (or denotation-preserving) for* ϕ, *if it is first-order admissible and, during the process of substituting* s *by* t *in* ϕ *for the formation of* ϕ_s^t, *neither* s *nor* t *trespass modalities for which they are not rigid, i.e. no* s *occurs in the scope of a modality updating a constant symbol of* s *or* t. [33]

At this stage of the iterative development of CDL in the thesis the item 2 of definition 3.18 means that a substitution must not trespass any modality because it is unknown in which cases terms are rigid or not rigid for programs. In the next chapter we introduce the modality "update" for which it can be determined in some cases whether a term is rigid for a particular update.

As will be shown in the next section the substitution is important for the application of derived equations on sub-terms of formulas. The drawback of substitutions is however the strong restriction that only elements in $V \cup \Sigma$ may be substituted.

An alternative technique is provided by rewrite rules. Rewrite rules can replace complex terms by other complex terms if this replacement is justified by an *axiom*. An asiom is an equation — formula with top-level predicate $\doteq$ — that holds in any interpretation and in any state and is therefore a tautology. A set of axioms constitutes an equational system.

"The idea of a term rewriting system is to orient an equation $r \doteq s$ into a rule $r \rightsquigarrow s$ indicating that instances of r may be replaced by instances of s but not vice versa." [18] "A *term rewriting system* R is a set of rules of the form $r \rightsquigarrow s$, where r and s are terms. It is common to require that any variable that appears in s must also appear in r." [18]

Definition 3.19. (Rewrite Relation) *A rewrite rule $r \rightsquigarrow s$ holds iff $r \doteq s$ is an axiom and r and s have the same variables.*

Definition 3.20. (Transitive Closure) *The relation R^* is the (reflexive)* transitive closure *of the relation R and is defined as follows.*

$$x R^* y \Longleftrightarrow \text{there are } x = x_0, x_1, \ldots, x_n = y \text{ such that } x_i R x_{i+1} \text{ for each } i$$

[33]

Definition 3.21. (Confluence) *A relation R on a set M is* confluent *if for each $x, y_1, y_2 \in M$ with $x R y_1$ and $x R y_2$ there is $z \in M$ such that $y_1 R^* z$ and $y_2 R^* z$.* [33]

Definition 3.22. *A relation R on a set M is* Noetherian *(or termination) if there is no infinite sequence $x_1, x_2, x_3, \ldots \in M$ with $x_i R x_{i+1}$ for each i.* [33]

Definition 3.23. (Evaluation by Fixed-Point Rewriting) *The relation $\rightsquigarrow^*$ is the* fixed-point *rewrite version of $\rightsquigarrow$. $s \rightsquigarrow^* t$ holds if and only if there is a finite sequence $s = s_0, s_1, \ldots, s_n = t \in$* Trm *such that for each i $s_i \rightsquigarrow s_{i+1}$ holds and there is no s_{n+1} with $s_n \rightsquigarrow s_{n+1}$. In this case, we say that s* evaluates *to t (by rewrite).* [33]

3.3 Sequent Calculus

A calculus is a set of rules which describe transformations on a formal language; in this case dynamic logic. A rule is a relation on syntactical elements. The purpose of the transformations is in the context of the thesis to prove that a program is correct with respect to a specification, i.e. that $\varphi \rightarrow \langle \alpha \rangle \phi$ is a tautology. The requirements on the calculus are that it is correct with respect to the semantic of the logic; this is called soundness.

Definition 3.24. (Sequent) *A sequent is of the form $\Gamma \vdash \Delta$, where Γ, Δ are duplicate-free lists of formulas. The left-hand side Γ is called antecedent and the right-hand side Δ is called succedent of the sequent. The semantics of a sequent $\Gamma \vdash \Delta$ is the same as that of the formula $\bigwedge \Gamma \rightarrow \bigvee \Delta$.* [11]

Remark: The symbol "$\vdash$" is often used to represent a set of inference rules in other literature. It must not be confused with the sequent symbols.

Definition 3.25. (Rule) *A* rule *R is a binary relation between (a) the set of all tuples of sequence and (b) the set of all sequence. If* $R(\langle P_1, \ldots, P_k\rangle, C)(k \geqslant 0)$, *then the* conclusion *C is* derivable *from the* premises $P_1, \ldots, P_k$ *using rule R.*

Definition 3.26. (Calculus) *A calculus is a set of rules.*

Definition 3.27. *The set of sequence that are derivable in a calculus C is the smallest set such that: If there is a rule in C that allows to derive a sequent S from premises that are all derivable in C, then S is derivable in C.*

Definition 3.28. (Rule Schema) *A rule schema is of the form*

$$\frac{P_1 \;\; P_2 \;\; \ldots \;\; P_k}{C} \quad (k \geqslant 0)$$

where $P_1, \ldots, P_k$ *and C are schematic sequence, i.e., sequence containing schema variables.*

A rule schema $P_1 \ldots P_k/C$ *represents a rule R if the following equivalence holds: a sequent* C^* *is derivable from premises* $P_1^* \ldots P_k^*$ *iff* $P_1^* \ldots P_k^*/C^*$ *is an instance of the rule schema. Schema instances are constructed by instantiating the schema variables with syntactical constructs (terms, formulas, etc) which are compliant to the types of the schema variables.*

Definition 3.29. (Soundness) *A rule R is sound with respect to* $\vDash_l$ *if the following implication holds*

$$\textit{if } (\langle P_1, \ldots, P_k\rangle, C) \in R \textit{ then } P_1, \ldots, P_k \vDash_l C$$

and it is sound with respect to $\vDash_g$ *if the following implication holds*

$$\textit{if } (\langle P_1, \ldots, P_k\rangle, C) \in R \textit{ then } P_1, \ldots, P_k \vDash_g C$$

In the if-part $P_1, \ldots, P_k$ *represents a tuple of sequence and in the then-part each P represents its equivalent formula as defined in def 3.24.*

A rule schema is sound wrt. $\vDash_l$ *or* $\vDash_g$ *if all possible instantiations of the rule schema are sound w.r.t.* $\vDash_l$ *or* $\vDash_g$ *respectively.*

A calculus is sound wrt. $\vDash_l$ *or* $\vDash_g$ *if all rules of the calculus are sound w.r.t.* $\vDash_l$ *or* $\vDash_g$ *respectively.*

3.3.1 First-order Calculus

In the following tables we present the rule schema of propositional logic and first-order logic. All rules we present are part of the calculus of CDL.

(R1) $\neg$ left
$$\frac{\vdash \mathrm{A}}{\neg A \vdash}$$

(R2) $\wedge$ left
$$\frac{A, B \vdash}{A \wedge B \vdash}$$

(R3) $\vee$ left
$$\frac{A \vdash \qquad \vdash B}{A \vee B \vdash}$$

(R4) $\rightarrow$ left
$$\frac{\vdash A \qquad B \vdash}{A \rightarrow B \vdash}$$

(R5) cut
$$\frac{A \vdash \qquad \vdash A}{\vdash}$$

(R6) weakening (left)
$$\frac{\vdash}{A \vdash}$$

(R7) $\neg$ right
$$\frac{A \vdash}{\vdash \neg A}$$

(R8) $\wedge$ right
$$\frac{\vdash A \qquad \vdash B}{\vdash A \wedge B}$$

(R9) $\vee$ right
$$\frac{\vdash A, B}{\vdash A \vee B}$$

(R10) $\rightarrow$ right
$$\frac{A \vdash B}{\vdash A \rightarrow B}$$

(R11) axiom
$$\frac{\vdash}{A \vdash A}$$

(R12) weakening (right)
$$\frac{\vdash}{\vdash A}$$

Table 3.1 Propositional Inference Rules

(R13) $\forall$ left
$$\frac{A_x^t, \forall x\, A \vdash}{\forall x\, A \vdash}$$

(R14) $\exists$ left
$$\frac{A_x^X \vdash}{\exists x\, A \vdash}$$

(R15) induction
$$\frac{\vdash \phi(0) \qquad \phi(n) \vdash \phi(n+1)}{\vdash \forall n \phi(n)}$$

$\Longleftarrow n$ new variable

(R16) $\doteq$ subst
$$\frac{\Gamma_s^t, s \doteq t \vdash \Delta_s^t}{\Gamma, s \doteq t \vdash \Delta}$$

(R17) $\forall$ right
$$\frac{\vdash A_x^X}{\vdash \forall x\, A}$$

(R18) $\exists$ right
$$\frac{\vdash A_x^t, \exists x\, A}{\vdash \exists x\, A}$$

(R19) $\doteq$ reflexive
$$\frac{\vdash}{\vdash t \doteq t}$$

(R20) $\doteq$ subst
$$\frac{\Gamma_s^t, t \doteq s \vdash \Delta_s^t}{\Gamma, t \doteq s \vdash \Delta}$$

Table 3.2 First-Order Inference Rules.

In table 3.2 t is a term, X is a new logical variable in the sequent, and all substitutions are admissible (def. 3.18).

These rules can be further generalized by the contextual lifting lemma 3.30 and context free inference lemma 3.31 which will be given below.

3.3.2 Integration of Rewrite Rules

Rule schema have the "disadvantage", that they allow to specify only rules on the level of sequences or — when considering the generalizations of the above lemmas — on the level of formulas. Rules describing transformations on terms are given by term rewrite rules. In addition to the propositional and first-order rules we present here the rules which *plug-in* term rewriting system into the sequent calculus.

(R35) term rewrite (left)

$$\frac{\phi(t) \vdash}{\phi(s) \vdash} \Longleftarrow (s \leadsto t) \text{ holds}$$

(R36) term rewirte (right)

$$\frac{\vdash \phi(t)}{\vdash \phi(s)} \Longleftarrow (s \leadsto t) \text{ holds}$$

Table 3.3. Rewrite rule application

$\phi(t)$ denotes the formula obtained by substituting s by t in $\phi(s)$. The restrictions on the substitution are implicitly given by the restriction on rewrite rules, which must meets the required conditions of def. 3.19. "By convention, the term rewrite rules are further subject to the constraint that s really occurs within $\phi(s)$, otherise no proper inference rule application of any visible effect could happen anyway." [33]

3.3.3 Generalisations for Dynamic Logic

The following two lemmas allows a further generalization of rule schemata. The lemmas are taken from [33] where also proofs of the lemmas can be found.

Lemma 3.30. (Contextual Lifting) *Provided that Γ, Δ are not both empty,*

$$\frac{\Gamma' \vdash \Delta'}{\Gamma \vdash \Delta} \; \textit{sound wrt.} \models_l \; \Rightarrow \; \frac{[\alpha]\Gamma' \vdash \langle\alpha\rangle\Delta'}{[\alpha]\Gamma \vdash \langle\alpha\rangle\Delta} \; \textit{sound wrt.} \models_l$$

Expecially, in case of deterministic termination programs like updates or cascades of conditional updates this statement can be refined as follows and generalized to $n \geqslant 1$ *premises.*

$$\frac{\Gamma' \vdash \Delta'}{\Gamma \vdash \Delta} \text{ sound wrt.} \vDash_l \;\Rightarrow\; \frac{\langle\alpha\rangle\Gamma' \vdash \langle\alpha\rangle\Delta'}{\langle\alpha\rangle\Gamma \vdash \langle\alpha\rangle\Delta} \text{ sound wrt.} \vDash_l$$

For a sequent context Δ *of the form* $\phi_1, ..., \phi_n$ *the symbolic notation* $\langle\alpha\rangle\Delta$ *is an abbreviation for* $\langle\alpha\rangle\phi_1, ..., \langle\alpha\rangle\phi_n$ *rather than* $\langle a\rangle(\phi_1 \vee ... \vee \phi_n)$*, here. Similarly,* $[\alpha]\Delta$ *abbreviates* $[\alpha]\phi_1, ..., [\alpha]\phi_n$.

Lemma 3.31. (Context-free Inference) *If*

$$\frac{\Phi_1 \vdash \Psi_1 \quad ... \quad \Phi_n \vdash \Psi_n}{\Phi \vdash \Psi}$$

is sound wrt. $\vDash_l$ *then the following inference rule is sound wrt.* $\vDash_l$

$$\frac{\Gamma, \Phi_1 \vdash \Psi_1, \Delta \quad ... \quad \Gamma, \Phi_n \vdash \Psi_n, \Delta}{\Gamma, \Phi \vdash \Psi, \Delta}$$

The proofes for lemma 3.30 and lemma 3.31 are given in [33].

Within this context we also give two rules which are sound only wrt. $\vDash_g$

(R46) $\langle\rangle$ generalisation

$$\frac{A \vdash B}{\langle\alpha\rangle A \vdash \langle\alpha\rangle B}$$

(R47) $[]$ generalisation

$$\frac{A \vdash B}{[\alpha]A \vdash [\alpha]B}$$

Table 3.4. Global inference rules

Chapter 4

KeY Concepts

4.1 The KeY-System

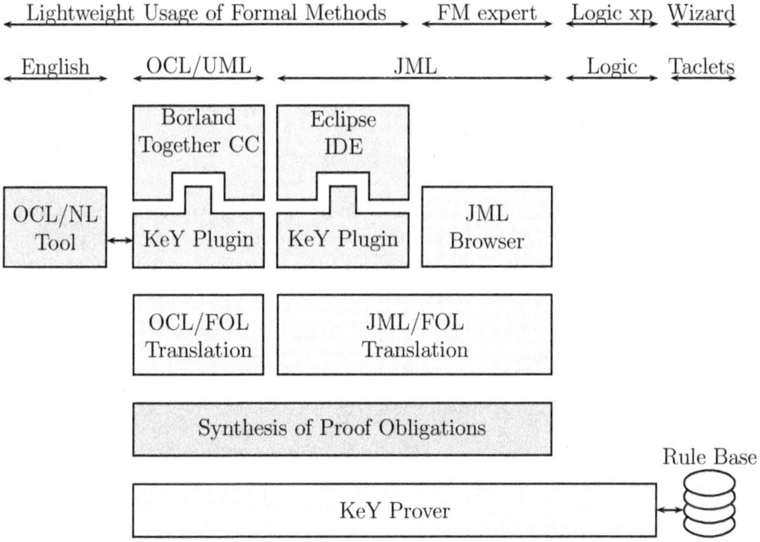

Figure 4.1. KeY's architecture

The idea behind KeY is the close integration of formal specification and verification into the object-oriented development process. This way formal methods become applicable and accessible to people who already use object-oriented development techniques.[27]p.5. The specification is done by annotation of an UML[30] diagram with OCL constrains which can subsequently be automatically translated into DL formulas for the verification process.

The KeY-tool is an extension/plug-in of the CASE-tool TogetherCC from Borland[4.1] and a version of KeY for the CASE-tool Eclipse[4.2] is currently in development. The advantage of this approach is that all features of the existing tool can be reused and usage of the tool becomes more feasible for the developer, especially if he is already familiar with the tools.

On the top level the KeY-system is composed from three components. The modeling component, verification middleware, and the deduction component.

1. The modeling component consists of the Together CC-tool for creating UML diagrams and source code and is extended with features for editing OCL constrains

2. The verification middleware is responsible for translating the UML diagram, the source code, and the OCL constrains into proof obligations for the deduction components. The proof obligations are formulas of JavaCardDL.

3. The deduction component is an interactive and automatic theorem prover which is used to construct proofs from the proof obligations obtained from the verification middleware.

The implementation part of the thesis deals only with the extension of the deduction component so that the further descriptions of the modeling component and the verification middleware will be omitted in the implementation part of the thesis.

The rule base of the deduction component is implemented in the taclet language described next.

4.1.1 Taclets

The idea behind *taclets* is derived from tactics of tactical theorem provers. Tactics are programs which act on a proof tree by execution of primitive rules from a small, fixed set. To extend the prover, for example to support a new datatype theory, the user may program special tactics for that purpose by using a tactical programming language with conditional statements, loops, and method invocations. This however, requires the user to have expert knowledge of the theorem prover. [11]

4.1. http://www.borland.com/together/

4.2. http://www.eclipse.org

The taclet language is restricted in the expressibility of syntactic operations but it provides sufficient means for implementing rules for first order dynamic logic including program transformations.

A *schema variable* is a syntactic entity on the meta level of the syntax of a logic and programs. This means that the instantiations of schema variables are syntactic entities of logic (function-, predicate-, variable- symbols, connectors, quantifiers, modal operators, terms, and formulas) and programs (any program elements). A schema variable has a type which determines what syntactic elements of the logic or program it may represent. Just like the syntactic elements of the logic or program can be composed to build terms and formulas or expressions and statements, schema variables of the corresponding types can be composed to schematic terms, schematic formulas, schematic program elements, or schematic sequents.

A *taclet* is a representation of a schema rule or a rewrite rule. The general form of a taclet is:

$$
\begin{array}{rl}
\texttt{assumes}(\mathit{cond}) & \texttt{find}(\mathit{target})\ \texttt{varcond}(\mathit{vc}) \\
\texttt{replacewith}(\mathit{rw}) & \texttt{add}(\mathit{add}_1)\ \texttt{addrules}(\mathit{addTac}_1) \\
 & \vdots \\
 & \texttt{add}(\mathit{add}_n)\ \texttt{addrules}(\mathit{addTac}_m)
\end{array}
$$

cond, *target*, *vc*,*rw*,*add*, and *addTac* are schematic patterns which may represent schematic terms, schematic formula etc. The **target** determines the syntactic entity on which the taclet can be applied; it determines the syntactic entity that may be in focus of the taclet. If **target** is a schematic sequent or a formula then the taclet represents a rule schema. If the **target** is a schematic term then it represents a (schematic) rewrite rule. Since schema variables may represent program elements a taclet may be applied on a program to perform program transformations.

When a taclet is applied on a syntactic entity then the schema variables occurring in **target** are instantiated. The instantiation takes place for all respective occurrences of schematic variables in the taclet. The application of the taclet performs a syntactic substitution of **target** by *rw* if the the **replacewith** construct is present. This way only the syntactic *replacement* can be realized. In order to add formulas to a sequent, the add construct is used. The schema variables of add_i are instantiated and the instantiated version of add_i is added to the sequent. By using the construct **addrules** the set of taclets can be extended by taclet application. This is useful when an equation is used for substitution. In this case one taclet matches via find(*target*) an equation and creates a taclet via addrules(addTac_m). The later can then be used to perform a substitution according to the equation.

The applicability of a taclet can be restricted by the constraint `cond`. If the construct `assumes(cond)` is present in the taclet definition then the taclet is only applicable if `cond` occurs in the sequent. When substitutions of variables are performed then it is important meat some constrains. For example a bound variable must not be replaced by another variable and a free variable must not be replaced such that it becomes bound. Constrains of this kind can be specified by variable conditions `vc`. Variable conditions are also used for the creation of program variables when a taclet is applied on a program.

Furthermore, schematic programs are extended by *meta constructs* which may occur in `rw`, `add` and `addTac`. A meta construct is a procedure that can be implemented by Java classes in the KeY prover. It may take some arguments of (usually) schematic variables and perform any syntactical operations. The meta construct is then replaced by the syntactic result it returns. This way syntactic operations can be implemented which would otherwise not be possible to be expressed in the taclet language; e.g, the replacement of a function call by its body.

4.2 Updates

An *update* is a special modal operator extending the syntax of dynamic logic. Updates don't change the expressibility of the logic but they are associated with a special calculus for "handling" of assignments and the evaluation of program variables or terms in the presence of aliasing. More on this can be found in [10], [33], and [34]. In its basic form an update is a side-effect-free assignment to a term, program variable or non-rigid function[4.3]. The innovative aspect of updates is that embedded updates can be merged resulting in a *simultaneous* (or *parallel*) update. A simultaneous update can be viewed as table or *list* of parallel assignments which represents a state (or a partial state) while care is taken for the aliasing problem. In contrast to the assignment rule of Hoare logic the effect of assignments can be delayed while a program is syntactically executed; which is due to lemma 3.30. Another advantage of updates is that this concepts is flexible and allows further extensions like quantified updates. In contrast to a single update which represents only one assignment or to a simultaneous updates which requires explicit listing of sub-updates, a quantified update represents a set of updates/assignments in a short form.

4.3. This is the intuitive understanding, but updates are actually assignments to locations.

4.2.1 Syntax

Definition 4.1. (Syntactic Updates) *The set of updates is inductively defined as the smallest set with*

- skip *is an (ineffective) update.*
- *If* $s, t \in \mathrm{Trm}$ *are terms and the top-level symbol of* s *is a non-rigid function/constant symbol, then* $\{s := t\}$ *is an (elementary) update. The left-hand side of an elementary update (here* s*) is called location term and the right-hand side (here* t*) is called value term.*
- *If a (parallel or simultaneous) update consisting of the (sub-)updates* $\{\mathcal{U}_1\} \ldots \{\mathcal{U}_n\}$ *is written as* $\{\mathcal{U}_1, \ldots, \mathcal{U}_n\}$ *or alternatively as* $\{\mathcal{U}_1\} | \ldots | \{\mathcal{U}_n\}$
- *If* $\mathcal{U}_1, \mathcal{U}_2$ *are updates, then* $\mathcal{U}_1; \mathcal{U}_2$ *is a (sequential) update*
- *If* $\mathcal{U}$ *is an update,* $x \in V$ *a variable and* $\varphi \in \mathrm{Fml}$ *a formula, then* $\{\mathrm{for}\, x; \varphi; \mathcal{U}\}$ *is a (quantified) update.*

[34]

Definition 4.2. (Extension Terms) *The set* Trm *of terms in CDL as defined in def. 3.4 is inductively extended by:*

- *If* $e \in \mathrm{Fml}$ *is a formula without the modalities* $\langle\!\{\,\}\!\rangle$ *and* $[\!\{\,\}\!]$ *and* $s, t \in \mathrm{Trm}_\tau$ *then* $\mathrm{if}\, e\, \mathrm{then}\, s\, \mathrm{else}\, t\, \mathrm{fi} \in \mathrm{Trm}_\tau$.[4.4]
- *If* $t \in \mathrm{Trm}$ *and* $\{\mathcal{U}\}$ *is an update then* $\{\mathcal{U}\} t \in \mathrm{Trm}$*. In this context* t *is called* target *(Term)*

Definition 4.3. (Extension Formulas) *The set* Fml *of formulas of CDL as defined in def.3.5 is inductively extended by*

- *If* $\phi \in \mathrm{Fml}$ *and* $\{\mathcal{U}\}$ *is an update then* $\{\mathcal{U}\}\phi \in \mathrm{Fml}$*. In this context* ϕ *is called* target *(Formula)*

4.2.2 Semantic

Definition 4.4. (Location) *The set* $\mathbb{L}\mathrm{oc}$ *of locations consists of tuples* $f\!: (a_1, \ldots, a_n)$ *and* $x\!:$ *where* $f \in \mathbf{\Sigma}$, $a_1, \ldots, a_n \in \boldsymbol{U}$ *and* $x \in \boldsymbol{V}$*. In case* $n = 0$ f *is a constant and we write* $f\!:$ *or* $f\!: ()$*, like in the case of variables* x*.*

4.4. That e is without the modalities $\langle\!\{\,\}\!\rangle$ *and* $[\!\{\,\}\!]$ *does not mean that e is a pure first-order formula like it is the case in [33]. e may contain updates.*

Definition 4.5. (Semantic Update) *The set of semantic updates $\mathbb{U}$ consists of partial functions from locations in $\mathbb{L}\mathrm{oc}$ to elements in U. It can also be regarded as a partial function from symbols in $\Sigma \cup V$ to partial functions on U.*[4.5] *A semantic update is denoted by*

$$[s\colon \bar{v} \mapsto v]$$

where $s\colon \bar{v} \in \mathbb{L}\mathrm{oc}$ and $v \in U$.

Depending of the view on semantic updates the notation can be understood according to one of the two possible syntax trees:

Partial functions from $\mathbb{L}\mathrm{oc}$ to U	Partial functions from Σ to functions on U
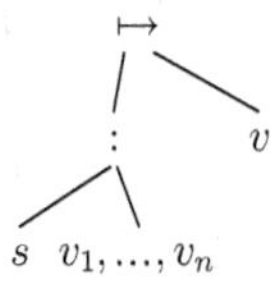	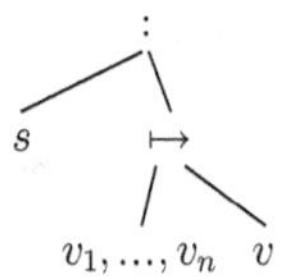

In this thesis all predicate symbols are rigid so that no updates to predicate symbols, or relations, occur.[4.6] Therefore, locations of the form $f\colon (a_1, \ldots, a_n)$ are implicitly restricted to non-rigid function symbols $f \in \Sigma_{\mathrm{nr}}^f$. For a variable x a semantic update looks like $[x\colon \mapsto v]$ and for a n-ary function symbol f it looks like $[f\colon (a_1, \ldots, a_n) \mapsto v]$. A semantic update which contains more than one element is denoted by a comma separated list like $[s_1\colon \bar{v}_1 \mapsto v_1, \ldots, s_m\colon \bar{v}_m \mapsto v_m]$ with $s_1\colon \bar{v}_1, \ldots, s_m\colon \bar{v}_m \in \mathbb{L}\mathrm{oc}$. If several locations share the same symbol of $f \in \Sigma$ we may write $f\colon [(a_{1_1}, \ldots, a_{n_1}) \mapsto v_1, \ldots, (a_{1_m}, \ldots, a_{n_m}) \mapsto v_m]$ instead of $[f\colon (a_{1_1}, \ldots, a_{n_1}) \mapsto v_1, \ldots, f\colon (a_{1_m}, \ldots, a_{n_m}) \mapsto v_m]$. The stress of this notation is on the view on updates as partial functions from Σ to functions on U.

From the definition follows that a semantic update is a partial interpretation or a variable assignment. Thus the interpretation of an update is an interpretation.

Definition 4.6. *(Semantic overriding) Given two semantic updates $u_1, u_2 \in \mathbb{U}$, we define the overriding $u_1 \lessdot u_2$ of u_1 by u_2 as it is common in the B Method:*

$$(u_1 \lessdot u_2)(\mathrm{loc}) = \begin{cases} u_1(\mathrm{loc}) \text{ \emph{for} } u_2(\mathrm{loc}) = \bot \\ u_2(\mathrm{loc}) \text{ \emph{otherwise}} \end{cases}$$

4.5. We do not distinguish strictly — mathematically correct — between a constant null-ary function and its value.

4.6. The two possibilities between updates to predicate symbols and updates to relations result from the two possible views on semantical updates in the definition. It makes no difference for our purposes whether the interpretation is modified or the function. We will make use of both views.

Where loc *is a location. Overriding can in particular be employed to interpretations (for instance* $I \lessdot u$*)* [34]

We extend the valuation $\mathrm{val}_l(s, .)$ to the valuation of updates. This may seem to be odd since updates are modal operators and their semantics is specified by using the accessibilty relation. By the extensions of the valuation the modal operators "updates" are treated like function symbols. In fact, updates embedding terms yielding again terms can be viewed as functions. Using a quantified variable in an update results therefore in quantification over function symbols yielding second-order (or higher-order) logic. Since updates don't change the expressibility of the logic it follows that first-order dynamic logic is a higher-order logic. There is however still a "semantic gap" between updates and function symbols so that we need to extend the definition of valuation.

Definition 4.7. (Extended Valuation) *The definition of the* valuation *as given in def.3.11 is extended by*

$$\mathrm{val}_l(s, \{\mathcal{U}\}) = \{t \mid s\rho_l(\{\mathcal{U}\})t\} \subset \mathbb{U}$$

In order to omit confusion between syntactic updates an sets we denote sets of semantic updates by using the brackets '[' and ']' as described above in stead of the brackets '{' and '}'.

Definition 4.8. *Suppose that* U *is a universe that is well-ordered by a relation* $\preccurlyeq$. *The evaluation of syntactic updates is defined inductively:*

- *Ineffective updates are ineffective:*

$$\mathrm{val}_l(w, \mathrm{skip}) = \emptyset$$

- *For terms* $f(s_1, \ldots, s_n)$, $t \in \mathrm{Trm}(\Sigma \cup V)$ *the value of the update* $\{f(s_1, \ldots, s_2) := t\}$ *is a singleton set:*

$$\mathrm{val}_l(w, \{f(s_1, \ldots, s_2) := t\}) = [f\colon (\mathrm{val}_l(w, s_1), \ldots, \mathrm{val}_l(w, s_n)) \mapsto \mathrm{val}_l(w, t)]$$

- *The evaluation of a parallel (or simultaneous) update* $\{\mathcal{U}_1, \ldots, \mathcal{U}_n\}$ *is:*

$$\mathrm{val}_l(w, \{\mathcal{U}_1, \ldots, \mathcal{U}_n\}) = \mathrm{val}_l(w, \{\mathcal{U}_1\}) \lessdot \ldots \lessdot \mathrm{val}_l(w, \{\mathcal{U}_n\})$$

- *If* $\mathcal{U}_1, \mathcal{U}_2$ *are updates, then the value of the sequential update* $\mathcal{U}_1; \mathcal{U}_2$ *is again obtained by overriding, but the evaluation of the second update is affected by the first one:*

$$\mathrm{val}_l(w, \mathcal{U}_1; \mathcal{U}_2) = \mathrm{val}_l(w \lessdot \mathrm{val}_l(w, \mathcal{U}_1), \mathcal{U}_2)$$

- *If* $\mathcal{U}$ *is an update,* x *is a variable and* φ *is a formula, then the value of the quantified update* $\{\mathrm{for}\, x;\, \varphi; \mathcal{U}\}$ *is defined as follows:*

$$\mathrm{val}_l(w, \{\mathrm{for}\, x;\, \varphi; \mathcal{U}\})(\mathrm{loc}) = \begin{cases} u_{\min_{\preccurlyeq} \mathrm{Def(loc)}}(\mathrm{loc}) \text{ for } \mathrm{Def(loc)} \neq \emptyset \\ \bot, \text{ otherwise} \end{cases}$$

The symbols of the right side are:

$$I_a = I \lessdot [x{:} \mapsto a] \quad (a \in U)$$

u_a *is the value of the sub-update* u *when assigning* x *the individual* a*:*

$$u_a = \mathrm{val}_{I_a}(u) \quad (a \in U)$$

Def(loc) *is the range of* x *for which* u *affects the particular location* loc*:*

$$\mathrm{Def(loc)} = \{a \in U{:}\, u_a(\mathrm{loc}) \neq \bot \text{ and } \mathrm{val}_{I_a}(\varphi) = \mathrm{true}\} \quad (\mathrm{loc} \in \mathbb{L}\mathrm{oc})$$

Note that $\min_{\preccurlyeq} \mathrm{Def(loc)}$ *exists for* $\mathrm{Def(loc)} \neq \emptyset$*, because* $\preccurlyeq$ *is a well-ordering.* [34]

Definition 4.9. (Extension Valuation of Terms and Formulas) *Let* w *be a state of an interpretation* l*. The valuation of terms with respect to* l *and* w *is extended as follows.*

1. *if* $r, t \in \mathrm{Trm}$ *are terms and* $\varphi \in \mathrm{Fml}$ *is a formula without the modalities* $\langle\!\{\}\!\rangle$ *and* $[\![\{\}]\!]$

$$\mathrm{val}_l(w, \mathrm{if}\ \varphi\ \mathrm{then}\ r\ \mathrm{else}\ t\ \mathrm{fi}) := \begin{cases} \mathrm{val}_l(w, r), \mathrm{if}\ \mathrm{val}_l(w, \varphi) = \mathit{true} \\ \mathrm{val}_l(w, t), \mathrm{if}\ \mathrm{val}_l(w, \varphi) = \mathit{false} \end{cases}$$

2. $\mathrm{val}_l(w, \{\mathcal{U}\}t) := \mathrm{val}_l(w', t)$ *with* $w\, \rho_l(\{\mathcal{U}\})\, w'$, *or alternatively* $\mathrm{val}_l(w, \{\mathcal{U}\}t) := \mathrm{val}_l(w \lessdot \mathrm{val}_l(w, \{\mathcal{U}\}), t)$.

In contrast to programs, which are contained in the modalities $\langle\!\{\,\}\!\rangle$ and $[\!\{\,\}\!]$, updates are deterministic and terminating. This allows to provide a well defined semantics of terms that are directly embedded in updates as target terms.

Definition 4.10. (Extension the Equivalence Relation) *The equivalence relation $\equiv$ is extended for updates u_1, u_2 as follows:*

$u_1 \equiv u_2$ *iff for all interpretations l and all states $w \in S^l$* $\mathrm{val}_l(w, u_1) = \mathrm{val}_l(w, u_2)$

4.2.3 Substitution and Rewriting Revised

Lemma 4.11. (Generalised Substitution Lemma) *Let σ be an admissible constant or variable substitution on a term (or formula) t, then the substitution principle holds, i.e.*

for each interpretation l for each state w: $\mathrm{val}_l(w, \sigma t) = \mathrm{val}_{\sigma * l}(\sigma * w, t)$

where $\sigma * l := l[X :\mapsto \mathrm{val}_l(\sigma X)]$ for each $X \in V$ and $\sigma * w := w[X :\mapsto \mathrm{val}_w(\sigma X)]$ for each $X \in \Sigma$ are semantic modification adjoint to σ.

A proof of the generalised substitution lemma can be found in [33].

In the following the "schematic symbol Υ matches all formula and term constructor symbols except, modalities and program constructors. Υ also concerns logical constant symbols like $+$, if then else fi, $\wedge$. Likewise, in this context, u is a generalized formal parameter and may as well represent an n-tuple of arguments for $0 \leqslant n \in \mathbb{N}$." [33]

(R28) update (promotion)
$\{f(s) := t\}\Upsilon(u) \rightsquigarrow \Upsilon(\{f(s) := t\}u)$
$\Longleftarrow f \neq \Upsilon \in \Sigma$
(R31) update (distinct)
$\{\mathcal{U}\}\Upsilon(u) \rightsquigarrow \Upsilon(\{\mathcal{U}\}u)$
$\Longleftarrow \mathcal{U}$ contains no updates to $\Upsilon \in \Sigma$
(R32) update merge
$\{\mathcal{U}\}\{\mathcal{U}'\}\phi \rightsquigarrow \{\mathcal{U}, f_1'(\{\mathcal{U}\}s_1') := \{\mathcal{U}\}t_1', \ldots, f_m'(\{\mathcal{U}\}s_m') := \{\mathcal{U}\}t_m'\}\phi$
(R34) update on formula
$\{f(s) := t\}p(u) \rightsquigarrow p(\{f(s) := t\}u)$
$\Longleftarrow p \in \Sigma$ predicate

The rewrite rules (R29), (R31), (R32), and (R34) originate from [33]. In cases where $\Upsilon(u)$ is a formula the so obtained formula after rewriting is correct but this does not comply to the definition of the rewrite relation $\rightsquigarrow$, which is a relation between terms. A correct treatement would be to give additional schema rules for formulas which have the same effect. The rule schemata presented below subsume (R28), (R31), and (R34) because predicates are rigid in the KeY logics (including CDL). In the following Υ_φ may match formula constructors except for modalities.

(R31b) update promotion(right)	(R31c) update promotion(right)
$\dfrac{\vdash \Upsilon_\varphi(\{\mathcal{U}\}u)}{\vdash \{\mathcal{U}\}\Upsilon_\varphi(u)}$	$\dfrac{\Upsilon_\varphi(\{\mathcal{U}\}u) \vdash}{\{\mathcal{U}\}\Upsilon_\varphi(u) \vdash}$

Since $\Upsilon_\varphi(\{\mathcal{U}\}u) \equiv \{\mathcal{U}\}\Upsilon_\varphi(u)$, the rewrite rules (R29), (R31), (R32), and (R34) can be applied *indirectly* on formulas. For instance, given the formula $\{\mathcal{U}_1\}\{\mathcal{U}_2\}\Upsilon_\varphi(u)$ the two updates can be promoted to terms, merged by the application of rule (R32), and then be "unpromoted" back "in front of" the formula yielding $\{\mathcal{U}_1, \mathcal{U}_2'\}\Upsilon_\varphi(u)$. We assume that this strategy is applied without giving a rule for "unpromotion" because this would allow repetitive application of promotion and "unpromotion" without effect leading to a termination problem.

Notation: Due to this (desired) merging of updates before they are applied on formulas, we abbreviate those compositions of rewrite rules and schema rules by allowing rewrite rules between formulas. Furthermore we allow rewrite rules between updates, meaning that the rewrite rule can be instantiated with arbitrary terms (and consequently formulas) following them. Thus this yields two kinds of rewrite rules. The first one is the *normal* kind of rewrite rules where a rewrite rule represents an equation ($\doteq$) on the level of the logic. The second kind of rewrite rules represents an "equation" on the meta level of the logic, namely the equivalence relation ($\equiv$).

The idea of rewrite rules between updates complies with the idea of rewriting. As described in the previous section an update that is the top-level "symbol" of a term can be viewed as higher order function symbol. "In addition, a functional program is essentially a set of equations, typically with higher order functions, and the execution of a program is then a kind of equational reasoning." [18]

4.2.4 Update Calculus

The rules presented here originate from [33] and [34].

(R37) conditional term split (left)

$$\frac{(e \rightarrow \phi(s)) \wedge (\neg e \rightarrow \phi(t)) \vdash}{\phi(\text{if } e \text{ then } s \text{ else } t \text{ fi}) \vdash}$$

(R38) conditional term split (right)

$$\frac{\vdash (e \rightarrow \phi(s)) \wedge (\neg e \rightarrow \phi(t))}{\vdash \phi(\text{if } e \text{ then } s \text{ else } t \text{ fi})}$$

Table 4.1 Conditional Term

In table 4.1 $\phi(s)$ is the formula obtained from ϕ by an implicit admissible substitution $\phi(s) = \phi^s_z$. In the following table the "schematic symbol Υ matches all formula and term constructor symbols except, modalities and program constructors. Υ also concerns logical constant symbols like $+$, if then else fi, $\wedge$. Likewise, in this context, u is a generalized formal parameter and may as well represent an n-tuple of arguments for $0 \leqslant n \in \mathbb{N}$." [33]

(R27) update (match)

$\{f(s) := t\} f(u) \rightsquigarrow \text{if } s \doteq \{f(s) := t\} u \text{ then } t \text{ else } f(\{f(s) := t\} u) \text{ fi}$

(R28) update (promotion)

$\{f(s) := t\} \Upsilon(u) \rightsquigarrow \Upsilon(\{f(s) := t\} u)$

$\Longleftarrow f \neq \Upsilon \in \Sigma$

(R29) update ($\forall$)

$\{\mathcal{U}\} \forall x \phi \rightsquigarrow \forall x \{\mathcal{U}\} \phi$

$\Longleftarrow x$ not in $\mathrm{FV}(\mathcal{U})$

(R30) update (match)

$\{\mathcal{U}\} f(u) \rightsquigarrow \text{if } s_{i_r} \doteq \{\mathcal{U}\} u \text{ then } t_{i_r} \text{ else} \ldots \text{ if } s_{i_1} \doteq \{\mathcal{U}\} u \text{ then } t_{i_1} \text{ else } f(\{\mathcal{U}\} u) \text{fi fi}$

$\Longleftarrow (i_1, \ldots, i_r) = (i\colon f_i = f)$

(R31) update (distinct)

$\{\mathcal{U}\} \Upsilon(u) \rightsquigarrow \Upsilon(\{\mathcal{U}\} u)$

$\Longleftarrow \mathcal{U}$ contains no updates to $\Upsilon \in \Sigma$

(R32) update merge

$\{\mathcal{U}\}\{\mathcal{U}'\} \phi \rightsquigarrow \{\mathcal{U}, f'_1(\{\mathcal{U}\} s'_1) := \{\mathcal{U}\} t'_1, \ldots, f'_m(\{\mathcal{U}\} s'_m) := \{\mathcal{U}\} t'_m\} \phi$

(R34) update on formula

$\{f(s) := t\} p(u) \rightsquigarrow p(\{f(s) := t\} u)$

$\Longleftarrow p \in \Sigma$ predicate

Table 4.2 Term Rewrite Rules.

In the table 4.2, "$\{\mathcal{U}\}$ is a short notation for the (simultaneous) parallel update $\{f_1(s_1) := t_1, \ldots, f_n(s_n) := t_n\}$, and $\{\mathcal{U}'\}$ short for $\{f'_1(s'_1) := t'_1, \ldots,$

$f'_m(s'_m) := t'_m\}$. The free variables of an update are defined as expected $\mathrm{FV}(\{f_1(s_1) := t_1, ..., f_n(s_n) := t_n\}) := \mathrm{FV}(\{s_1, ..., s_n, t_1, ..., t_n\})$. Further, the notation $(i_1, ..., i_r) = (i\colon f_i = f)$ selects all indices of top-level function symbol f without changing the order." [33]

(RQuan) quantified parallel update

for a $\{\mathcal{U}\} = \{\text{for}\,\bar{x_1};\, \varphi_1;\, s_1 := t_1, ..., \text{for}\,\bar{x_n};\, \varphi_n;\, s_n := t_n\}$

where each $\text{for}\,\bar{x_i};\, \varphi_i;\, s_i := t_i$ is of the form

$\text{for}(y_1, ..., y_l);\, \varphi_i;\, g(b_1, ..., b_m) := t_i$

we have

$$\{\mathcal{U}\}\, f(a_1, ..., a_k) \rightsquigarrow \text{if}\, C_n\, \text{then}\, T_n\, \text{else} ... (\text{if}\, C_1\, \text{then}\, T_1\, \text{else}\, f(\{\mathcal{U}\}a_1, ..., \{\mathcal{U}\}a_k$$

with

$$C_i = \begin{cases} \exists y_1 ... \exists y_l . C'_i \text{ for } f = g, k = m \\ \text{false, otherwise} \end{cases}$$

$$C'_i = \varphi_i \wedge \{\mathcal{U}\}a_1 \doteq b_1 \wedge ... \wedge \{\mathcal{U}\}a_k \doteq b_k$$

and the term T_i evolves from t_i by assigning occurring variables the smallest possible values:

$$[y_1 \mapsto \min_{\preccurlyeq} y_1 . \exists y_2 . ... \exists y_l . C'_i][y_2 \mapsto \min_{\preccurlyeq} y_2 . \exists y_2 . ... \exists y_l . C'_i] ... [y_l \mapsto \min_{\preccurlyeq} y_1 . C'_i] t_i$$

Table 4.3 Quantified update application

Note that here we use only syntactic entities. Thus "$[X \mapsto Y]$" is a substitution. The rule for quantified update application originates from [34]. Furthermore the following derived rules are useful.

(R48) update occurrence

$\{\mathcal{U}\}\phi \rightsquigarrow \{\mathcal{U}'\}\phi$

$\{\mathcal{U}'\}$ equals $\{\mathcal{U}\}$ with location not occurring admissible in in ϕ removed, i.e. remove $f(s) := t$ iff $\phi_f^{f'} = \phi$

(R49) update deletion

$\{..., f(s) := t, ..., f(s) := t'\} \rightsquigarrow \{..., f(s) := t'\}$

(R50) update no-op

$\{\mathcal{U}, f(s) := f(s), ...\} \rightsquigarrow \{\mathcal{U}, ...\}$

$\Longleftarrow f(s') := t'$ not in $\mathcal{U}$

Table 4.4 Derived Inference Rules

4.3 Datatype Refinement for Integer Arithmetic

This section is based on [36]. We transfer the ideas and definitions from the source document and adjust them according the needs for constructing the logic CDL. The transfer of the associated calculus is done in section 7.4.2.

4.3.1 Motivation

We motivate the datatype refinement for integer arithmetic as it is done in [12].

In the following we denote with S_{C0} the semantics of finite integer types that correspond exactly to the integer semantics of C0. During programming, however, programmers often think using infinite integer semantics. If overflow occurs, then the behavior of the program may diverge from the understanding of the programer. This may equaly apply to the meaning of the specification and the understanding of the programmer about the specification. Thus if the verification calculus uses the S_{C0} semantics a program may be verified against a given specification, yet both the specification and the program may describe a behavior not intended by the programmer. For instance consider the formula $i > 0 \rightarrow \langle\!\{\texttt{i=i+1; i=i-1}\}\!\rangle i > 0$ using S_{C0}. The formula is valid but in the case where i is MAX_`int` before the execution it becomes negative after the first statement. This behavior is likely to be different from what the programmer expects.

Programs that are correct with respect to a given specification using S_{C0} event when overflows occur are likely to be not really well understood by the programmer. We therefore call such programs "incidentally" correct.

Furthermore formulas like $\forall x. \exists y. y > x$ are valid in the context of infinite integer semantics but not in the context of finite integer semantics. The datatype refinement for integer arithmetic provides also a nice handling of such cases.

By extending C0 with new types and the definition of operators for these types we change the semantic of C0 to which we refer by S_{KeY}. By $S_{\mathbb{Z}}$ we refer to a semantic of C0 where all integral types have an infinite range and therefore the operators of C0 are defined to the the usual mathematical functions which do not cause overflow.

4.3.2 Syntax

The set of types of CDL is extended by an arithmetic type for every integral type.

Definition 4.12. (Types of CDL)

- *The type system (the set TYP) contains the set* TYP^{C0} *of C0 types*
- *For every integral type of C0* $t \in \mathrm{TYP}^{C0}_{\mathrm{int}} \subset \mathrm{TYP}^{C0}_{0}$ *the* $arith(t) \in \mathrm{TYP}$

On the set of integral types and the corresponding arithmetic types we define a strict order $\prec$ in the following definition. Since the handling of integer arithmetic concerns only the mentioned types we define the set $\mathrm{TYP}^{C0}_{\mathrm{exint}}$ which excludes types which are not subject of arithmetic operations like `bool`, *struct*, and $a[n]$.

Definition 4.13. (Strict Order $\prec$ on Elementary Types) *The strict order $\prec$ on the set*

$$\mathrm{TYP}^{C0}_{\mathrm{exint}} = \{\texttt{char}, \texttt{int}, \texttt{unsigned int}, arith_{\texttt{char}}, arith_{\texttt{int}}, arith_{\texttt{unsigned int}}\}$$

of extended integral types is defined as:

$$\begin{aligned} \texttt{char} &\prec \texttt{int} \\ \texttt{char} &\prec \textit{unsigend int} \\ \texttt{char} &\prec arith_{\texttt{char}} \\ \texttt{int} &\prec arith_{\texttt{int}} \\ \texttt{unsigned int} &\prec arith_{\texttt{unsigend int}} \end{aligned}$$

Definition 4.14. (Transitive Closure $\prec^*$) *The strict total order $\prec^*$ denotes the transitive closure of $\prec$.*

Since C0 does not provide type promotion rules like MISRA C the operands of operators and the assignment must have equal types.[4.7] If two expressions of different type need to be used as operands of an operator or in an assignment a type conversion has to be done explicitly. We define the term *assignment compatibility* in a similar way as it is done in [36]. In contrast to the definition in [36] our notion of assignment compatibility does not imply that an assignment or operation between assignment compatible types may be performed without an explicit type cast.

4.7. For simplicity we call the left-hand side and right-hand side of an assignment operators of the assignment.

Definition 4.15. (Assignment Compatibility) *Let* $S, T \in \mathrm{TYP}^{C0}_{\mathrm{exint}}$. *S is assignment compatible to T if and only if S and T are equal or* $S \prec^* T$.

Definition 4.16. (Extension of the Signature Σ) *The signature* Σ *as it is defined in def. 3.4 is extended to contain for the build-in types* $\mathrm{TYP}^{C0}_{\mathrm{el}}$ *of C0 the following rigid function and predicate symbols. Most of the function symbols are the logical counterpart of the arithmetical C0 operators and their semantics is the same as that of the corresponding C0 operator defined in* [36].

- *The binary function* $CMul_T$ *(corresponds to the C0 operator* `*` *for multiplication).*
- *The binary function* $CDiv_T$ *(corresponds to the C0 operator* `/`*)*
- *The binary function* $CPlus_T$ *(corresponds to the C0 operator* `+`*).*
- *The binary function* $CMinus_T$ *(corresponds to the C0 operator* `-`*).*
- *The unary function* $CUMinus_T$ *(corresponds to the C0 unary operator* `-`*)*
- *The unary functions* $\overline{T}$ *where T is the* name *of a build-in integral or an arithmetical type*
- *The unary function* $overflow_T$
- *The unary predicate* in_T *(For build-in and arithmetical types)*

Definition 4.17. (Subset of Σ for the Arithmetical Types) *The signature* Σ *contains for the arithmetical types* $T = \{arith_{\texttt{char}}, arith_{\texttt{int}}, arith_{\texttt{unsigned int}}\}$ *the following function and predicate symbols*

- *The functions* $*, /, \mathrm{mod}, +, -$ *and unary* $-$ *are also available for the arithmetical types and have the regular meaning.*
- *The unary predicate* in_T

Definition 4.18. (Extension of Terms and Formulas) *The sets* Trm *and* Fml *as they are defined in def. 3.4 and def. 3.5 and extended in def. 4.2 and def. 4.3 respectively are inductively extended by using the extended signature of definition 4.16.*

Definition 4.19. (Extension of C0 Syntax) *The syntax of C0 consist of the syntax definition given in section 2.4 extended as follows:*

- *The additional arithmetical integral types* $\texttt{arith}_{\texttt{int}}$, $\texttt{arith}_{\texttt{unsigned int}}$, *and* $\texttt{arith}_{\texttt{char}}$ *resulting in a new set of types* TYP^{C0}. *This has immediate effect on the rest of the definition*

- *The type cast operators* $\texttt{arith}_{\text{int}}$`()`,$\texttt{arith}_{\text{unsigned}}$`()`*, and* $\texttt{arith}_{\text{char}}$`()`
- *The functions with the type specification*
  - $\texttt{arith}_T$ `overflow(`$\texttt{arith}_T$`,'op')`
  - $\texttt{arith}_T$ `overflow(`$\texttt{arith}_T$`,`$\texttt{arith}_T$`,'op')`

  for every extended integral type $arith_T \in \mathrm{TYP}^{C0}_{\mathrm{exint}}$.
-

Operator	*Signature*	*Abbreviations*
`+, -, *, /,&,|,^`	$T \times T \to T$	$T \in \mathrm{TYP}^{C0}_{\mathrm{exint}}$
`>,<,>=,<=,==`	$T \times T \to$ `bool`	$T \in \mathrm{TYP}^{C0}_{\mathrm{exint}}$
`[]`	$T_2[\in \mathbb{N}] \times T_1 \to T_2$	$T_1 \in \mathrm{TYP}^{C0}_{\mathrm{exint}}$ $T_2 \in \mathrm{TYP}^{C0}$
`.`	$struct\{T_0 n_0, ..., T_s n_s\} \to T_i$	$0 \leqslant i \leqslant s$ $T_i \in \mathrm{TYP}^{C0}$
`*`	$ptr(T) \to T$	$T \in \mathrm{TYP}^{C0}$
`&`	$T \to ptr(T)$	$T \in \mathrm{TYP}^{C0}$
`int()`	$T \to$ `int`	$T \in \{$`char`, `unsigend int`$\}$
`unsigned()`	$T \to$ `unsigned int`	$T \in \{$`int`, `char`$\}$
`char()`	$T \to$ `char`	$T \in \{$`int`, `unsigend int`$\}$
$\texttt{arith}_{\text{int}}$`()`	$T \to arith_{\texttt{int}}$	$T \in \{$`char`, `unsigend int`, $\texttt{arith}_{\text{char}}$, $\texttt{arith}_{\text{unsigned int}}\}$
$\texttt{arith}_{\text{unsigned}}$`()`	$T \to$ `unsigned int`	$T \in \{$`int`, `char` $\texttt{arith}_{\text{int}}$, $\texttt{arith}_{\text{unsigned int}}\}$
$\texttt{arith}_{\text{char}}$`()`	$T \to arith_{\texttt{char}}$	$T \in \{$`int`, `unsigend int` $\texttt{arith}_{\text{int}}$, $\texttt{arith}_{\text{unsigned}}\}$

where `'op'` *denotes a number which is unique for every operator.*

Note that the C0 operators `<<,>>,&,|,^,~` operating on bits and the relational operators `&&,||,!` are not allowed to have operands of arithmetical integral types.

Definition 4.20. (ptransf) *Let p be a program containing arithmetical types. Then the program ptransf(p) is the result of replacing in p all occurrences of arithmetical types with the corresponding built-in C0 types.* [12]

Theorem 4.21. (Well typedness) *If a C0 program p is well-typed, then the program ptransf (p) is well-typed.*

Informally, a close look at the definition of the signature of operators in definition 4.19 should not give rise to any doubts.

Remark 4.22. ***(Notation of Terms and Expressions)*** In this thesis we distinguish between expressions and terms. In order to simplify notation we allow expressions to occur in the logic-part — this means, as terms. Expressions are written in a monospaced font and are implicitly assumed subject to conversion by the rules given in section 4.3.5.

4.3.3 Semantic

Definition 4.23. (Range of Arithmetical Types) *The arithmetical types* $arith_{\texttt{char}}$, $arith_{\texttt{int}}$, and $arith_{\texttt{unsigned int}}$ *all have an infinite range and are therefore isomorphic to the set of integers* $\mathbb{Z}$.

Definition 4.24. (Unary Predicate in_T) *Let* $T \in \mathrm{TYP}^{C0}_{\mathrm{int}}$ *be an elementary built-in integral type of C0 and let t be a logical term of one of these types. If T is an arithmetical type, let T′ be the corresponding built-in type, otherwise T′ is equal to T. Then, the unary predicate* $in_T(t)$ *is defined as:*

$$in_T(t) :\Leftrightarrow \mathrm{MIN\_}T' \leqslant t \wedge t \leqslant \mathrm{MAX\_}T'$$

[12]

Definition 4.25. (Unary Function $overflow_T$) *Let* $T \in \mathrm{TYP}^{C0}_{\mathrm{int}}$ *be an elementary built-in integral type of C0 and let t be a logical term of one of these types. The function* $overflow_T(t)$ *is a short form defined by:*

$$overflow_T(t) \doteq (t - \mathrm{MIN\_}T)\ mod\ (\mathrm{MAX\_}T + 1 - \mathrm{MIN\_}T) + \mathrm{MIN\_}T$$

The idea of this definition is the following. For the type $T =$ `unsigend int` $\mathrm{MIN\_}T = 0$ and we get $t\ mod\ \mathrm{MAX\_}T + 1$ which is clear. In case of a signed type the size of the range of the type is $(\mathrm{MAX\_}T + 1 - \mathrm{MIN\_}T)$. Before applying the modulo operator the value of t is first *transformed* to a positive value by $(t - \mathrm{MIN\_}T)$ and then back to the original range by $+\mathrm{MIN\_}T$.

This definition of the function $overflow_T$ is equivalent to

$$\begin{aligned} overflow_T(t) \doteq\ & \text{if } in_T(t) \text{ then } t \\ & \text{else if } t > \mathrm{MAX\_}T \text{ then } t - 2^{n_T} \\ & \text{else } t + 2^{n_T} \text{ fi fi fi} \end{aligned}$$

for C0 where n is the bit-width of type T and the value of 2^{n_T} is a constant expression. The value of an expression (when computing with the usual arithmetic operators $+$, $-$, $*$, $/$) cannot exceed the bounds $\mathrm{MIN\_}T * 2$ and $\mathrm{MAX\_}T * 2$. This is because the operands in and expression and the target variable to which the value is assigned must have the same type. The definition using addition or substraction of 2^{n_T} is equivalent to the semantic definition of operands in C0 in case of overflow. We prefer however the "more general" definition 4.25 since it can be reused for other C dialects.

The semantic of the C0 function `overflow` is left intentionally unspecified; it may even not terminate. The motivation for this is given in the following excerpt from [12] (which has been partially modified to meet its purpose in the context of the thesis):

> If the values of the arguments of an operator application in S_{KeY} are in valid range but the (mathematical) result is not (i.e., overflow would occur if the arithmetical types were replaced with the corresponding built-in types), then the result of the operation is unknown; it remains unspecified. Otherwise, i.e., if the result is in valid range, it is the same as in S_{C0}. Technically this is achieved by defining that the result is calculated in the overflow case by invoking a function `overflow(x,y,'op')` (the third parameter op is the operator that caused overflow and x,y are the arguments), whose behavior remains unspecified.
>
> The C0 function `overflow` is not invoked if at least one argument of the operation is already out of valid range. In that case, the semantics of the operation in our semantics S_{KeY} is the same as in $S_{\mathbb{Z}}$. This definition cannot lead to incorrect program behavior because the program state before executing the operation is unreal and cannot be reached in an actual execution of the program.

Definition 4.26. (Valid Range) *An implicit variable that has an arithmetical type T is in valid range (in a certain state) if its value v satisfies the inequations*

$$\mathrm{MIN\_}T' \leqslant v \text{ and } v \geqslant \mathrm{MAX\_}T'$$

, where T' is the built-in C0 type corresponding to T. [12]

Definition 4.27. (Real and Unreal States) *A CDL state s is called a* real state *if all implicit program variables with an arithmetical type are in valid range. Otherwise, s is called an* unreal state. [12]

The semantic of the functions $CMul_T$, $CDiv_T$, etc. is as defined in [14]. The definitions are translated according to our notation in section 6.2.1. The reason for this organization of the text is that the semantic of C0 operators is too C0-specific and does not belong into this chapter. Contrary, the extension of the semantic of C0 operators by the arithmetical types does belong in this section since this is the actual data type refinement.

Definition 4.28. (Undefined Semantic of C0 Operators) *If the semantic of a C0 operator is undefined (like overflow of multiplication in C0) the result is the value returned by the function* `overflow` *for any type.*

The previous definition takes effect on the following definitions.

Definition 4.29. (Semantic of Type Casts) *If the type T to be converted is a built-in C0 type, a conversion to a type $S \prec^* T$ or between* `int` *and* `unsigned int` *may change the value of the expression, whose type is to be converted, if it is not representable in the target type. In this case the result of the conversion is that of the conversion functions $\overline{T}$* [4.8]*.*

On the other hand, if overflow occurs in a conversion from an arithmetical type to another arithmetical type or to a built-in type, the result is that of the function `overflow`*.* [12]

Definition 4.30. (Semantic of Unary Minus) *If the type T of the operand is a build-in type the semantic is that of the function $CUMinus_T$. for arithmetical types we have to make a case distinction:*

- *If the value of the operand* `a` *is in valid range and $CUMinus_T$(*`a`*) $\doteq$* `a` *then the result is the return value of the C0 function* `overflow(a, '-')`*.*
- *other wise the semantic is the same as of mathematical negation.* [12]

Definition 4.31. (Semantic of Additive Operators and Multiplication) *For build-in integral types T the semantic is that of $CPlus_T$, and $CMinus_T$. If the types are arithmetical types, then, two cases have to be distinguished.*

1. *If both operands* `a1` *and* `a2` *are in valid range, then the result is the mathematical sum, difference, or product, respectively, if it is in valid range. Otherwise the result is the return value of the C0 function invocation* `overflow(a1,a2,'+')` *,*`overflow(a1,a2,'-')`*, or* `overflow(a1,a2,'*')` *respectively.*
2. *If at least one operand is not in valid range, then the result is the mathematical sum or difference, respectively, and C0 function* `overflow` *is not invoked.*

[12]

4.8. $\overline{T}$: The syntax is describe above, the semantic is given later.

The reason for the definition of the second situation is that the machine executing a C0 program cannot reach a state where one operand is not in valid range. This is an unreal stated and is not subject to the handling by overflow.

Definition 4.32. (Semantic of the Division Operator) *The operand on the left-hand side is called* dividend *and the operand on the right-hand side is call* divisor. *If the type T of the operands is a build-in type then the semantic remains as defined in C0 (the definition of the semantic is missing in* [14]*). For arithmetical types two cases have to be distinguished.*

- *If both arguments* `a1` *and* `a2` *are in valid range, then the result of the division operation is the mathematical integer quotient if it is in valid range. otherwise the result is the return value of the method invocation* `overflow(a1,a2,'/')`.
- *If at least one argument is not in valid range, then the result is the mathematical integer quotient of dividend and divisor but only if the semantic of division in C0 is the same as that of mathematical integer division within valid range.*

[12]

Note that division by zero is handled by def. 4.28.

4.3.4 Properties of S_{KeY}

Example: In S_{KeY} the formula $\langle\{\texttt{j=i+1}\}\rangle \texttt{j} \doteq \texttt{i}+1$ is not valid because `j=i+1` may cause an overflow after which $\texttt{j} \doteq \texttt{i}+1$ does not hold. [12]
Example: In S_{KeY} the formula $\texttt{i} > \mathrm{MAX\_}T \rightarrow \langle\{\texttt{j=i+1}\}\rangle \texttt{j} \doteq \texttt{i}+1$ is valid. "This is reasonable as the premiss $\texttt{i} > \mathrm{MAX\_}T$ is never true during the actual execution of a [C0] program." [12]

In the following theorem C0 referes to the extended version of C0 with arithemtic types.

Theorem 4.33. *If $\models_{S_{\mathrm{KeY}}} \phi$, then both $\models_{S_{\mathbb{Z}}} \phi$ and $\models_{S_{C0}} \phi$.* [12]

Definition 4.34. (Isomorphic State) *Let s be a real CDL state. The* isomorphic *state* iso(s) *to s is the state of the machine execution the C0 program in which all state elements (program variables) with an arithmetical type in s are of the corresponding built-in type and are assigned the same values as in s.* [12]

Corollary 4.35. *Let Γ, ψ be pure first-order predicate logic formulas, let* p *be an arbitrary C0 program that may contain arithmetical types, and let s be an arbitrary CDL state.*

*If (i) $\models_{S_{\mathrm{KeY}}} \Gamma \rightarrow \langle\!\langle \mathtt{p} \rangle\!\rangle \psi$, (ii) $s \models_{S_{\mathrm{KeY}}} \Gamma$, and (iii) s is a real state, then when the transformed program ptransf(*p*) is tarted* iso(s)*, (a) no overflow occurs and (b) the execution terminates in a state in which ψ holds.* [12]

4.3.5 Calculus

The calculus we present here does not occur in this form in [12]. We don't use the calculus presented in [12] in its original form because it does not comply with our concepts and it is not as general as our approach. The main reason for this is that we distinguish stronger between terms and expressions. Why the distinction is imporant will be explained in the next chapter. In contrast to [12] we give rewrite rules instead of rule schemata. However some of the rewrite rules contain conditional terms. By the useage of the rewrite application inference rules (R37) and (R38) (on page 55) formulas generated by the assignment rule (presented later) can be transformed to formulas as they would occur in proof obligations generated by the rule schemata of the calculus in [12].

We extend the rewrite relation $\rightsquigarrow$ to the rewriting of expressions to terms. Even though expressions are not part of the logic this extension is harmless. Expression could be simply defined as special terms, or terms "embeded" as arguments of a function *conv* or as terms with a special type decorator.

Notation: The calculus we present here is more than a calculus; it is a also a definition of the *notation* we use in the following chapters. Expressions are written in a monospaced font and are assumed to be converted by the following rules when they occur in the logic-part (where terms are exptected).

Rule 1.1.0 *cast-expression-conversion-form-build-in-type*

Purpose Symbolic execution of a type cast expression.

Requirements The type of the expression X must be a build-in integral type.

$$\boxed{T(X) \rightsquigarrow \bar{\mathtt{T}}(X)}$$

Description T is the name of a build-in integral type. The expression T(X) is converted to the term $\bar{\mathtt{T}}(X)$. $\bar{\mathtt{T}}$ are function symbols as defined in def. 4.16 and their semantics is be given in section 6.2.1.

Remark The sub-expression X is subject to further conversion.

Rule 1.1.1 *cast-expression-conversion-from-arithmetical-type*

Purpose Symbolic execution of a type cast expression

Requirements The type of the expression `X` must be an arithmetical type.

$$\boxed{T(X) \leadsto \left(\begin{array}{c} \text{if } in_S(X) \wedge in_T(X) \text{ then} \\ X \\ \text{else if} \neg in_S(X) \text{ then} \\ X \\ \text{else } \texttt{overflow}(X, Y, \prime\circ\prime) \text{ fi fi} \end{array}\right)}$$

Description S is the type of the expression `X`. `T` is the name of an integral or arithmetical type T. The expression `T(X)` is converted to a conditional term containing another conditional term. The term structure follows directly from the description of the semantic of type casts.

Remark The sub-expression `X` is subject to further conversion.

Rule 1.1.2 *built-in-binary-expression-execution*

Purpose Symbolic execution of an expression with a binary operator

Requirements The type of `X`, `Y` is a build-in type T

$$\boxed{X \ op \ \ Y \leadsto CFunc_T(X, Y)}$$

Description `op` is one of the binary C0 operators. $CFunc_T$ is the corresponding function to the operator.

Remark The sub-expressions `X` and `Y` are subject to further conversion.

Rule 1.1.3 *arithmetical-binary-expression-execution*

Purpose Symbolic execution of a binary expression of an arithmetical type for the box operator.

Requirements The type of `X`, `Y` is an arithmetical type T

$$\boxed{X \ op \ \ Y \leadsto \left(\begin{array}{c} \text{if } in_T(X) \wedge in_T(Y) \wedge in_T(X \ \texttt{logOp} \ Y) \text{ then} \\ X \ \texttt{logOp} \ Y \\ \text{else if} \neg in_T(X) \vee \neg in_T(Y) \text{ then} \\ X \ \texttt{logOp} \ Y \\ \text{else } \texttt{overflow}(X, Y, \prime\circ\prime) \text{ fi fi} \end{array}\right)}$$

Description

- *op* is one of the binary operators `*`, `/`, `+`, `-`
- *logOp* is the corresponing logical function to the C0 operator *op*:
  - If *op* is `*`, then *logOp* is $*$.
  - If *op* is `/`, then *logOp* is $/$.
  - If *op* is `+`, then *logOp* is $+$.
  - If *op* is `-`, then *logOp* is $-$.
- T is the type of `X` and `Y`.

The term structure of the conditional term follows directly from the description of the semantic of the operators. The handling of division by zero is done by other rules.

Remark The sub-expressions X and Y are subject to further conversion.

Rule 1.1.4 *build-in-unary-minus-execution*

Purpose Symbolic execution of an expression with the unary minus operator

Requirements The type of X is a build-in type T

$$\boxed{\texttt{-}X \rightsquigarrow \mathit{CUMinus}_{\mathrm{T}}(X)}$$

Description Conversion of the expression $\texttt{-}X$ to the term $\mathit{CUMinus}_{\mathrm{T}}(X)$. The semantic of the function symbol $\mathit{CUMinus}_{\mathrm{T}}$ is defined in section 6.2.1.

Remark The sub-expression X is subject to further conversion.

Rule 1.1.5 *arithmetical-unary-minus-execution*

Purpose Symbolic execution of an expression with the unary minus operator

Requirements The type of X is an arithmetical type T

$$\boxed{\texttt{-}X \rightsquigarrow \left(\begin{array}{l} \text{if } in_T(X) \wedge \mathit{CUMinus}_T(X) \doteq X \text{ then} \\ \qquad \texttt{overflow}(X, \prime - \prime) \\ \text{else} - X \text{ fi} \end{array}\right)}$$

Description The term structure corresponds exactly to the description of the semantic of the overloaded unary minus operator. Note that $\texttt{-}X$ is an expression and $-X$ (with the longer minus symbol) is a term.

Remark The sub-expression X is subject to further conversion.

Chapter 5

Handling of Special Concepts in C: Program Variables, Pointer Operators and Assignments

5.1 Preliminaries

5.1.1 Notation

Elements of the program part are written in monospaced font. The conventional notations for symbols of the logic part remains as in the previous chapters. We use the following abbreviations for elements of the program part with respect to the syntax definition of C0 2.4.

BNF notation	Abbreviation
`lexpression`	`lexpr`
`rexpression`	`rexpr`
for the substring `statement` we write	`stmt`

Schematic program symbols are written in an italicized mono-spaced font like *`lexpr`* if they are surrounded by a text written in a regular font. Otherwise, just a monospaced font is used. Furthermore, we use a pseudo code representation for updates. The notation `a=b` represents an update where `a` and `b` are program variables that are subject to conversion as will be described in section 5.2. The notation `a=b:c` represents the application of the update `a=b` on the program variable or term `c`. Similarly, `a=b:c=d` is the application of the update `a=b` on the update `c=d`. A parallel update is abbreviated by using a comma like in the example `a=b,c=d`.

In the specification of C0 in [14] the predicate *valid* is used. The predicate *valid* is replaced in this thesis by the *intentional* equivalent predicate *isdef* according to the convention in [10] and [36].

In the following we will refer to the updates described in section 4.2 by the term "KeY updates".

We use the notion of a program variable as described in section 2.4.4.

5.1.2 Motivation

In this section we explain what we consider as special issues of C, how we interpret them, and how we develop our solutions for handling them.

This part of the thesis deals with the handling of pointer operators and assignments. The pointer operators in C are the reference (`&`) and the dereference (`*`) operators. The pointer operators are not present in JAVA, and therefore no *direct* treatment of this concept is available within the KeY project. Considering the assignment `a = new int;` the C0 key-word `new` for the creation of objects seems to be an operator as well but the C0 specification [14] treats dynamic creation as a statement, which means that the assignment symbol `=` and the key-word `new` form a single statement.

Another issue is the semantic of assignments concerning arrays and structures in C. For further explanation we need the following definitions.

Definition 5.1. (Deep copy/Value assignment) *A* value assignment *is an assignment that creates a copy of a value from a* source *expression or term and assigns this value to a* target *program variable or non-rigid term. Modifications of the value of the* target *occurring after the* value assignment *have no influence on the value of the* source*. We use the terms* deep copy assignment *and* value assignment *interchangeably.*

Definition 5.2. (Reference Assignment and Aliasing) *A* reference assignment *is an assignment that does not create a copy of a value from a* source *expression or term in contrast to value assignments. It assigns a reference of an object (or primitive value) to a* target *program variable or non-rigid term in such a way that both share the same object (or primitive value). Modifications of the object (or primitive value) of the target occurring after the* reference assignment *are also modifications of the value of the source.*

The concept of modifying the value of one term (or program variable) by an assignment to another term (or program variable) is called aliasing.

In JAVA the assignment of primitive values (integers, boolean) is done via value assignments. The assignment of objects is done via reference assignments. Actually, in the latter case a value assignment is performed — however, not on the level of objects but on the level of references to objects. Therefore the notion of value assignments and reference assignment is *relative*, depending on which entities are recognized as values.

C supports value assignments for elementary types and for structure types. This means that assigning the value of a program variable `b` to another program variable `a`, where both are of a structure type, results in the assignment of a new copy of the structure value of `b` assigned to `a` . When using KeY updates a set of updates has to be created in this case for the assignment between all corresponding members of the structures. We call this concept *unfolding*.

Definition 5.3. (Unfolding) *The term* unfolding *refers to the concept of syntactically expanding some* operation *between terms or expressions of a compound type, i.e., a structure type or array type. Operations in this context may be, for instance, a deep copy assignment, a bit-wise operation, element-wise comparison etc.*

C0 supports — in contrast to MISRA C — value assignments between arrays (it considers arrays as proper types) which results in copying the value from all elements of one array to the other. However, MISRA C does support value assignments of arrays indirectly, namely if an array is nested in a structure. If this structure is copied, then also all the elements of the contained array are copied as well. We recognize the value assignment of arrays and structures as a special concept and therefore provide a special solution called deep copy updates.

Definition 5.4. (Deep Copy/Value Update) *A* deep copy update *or* value update *is an update that performs a deep copy assignment without unfolding of the update.*

Definition 5.5. (Reference Update) *A* reference update *is an update that performs a reference assignment.*

Another aspect is that an integral type can be viewed — in a broader sense — as a structure composed of bits. Note that this is the idea of bit-fields in MISRA C. If direct access to bits or sequences of bits *shall* be given in a way like the members of a structure are accessed, then integral types have to be treated *as* structures or arrays. This applies in particular to the treatment of assignments between variables of integral types. In this case, a simple assignment between integral types must be unfolded to a set of updates for each bit. Ignoring this expansion the assignment of one program variable of integral type to another would merely lead to the assignment of the "reference to the value" between the variables. In this case, both variables refer to the same value instead of separate copies of the value. In other words, using regular updates, program variables are treated like JAVA objects when giving access to bits in a way like to member variables. One way to assign a value to a bit without treating the integral type as a structure is to use a function of the from $v(\texttt{a}, \mathit{bitnr}, \mathit{newval})$. This function represents a value of the integral type derived from the value of the program variable `a` which is modified at bit number *bitnr* to the value *newval*. This value of that function may then be assigned to a program variable. To update bit 4 of program variable `a` to the value 0 one would write `a = v(a,4,0)`.

5.1.3 Lambda Calculus

The following description of the lambda calculus is base on [3]. The lambda calculus is also presented in [23].

5.1.3.1 Syntax

The syntax of lambda expressions is defined the follwoing grammar in BNF.

$$
\begin{aligned}
1.\ \textit{expression} &::= \textit{identifier} \\
2.\ \textit{expression} &::= (\lambda\, \textit{identifier}\, .\, \textit{expression}) \\
3.\ \textit{expression} &::= (\textit{expression}\ \textit{expression})
\end{aligned}
$$

For identifiers we use lower-case letters. Rule one defines functions. Rule two also defines function called lambda abstraction. Rule three defines function application. If parentheses are omitted than the application of functions is left-associative. We can therefore abbreviate for example the expression $((\lambda x.(xx))(\lambda y.y))$ by the expression $(\lambda x.xx)\lambda y.y$.

The lambda calculus defines rules for transforming lambda expressions into equivalent lambda expression. The calculus defines therefore an equivalence relation on lambda expressions. The goal in using the lambda calculus is therefore the determine if two lambda expressions are equivalent or to find given a lambda expression a "smaller" or simplified lambda expression. The calculus defines two transformation rules: the α-conversion and the β-conversion.

5.1.3.2 α-conversion

Let E be a lambda expression with a free occurence of the variable V. If E' is obtained by replacing all occrences of V by the variable W that does not coccur freelz in E, then

$$\lambda V.E \text{ is equivalen to } \lambda W.E'$$

Thus the naming of variables is irrelevant for the meaning of a lambda expression

5.1.3.3 β-reduction

Let E_1 and E_2 be lambda expression and V a variable. The expression

$$(\lambda V.E_1)E_2$$

is equivalent to the expression E_1' that is equal to E_1 except that every occurence of V in E_1 is replace by E_2.

5.2 Representation of Program Variables as Terms

In this section we describe in an informal way the syntax and the semantic of terms which represent program variables.

5.2.1 Motivation

In C a program variable is an object. It has a value and it has an address which can be determined by using the reference operator `&`. Thus, there must be a distinction in the representation of program variables as terms in updates or in formulas. On the one hand, there must be terms that represent the value of program variables and on the other hand there must be terms representing their addresses.

Since this distinction is not explicitly made in programs, program variables must be syntactically *converted* when they are moved into the logic part; this is meant if they are used as terms.

Notation: We use the mono-spaced font for program variables in the program part. If the name of a program variable occurs in a mono-spaced font in the logic part — this is where a logical term is expected — the program variable is subject to conversion. A program variable which is not written in mono-spaced font has a special meaning, depending on the way how program variables are represented as terms.

Three representations have been analyzed during the development of the calculus for C which we call mono, dual, and accessor path representations.

5.2.2 Representation of Simple Program Variables

5.2.2.1 Mono Representation

The address of a program variable `a` is represented in the logic part as the constant a. The value of the program variable is represented by the term ${}^v a$ where ^{v} is a function symbol[5.1]. Thus, a program variable is treated like an object reference, and its value is represented by an attribute in the sense of ODL [33] and JavaCardDL [10]. Thus, when converting a reference variable `&a` to the logic part the result is a. Given the address a of a program variable `a` the dereferenciation of this address must yield a term that represents the value of the program variable. Thus, $*a$ must consequently yield ${}^v a$. This concept can now be further generalized to arbitrary dereferenciation chains so that the expression $*_0 \ldots *_n$`a` is represented as a term by ${}^v_0 \ldots {}^v_{n+1} a$. In other words, $*$ adds a ^{v} and `&` removes a ^{v}.

5.1. ${}^v a$ is a short notation for ${}^v(a)$.

5.2.2.2 Dual Representation

The address of a program variable `a` is represented in the logic part by the term ${}^{\&}a$ where ${}^{\&}$ is a function symbol. The value of the program variable is represented by the term ${}^{v}a$ like in the mono representation. Thus a is an abstract object which has an address attached to it by the function ${}^{\&}$. When converting the referenced program variable `&a` to the logic part we therefore obtain the term ${}^{\&}a$. Furthermore, we map the reference `&` and dereference `*` operators to the logic part providing the function symbols $\&$ and *. A referenced program variable `&a` can therefore also be converted to $\&^{v}a$ and by a calculus rule to ${}^{\&}a$. Consequently, dereferencing an address ${}^{*}({}^{\&}a)$ must yield ${}^{v}a$.

5.2.2.3 Accessor Path Representation

The accessor path representation is equivalent to the dual representation for simple program variables. It differs, however, for the representation for structure and array access. The accessor path representation defines the construction of terms. It was used at some time in the development of the calculus but a suitable calculus with this kind of terms could not be found for deep copy updates. In the semantic section of this chapter an accessor path-like representation is used but the entities are not terms.

5.2.3 Program Variables and Substructures

Remark: The notion of a substructure is explained in section 2.4.4.

Structures and arrays have the common property that they aggregate objects. Without regarding pointers to program variables an array `a[i]` can be represented as a function $\mathrm{arr}(a, i)$. Note that `a` may be an expression, e.g., another array or a dereferenciation expression etc.

A structure member `a.m` can be represented as term by ${}^{\cdot\mathtt{m}}a$ where `.m` is a function symbol giving access to the structure member. A member of a nested structure `a.m.n` can be either represented using a single function like ${}^{\cdot\mathtt{m}\cdot\mathtt{n}}(a)$ or using a concatenation of two functions ${}^{\cdot\mathtt{m}}({}^{\cdot\mathtt{n}}(a))$. The problem of the first approach is that the part `a.m` may be the result of a dereferenciation of some expression `*e`; the first representation is not compatible if we have an expression like `(*e).n` because then we are missing the "unconcatenated" function ${}^{\cdot\mathtt{n}}$ in the logic. If we add both function symbols ${}^{\cdot\mathtt{m}\cdot\mathtt{n}}$ and ${}^{\cdot\mathtt{n}}$ to the logic then we introduce an unnecessary aliasing problem. The choice of having a single function symbol ${}^{\cdot\mathtt{m}}$ and ${}^{\cdot\mathtt{n}}$ etc. for the access to a structure member of each level is therefore better.

A third possibility to represent a structure member is to treat the attribute name as a value from a set *Acc* of accessors and introduce a binary accessor function symbol $^\circ$ [5.2] which represents a structure member for a given structure and accessor as arguments. Thus, a structure member `a.m` is represented as the term $^\circ$(`a`, m) where m is of type *Acc*. In this way, it is possible to quantify over members of a structure which is not possible if the members would be represented by individual function symbols. The oddness of this representation is first that the number of structure members — which is limited — is staticaly known for each program and secondly that the types of the members differ in general in contrast to the elements of an array. This does not cause any problems when the quantification over the set of accessors (and therefore over different types) is done in the right context.

A context where the quantification over the members of a structure is safe and very useful is the replacing of *unfolding* of assignments by a single value assignment. This is the actual motivation of this part of the thesis. Since this representation corresponds exactly to the representation of arrays, we can use syntax, semantic and calculus of value assignments without unfolding for arrays and structures. Especially this allows a homogeneous treatment if arrays and structures are nested in each other. We will therefore use only the term "structures" and mean implicitly also "arrays".

5.2.4 Representation of Program Variables

Instead of a lengthy text we show how program variables are represented in the mono, dual, and access path representation by presenting the following table:

	Mono	**Dual**	**Accessor path**
the pointer of the program variable `a`	a	$^{\&}a$	$^{\&}(a,\#)$
the value of the program variable `a`	^{v}a	^{v}a	$^{v}(a,\#)$
the pointer of the substructure `a.m`	$^{\bullet}(^{v}a,m)$	$^{\&}(^{\&}a,m)$	$^{\&}(a,{}^{\bullet}(m,\#))$
the value of the substructure `a.m`	$^{v}(^{\bullet}(^{v}a,m))$	$^{v}(^{v}a,m)$	$^{v}(a,{}^{\bullet}(m,\#))$
the pointer of the substructure `a.m`$_1$`.`...`.m`$_n$	$^{\bullet}(...^{v}(^{\bullet}(^{v}a,m_1))...,m_n)$	$^{\&}(...^{\&}(^{\&}a,m_1)...,m_n)$	$^{\&}(a,{}^{\bullet}(m_1,...^{\bullet}(m_n,\#)...))$
the value of the substructure `a.m`$_1$`.`...`.m`$_n$	$^{v}(^{\bullet}(...^{v}(^{\bullet}(^{v}a,m_1))...,m_n))$	$^{v}(...^{v}(^{v}a,m_1)...,m_n)$	$^{v}(a,{}^{\bullet}(m_1,...^{\bullet}(m_n,\#)...))$

5.2. We abstract using the symbol $\circ$ from a concrete "implementation" in the mono, dual, or access path representation.

The symbol # is a skolem constant so that it may represent any chain of accessors. In the semantic section of this chapter an accessor path-like representation is used but the entities are not terms so the meaning of # is irrelevant in the semantic section.

The mono representation has been used at an earlier time during the writing of the thesis than the dual representation. The mono representation is used in the implementation part and is not relevant here. The representation used in the calculus we present is the dual representation and therefore we define the conversion from program variables of the program part (written in a mono-spaced font) to terms in the logic part in definition 5.8.

5.2.5 Syntax

Definition 5.6. (Extension of the type system) *The type system is extended by the type* ACC *of accessors that is a supertype of every build-in C0 type.*

Definition 5.7. (Extension of the signature) *The signature* Σ *as it is defined in def. 4.17 is extended by the following symbols.*

- *The non-rigid unary value function* ^{v}.
- *The non-rigid binary value function* ^{v}.
- *The rigid unary address function* $^\&$.
- *The rigid binary address function* $^\&$.
- *The rigid unary reference function* &.
- *The rigid unary dereference function* *
- *local program variables are rigid constants*
- *(eventually the unary function* bit_T *of type* ACC*)*

The set Trm of terms is extended inductively by using definition 5.7. The semantic of the terms is described informaly above. A formal definition of the semantic is given in section 5.4.2.

5.2.6 Calculus

The definition of the conversion of program variables to terms is part of the calculus but it serves also the definition of our notation, namely that program variables in the logic part written in monospaced font are subject to the rule in definition 5.8. The conversion of other expressions with operators is defined in section 4.3.5.

Definition 5.8. (Conversion of Expressions to Terms) *The conversion of an expression to a term as defined by the rewrite rules in section 4.3.5 is extended for the conversion of program variables and program variables with pointer operators.*

$$X \leadsto \begin{cases} {}^{v}(X), \textit{ if } \mathtt{X} \textit{ is a simple local program variable} \\ {}^{v}(\mathrm{obj}_T(n)), \textit{ if } \mathtt{X} \textit{ is a simple global program variable} \\ {}^{v}(A\,, \mathrm{aconv}(B)), \textit{ if } \mathtt{X} = \mathtt{A.B} \textit{ is a structure member access} \\ {}^{v}(A\,, I\,), \textit{ if } \mathtt{X} = \mathtt{A[I]} \textit{ is an array access} \\ \&(A\,), \textit{ if } \mathtt{X}{=}\mathtt{\&A} \\ {}^{*}(A\,), \textit{ if } \mathtt{X}{=}\mathtt{*A} \end{cases}$$

$$\mathrm{aconv}(B) = B \textit{ but members with equal names which belong to different structures are distinct}$$

n is the static number of the global program variable.

Note that the expressions (in monospaced font) A, B, I *are subject to further conversion.*

5.3 Unfolding

KeY updates perform *lazy evaluation* in contrast to the assignment rule from Hoare logic. Therefore KeY updates provide an improvement in handling of assignments. In presence of deep copy assignments, however, a KeY update must be unfolded into a simultaneous update that contains as subupdate for every element of nested structures or arrays. For an assignment of arrays quantified updates can be used. However, in case of nested arrays, also nested quantified updates have to be constructed. If the elements of an array are structures, then there must be a quantified update for each member of the structure. Because of arbitrary nesting of arrays and structures this procedure must be implemented in a general recursive manner as follows.

$$\{X := Y\} \leadsto \begin{cases} \{X.m_1 := Y.m_1\}...\{X.m_n := Y.m_n\}, \text{if } \mathtt{X},Y \text{ have structure types} \\ \{\text{for } x;\, ; X[x] := Y[x]\}\,, \text{if } \mathtt{X},Y \text{ have array types} \end{cases}$$

The rule must be applied recursively. Note that the program variables are subject to conversion.

During the symbolic execution of programs, updates are created embedding the "remaining" formula as target (formula). Before updates can be merged to simultaneous updates they have to be unfolded, so that they are growing in size *rapidly* if assignments between structures, or nested structures and arrays occur. The final first-order target term (after symbolic execution) on which the simultaneous-unfolded update is applied will *usually* not need to be updated by all the sub-updates but only by a subset of them. Thus in the unfolding approach updates may be created unnecessarily.

A Strategy how to minimize unfolding is the following. Firstly, *collect* all updates while the program is symbolically executed up to the point where a first-order term or formula (the program is completely executed) is reached. While the updates are collected, *do not* perform any simplifications (merging), because it is unknown in which cases terms represent overlapping locations. When the sequence of embedded updates is created embedding a term or formula after symbolic program execution, then unfold the *inner most* update and apply it on the term or formula. The point is that location terms which may not be aliased by the target can be removed. Then unfold the next-outer update and apply it on the term or formula (possibly preceeded by "parts" of the previously unfolded update) etc. Intuitively, in this way only relevant sub-updates (of the unfolded updates) are pulled out from the innermost (last or right-most) update near the target to the outermost (first or left-most). The drawback of this approach is that during the symbolic execution of a program simultaneous updates cannot be created; this means that overwritten updates like $\{a := b\}...\{a := c\}$ may not be simplified and dereferenciations must no take place.

5.4 Deep copy updates

The application of deep copy updates on terms or formulas has the same effect as the application of unfolded KeY updates. In contrast to KeY updates no unfolding has to be performed and, yet, they can be merged and simplified to simultaneous (focal) updates during symbolic execution of programs.

5.4.1 Syntax

Definition 5.9. (Extension of the signature) *The signature* Σ *as it is defined in def. 5.7 is extended by the following symbols.*

- *The binary predicates* $\sqsubset, \sqsubseteq, \sqsubset^*, \sqsubseteq^*, \sqsupset, \sqsupseteq, \sqsupset^*, \sqsupseteq^*$

Definition 5.10. (Extension of Terms and Formulas) *The sets Trm and Fml as they are defined in def. 3.4 and def. 3.5 respectively and extended by def. 4.18 are extended by using the extended signature of definitions 5.7, 4.17, and 5.9. And furthermore*

- *global program variables of type* T *are represented by distinct terms* $\mathrm{obj}_T(n)$ *where* $n \in \mathrm{Trm}_{\mathrm{nat}}$ *enumerates the global program variables starting from 0.*

- next_T *is an* abbreviation *for* ${}^v\text{next}_T$
- $x_{[F]}$ *is an epsilon term if* $x \in V$ *and* $F \in \text{Fml}$
- *The structural update* $\lhd \langle Y := Z \rangle$ *is a modal operator in* postfix *notation so that* $X \lhd \langle Y := Z \rangle$ *is a term if* X *is a term where* Y, $Z \in \text{Trm}$
- *All updates are deep copy updates. The way how deep copy updates can be composed with terms and formulas to build new terms and formulas remains the same as that of KeY updates. The syntax for an elementary deep copy update is*

$$\{a := b\}$$

, where $a, b \in \text{Trm}$.

Simultaneous deep copy updates (or focal updates) are of the form

$$\{a_1 := b_1, \ldots, a_n := b_n\}_k^n$$

, where $0 \leqslant k \leqslant n$. *The notation* U *for an update without indices is an abbreviation for* U_n^n.

When we use a program variable name written in a monospaced font at positions where a term is expected the program variable is subject to conversion as defined in 5.8.

5.4.2 Semantic

Definition 5.11. (Semantic of an Epsilon Term) *The semantic of an epsilon term* $x_{[\phi_x]}$ *is defined by the constraint*

$$\exists y.\, y \doteq x_{[\phi_x]} \wedge \phi_x(y) \equiv \mathit{true}$$

We restrict ϕ_x *only to those formulas where the value of the epsilon is unique.*

Definition 5.12. (Extension of the Universe) *The universe* U *of our Interpretations (Kripke structures) is extended by lambda expressions. Lambda expressions of the form* $\lambda w.\, {}^\bullet(Y, w)$ *are called accessor paths and are collected in the subset* AP *of* U.

Definition 5.13. (Semantic of Function Symbols) *The valuation (or interpretation) of the function symbols defined in def. 5.7 is defined as*

- ${}^v\!: (X, Y) \mapsto \lambda z.(X\, {}^\bullet(Y, z))$

- ${}^{v}\!: (X) \mapsto \lambda z.\, {}^{\mathrm{va}}(X, z)$
- $\&\!: (\lambda z.\, {}^{\mathrm{va}}(X, z)) \mapsto \lambda z.\, {}^{\mathrm{adr}}(X, z)$
- ${}^{\&}\!: (X) \mapsto \lambda z.\, {}^{\mathrm{adr}}(X, z)$
- ${}^{\&}\!: (X, Y) \mapsto \lambda z.(X\, {}^{\bullet}(Y, z))$ *defined only for pointers so that* ${}^{\&}\!: (\lambda x.\, {}^{\mathrm{adr}}(X, x), Y) \mapsto \lambda z.({}^{\mathrm{adr}}(X, {}^{\bullet}(Y, z)))$
- ${}^{*}\!: (\lambda z.\, {}^{\mathrm{adr}}(X, z)) \mapsto \lambda z.\, {}^{\mathrm{va}}(X, z)$
- $\mathrm{val}_I(s, a) = a^I$ for local program variables
- $\mathrm{val}_I(s, \mathrm{next}_T) \in \mathbb{N}$ *is initially set to a value for every type* T *that is greater than the number of global program variables.*

  ${}^{\mathrm{va}}, {}^{\mathrm{adr}}, {}^{\bullet}$ *are categories of combinators. For instance, there may be versions of* ${}^{\mathrm{va}}$ *for representing numbers and* ${}^{\bullet}$ *can be a set of* accessor combinators *with some annotations i such that e.g. for some* i ${}^{\bullet_i}(X, {}^{\bullet_{i+1}}(Y, Z)) == {}^{\bullet_i}(X, Y)$ *or* ${}^{\bullet_i}(X, {}^{\bullet'_{i+1}}(Y))$. *(See Discussion below)*

Definition 5.14. (Semantic of Structural Updates) *The semantic of a structural update is defined by the application of structural updates on terms*

$$\mathrm{val}_l(s, a \lhd \langle m := v \rangle) = \lambda z.(\mathrm{if}\ z == m\ \mathrm{then}\ v\ \mathrm{else}\ (a\, z))$$

,where if C then A else B *is a lambda expression which is defined such that*

$$\mathrm{if}\ C\ \mathrm{then}\ A\ \mathrm{else}\ B = \begin{cases} A, \mathrm{if}\ z == m \\ B, \mathrm{otherwise} \end{cases}$$

With this semantic of function symbols it is easy to define the semantic of deep copy updates.

Definition 5.15. (Semantic of a Deep Copy Update) *The semantic of an elementary deep copy update is defined as*

$$\mathrm{val}_l(s, \{{}^{v}X := Y\}) = [{}^{v}\!: \mathrm{val}_l(s, X) \mapsto \mathrm{val}_l(s, Y)]$$

The semantic of a focal update U_k^0 *is* $[]$, *i.e, it is ineffective.*

The semantic of a focal update U_1^1 *is equal to the semantic of the elementary deep copy update U.*

The semantic of the application of a focal update on a term/formula $U_0^1 t$ *is the same as that of the term* ${}^{*}(U_1^1 \&(t))$.

We give no formal definition of the semantic of focal updates (deep copy updates) U_k^n $n > 1$. Informally the semantic of a focal update is that when applying it on a term $f(a)$ only the sub-updates $0 < i \leqslant k$ are applied on f and the rest of the update is propagated to update a. The semantic definition formalizes arbitrary chains of application of elementary updates on terms and formulas. If it can be shown that the application of a chain of elementary updates on a term is equivalent to the application of the focal update resulting from merging of the elementary update, then the semantic of focal updates is indirectly defined. Focal updates are generated and used by the calculus rules.

Definition 5.16. (Semantic of Substruct Predicate $\sqsubset$) *The semantic of the* strict substruct *predicate* $\sqsubset$ *is defined by*

$$A \sqsubset B :\Leftrightarrow A \textit{ is direct substructure of } B \textit{ (see def.2.12)}$$

Furthermore

$$A \sqsubseteq B :\Leftrightarrow A \sqsubset B \vee A \doteq B$$

and

$$\sqsubset^* :\Leftrightarrow \text{transitive closure of} \sqsubset$$

The predicates $\sqsubseteq^*$, $\sqsupset$, $\sqsupseteq$, and $\sqsupseteq^*$ *are defined analogically.*

Definition 5.17. (Isomorphism of Finite Numbers) *There is an isomorphism between the finite set of representable numbers of the C0 integral types and some subset of the lambda expressions in U.*

The definition 5.17 allows the assignment of numbers of integral types to program variables. Furthermore, it is possible to access individual bits like `5.bit1` which is the term ${}^{v}(5, \text{bit1})$. We make, however, no statement about the relation between all integers in $\mathbb{Z}$ and lambda expressions.

5.4.2.1 Valuation Examples

For a simpler notation we write $\text{val}_I(x)$ instead of $\text{val}_L(I, x)$ which is possible because we will not consider variables but only function symbols (including constants and thus program variables) which are evaluated in the state I. We use α conversion and β reduction to simplify lambda expression.

Example 1. Valuation of a simple program variable `a`

$$
\begin{aligned}
\mathrm{val}_I({}^{v}a) &= \mathrm{val}_I({}^{v})(\mathrm{val}_I(a)) \\
&= \mathrm{val}_I({}^{v})a^I \\
&= \lambda z.\, {}^{\mathrm{va}}(a^I, z)
\end{aligned}
$$

Example 2. Valuation of a program variable `a.m` or `a[m]`

$$
\begin{aligned}
\mathrm{val}_I({}^{v}({}^{v}a, m)) &= \mathrm{val}_I({}^{v})(\mathrm{val}_I({}^{v}a), \mathrm{val}_I(m)) \\
&= \mathrm{val}_I({}^{v})(\underbrace{\lambda z_1.\, {}^{\mathrm{va}}(a^I, z_1)}_{X_1}, \underbrace{m^I}_{Y_1}) \\
&= \lambda z_2.(\underbrace{\lambda z_1.\, {}^{\mathrm{va}}(a^I, z_1)}_{X_1}\, {}^{\bullet}(\underbrace{m^I}_{Y_1}, z_2)) \\
&= \lambda z_2.(\, {}^{\mathrm{va}}(a^I, {}^{\bullet}(m^I, z_2)))
\end{aligned}
$$

Example 3. Valuation of a program variable `a.m.n` or `a[m].n` or `a.m[n]` or `a[m][n]`

$$
\begin{aligned}
\mathrm{val}_I({}^{v}({}^{v}(a, m), n)) &= \ldots \text{see above} \\
&= {}^{v^I}(\underbrace{\lambda z_2.(\, {}^{\mathrm{va}}(a^I, {}^{\bullet}(m^I, z_2)))}_{X_3}, \underbrace{n^I}_{Y_3}) \\
&= \lambda z_3.(\underbrace{\lambda z_2.(\, {}^{\mathrm{va}}(a^I, {}^{\bullet}(m^I, z_2)))}_{X_3}\, {}^{\bullet}(\underbrace{n^I}_{Y_3}, z_3)) \\
&= \lambda z_3.(\, {}^{\mathrm{va}}(a^I, {}^{\bullet}(m^I, {}^{\bullet}(\underbrace{n^I}_{Y_3}, z_3))))
\end{aligned}
$$

Example 4. Valuation of a referenced simple program variable `&a`

$$
\begin{aligned}
\mathrm{val}_I({}^{\&}a) &= \mathrm{val}_I({}^{\&})(\mathrm{val}_I(a)) \\
&= \mathrm{val}_I({}^{\&})(a^I) \\
&= \lambda z_1.\, {}^{\mathrm{adr}}(a^I, z_1)
\end{aligned}
$$

Example 5. Valuation of a referenced program variable `&a.m`

$$
\begin{aligned}
\mathrm{val}_I({}^{\&}({}^{\&}a, m)) &= \mathrm{val}_I({}^{\&})(\, \mathrm{val}_I({}^{\&}a), \mathrm{val}_I(m)) \\
&= \mathrm{val}_I({}^{\&})(\underbrace{\lambda z_1.\, {}^{\mathrm{adr}}(a^I, z_1)}_{X_1}, \underbrace{m^I}_{Y_1}) \\
&= \lambda z_2.(\, {}^{\mathrm{adr}}(a^I, {}^{\bullet}(\underbrace{m^I}_{Y_1}, z_2)))
\end{aligned}
$$

Example 6. Valuation of a syntactical deep copy update `a=b`

$$\begin{aligned}\mathrm{val}_I(\{\,{}^v a := {}^v b\}) &= [{}^v\!: \mathrm{val}_I(a) \mapsto \mathrm{val}_I({}^v b)]\\ &= [{}^v\!: a^I \mapsto \mathrm{val}_I({}^v)(\mathrm{val}_I(b))]\\ &= [{}^v\!: a^I \mapsto {}^{v^I}(b^I)]\end{aligned}$$

Example 7. Valuation of the application of a syntactical deep copy update `a=b:a`

$$\begin{aligned}\mathrm{val}_I(\{\,{}^v a := {}^v b\}\,{}^v a) &= \mathrm{val}_{I \lessdot \mathrm{val}_I(\{\,{}^v a := {}^v b\})}({}^v a)\\ &= \mathrm{val}_{\underbrace{I \lessdot [{}^v: a^I \mapsto {}^{v^I}(b^I)]}_{I_2}}({}^v a)\\ &= \mathrm{val}_{I_2}({}^v)(\mathrm{val}_{I_2}(a))\\ &= {}^{v^{I_2}}(a^{I_2})\\ &\overset{a \text{ is rigid}}{=} {}^{v^{I_2}}(a^I)\\ &= {}^{v^I}(b^I)\\ &= \lambda z.{}^{\mathrm{va}}(b^I, z)\end{aligned}$$

5.4.3 Calculus

The application of the rules must be done in order. Practically this is only important for the rules (dR) and (Rd) because these rules have to be applied before any update application rules are applied.

Abbr.	Rewrite rule schema
dr1	$^*({}^{\&}a) \rightsquigarrow {}^v a$ only if a is a program variable
dr2	$^*({}^{\&}(x, m)) \rightsquigarrow {}^v({}^*(x), m)$
dR	$^*(\&x) \rightsquigarrow x$

Table 5.1. Dereferenciation Rules

Abbr	Rewrite rule schema
Rd	$\&({}^*x) \rightsquigarrow x$
Rv1	$\&\,{}^v a \rightsquigarrow {}^{\&}a$
Rv2	$\&\,{}^v(x, y) \rightsquigarrow {}^{\&}(\&x, y)$
Rs	$\&(a \lhd \langle m := b\rangle) \rightsquigarrow \&a$

Table 5.2. Referenciation Rules

Abbr.	Rewrite rules schema
uu	$U;\{a:=b\} \leadsto \{U, {}^*U\&a:=Ub\}$

uv	$\{X_1:=y_1,\ldots,X_k:=y_k,\ldots,X_n:=y_n\}_k\,{}^vZ \leadsto$
	if $\&X_k \doteq U\&{}^vZ$ then y_n else
	if $\&X_k \sqsubset^* U\&{}^vZ$ then
	$(U_{k-1}({}^vZ)) \lhd \langle x_{[\&X \sqsubseteq^* {}^\&(U\&{}^vZ,x)]} := U_k\,({}^vZ, x_{[\&X \sqsubseteq^* {}^\&(U\&{}^vZ,x)]})\rangle$
	else if $\&X_k \sqsupset^* U\&{}^vZ$ then ${}^v(UZ)$ else
	else $U_{k-1}({}^vZ)$ fi fi fi
	//for $k>0$ and $X_k \neq {}^\&(\ldots)$ ignore updates to pointers

u0	$U_0\,{}^vt \leadsto {}^*U\&\,{}^vt$
ur	$U\,{}^\&X \leadsto {}^\&(UX)$
uRr	$U\&^\&c \leadsto \&^\&(Uc)$
ud	$U\,{}^*({}^vX) \leadsto \overset{*}{U}\lvert U\,{}^vX$
ud2	$U_k\,{}^*Z \leadsto$ if $\&X_k \doteq UZ \vee \&X_k \sqsubset^* UZ \vee \&X_k \sqsupset^* UZ$ then $\overset{*}{U_k}\lvert UZ$ else $U_{k-1}\,{}^*Z$ fi
udr	$\overset{*}{U}\lvert\,{}^\&X \leadsto U({}^*({}^\&X))$
uud	$U'\overset{*}{U}\lvert X \leadsto \overset{*}{U';U}\lvert U'X$
us	$U(x \lhd \langle y:=z\rangle) \leadsto (Ux) \lhd \langle (Uy):=(Uz)\rangle)$
ue	$Ux_{[F]} \leadsto x_{[UF]}$ update epsilon term
ua	$Ua \leadsto a$ for rigid constants (program variables)
uf	$Uf(x_1,\ldots,x_n) \leadsto f(Ux_1,\ldots,Ux_n)$, f is a rigid function like if-then-else-fi. We use also the notation $Uf(x_1,\ldots,x_m) \leadsto fU(x_1,\ldots,x_n)$
uF	$U\phi(x_1,\ldots,x_n) \leadsto \phi(Ux_1,\ldots,Ux_n)$ where $\phi \in \mathrm{Fml}$ propagation of updates to the terms of formulas. (should be explicitly listed for all constructors of formulas)

Table 5.3. Update Application Rules

Abbr.	Rewrite rule schema
vs	${}^v(a \lhd \langle m:=b\rangle, n) \leadsto$ if $m \doteq n$ then b else ${}^v(a,n)$ fi
co	`x=y` $\leadsto \{{}^vx := {}^vy\}$ this rule just symbolizes the conversion defined in def. 5.8

Table 5.4. Program Variable Rules

Abbr.	Rewrite rule schema
eps	substitution of an epsilon term $x_{[F]}$ such that F is true which can be computed in easy cases.
eq	decision procedure for $\doteq$ in simple cases
ss	decision procedure for $\sqsupset$, $\sqsupseteq$ etc. in simple cases
if	$\text{if } C \text{ then } p \text{ else } q \text{ fi} = \begin{cases} p \text{ if } C = \text{true} \\ q \text{ otherwise} \end{cases}$
subcal	This is not a rule. Calculations in a subbox.
subst	Substitution (usually of a sub-term simplified in a subbox

Table 5.5. Utility Rules

5.4.4 Discussion

5.4.4.1 Semantic

The set AP of accessor paths can be semantically restricted to contain only accessor paths which really exist, according to the type definitions in the program. Syntactically the set of terms of type ACC could be restricted as well. There is, however, no reason why the set of accessor paths should be restricted only to those accessors paths which correspond to the type definitions of the program. If we put no restrictions on the accessor paths, then deep copy updates perform a deep copy between arbitrarily large virtual structures. As the virtual structures are copied, the structure that the program variables a and b represent is copied *on the way*. In other words, this is a very general mechanism of value assignments by which the special case of assignments between C structures can be handled. This is similar to treating arithmetic on integers of a programming language by using arithmetic mathematical integers of infinite size.

We assume that any C structure fits or can be represented by a virtual structure of a possibly larger size. When the accessor paths reach members of basic types and then possibly bits then we allow the set ACC to contain accessor paths which would virtually reach even deeper substructures, but the lambda combinators $^\bullet$ could be defined as such that they truncate these impossible accessor paths — in a similar sense a bit vector is truncated in a bit shift operation when it exceeds the boundary of the bit vector which will hold the result of the shift operation.

One limitation has to be put on the possible accessors paths: the accessor paths may have arbitrary length, but they must be finite because otherwise the set of accessors is not a countable set.

5.4.4.2 Calculus

The presented calculus has been developed by trial and error. We can't prove the correctness of the calculus in the scope of the thesis but instead we provide a set of experiments that show the application of the calculus to simplify terms with updates. A correctness proof for deep copy updates would consist of the proofs:

1. The relation $\rightsquigarrow^*$ is a fixed-point rewrite relation (def. 3.23).
2. For all terms A, B, C it holds that $\text{val}_l(s, (\{A := B\}C) \rightsquigarrow^*) = \text{val}_l(s \lessdot \text{val}_l(s, \{A := B\}), C)$
   , where $\{A := B\}C) \rightsquigarrow^*$ is the result of the evaluation of fixed-point rewriting.
3. The merging of updates by rule (uu) and application of focal (simultan) deep copy updates (especially rule (uv)) are correct. This means it has to be shown that $\rightsquigarrow^*$ is confluent (def. 3.21)

In an attempt of proving the third "proof obligation" we have found out that rule (ud) has to be replaced by rule (ud2). The effect of rule (ud2) — even though is looks much more complicated — is the same as that of (ud) but in some situations the application of an update on the top-most function symbols of a term is skipped and propagated to the next sub-term. Intuitively (ud2) sub-sums (ud) in the sense that all calculations using (ud) which yield a correct result also yield a correct result when using (ud2). The case where (ud) fails to work correctly is too complicated to be explained here.

We believe that the calculus is correct when using (ud2). In the next section we present 65 experiments (using (ud)) which all yield the desired results supporting our believe that the calculus does correctly implement deep copy assignments. Furthermore we believe that these experiments yield also the same results when using (ud2) in place of (ud).

A much simpler solution has been developed after the writing of this thesis in [20].

5.5 Experiments

Notation: Sub-calculations are done in sub-boxes. The result of a sub-calculation is then substituted in the following term for some sub-terms. Terms that reach over several lines in size are separated from other terms by a horizontal line. The final result is presented in a non-indented box.

5.5.1 List of Experiments

Nr	Abbreviations	Updated terms	Resulting terms
1	`a=b :a`	$\{ {}^{v}a := {}^{v}b \} {}^{v}a$	${}^{v}b$
2	`a=b :&a`	$\{ {}^{v}a := {}^{v}b \} \&^{v}a$	${}^{\&}a$
3	`a=b :c`	$\{ {}^{v}a := {}^{v}b \} {}^{v}c$	${}^{\&}c$
4	`a=b :a.m`	$\{ {}^{v}a := {}^{v}b \} {}^{v}({}^{v}a, m)$	${}^{v}({}^{v}b, m')$
5	`a=b :&a.m`	$\{ {}^{v}a := {}^{v}b \} \&^{v}({}^{v}a, m)$	${}^{\&}({}^{\&}a, m')$
6	`a.m=b :a`	$\{ {}^{v}({}^{v}a, m) := {}^{v}b \} {}^{v}a$	${}^{v}a \lhd \langle m := {}^{v}b \rangle$
7	`*a=b :a`	$\{ {}^{*}({}^{v}a) := {}^{v}b \} {}^{v}a$	$\text{if}\ {}^{v}a \doteq {}^{\&}a\ \text{then}\ {}^{v}b\ \text{else}$ $\text{if}\ {}^{v}a \sqsubset^{*} {}^{\&}a\ \text{then}\ (U_0\, {}^{v}a) \lhd$ $\langle x_{[{}^{v}a \sqsubseteq^{*} {}^{\&}({}^{\&}a, x)]} := U_1\, {}^{v}({}^{v}a, x_{[{}^{v}a \sqsubseteq^{*} {}^{\&}({}^{\&}a, x)]}) \rangle$ $\text{else if}\ {}^{v}a \sqsupset^{*} {}^{\&}a\ \text{then}\ {}^{v}(Ua)$ $\text{else}\ U_0({}^{v}a)\ \text{fi fi fi}$
8	`*a=b :c`	$\{ {}^{*}({}^{v}a) := {}^{v}b \} {}^{v}c$	$\text{if}\ {}^{v}a \doteq {}^{\&}c\ \text{then}\ {}^{v}b\ \text{else}$ $\text{if}\ {}^{v}a \sqsubset^{*} {}^{\&}c\ \text{then}\ (U_0({}^{v}c)) \lhd$ $\langle x_{[{}^{v}a \sqsubseteq^{*} {}^{\&}({}^{\&}c, x)]} := U_1\, {}^{v}({}^{v}c, x_{[{}^{v}a \sqsubseteq^{*} {}^{\&}({}^{\&}c, x)]}) \rangle$ $\text{else if}\ {}^{v}a \sqsupset^{*} {}^{\&}c\ \text{then}\ {}^{v}(Uc)$ $\text{else}\ U_0({}^{v}c)\ \text{fi fi fi}$
9	`a=b :*a`	$\{ {}^{v}a := {}^{v}b \} {}^{*}({}^{v}a)$	$\overset{*}{\{ {}^{v}a := {}^{v}b \}} \vert {}^{v}b$
10	`a=b :&(*a)`	$\{ {}^{v}a := {}^{v}b \} \&^{*}({}^{v}a)$	${}^{v}b$
11	`a=&b :*a`	$\{ {}^{v}a := {}^{\&}b \} {}^{*}({}^{v}a)$	${}^{v}b$
12	`a=&b :&*a`	$\{ {}^{v}a := \&^{v}b \} \&^{*}({}^{v}a)$	${}^{\&}b$
13	`a=&a :*a`	$\{ {}^{v}a := \&^{v}a \} {}^{*}({}^{v}a)$	${}^{\&}a$
14	`a=&a :**a`	$\{ {}^{v}a := \&^{v}a \} {}^{*}({}^{*}({}^{v}a))$	${}^{\&}a$
15	`a=&b :(*a).m`	$\{ {}^{v}a := {}^{\&}b \} {}^{v}({}^{*}({}^{v}a), m)$	${}^{v}({}^{v}b, m')$
16	`a=&b :&(*a).m`	$\{ {}^{v}a := {}^{\&}b \} \&^{v}({}^{*}({}^{v}a), m)$	${}^{\&}({}^{\&}b, m')$
17	`a=a.m :a`		must be excluded by the type system
18	`a=&a.m:*a`		must be excluded by the type system
19	`a=&a.m:(*a).m`		must be excluded by the type system

Table 5.6. Application of deep copy updates on terms

Nr	Abbreviation	Resulting terms	
20	`a.m=&a:(*a.m).m`	$\{ {}^{v}({}^{v}a, m) := {}^{\&}a \} {}^{v}({}^{*}({}^{v}({}^{v}a, m)), m)$	${}^{\&}a$

The resulting "big" terms of experiments 7 and 8 are due to the dereferenciation of the uninitialized pointer variable a. The resulting if-cascade is important to handle "upcoming updates from the left", i.e., to handle update merging from right to left or from the inner updates to outer updates. The idea and motivation behind deep copy updates is, however, to merge updates from left to right or from outer updates to inner updates as programs are symbolically executed. Therefore results like in the experiments 7 and 8 do not occur if uninitialized pointers are not dereferenced.

Nr	Abbreviations	Updating an update	Merged updates
21	`a=b ; a=c`	$\{{}^{v}a := {}^{v}b\}\{{}^{v}a := {}^{v}c\}$	$\{{}^{v}a := {}^{v}b, {}^{v}a := {}^{v}c\}$
22	`a=b ; c=a`	$\{{}^{v}a := {}^{v}b\}\{{}^{v}c := {}^{v}a\}$	$\{{}^{v}a := {}^{v}b, {}^{v}c := {}^{v}b\}$
23	`a=b ;a.m=c`	$\{{}^{v}a := {}^{v}b\}\{{}^{v}({}^{v}a, m) := {}^{v}c\}$	$\{{}^{v}a := {}^{v}b, {}^{v}({}^{v}a, m') := {}^{v}c\}$
24	`a.m=b ; a=c`	$\{{}^{v}({}^{v}a, m) := {}^{v}b\}\{{}^{v}a := {}^{v}c\}$	$\{{}^{v}({}^{v}a, m) := {}^{v}b, {}^{v}a := {}^{v}c\}$
25	`a=b ; c=a.m`	$\{{}^{v}a := {}^{v}b\}\{{}^{v}c := {}^{v}({}^{v}a, m)\}$	$\{{}^{v}a := {}^{v}b, {}^{v}c := {}^{v}({}^{v}b, m')\}$
26	`a.m=b ; c=a`	$\{{}^{v}({}^{v}a, m) := {}^{v}b\}\{{}^{v}c := {}^{v}a\}$	$\{{}^{v}({}^{v}a, m) := {}^{v}b, {}^{v}c := {}^{v}a \lhd \langle m := {}^{v}b \rangle\}$
27	`a=c ; b=&a`	$\{{}^{v}a := {}^{v}c\}\{{}^{v}b := {}^{\&}a\}$	$\{{}^{v}a := {}^{v}c, {}^{v}b := {}^{\&}a\}$
28	`a.m=c ; b=&a`	$\{{}^{v}({}^{v}a, m) := {}^{v}c\}\{{}^{v}b := {}^{\&}a\}$	$\{{}^{v}({}^{v}a, m) := {}^{v}c, {}^{v}b := {}^{\&}a\}$
29	`a=b ; b=c`	$\{{}^{v}a := {}^{v}b\}\{{}^{v}b := {}^{v}c\}$	$\{{}^{v}a := {}^{v}b, {}^{v}b := {}^{v}c\}$
30	`a=b ;b.m=c`	$\{{}^{v}a := {}^{v}b\}\{{}^{v}({}^{v}b, m) := {}^{v}c\}$	$\{{}^{v}a := {}^{v}b, {}^{v}({}^{v}b, m') := {}^{v}c\}$
31	`a=&b; b=c`	$\{{}^{v}a := \&{}^{v}b\}\{{}^{v}b := {}^{v}c\}$	$\{{}^{v}a := {}^{\&}b, {}^{v}b := {}^{v}c\}$
32	`a=&b;b.m=c`	$\{{}^{v}a := \&{}^{v}b\}\{{}^{v}({}^{v}b, m) := {}^{v}c\}$	$\{{}^{v}a := {}^{\&}b, {}^{v}({}^{v}b, m') := {}^{v}c\}$
33	`a=&b; c=a`	$\{{}^{v}a := \&{}^{v}b\}\{{}^{v}c := {}^{v}a\}$	$\{{}^{v}a := {}^{\&}b, {}^{v}c := {}^{\&}b\}$
34	`a=&b; c=*a`	$\{{}^{v}a := \&{}^{v}b\}\{{}^{v}c := {}^{*}({}^{v}a)\}$	$\{{}^{v}a := {}^{\&}b, {}^{v}c := {}^{v}b\}$
35	`a=&b; *a=c`	$\{{}^{v}a := \&{}^{v}b\}\{{}^{*}({}^{v}a) := {}^{v}c\}$	$\{{}^{v}a := {}^{\&}b, {}^{v}b := {}^{v}c\}$
36	`a=&b;(*a).m=c`	$\{{}^{v}a := {}^{\&}b\}\{{}^{v}({}^{*}({}^{v}a), m) := {}^{v}c\}$	$\{{}^{v}a := {}^{\&}b, {}^{v}({}^{v}b, m') := {}^{v}c\}$
37	`a=&b;c=(*a).m`	$\{{}^{v}a := {}^{\&}b\}\{{}^{v}c := {}^{v}({}^{*}({}^{v}a), m)\}$	$\{{}^{v}a := {}^{\&}b, {}^{v}c := {}^{v}({}^{v}b, m')\}$

Table 5.7. Application of deep copy updates on deep copy updates

Nr	Abbreviations	Updating a term	Resulting term
38	`(a=b;a=c):a`	$\{{}^{v}a := {}^{v}b, {}^{v}a := {}^{v}c\}_2 \; {}^{v}a$	${}^{v}c$
39	`(a=b;c=a):a`	$\{{}^{v}a := {}^{v}b, {}^{v}c := {}^{v}b\}_2 \; {}^{v}a$	${}^{v}b$
40	`(a=b;c=a):c`	$\{{}^{v}a := {}^{v}b, {}^{v}c := {}^{v}b\}_2 \; {}^{v}c$	${}^{v}b$
41	`(a=b;a.m=c):a`	$\{{}^{v}a := {}^{v}b, {}^{v}({}^{v}a, m) := {}^{v}c\}_2 \; {}^{v}a$	${}^{v}b \lhd \langle m := {}^{v}c \rangle$
42	`(a=b;c=a.m):c`	$\{{}^{v}a := {}^{v}b, {}^{v}c := {}^{v}({}^{v}b, m')\}_2 \; {}^{v}c$	${}^{v}({}^{v}b, m')$
43	`(a.m=b;c=a):c`	$\{{}^{v}({}^{v}a, m) := {}^{v}b, {}^{v}c := {}^{v}a \lhd \langle m := {}^{v}b \rangle\}_2 \; {}^{v}c$	${}^{v}a \lhd \langle m := {}^{v}b \rangle$
44	`(a=&b;c=*a):c`	$\{{}^{v}a := {}^{\&}b, {}^{v}c := {}^{v}b\} \; {}^{v}c$	${}^{v}b$
45	`(a.m=b;c=a):a`	$\{{}^{v}({}^{v}a, m) := {}^{v}b, {}^{v}c := {}^{v}a \lhd \langle m := {}^{v}b \rangle\}_2 \; {}^{v}a$	${}^{v}a \lhd \langle m := {}^{v}b \rangle$

Table 5.8. Application of merged deep copy updates on simple program variables

Nr	Abbreviations	Updating a term	Result
46	`(a=b;a=c):a.m`	$\{{}^{v}a := {}^{v}b, {}^{v}a := {}^{v}c\}_2 \; {}^{v}({}^{v}a, m)$	${}^{v}({}^{v}c, m')$
47	`(a=b;c=a):a.m`	$\{{}^{v}a := {}^{v}b, {}^{v}c := {}^{v}a\}_2 \; {}^{v}({}^{v}a, m)$	${}^{v}({}^{v}b, m')$
48	`(a=b;a.m=c):a.m`	$\{{}^{v}a := {}^{v}b, {}^{v}({}^{v}a, m) := {}^{v}c\}_2 \; {}^{v}({}^{v}a, m)$	${}^{v}c$
49	`(a.m=b;a=c):a.m`	$\{{}^{v}a := {}^{v}b, {}^{v}a := {}^{v}c\}_2 \; {}^{v}({}^{v}a, m)$	${}^{v}({}^{v}c, m')$
50	`(a.m=b;c=a):c.m`	$\{{}^{v}({}^{v}a, m) := {}^{v}b, {}^{v}c := {}^{v}a \lhd \langle m := {}^{v}b \rangle\}_2 \; {}^{v}({}^{v}c, m)$	${}^{v}b$
51	`(a.m=b;c=a):c.w`	$\{{}^{v}({}^{v}a, m) := {}^{v}b, {}^{v}c := {}^{v}a \lhd \langle m := {}^{v}b \rangle\}_2 \; {}^{v}({}^{v}c, w)$	${}^{v}({}^{v}a, w)$
52	`(a=&b;c=*a):c.m`	$\{{}^{v}a := {}^{\&}b, {}^{v}c := {}^{v}b\} \; {}^{v}({}^{v}c, m)$	${}^{v}({}^{v}b, m')$

Table 5.9. Application of merged deep copy updates on sub-structures

Nr	Abbreviations	Updating a term	Resulting term
53	`(a=b;c=a):*c`	$\{{}^{v}a:={}^{v}b,{}^{v}c:={}^{v}a\}\,{}^{*}({}^{v}c)$	$\overset{*}{\{{}^{v}a:={}^{v}b,\,{}^{v}c:={}^{v}a\}}\mid{}^{v}b$
54	`(a=c;b=&a):*b`	$\{{}^{v}a:={}^{v}c,{}^{v}b:={}^{\&}a\}\,{}^{*}({}^{v}b)$	${}^{v}c$
55	`(a.m=c;b=&a):*b`	$\{{}^{v}({}^{v}a,m):={}^{v}c,{}^{v}b:={}^{\&}a\}\,{}^{*}({}^{v}b)$	${}^{v}a\lhd\langle m:={}^{v}c\rangle$
56	`(a=&b;b=c):*a`	$\{{}^{v}a:={}^{\&}b,{}^{v}b:={}^{v}c\}{}^{*}({}^{v}a)$	${}^{v}c$
57	`(a=&b;b.m=c):*a`	$\{{}^{v}a:={}^{\&}b,\,{}^{v}({}^{v}b,m):={}^{v}c\}{}^{*}({}^{v}a)$	${}^{v}b\lhd\langle m:={}^{v}c\rangle$
58	`(a=&b;c=a):*c`	$\{{}^{v}a:={}^{\&}b,{}^{v}c:={}^{\&}b\}{}^{*}({}^{v}c)$	${}^{v}b$
59	`(a=&b;*a=c):*a`	$\{{}^{v}a:={}^{\&}b,{}^{v}b:={}^{v}c\}{}^{*}({}^{v}a)$	${}^{v}c$
60	`(a=&b;(*a).m=c):*a`	$\{{}^{v}a:={}^{\&}b,\,{}^{v}({}^{v}b,m'):={}^{v}c\}\,{}^{*}({}^{v}a)$	${}^{v}b\lhd\langle m':={}^{v}c\rangle$

Table 5.10. Application of deep copy updates on dereferenced program variables

Nr	Abbreviation	Updating a term
61	`(a=b;c=a):(*c).m`	$\{{}^{v}a:={}^{v}b,{}^{v}c:={}^{v}a\}_2\,{}^{v}({}^{*}({}^{v}c),m)$

Result

if ${}^{\&}c \doteq {}^{\&}({}^{v}a,m')$ then ${}^{v}a$ else
if ${}^{\&}c \sqsubset^{*} {}^{\&}({}^{v}a,m')$ then $(U_1({}^{v}({}^{*}({}^{v}c),m)))\lhd$
$\langle x_{[\&^{v}c\sqsubseteq^{*}\,{}^{\&}({}^{\&}(\&\overset{*}{U}|{}^{v}a,m'),x)]} := U_2\,({}^{v}({}^{*}({}^{v}c),m),x_{[\&^{v}c\sqsubseteq^{*}\,{}^{\&}({}^{\&}(\&\overset{*}{U}|{}^{v}a,m'),x)]})\rangle$ else
if ${}^{\&}c \sqsupset^{*} {}^{\&}({}^{v}a,m')$ then ${}^{v}(\overset{*}{U}|{}^{v}a,m')$
else $U_1({}^{v}({}^{*}({}^{v}c),m))$ fi fi fi

The reason for this result is that the dereferenced value of ${}^{*}({}^{v}c)$ is unknown at this point; this means that an uninitialized pointer is dereferenced. Alternatively, in such cases, the application of the rules can be delayed if the results end up in bigger terms than the original terms are.

Nr	Abbreviations	Updating a term	Result
62	`(a=c;b=&a):(*b).m`	$\{{}^{v}a:={}^{v}c,{}^{v}b:={}^{\&}a\}_2\,{}^{v}({}^{*}({}^{v}b),m)$	${}^{v}({}^{v}c,m')$
63	`(a.m=c;b=&a):(*b).m`	$\{{}^{v}({}^{v}a,m):={}^{v}c,{}^{v}b:={}^{\&}a\}_2\,{}^{v}({}^{*}({}^{v}b),m)$	${}^{v}c$
64	`(a=&b;b=c):(*a).m`	$\{{}^{v}a:={}^{\&}b,{}^{v}b:={}^{v}c\}_2\,{}^{v}({}^{*}({}^{v}a),m)$	${}^{v}({}^{v}c,m')$
65	`(a=&b;b.m=c):(*a).m`	$\{{}^{v}a:={}^{\&}b,{}^{v}({}^{v}b,m):={}^{v}c\}_2\,{}^{v}({}^{*}({}^{v}a),m)$	${}^{v}c$

Table 5.11. Application of deep copy updates on dereferenced sub-structures

5.5.2 Apply Update on Term

Experiment 1

```
a=b:a
```

$$\{\underbrace{{}^{v}a}_{X_1} := \underbrace{{}^{v}b}_{y_1}\}_1 \underbrace{{}^{v}a}_{{}^{v}Z} \overset{(uv)}{\rightsquigarrow}$$

$$\text{if}\,\&\underbrace{{}^{v}a}_{X_1} \doteq U\&\underbrace{{}^{v}a}_{{}^{v}Z}\ \text{then}\ \underbrace{{}^{v}b}_{y_1}\ \text{else}$$
$$\text{if}\,\&X_1 \sqsubset^* U\&{}^{v}Z\ \text{then}\,(U_{1-1}({}^{v}Z)) \lhd \langle x_{[\ldots]} := U_1{}^{v}({}^{v}Z, x_{[\ldots]})\rangle\ \text{else}$$
$$\text{if}\,\&X_1 \sqsupset^* U\&{}^{v}Z\ \text{then}\,{}^{v}(U\,Z)$$
$$\text{else}\ U_{1-1}({}^{v}Z)\ \text{fi fi fi} \overset{(subcal)}{\rightsquigarrow}$$

$$\&\underbrace{{}^{v}a}_{X_1} \doteq U\&\underbrace{{}^{v}a}_{{}^{v}Z} \overset{(rv1)}{\rightsquigarrow}$$
$${}^{\&}a \doteq U\,{}^{\&}a \overset{(ur)}{\rightsquigarrow}$$
$${}^{\&}a \doteq {}^{\&}(Ua) \overset{(ua)}{\rightsquigarrow}$$
$${}^{\&}a \doteq {}^{\&}a \overset{(eq)}{\rightsquigarrow}$$
$$\mathit{true}$$
$$\overset{(subst)}{\rightsquigarrow}$$

$$\text{if}\ \mathit{true}\ \text{then}\ {}^{v}b\ \text{else} \ldots \text{fi} \overset{(if)}{\rightsquigarrow}$$

$${}^{v}b$$

Experiment 2

```
a=b:&a
```

$$\{{}^{v}a := {}^{v}b\}\,\&{}^{v}a \overset{(rv1)}{\rightsquigarrow}$$
$$\{{}^{v}a := {}^{v}b\}\,{}^{\&}a \overset{(ur)}{\rightsquigarrow}$$
$${}^{\&}(\{{}^{v}a := {}^{v}b\}\,a) \overset{(ua)}{\rightsquigarrow}$$

$${}^{\&}a$$

Experiment 3

```
a=b:c
```

$$\{\underbrace{{}^{v}a}_{X_1} := \underbrace{{}^{v}b}_{y_1}\}_1 \underbrace{{}^{v}c}_{{}^{v}Z} \overset{(uv)}{\rightsquigarrow}$$

$$\text{if}\,\&\underbrace{{}^{v}a}_{X_1} \doteq U\&\underbrace{{}^{v}c}_{{}^{v}Z}\ \text{then}\ \underbrace{{}^{v}b}_{y_1}\ \text{else}$$
$$\text{if}\,\&X_1 \sqsubset^* U\&{}^{v}Z\ \text{then}\,(U_{1-1}({}^{v}Z)) \lhd \langle x_{[\ldots]} := U_1{}^{v}({}^{v}Z, x_{[\ldots]})\rangle\ \text{else}$$
$$\text{if}\,\&X_1 \sqsupset^* U\&{}^{v}Z\ \text{then}\,{}^{v}(U\,Z)$$
$$\text{else}\ U_{1-1}({}^{v}Z)\ \text{fi fi fi} \overset{(subcal)}{\rightsquigarrow}$$

$$\boxed{\begin{array}{l} \underbrace{\& \, {}^{v}a}_{X_1} \doteq \underbrace{U\& \, {}^{v}c}_{{}^{v}Z} \overset{(\mathrm{Rv1})}{\rightsquigarrow} \\ {}^{\&}a \doteq U\, {}^{\&}c \overset{(\mathrm{ur})}{\rightsquigarrow} \\ {}^{\&}a \doteq {}^{\&}(Uc) \overset{(\mathrm{ua})}{\rightsquigarrow} \\ {}^{\&}a \doteq {}^{\&}c \overset{(\mathrm{eq})}{\rightsquigarrow} \\ \mathit{false} \end{array}} \overset{(\mathrm{subst})}{\rightsquigarrow}$$

$$\begin{array}{l} \text{if } \mathit{false} \text{ then } {}^{v}b \text{ else} \\ \text{if } \&X_1 \sqsubset^{*} U\&{}^{v}Z \text{ then } (U_0({}^{v}Z)) \lhd \langle x_{[\ldots]} := U_1\,{}^{v}({}^{v}Z, x_{[\ldots]})\rangle \text{ else} \\ \text{if } \&X_1 \sqsupset^{*} U\&{}^{v}Z \text{ then } {}^{v}(U\,Z) \\ \text{else } U_0({}^{v}Z) \text{ fi fi fi} \overset{(\mathrm{if})}{\rightsquigarrow} \end{array}$$

$$\begin{array}{l} \text{if } \underbrace{\& \, {}^{v}a}_{X_1} \sqsubset^{*} \underbrace{U\& \, {}^{v}c}_{{}^{v}Z} \text{ then } (U_0({}^{v}Z)) \lhd \langle x_{[\ldots]} := U_1\,{}^{v}({}^{v}Z, x_{[\ldots]})\rangle \text{ else} \\ \text{if } \&X_1 \sqsupset^{*} U\&{}^{v}Z \text{ then } {}^{v}(U\,Z) \\ \text{else } U_0({}^{v}Z) \text{ fi fi} \overset{(\mathrm{subcal})}{\rightsquigarrow} \end{array}$$

$$\boxed{\underbrace{\& \, {}^{v}a}_{X_1} \sqsubset^{*} \underbrace{U\& \, {}^{v}c}_{{}^{v}Z} \overset{(\mathrm{Rv1})}{\rightsquigarrow} \ldots \overset{(\mathrm{ua})}{\rightsquigarrow} {}^{\&}a \sqsubset^{*} {}^{\&}c \overset{(\mathrm{eq})}{\rightsquigarrow} \mathit{false}} \overset{(\mathrm{subst})}{\rightsquigarrow}$$

$$\begin{array}{l} \text{if } \mathit{false} \text{ then } (U_{1-1}({}^{v}Z)) \lhd \langle x_{[\ldots]} := U_1\,{}^{v}({}^{v}Z, x_{[\ldots]})\rangle \text{ else} \\ \text{if } \&X_1 \sqsupset^{*} U\&{}^{v}Z \text{ then } {}^{v}(U\,Z) \\ \text{else } U_0({}^{v}Z) \text{ fi fi} \overset{(\mathrm{if})}{\rightsquigarrow} \end{array}$$

$$\begin{array}{l} \text{if } \underbrace{\& \, {}^{v}a}_{X_1} \sqsupset^{*} \underbrace{U\& \, {}^{v}c}_{{}^{v}Z} \text{ then } {}^{v}(U\,Z) \\ \text{else } U_0({}^{v}Z) \text{ fi} \overset{(\mathrm{subcal})}{\rightsquigarrow} \end{array}$$

$$\boxed{\underbrace{\& \, {}^{v}a}_{X_1} \sqsupset^{*} \underbrace{U\& \, {}^{v}c}_{{}^{v}Z} \overset{(\mathrm{Rv1})}{\rightsquigarrow} \ldots \overset{(\mathrm{ua})}{\rightsquigarrow} {}^{\&}a \sqsupset^{*} {}^{\&}c \overset{(\mathrm{ss})}{\rightsquigarrow} \mathit{false}} \overset{(\mathrm{subst})}{\rightsquigarrow}$$

$$\begin{array}{l} \text{if } \mathit{false} \text{ then } {}^{v}(U\,Z) \text{ else } U_0(\underbrace{{}^{v}c}_{{}^{v}Z}) \text{ fi} \overset{(\mathrm{if})}{\rightsquigarrow} \\ U_0({}^{v}c) \overset{(\mathrm{u0})}{\rightsquigarrow} \\ {}^{*}U\&({}^{v}c) \overset{(\mathrm{Rv})}{\rightsquigarrow} \\ {}^{*}(U\,{}^{\&}c) \overset{(\mathrm{ur})}{\rightsquigarrow} \\ {}^{*}({}^{\&}(Uc)) \overset{(\mathrm{ua})}{\rightsquigarrow} \end{array}$$

$$\boxed{{}^{v}c}$$

Experiment 4

```
a=b:a.m
```

$$\{\underbrace{{}^v a}_{X_1} := \underbrace{{}^v b}_{y_1}\}_1\, {}^v\underbrace{({}^v a, m)}_{{}^v Z} \overset{(uv)}{\rightsquigarrow}$$

$$\text{if}\,\&\underbrace{{}^v a}_{X_1} \doteq U\&{}^v\underbrace{({}^v a, m)}_{{}^v Z}\ \text{then}\ \underbrace{{}^v b}_{y_1}\ \text{else}$$

$$\text{if}\,\&\underbrace{{}^v a}_{X_1} \sqsubset^* U\&{}^v\underbrace{({}^v a, m)}_{{}^v Z}\text{then}\,(U_{1-1}({}^v Z)) \lhd \langle x_{[\ldots]} := U_1\, {}^v({}^v Z, x_{[\ldots]})\rangle\ \text{else}$$

$$\text{if}\,\&\underbrace{{}^v a}_{X_1} \sqsupset^* U\&{}^v\underbrace{({}^v a, m)}_{{}^v Z}\ \text{then}\, {}^v(U\, Z)$$

$$\text{else}\ U_{1-1}({}^v Z)\ \text{fi fi fi} \overset{(subcal)}{\rightsquigarrow}$$

$$\&\underbrace{{}^v a}_{X_1} \doteq U\&{}^v\underbrace{({}^v a, m)}_{{}^v Z} \overset{(Rv1)(Rv2)}{\rightsquigarrow}$$

$${}^\& a \doteq U\, {}^\&({}^\& a, m) \overset{(ur)}{\rightsquigarrow}$$

$${}^\& a \doteq {}^\&(U\, {}^\& a, Um) \overset{(ur)(ua)}{\rightsquigarrow}$$

$${}^\& a \doteq {}^\&({}^\& a, m') \overset{(eq)}{\rightsquigarrow}$$

false

$$\&{}^v a \sqsubset^* U\&{}^v({}^v a, m) \overset{(Rv1)(Rv2)}{\rightsquigarrow}$$

$${}^\& a \sqsubset^* U\, {}^\&({}^\& a, m) \overset{(ur)}{\rightsquigarrow}$$

$${}^\& a \sqsubset^* {}^\&(U\, {}^\& a, Um) \overset{(ur)(ua)}{\rightsquigarrow}$$

$${}^\& a \sqsubset^* {}^\&({}^\& a, m') \overset{(ss)}{\rightsquigarrow}$$

false

$$\&{}^v a \sqsupset^* U\&{}^v({}^v a, m) \overset{(Rv1)(Rv2)}{\rightsquigarrow}$$

$${}^\& a \sqsupset^* U\, {}^\&({}^\& a, m) \overset{(ur)}{\rightsquigarrow}$$

$${}^\& a \sqsupset^* {}^\&(U\, {}^\& a, Um) \overset{(ur)(ua)}{\rightsquigarrow}$$

$${}^\& a \sqsupset^* {}^\&({}^\& a, m') \overset{(ss)}{\rightsquigarrow}$$

true

$$\overset{(subst)}{\rightsquigarrow}$$

$$\text{if}\ \textit{false}\ \text{then}\, {}^v b\ \text{else}$$

$$\text{if}\ \textit{false}\ \text{then}\,(U_{1-1}({}^v Z)) \lhd \langle x_{[\ldots]} := U_1\, {}^v({}^v Z, x_{[\ldots]})\rangle\ \text{else}$$

$$\text{if}\ \textit{true}\ \text{then}\, {}^v(U\, \underbrace{({}^v a, m)}_{Z})$$

$$\text{else}\ U_{1-1}({}^v Z)\ \text{fi fi fi} \overset{(if)}{\rightsquigarrow}$$

$${}^v(U\,({}^v a, m)) \overset{(uf)}{\rightsquigarrow}$$

$${}^v(U{}^v a, Um) \overset{(subcal)}{\rightsquigarrow}$$

$$\boxed{U{}^v a \rightsquigarrow \text{see above} \rightsquigarrow {}^v b} \overset{(subst)}{\rightsquigarrow}$$

${}^v({}^v b, m')$ //where m' is the updated version of m. For attributename m is rigid

Experiment 5

```
a=b:&a.m
```

$$\{{}^va := {}^vb\}\,\&^v({}^va, m) \overset{(Rv1)(Rv2)}{\rightsquigarrow}$$
$$\{{}^va := {}^vb\}\,{}^{\&}({}^{\&}a, m) \overset{(ur)}{\rightsquigarrow}$$
$${}^{\&}(\{{}^va := {}^vb\}{}^{\&}a, \{{}^va := {}^vb\}m) \overset{(ur)(ua)}{\rightsquigarrow}$$

whether m is modified depends on whether it is rigid or not

$${}^{\&}({}^{\&}(\{{}^va := {}^vb\}a), m') \overset{(ua)}{\rightsquigarrow}$$

$${}^{\&}({}^{\&}a, m')$$

Experiment 6

```
a.m=b:a
```

$$\{\underbrace{{}^v({}^va, m)}_{X_1} := \underbrace{{}^vb}_{y_1}\}_1 \underbrace{{}^va}_{{}^vZ} \overset{(uv)}{\rightsquigarrow}$$

$$\text{if}\ \&\underbrace{{}^v({}^va, m)}_{X_1} \doteq U\&\underbrace{{}^va}_{{}^vZ}\ \text{then}\ \underbrace{{}^vb}_{y_1}\ \text{else}$$
$$\text{if}\ \&\underbrace{{}^v({}^va, m)}_{X_1} \sqsubset^* U\&\underbrace{{}^va}_{{}^vZ}\ \text{then}\ (U_{1-1}({}^vZ)) \lhd \langle x_{[\ldots]} := U_1\,{}^v({}^vZ, x_{[\ldots]})\rangle\ \text{else}$$
$$\text{if}\ \&X_1 \sqsupset^* U\&^vZ\ \text{then}\ {}^v(U\,Z)$$
$$\text{else}\ U_{1-1}({}^vZ)\ \text{fi fi fi} \overset{(subcal)}{\rightsquigarrow}$$

$$\&^v\underbrace{({}^va, m)}_{X_1} \doteq U\&\underbrace{{}^va}_{{}^vZ} \overset{(Rv1)(Rv2)}{\rightsquigarrow}$$
$${}^{\&}({}^{\&}a, m) \doteq U^{\&}a \overset{(ur)}{\rightsquigarrow}$$
$${}^{\&}({}^{\&}a, m) \doteq {}^{\&}(Ua) \overset{(ua)}{\rightsquigarrow}$$
$${}^{\&}({}^{\&}a, m) \doteq {}^{\&}(a) \overset{(eq)}{\rightsquigarrow}$$
false

$$\&^v({}^va, m) \sqsubset^* U\&^va \overset{(Rv1)(Rv2)}{\rightsquigarrow}$$
$${}^{\&}({}^{\&}a, m) \sqsubset^* U\,{}^{\&}a \overset{(ur)}{\rightsquigarrow}$$
$${}^{\&}({}^{\&}a, m) \sqsubset^* {}^{\&}(Ua) \overset{(ua)}{\rightsquigarrow}$$
$${}^{\&}({}^{\&}a, m) \sqsubset^* {}^{\&}a \overset{(ss)}{\rightsquigarrow}$$
true

$$\text{if}\ \mathit{false}\ \text{then}\ {}^vb\ \text{else}$$
$$\text{if}\ \mathit{true}\ \text{then}\ (U_0(\underbrace{{}^va}_{{}^vZ})) \lhd \langle x_{[\&X \sqsubseteq^* {}^{\&}(U\&^vZ, x)]} := U_1\,{}^v(\underbrace{{}^va}_{{}^vZ}, x_{[\&X \sqsubseteq^* {}^{\&}(U\&^vZ, x)]})\rangle$$
$$\text{else if}\ \&X_1 \sqsupset^* U\&^vZ\ \text{then}\ {}^v(U\,Z)$$

$\text{else } U_{1-1}({}^{v}Z) \text{ fi fi fi} \overset{(\text{if})}{\leadsto}$

$(U_0(\underbrace{{}^{v}a}_{{}^{v}Z})) \lhd \langle x_{[\&X \sqsubseteq^* \&(U\&^{v}Z,x)]} := U_1{}^{v}(\underbrace{{}^{v}a}_{{}^{v}Z}, x_{[\&X \sqsubseteq^* \&(U\&^{v}Z,x)]})\rangle$

$[\underbrace{\&^{v}({}^{v}a,m)}_{X_1} \sqsubseteq^* {}^{\&}(U\& \underbrace{{}^{v}a}_{{}^{v}Z}, x)] \overset{(\text{Rv1})(\text{Rv2})}{\leadsto}$ $[{}^{\&}({}^{\&}a,m) \sqsubseteq^* {}^{\&}(U{}^{\&}a,x)] \overset{(\text{ur})}{\leadsto}$ $[{}^{\&}({}^{\&}a,m) \sqsubseteq^* {}^{\&}({}^{\&}a,x)] \overset{(\text{ss})}{\leadsto}$ $x \doteq m$	$\overset{(\text{subst})}{\leadsto}$

$(U_0({}^{v}a)) \lhd \langle m := U_1{}^{v}({}^{v}a,m)\rangle \overset{(\text{subcal})}{\leadsto}$

$U_1{}^{v}({}^{v}a,m) = \{{}^{v}({}^{v}a,m) := {}^{v}b\}_1{}^{v}({}^{v}a,m) \leadsto$ similar to $\{X := Y\}X \overset{[1]}{\leadsto} Y$ $\leadsto {}^{v}b$

$(U_0({}^{v}a)) \lhd \langle m := {}^{v}b\rangle \overset{(\text{subcal})}{\leadsto}$

$U_0({}^{v}a) \overset{(\text{u0})}{\leadsto} {}^{*}U\&{}^{v}a \overset{(\text{Rv1})}{\leadsto} {}^{*}U{}^{\&}a \overset{(\text{ur})}{\leadsto} {}^{*}({}^{\&}(Ua)) \overset{(\text{ua})}{\leadsto} {}^{v}a$

${}^{v}a \lhd \langle m := {}^{v}b\rangle$

Experiment 7

```
*a=b:a
```

$\{\underbrace{{}^{*}({}^{v}a)}_{X_1} := \underbrace{{}^{v}b}_{y_1}\}_1 \underbrace{{}^{v}a}_{{}^{v}Z} \overset{(\text{uv})}{\leadsto}$

$\text{if } \underbrace{\&^{*}({}^{v}a)}_{X_1} \doteq U\& \underbrace{{}^{v}a}_{{}^{v}Z} \text{ then } \underbrace{{}^{v}b}_{y_1} \text{ else}$

$\text{if } \underbrace{\&^{*}({}^{v}a)}_{X_1} \sqsubset^* U\& \underbrace{{}^{v}a}_{{}^{v}Z} \text{ then } (U_0({}^{v}Z)) \lhd$

$\langle x_{[\&X \sqsubseteq^* \&(U\&^{v}Z,x)]} := U_1 {}^{v}({}^{v}Z, x_{[\&X \sqsubseteq^* \&(U\&^{v}Z,x)]})\rangle$ else

$\text{if } \underbrace{\&^{*}({}^{v}a)}_{X_1} \sqsupset^* U\& \underbrace{{}^{v}a}_{{}^{v}Z} \text{ then } {}^{v}(U\,Z)$

$\text{else } U_{1-1}({}^{v}Z) \text{ fi fi}$

$\&^{*}({}^{v}a) \overset{(\text{Rd})}{\leadsto} {}^{v}a$

$U\&{}^{v}a \overset{(\text{Rv1})}{\leadsto} U{}^{\&}a \overset{(\text{ur})}{\leadsto} {}^{\&}(Ua) \overset{(\text{ua})}{\leadsto} {}^{\&}a$

$\text{if } {}^{v}a \doteq {}^{\&}a \text{ then } {}^{v}b \text{ else}$ $\text{if } {}^{v}a \sqsubset^* {}^{\&}a \text{ then } (U_0({}^{v}a)) \lhd \langle x_{[{}^{v}a \sqsubseteq^* \&({}^{\&}a,x)]} := U_1{}^{v}({}^{v}a, x_{[{}^{v}a \sqsubseteq^* \&({}^{\&}a,x)]})\rangle \text{ else}$ $\text{if } {}^{v}a \sqsupset^* {}^{\&}a \text{ then } {}^{v}(Ua)$ $\text{else } U_0({}^{v}a) \text{ fi fi fi}$

Experiment 8

```
*a=b:c
```

$$\{\underbrace{{}^*({}^v a)}_{X_1} := \underbrace{{}^v b}_{y_1}\}_1 \underbrace{{}^v c}_{{}^v Z} \overset{(uv)}{\rightsquigarrow}$$

$$\text{if}\ \underbrace{\&^*({}^v a)}_{X_1} \doteq U\&\ \underbrace{{}^v c}_{{}^v Z}\ \text{then}\ \underbrace{{}^v b}_{y_1}\ \text{else}$$

$$\text{if}\ \underbrace{\&^*({}^v a)}_{X_1} \sqsubset^*\ U\&\ \underbrace{{}^v c}_{{}^v Z}\ \text{then}\ (U_0({}^v Z)) \lhd \langle x_{[\& X \sqsubseteq^* \&(U\&{}^v Z, x)]} := U_1\ {}^v({}^v Z,$$

$$x_{[\& X \sqsubseteq^* \&(U\&{}^v Z, x)]})\rangle\ \text{else}$$

$$\text{if}\ \underbrace{\&^*({}^v a)}_{X_1} \sqsupset^*\ U\&\ \underbrace{{}^v c}_{{}^v Z}\ \text{then}\ {}^v(U\, Z)$$

$$\text{else}\ U_{1-1}({}^v Z)\ \text{fi fi fi}$$

$$\boxed{\&^*({}^v a) \overset{(Rd)}{\rightsquigarrow} {}^v a}$$

$$\boxed{U\&\ {}^v c \overset{(Rv1)}{\rightsquigarrow} U\,{}^{\&}c \overset{(ur)}{\rightsquigarrow} {}^{\&}(Uc) \overset{(ua)}{\rightsquigarrow} {}^{\&}c}$$

$$\boxed{\begin{array}{l}\text{if}\ {}^v a \doteq {}^{\&}c\ \text{then}\ {}^v b\ \text{else}\\ \text{if}\ {}^v a \sqsubset^* {}^{\&}c\ \text{then}\ (U_0({}^v c)) \lhd \langle x_{[{}^v a \sqsubseteq^* \&({}^{\&}c, x)]} := U_1\ {}^v({}^v c, x_{[{}^v a \sqsubseteq^* \&({}^{\&}c, x)]})\rangle\ \text{else}\\ \text{if}\ {}^v a \sqsupset^* {}^{\&}c\ \text{then}\ {}^v(Uc)\\ \text{else}\ U_0({}^v c)\ \text{fi fi fi}\end{array}}$$

Experiment 9

```
a=b:*a
```

$$\{{}^v a := {}^v b\}\ {}^*({}^v a) \overset{(ud)}{\rightsquigarrow}$$

$$\overset{*}{}_{\{{}^v a := {}^v b\}}|\{{}^v a := {}^v b\}{}^v a \overset{(subcal)}{\rightsquigarrow}$$

$$\boxed{\{{}^v a := {}^v b\}{}^v a \rightsquigarrow \text{see above} \overset{[1]}{\rightsquigarrow} {}^v b}$$

$$\boxed{\overset{*}{}_{\{{}^v a := {}^v b\}}|{}^v b}$$

Experiment 10

```
a=b:&(*a)
```

$$\{{}^v a := {}^v b\}\ \&^*({}^v a) \overset{(Rd)}{\rightsquigarrow}$$

$$\{{}^v a := {}^v b\}\ {}^v a \overset{(uv)}{\rightsquigarrow}$$

$$\boxed{\{{}^v a := {}^v b\}{}^v a \rightsquigarrow \text{see above} \overset{[1]}{\rightsquigarrow} {}^v b}$$

$\boxed{{}^{v}b}$

Experiment 11

`a=&b:*a`

$\{\,{}^{v}a := \&{}^{v}b\}\,{}^{*}({}^{v}a) \overset{(Rv1)}{\rightsquigarrow}$

$\{\,{}^{v}a := {}^{\&}b\}\,{}^{*}({}^{v}a) \overset{(ur)}{\rightsquigarrow}$

$\overset{*}{\{{}^{v}a:={}^{\&}b\}}|\{\,{}^{v}a := {}^{\&}b\}{}^{v}a \overset{(subcal)}{\rightsquigarrow}$

$\boxed{\{\,{}^{v}a := {}^{\&}b\}{}^{v}a \rightsquigarrow \text{see above} \overset{[1]}{\rightsquigarrow} {}^{\&}b}$

$\overset{*}{\{{}^{v}a:={}^{\&}b\}}|\,{}^{\&}b \overset{(udr)}{\rightsquigarrow}$

$\{\,{}^{v}a := {}^{\&}b\}({}^{*}({}^{\&}b)) \overset{(dr1)}{\rightsquigarrow}$

$\{\,{}^{v}a := {}^{\&}b\}\,{}^{v}b \overset{(subcal)}{\rightsquigarrow}$

$\boxed{\{\,{}^{v}a := {}^{\&}b\}\,{}^{v}b \rightsquigarrow \boxed{\text{similar to } \{X := Y\}X \overset{[1]}{\rightsquigarrow} Y} \overset{(subst)}{\rightsquigarrow} {}^{v}b}$

$\boxed{{}^{v}b}$

Experiment 12

`a=&b:&*a`

$\{\,{}^{v}a := \&{}^{v}b\}\,\&{}^{*}({}^{v}a) \overset{(Rd)}{\rightsquigarrow}$

$\{\,{}^{v}a := {}^{\&}b\}\,{}^{v}a \overset{(subcal)}{\rightsquigarrow}$

$\boxed{\{\,{}^{v}a := {}^{\&}b\}{}^{v}a \rightsquigarrow \text{see above} \overset{[1]}{\rightsquigarrow} {}^{\&}b}$

$\boxed{{}^{\&}b}$

Experiment 13

`a=&a:*a`

$\{\,{}^{v}a := \&{}^{v}a\}\,{}^{*}({}^{v}a) \overset{(Rv1)}{\rightsquigarrow}$

$\{\,{}^{v}a := {}^{\&}a\}\,{}^{*}({}^{v}a) \overset{(ud)}{\rightsquigarrow}$

$\overset{*}{\{{}^{v}a:={}^{\&}a\}}|\{\,{}^{v}a := {}^{\&}a\}{}^{v}a \overset{(subcal)}{\rightsquigarrow}$

$\boxed{\{\,{}^{v}a := {}^{\&}a\}{}^{v}a \rightsquigarrow \boxed{\text{similar to } \{X := Y\}X \overset{[1]}{\rightsquigarrow} Y} \overset{(subst)}{\rightsquigarrow} {}^{\&}a}$

$\overset{*}{\{{}^{v}a:={}^{\&}a\}}|\,{}^{\&}a \overset{(udr)}{\rightsquigarrow}$

$\{\,{}^{v}a := {}^{\&}a\}({}^{*}({}^{\&}a)) \overset{(dr1)}{\rightsquigarrow}$

$\{\,{}^{v}a := {}^{\&}a\}\,{}^{v}a \overset{(subcal)}{\rightsquigarrow}$

$\boxed{\{\,{}^{v}a := {}^{\&}a\}\,{}^{v}a \rightsquigarrow \boxed{\text{similar to } \{X := Y\}X \overset{[1]}{\rightsquigarrow} Y} \overset{(subst)}{\rightsquigarrow} {}^{\&}a}$

$\boxed{{}^{\&}a}$

Experiment 14

```
a=&a:**a
```

$\{{}^v a := \&^v a\}\, {}^*({}^*({}^v a)) \overset{(\mathrm{Rv})}{\rightsquigarrow}$

$\{{}^v a := {}^{\&} a\}\, {}^*({}^*({}^v a)) \overset{(\mathrm{ud})}{\rightsquigarrow}$

$\overset{*}{}_{\{{}^v a := {}^{\&} a\}} | \{{}^v a := {}^{\&} a\} {}^*({}^v a) \overset{(\mathrm{subcal})}{\rightsquigarrow}$

$\boxed{\{{}^v a := {}^{\&} a\} {}^*({}^v a) \rightsquigarrow \text{see above} \overset{[1]}{\rightsquigarrow} {}^{\&} a}$

$\overset{*}{}_{\{{}^v a := {}^{\&} a\}} | {}^{\&} a \overset{(\mathrm{udr})}{\rightsquigarrow}$

$\{{}^v a := {}^{\&} a\} ({}^*({}^{\&} a)) \overset{(\mathrm{dr1})}{\rightsquigarrow}$

$\{{}^v a := {}^{\&} a\}\, {}^v a \overset{(\mathrm{subcal})}{\rightsquigarrow}$

$\boxed{\{{}^v a := {}^{\&} a\}\, {}^v a \rightsquigarrow \boxed{\text{similar to } \{X := Y\} X \overset{[1]}{\rightsquigarrow} Y} \overset{(\mathrm{subst})}{\rightsquigarrow} {}^{\&} a}$

$\boxed{{}^{\&} a}$

Experiment 15

```
a=&b:(*a).m
```

$\{ \underbrace{{}^v a}_{X_1} := \underbrace{{}^{\&} b}_{y_1} \}_1 \underbrace{{}^v({}^*({}^v a), m)}_{{}^v Z} \overset{(\mathrm{uv})}{\rightsquigarrow}$

$\text{if}\, \& \underbrace{{}^v a}_{X_1} \doteq U \& \underbrace{{}^v({}^*({}^v a), m)}_{{}^v Z} \text{ then } \underbrace{{}^{\&} b}_{y_1} \text{ else}$

$\text{if}\, \& \underbrace{{}^v a}_{X_1} \sqsubset^* U \& \underbrace{{}^v({}^*({}^v a), m)}_{{}^v Z} \text{then} (U_{1-1}({}^v Z)) \lhd \langle x_{[\ldots]} := U_1\, {}^v({}^v Z, x_{[\ldots]}) \rangle \text{ else}$

$\text{if}\, \& \underbrace{{}^v a}_{X_1} \sqsupset^* U \& \underbrace{{}^v({}^*({}^v a), m)}_{{}^v Z} \text{ then } {}^v(U\, Z)$

$\text{else } U_{1-1}({}^v Z) \text{ fi fi fi} \overset{(\mathrm{subcal})}{\rightsquigarrow}$

$\boxed{\& {}^v a \overset{(\mathrm{Rv1})}{\rightsquigarrow} {}^{\&} a}$

$U \& {}^v({}^*({}^v a), m) \overset{(\mathrm{Rv1})}{\rightsquigarrow}$

$U\, {}^{\&}(\&^*({}^v a), m) \overset{(\mathrm{Rd})}{\rightsquigarrow}$

$U\, {}^{\&}({}^v a, m) \overset{(\mathrm{ur2})}{\rightsquigarrow}$

${}^{\&}(U^v a, U m) \overset{(\mathrm{subcal})}{\rightsquigarrow}$

$\boxed{U^v a = \{{}^v a := {}^{\&} b\}\, {}^v a \rightsquigarrow \boxed{\text{similar to } \{X := Y\} X \overset{[1]}{\rightsquigarrow} Y} \overset{(\mathrm{subst})}{\rightsquigarrow} {}^{\&} b}$

${}^{\&}({}^{\&} b, m')$

$\text{if}\, {}^{\&} a \doteq {}^{\&}({}^{\&} b, m') \text{ then } {}^{\&} b \text{ else}$

$\text{if}\,{}^{\&}a \sqsubset^{*} {}^{\&}({}^{\&}b, m')\,\text{then}\,(U_{1-1}({}^{v}Z)) \lhd \langle x_{[\ldots]} := U_1\,{}^{v}({}^{v}Z, x_{[\ldots]})\rangle\,\text{else}$
$\text{if}\,{}^{\&}a \sqsupset^{*} {}^{\&}({}^{\&}b, m')\,\text{then}\,{}^{v}(U\,Z)$
$\text{else}\,U_{1-1}({}^{v}Z)\,\text{fi fi fi} \overset{(\text{subcal})}{\leadsto}$

${}^{\&}a \doteq {}^{\&}({}^{\&}b, m') \overset{(\text{eq})}{\leadsto} \mathit{false}$

${}^{\&}a \sqsubset^{*} {}^{\&}({}^{\&}b, m') \overset{(\text{ss})}{\leadsto} \mathit{false}$

${}^{\&}a \sqsupset^{*} {}^{\&}({}^{\&}b, m') \overset{(\text{ss})}{\leadsto} \mathit{false}$

$\overset{(\text{subst})}{\leadsto}$

$\text{if}\,\mathit{false}\,\text{then}\,{}^{\&}b\,\text{else}$
$\text{if}\,\mathit{false}\,\text{then}\,(U_{1-1}({}^{v}Z)) \lhd \langle x_{[\ldots]} := U_1\,{}^{v}({}^{v}Z, x_{[\ldots]})\rangle\,\text{else}$
$\text{if}\,\mathit{false}\,\text{then}\,{}^{v}(U\,Z)$
$\text{else}\,U_0(\underbrace{{}^{v}({}^{*}({}^{v}a), m)}_{{}^{v}Z})\,\text{fi fi fi} \overset{(\text{if})}{\leadsto}$

$U_0\,{}^{v}({}^{*}({}^{v}a), m) \overset{(\text{u0})}{\leadsto}$
${}^{*}U\&\,{}^{v}({}^{*}({}^{v}a), m) \overset{(\text{subcal})}{\leadsto}$

$U\&\,{}^{v}({}^{*}({}^{v}a), m) \leadsto$see in box above $\overset{(\text{subst})}{\leadsto} {}^{\&}({}^{\&}b, m')$

${}^{*}\,({}^{\&}({}^{\&}b, m')) \overset{(\text{dr2})}{\leadsto}$
${}^{v}({}^{*\&}b, m') \overset{(\text{dr1})}{\leadsto}$

${}^{v}({}^{v}b, m')$

Experiment 16

```
a=&b:&(*a).m
```

$\{{}^{v}a := {}^{\&}b\}\,\&^{v}({}^{*}({}^{v}a), m) \overset{(\text{Rv1})}{\leadsto}$
$\{{}^{v}a := {}^{\&}b\}\,{}^{\&}(\&\,{}^{*}({}^{v}a), m) \overset{(\text{Rd})}{\leadsto}$
$\{{}^{v}a := {}^{\&}b\}\,{}^{\&}({}^{v}a, m) \overset{(\text{ur2})}{\leadsto}$
${}^{\&}(\{{}^{v}a := {}^{\&}b\}{}^{v}a, \{{}^{v}a := {}^{\&}b\}m) \overset{(\text{subcal})}{\leadsto}$

$\{{}^{v}a := {}^{\&}b\}{}^{v}a \leadsto$ similar to $\{X := Y\}X \overset{[1]}{\leadsto} Y$ $\overset{(\text{subst})}{\leadsto} {}^{\&}b$

$\{{}^{v}a := {}^{\&}b\}m \leadsto$depends on whether m is rigid or not $\leadsto m'$

${}^{\&}({}^{\&}b, m')$

Experiment 17

```
a=a.m:a
```

This case could be computed but must be excluded by static type checks.

Experiment 18

```
a=&a.m:*a
```

This case could be computed but must be excluded by static type checks.

Experiment 19

```
a=&a.m:(*a).m
```

hypothetical computation

```
a=&a.m:(a.m).m
(a=&a.m:a.m).m
((&a.m).m).m
```

This case could be computed but must be excluded by static type checks.

Experiment 20

```
a.m=&a:(*a.m).m
```

$$\{\underbrace{{}^v({}^va,m)}_{X_1} := \underbrace{{}^{\&}a}_{y_1}\}_1 \underbrace{{}^v({}^*({}^v({}^va,m)),m)}_{{}^vZ} \overset{(uv)}{\rightsquigarrow}$$

$\text{if}\ \&\underbrace{{}^v({}^va,m)}_{X_1} \doteq U\&\ \underbrace{{}^v({}^*({}^v({}^va,m)),m)}_{{}^vZ}\ \text{then}\ \underbrace{{}^{\&}a}_{y_1}\ \text{else}$

$\text{if}\ \&\underbrace{{}^v({}^va,m)}_{X_1} \sqsubset^* U\&\ \underbrace{{}^v({}^*({}^v({}^va,m)),m)}_{{}^vZ}\ \text{then}\ (U_{1-1}({}^vZ)) \lhd$

$\langle x_{[\ldots]} := U_1\,{}^v({}^vZ, x_{[\ldots]})\rangle\ \text{else}$

$\text{if}\ \&\underbrace{{}^v({}^va,m)}_{X_1} \sqsupset^* U\&\ \underbrace{{}^v({}^*({}^v({}^va,m)),m)}_{{}^vZ}\text{then}\ (U\,Z)$

$\text{else}\ U_{1-1}({}^vZ)\ \text{fi fi fi} \overset{(subcal)}{\rightsquigarrow}$

$\&\,{}^v({}^va,m) \overset{(Rv2)}{\rightsquigarrow} {}^{\&}(\&{}^va,m) \overset{(Rv1)}{\rightsquigarrow} {}^{\&}({}^{\&}a,m)$

$U\&\,{}^v({}^*({}^v({}^va,m)),m) \overset{(Rv2)}{\rightsquigarrow}$

$U\,{}^{\&}(\&\,{}^*({}^v({}^va,m)),m) \overset{(Rd)}{\rightsquigarrow}$

$U\,{}^{\&}({}^v({}^va,m),m) \overset{(ur2)}{\rightsquigarrow}$

${}^{\&}(U^v({}^va,m),Um) \overset{(subcal)}{\rightsquigarrow}$

$U^v({}^va,m) = \{{}^v({}^va,m) := {}^{\&}a\}^v({}^va,m) \rightsquigarrow$

similar to $\{X := Y\}X \overset{[1]}{\rightsquigarrow} Y$ $\overset{(subst)}{\rightsquigarrow} {}^{\&}a$

${}^{\&}({}^{\&}a,m')$

$\text{if}\ {}^{\&}a \doteq {}^{\&}({}^{\&}a,m')\ \text{then}\ {}^{\&}b\ \text{else}$

if ${}^{\&}a \sqsubset^* {}^{\&}({}^{\&}a, m')$ then $(U_{1-1}({}^{v}Z)) \lhd \langle x_{[\ldots]} := U_1\, {}^{v}({}^{v}Z, x_{[\ldots]})\rangle$ else
if ${}^{\&}a \sqsupset^* {}^{\&}({}^{\&}a, m')$ then ${}^{v}(U\, Z)$
else $U_{1-1}({}^{v}Z)$ fi fi fi $\overset{\text{(subcal)}}{\rightsquigarrow}$

$\boxed{{}^{\&}a \doteq {}^{\&}({}^{\&}a, m') \overset{\text{(eq)}}{\rightsquigarrow} \mathit{false}}$

$\boxed{{}^{\&}a \sqsubset^* {}^{\&}({}^{\&}a, m') \overset{\text{(ss)}}{\rightsquigarrow} \mathit{false}}$

$\boxed{{}^{\&}a \sqsupset^* {}^{\&}({}^{\&}a, m') \overset{\text{(ss)}}{\rightsquigarrow} \mathit{true}}$

if *false* then ${}^{\&}b$ else
if *false* then $(U_{1-1}({}^{v}Z)) \lhd \langle x_{[\ldots]} := U_1\, {}^{v}({}^{v}Z, x_{[\ldots]})\rangle$ else
if *true* then ${}^{v}(U\, \underbrace{({}^{*}({}^{v}({}^{v}a, m)), m)}_{Z})$
else $U_0({}^{v}Z)$ fi fi fi $\overset{\text{(if)}}{\rightsquigarrow}$

${}^{v}(U\, ({}^{*}({}^{v}({}^{v}a, m)), m)) \overset{\text{(ud)}}{\rightsquigarrow}$

${}^{v}(\, {}^{*}_{U} | U\, {}^{v}({}^{v}a, m), Um) \rightsquigarrow$

${}^{v}(\, {}^{*}_{U} | U\, {}^{v}({}^{v}a, m), m') \overset{\text{(subcal)}}{\rightsquigarrow}$

$\boxed{\begin{array}{l} U^{v}({}^{v}a, m) = \{\, {}^{v}({}^{v}a, m) := {}^{\&}a\}\, {}^{v}({}^{v}a, m) \rightsquigarrow \\ \boxed{\text{similar to } \{X := Y\}\, X \overset{[1]}{\rightsquigarrow} Y} \overset{\text{(subst)}}{\rightsquigarrow} \\ {}^{\&}a \end{array}}$

${}^{v}(\, {}^{*}_{U} | {}^{\&}a, m') \overset{\text{(udr)}}{\rightsquigarrow}$

${}^{v}(\, U({}^{*}({}^{\&}a)), m') \overset{\text{(dr1)}}{\rightsquigarrow}$

${}^{v}(\, U^{v}a, m') \overset{\text{(subcal)}}{\rightsquigarrow}$

$\boxed{\begin{array}{l} U\, {}^{v}a = \{\, {}^{v}({}^{v}a, m) := {}^{\&}a\}\, {}^{v}a \overset{\text{subcal}}{\rightsquigarrow} \\ \boxed{\text{similar to } \{\, {}^{v}(X, m) := Y\}\, X \overset{[6]}{\rightsquigarrow} X \lhd \langle m := Y\rangle} \\ \overset{\text{subst}}{\rightsquigarrow} \\ {}^{v}a \lhd \langle m := {}^{\&}a\rangle \end{array}} \overset{\text{subst}}{\rightsquigarrow}$

${}^{v}(\, {}^{v}a \lhd \langle m := {}^{\&}a\rangle, m') \overset{\text{(vs)}}{\rightsquigarrow}$

if $m \doteq m'$ then ${}^{\&}a$ else ${}^{v}({}^{v}a, m')$ fi $\overset{\text{(eq)}}{\rightsquigarrow}$

if *true* then ${}^{\&}a$ else ${}^{v}({}^{v}a, m')$ fi $\overset{\text{(if)}}{\rightsquigarrow}$

$\boxed{{}^{\&}a}$

5.5.3 Apply Update on Update

Experiment 21

```
a=b;a=c
```

$$\{\underbrace{{}^v a := {}^v b}_{U^1}\}\{\underbrace{{}^v a := {}^v c}_{U^2}\} \overset{\text{(uu)}}{\leadsto}$$

$$\{\underbrace{{}^v a := {}^v b}_{U^1}, {}^*(\{\underbrace{{}^v a := {}^v b}_{U^1}\}\&\,{}^v a) := \{\underbrace{{}^v a := {}^v b}_{U1}\}{}^v c\} \overset{\text{(subcal)}}{\leadsto}$$

$$\boxed{\begin{array}{l} \{{}^v a := {}^v b\}\&\,{}^v a \overset{\text{(Rv1)}}{\leadsto} \{{}^v a := {}^v b\}{}^{\&}a \overset{\text{subcal}}{\leadsto} \\ \boxed{\text{similar to } \{X := Y\}X \overset{[1]}{\leadsto} Y} \\ \overset{\text{(subst)}}{\leadsto} {}^{\&}a \end{array}}$$

$$\boxed{\{{}^v a := {}^v b\}{}^v c \overset{\text{(subcal)}}{\leadsto} \boxed{\text{similar to } \{X := Y\}Z \overset{[3]}{\leadsto} Z} \overset{\text{(subst)}}{\leadsto} {}^v c}$$

$$\{{}^v a := {}^v b, {}^*({}^{\&}a) := {}^v c\} \overset{\text{(dr1)}}{\leadsto}$$

$$\boxed{\{{}^v a := {}^v b, {}^v a := {}^v c\}}$$

Experiment 22

```
a=b;c=a
```

$$\{{}^v a := {}^v b\}\{{}^v c := {}^v a\} \overset{\text{(uu)}}{\leadsto}$$

$$\{{}^v a := {}^v b, {}^*(\{{}^v a := {}^v b\}\&\,{}^v c) := \{{}^v a := {}^v b\}{}^v a\} \overset{\text{(subcal)}}{\leadsto}$$

$$\boxed{\{{}^v a := {}^v b\}{}^{\&}c \overset{\text{(subcal)}}{\leadsto} \boxed{\text{similar to } \{X := Y\}Z \overset{[3]}{\leadsto} Z} \overset{\text{(subst)}}{\leadsto} {}^{\&}c}$$

$$\boxed{\{{}^v a := {}^v b\}{}^v a \overset{\text{(subcal)}}{\leadsto} \boxed{\text{similar to } \{X := Y\}Z \overset{[3]}{\leadsto} Z} \overset{\text{(subst)}}{\leadsto} {}^v b}$$

$$\{{}^v a := {}^v b, {}^*({}^{\&}c) := {}^v b\} \overset{\text{(dr1)}}{\leadsto}$$

$$\boxed{\{{}^v a := {}^v b, {}^v c := {}^v b\}}$$

Experiment 23

```
a=b;a.m=c
```

$$\{{}^v a := {}^v b\}\{{}^v({}^v a, m) := {}^v c\} \overset{\text{(uu)}}{\leadsto}$$

$$\{{}^v a := {}^v b, {}^*(\{{}^v a := {}^v b\}\&\,{}^v({}^v a, m)) := \{{}^v a := {}^v b\}{}^v c\} \overset{\text{(subcal)}}{\leadsto}$$

$$\boxed{\{{}^v a := {}^v b\}\&{}^v({}^v a, m) \overset{\text{(Rv)}}{\leadsto} \{{}^v a := {}^v b\}{}^{\&}({}^{\&}a, m) \overset{\text{(ur)}}{\leadsto} \ldots \overset{\text{(ur)}}{\leadsto} {}^{\&}({}^{\&}a, m')}$$

$$\boxed{\{{}^v a := {}^v b\}{}^v c \overset{\text{(subcal)}}{\leadsto} \boxed{\text{similar to } \{X := Y\}Z \overset{[3]}{\leadsto} Z} \overset{\text{(subst)}}{\leadsto} {}^v c}$$

$$\{{}^v a := {}^v b, {}^*({}^{\&}({}^{\&}a, m')) := {}^v c\} \overset{\text{(dr2)}}{\leadsto}$$

$$\{{}^v a := {}^v b, {}^v({}^{*\&}a, m')) := {}^v c\} \overset{\text{(dr1)}}{\leadsto}$$

$$\boxed{\{{}^v a := {}^v b,\ {}^v({}^v a, m') := {}^v c\}}$$

Experiment 24

```
a.m=b;a=c
```

$$\{\underbrace{{}^v({}^va,m):={}^vb}_{U^1}\}\{\underbrace{{}^va:={}^vc}_{U^2}\} \overset{(\mathrm{uu})}{\rightsquigarrow}$$

$$\{\underbrace{{}^v({}^va,m):={}^vb}_{U^1}, {}^*(\{\underbrace{{}^v({}^va,m):={}^vb}_{U^1}\}\&{}^va):=\{\underbrace{{}^v({}^va,m):={}^vb}_{U^1}\}{}^vc\} \overset{(\mathrm{subcal})}{\rightsquigarrow}$$

$$\boxed{\{{}^v({}^va,m):={}^vb\}\&{}^va \overset{(\mathrm{Rv1})}{\rightsquigarrow} \{{}^v({}^va,m):={}^vb\}{}^{\&}a \overset{(\mathrm{ur1})}{\rightsquigarrow} {}^{\&}a}$$

$$\{{}^v({}^va,m):={}^vb\}{}^vc \overset{(\mathrm{subcal})}{\rightsquigarrow}$$

similar to $\{X:=Y\}Z \overset{[3]}{\rightsquigarrow} Z$ $\overset{(\mathrm{subst})}{\rightsquigarrow} {}^vc$

$$\{{}^v({}^va,m):={}^vb, {}^*({}^{\&}a):={}^vc\} \overset{(\mathrm{dr1})}{\rightsquigarrow}$$

$\{{}^v({}^va,m):={}^vb, {}^va:={}^vc\}$ //TODO write a rule for simplifying this case

Experiment 25

```
a=b;c=a.m
```

$$\{{}^va:={}^vb\}\{{}^vc:={}^v({}^va,m)\} \overset{(\mathrm{uu})}{\rightsquigarrow}$$

$$\{{}^va:={}^vb, {}^*(\{{}^va:={}^vb\}\&{}^vc):=\{{}^va:={}^vb\}{}^v({}^va,m)\} \overset{(\mathrm{subcal})}{\rightsquigarrow}$$

$\{{}^va:={}^vb\}{}^{\&}c \overset{(\mathrm{subcal})}{\rightsquigarrow}$ similar to $\{X:=Y\}Z \overset{[3]}{\rightsquigarrow} Z$ $\overset{(\mathrm{subst})}{\rightsquigarrow} {}^{\&}c$

$$\{{}^va:={}^vb\}{}^v({}^va,m) \overset{[4]}{\rightsquigarrow} {}^v({}^vb,m')$$

$$\{{}^va:={}^vb, {}^*({}^{\&}c):={}^v({}^vb,m')\} \overset{(\mathrm{dr1})}{\rightsquigarrow}$$

$$\{{}^va:={}^vb, {}^vc:={}^v({}^vb,m')\}$$

Experiment 26

```
a.m=b;c=a
```

$$\{{}^v({}^va,m):={}^vb\}\{{}^vc:={}^va\} \overset{(\mathrm{uu})}{\rightsquigarrow}$$

$$\{{}^v({}^va,m):={}^vb, {}^*(\{{}^v({}^va,m):={}^vb\}\&{}^vc):=\{{}^v({}^va,m):={}^vb\}{}^va\} \overset{(\mathrm{subcal})}{\rightsquigarrow}$$

$\{{}^v({}^va,m):={}^vb\}{}^{\&}c \overset{(\mathrm{subcal})}{\rightsquigarrow}$ similar to $\{X:=Y\}Z \overset{[3]}{\rightsquigarrow} Z$ $\overset{(\mathrm{subst})}{\rightsquigarrow} {}^{\&}c$

$$\{{}^v({}^va,m):={}^vb\}{}^va \overset{[6]}{\rightsquigarrow} {}^va \lhd \langle m:={}^vb\rangle$$

$$\{{}^v({}^va,m):={}^vb, {}^*({}^{\&}c):={}^va \lhd \langle m:={}^vb\rangle\} \overset{(\mathrm{dr1})}{\rightsquigarrow}$$

$$\{{}^v({}^va,m):={}^vb, {}^vc:={}^va \lhd \langle m:={}^vb\rangle\}$$

Experiment 27

```
a=c;b=&a
```

$$\{{}^v a := {}^v c\}\{{}^v b := {}^\& a\} \overset{(uu)}{\rightsquigarrow}$$
$$\{{}^v a := {}^v c, {}^*(\{{}^v a := {}^v c\}\& {}^v b) := \{{}^v a := {}^v c\}{}^\& a\} \overset{(subcal)}{\rightsquigarrow}$$
$$\boxed{\{{}^v a := {}^v c\}{}^\& b \overset{(subcal)}{\rightsquigarrow} \boxed{\text{similar to } \{X := Y\}Z \overset{[3]}{\rightsquigarrow} Z} \overset{(subst)}{\rightsquigarrow} {}^\& b}$$
$$\boxed{\{{}^v a := {}^v c\}{}^\& a \overset{(ur)}{\rightsquigarrow} {}^\& a}$$
$$\{{}^v a := {}^v c, {}^*({}^\& b) := {}^\& a\} \overset{(dr1)}{\rightsquigarrow}$$
$$\boxed{\{{}^v a := {}^v c, {}^v b := {}^\& a\}}$$

Experiment 28

```
a.m=c;b=&a
```

$$\{{}^v({}^v a, m) := {}^v c\}\{{}^v b := {}^\& a\} \overset{(uu)}{\rightsquigarrow}$$
$$\{{}^v({}^v a, m) := {}^v c, {}^*(\{{}^v({}^v a, m) := {}^v c\}\& {}^v b) := \{{}^v({}^v a, m) := {}^v c\}{}^\& a\} \overset{(subcal)}{\rightsquigarrow}$$
$$\boxed{\{{}^v({}^v a, m) := {}^v c\}{}^\& b \overset{(subcal)}{\rightsquigarrow} \boxed{\text{similar to } \{X := Y\}Z \overset{[3]}{\rightsquigarrow} Z} \overset{(subst)}{\rightsquigarrow} {}^\& b}$$
$$\boxed{\{{}^v({}^v a, m) := {}^v c\}{}^\& a \overset{(ur)}{\rightsquigarrow} {}^\& a}$$
$$\{{}^v({}^v a, m) := {}^v c, {}^*({}^\& b) := {}^\& a\} \overset{(dr1)}{\rightsquigarrow}$$
$$\boxed{\{{}^v({}^v a, m) := {}^v c, {}^v b := {}^\& a\}}$$

Experiment 29

```
a=b;b=c
```

$$\{{}^v a := {}^v b\}\{{}^v b := {}^v c\} \overset{(uu)}{\rightsquigarrow}$$
$$\{{}^v a := {}^v b, {}^*(\{{}^v a := {}^v b\}\& {}^v b) := \{{}^v a := {}^v b\}{}^v c\} \overset{(subcal)}{\rightsquigarrow}$$
$$\boxed{\{{}^v a := {}^v b\}{}^\& b \overset{(subcal)}{\rightsquigarrow} \boxed{\text{similar to } \{X := Y\}Z \overset{[3]}{\rightsquigarrow} Z} \overset{(subst)}{\rightsquigarrow} {}^\& b}$$
$$\boxed{\{{}^v a := {}^v b\}{}^v c \overset{(subcal)}{\rightsquigarrow} \boxed{\text{similar to } \{X := Y\}Z \overset{[3]}{\rightsquigarrow} Z} \overset{(subst)}{\rightsquigarrow} {}^v c}$$
$$\{{}^v a := {}^v b, {}^*({}^\& b) := {}^v c\} \overset{(dr1)}{\rightsquigarrow}$$
$$\boxed{\{{}^v a := {}^v b, {}^v b := {}^v c\}}$$

Experiment 30

```
a=b;b.m=c
```

$$\{{}^v a := {}^v b\}\{{}^v({}^v b, m) := {}^v c\} \overset{(uu)}{\rightsquigarrow}$$
$$\{{}^v a := {}^v b, {}^*(\{{}^v a := {}^v b\}\& {}^v({}^v b, m)) := \{{}^v a := {}^v b\}{}^v c\} \overset{(subcal)}{\rightsquigarrow}$$
$$\boxed{\{{}^v a := {}^v b\}{}^\&({}^\& b, m) \overset{(ur)}{\rightsquigarrow} {}^\&({}^\& b, m')}$$

$\{{}^v a := {}^v b\}{}^v c \overset{(subcal)}{\rightsquigarrow}$ similar to $\{X := Y\}Z \overset{[3]}{\rightsquigarrow} Z$ $\overset{(subst)}{\rightsquigarrow} {}^v c$

$\{{}^v a := {}^v b, {}^*({}^\&({}^\& b, m')) := {}^v c\} \overset{(dr1)}{\rightsquigarrow}$

$\{{}^v a := {}^v b, {}^v({}^{*\&} b, m')) := {}^v c\} \overset{(dr1)}{\rightsquigarrow}$

$\{{}^v a := {}^v b, {}^v({}^v b, m') := {}^v c\}$

//The challange of the following example is when the update is used to update `*a`, because updates to `b` that are executed after the address was obtained must become visible. This is in contrast to `a=b;b=c`. If `a` or any of its substructures is accessed the modification to `b` after the update to `a` must be invisible.

Experiment 31

```
a=&b; b=c
```

$\{{}^v a := \&{}^v b\}\{{}^v b := {}^v c\} \overset{(Rv1)}{\rightsquigarrow}$

$\{{}^v a := {}^\& b\}\{{}^v b := {}^v c\} \overset{(uu)}{\rightsquigarrow}$

$\{{}^v a := {}^\& b, {}^*(\{{}^v a := {}^\& b\}\&\,{}^v b) := \{{}^v a := {}^\& b\}{}^v c\} \overset{(subcal)}{\rightsquigarrow}$

$\{{}^v a := {}^\& b\}{}^\& b \overset{(subcal)}{\rightsquigarrow}$ similar to $\{X := Y\}Z \overset{[3]}{\rightsquigarrow} Z$ $\overset{(subst)}{\rightsquigarrow} {}^\& b$

$\{{}^v a := {}^\& b\}{}^v c \overset{(subcal)}{\rightsquigarrow}$ similar to $\{X := Y\}Z \overset{[3]}{\rightsquigarrow} Z$ $\overset{(subst)}{\rightsquigarrow} {}^v c$

$\{{}^v a := {}^\& b, {}^*({}^\& b) := {}^v c\} \overset{(dr1)}{\rightsquigarrow}$

$\{{}^v a := {}^\& b, {}^v b := {}^v c\}$

Experiment 32

```
a=&b; b.m=c
```

$\{{}^v a := \&{}^v b\}\{{}^v({}^v b, m) := {}^v c\} \overset{(Rv1)}{\rightsquigarrow}$

$\{{}^v a := {}^\& b\}\{{}^v({}^v b, m) := {}^v c\} \overset{(uu)}{\rightsquigarrow}$

$\{{}^v a := {}^\& b, {}^*(\{{}^v a := {}^\& b\}\&\,{}^v({}^v b, m)) := \{{}^v a := {}^\& b\}{}^v c\} \overset{(subcal)}{\rightsquigarrow}$

$\{{}^v a := {}^\& b\}\,{}^\&({}^\& b, m) \overset{(ur)}{\rightsquigarrow} {}^\&({}^\& b, m')$

$\{{}^v a := {}^\& b\}{}^v c \overset{(subcal)}{\rightsquigarrow}$ similar to $\{X := Y\}Z \overset{[3]}{\rightsquigarrow} Z$ $\overset{(subst)}{\rightsquigarrow} {}^v c$

$\{{}^v a := {}^\& b, {}^*(\,{}^\&({}^\& b, m')) := {}^v c\} \overset{(dr2)}{\rightsquigarrow}$

$\{{}^v a := {}^\& b, {}^v({}^v b, m') := {}^v c\}$

Experiment 33

`a=&b;c=a`

$$\{^v a := \&^v b\}\{^v c := {}^v a\} \overset{(\mathrm{Rv1})}{\leadsto}$$
$$\{^v a := {}^\& b\}\{^v c := {}^v a\} \overset{(\mathrm{uu})}{\leadsto}$$
$$\{^v a := {}^\& b, {}^*(\{^v a := {}^\& b\}\& {}^v c) := \{^v a := {}^\& b\}{}^v a\} \overset{(\mathrm{subcal})}{\leadsto}$$
$$\boxed{\{^v a := {}^\& b\}{}^\& c \overset{(\mathrm{ur})}{\leadsto} {}^\& c}$$
$$\boxed{\{^v a := {}^\& b\}{}^v a \overset{(\mathrm{subcal})}{\leadsto} \boxed{\text{similar to } \{X := Y\}X \overset{[1]}{\leadsto} X} \overset{(\mathrm{subst})}{\leadsto} {}^\& b}$$
$$\{^v a := {}^\& b, {}^*({}^\& c) := {}^\& b\} \overset{(\mathrm{dr1})}{\leadsto}$$
$$\boxed{\{^v a := {}^\& b, {}^v c := {}^\& b\}}$$

Experiment 34

`a=&b;c=*a`

$$\{^v a := \&^v b\}\{^v c := {}^*({}^v a)\} \overset{(\mathrm{Rv1})}{\leadsto}$$
$$\{^v a := {}^\& b\}\{^v c := {}^*({}^v a)\} \overset{(\mathrm{uu})}{\leadsto}$$
$$\{^v a := {}^\& b, {}^*(\{^v a := {}^\& b\}\& {}^v c) := \{^v a := {}^\& b\}\, {}^*({}^v a)\} \overset{(\mathrm{subcal})}{\leadsto}$$
$$\boxed{\{^v a := {}^\& b\}{}^\& c \overset{(\mathrm{ur})}{\leadsto} {}^\& c}$$
$$\boxed{\{^v a := {}^\& b\}\, {}^*({}^v a) \overset{[11]}{\leadsto} {}^v b}$$
$$\{^v a := {}^\& b, {}^*({}^\& c) := {}^v b\} \overset{(\mathrm{dr})}{\leadsto}$$
$$\boxed{\{^v a := {}^\& b, {}^v c := {}^v b\}}$$

Experiment 35

`a=&b;*a=c`

$$\{^v a := \&^v b\}\{{}^*({}^v a) := {}^v c\} \overset{(\mathrm{Rv1})}{\leadsto}$$
$$\{^v a := {}^\& b\}\{{}^*({}^v a) := {}^v c\} \overset{(\mathrm{uu})}{\leadsto}$$
$$\{^v a := {}^\& b, {}^*(\{^v a := {}^\& b\}\& {}^*({}^v a)) := \{^v a := {}^\& b\}{}^v c\} \overset{(\mathrm{subcal})}{\leadsto}$$
$$\boxed{\{^v a := {}^\& b\}{}^c c \overset{(\mathrm{subcal})}{\leadsto} \boxed{\text{similar to } \{X := Y\}Z \overset{[3]}{\leadsto} Z} \overset{(\mathrm{subst})}{\leadsto} {}^v c}$$
$$\boxed{\{^v a := {}^\& b\}\, \&{}^*({}^v a) \overset{[12]}{\leadsto} \& b}$$
$$\{^v a := {}^\& b, {}^*({}^\& b) := {}^v c\} \overset{(\mathrm{dr1})}{\leadsto}$$
$$\boxed{\{^v a := {}^\& b, {}^v b := {}^v c\}}$$

Experiment 36

```
a=&b;(*a).m=c
```

$$\{{}^v a := {}^\& b\}\{{}^v(*({}^v a), m) := {}^v c\} \overset{(uu)}{\rightsquigarrow}$$
$$\{{}^v a := {}^\& b, *(\{{}^v a := {}^\& b\}\&{}^v(*({}^v a), m)) := \{{}^v a := {}^\& b\}{}^v c\} \overset{(subcal)}{\rightsquigarrow}$$
$$\boxed{\{{}^v a := {}^v b\}{}^v c \overset{[3]}{\rightsquigarrow} {}^v c}$$
$$\boxed{\{{}^v a := {}^\& b\}\&{}^v(*({}^v a), m) \overset{[16]}{\rightsquigarrow} {}^\&({}^\& b, m')}$$
$$\{{}^v a := {}^\& b, *({}^\&({}^\& b, m')) := {}^v c\} \overset{(dr2)}{\rightsquigarrow}$$
$$\{{}^v a := {}^\& b, {}^v({}^{*\&} b, m')) := {}^v c\} \overset{(dr1)}{\rightsquigarrow}$$
$$\boxed{\{{}^v a := {}^\& b, {}^v({}^v b, m') := {}^v c\}}$$

Experiment 37

```
a=&b;c=(*a).m
```

$$\{{}^v a := {}^\& b\}\{{}^v c := {}^v(*({}^v a), m)\} \overset{(uu)}{\rightsquigarrow}$$
$$\{{}^v a := {}^\& b, *(\{{}^v a := {}^\& b\}\&{}^v c) := \{{}^v a := {}^\& b\}{}^v(*({}^v a), m)\} \overset{(subcal)}{\rightsquigarrow}$$
$$\boxed{\{{}^v a := {}^v b\}{}^\& c \overset{[3]}{\rightsquigarrow} {}^\& c}$$
$$\boxed{\{{}^v a := {}^\& b\}\&{}^v(*({}^v a), m) \overset{[16]}{\rightsquigarrow} {}^\&({}^\& b, m')}$$
$$\{{}^v a := {}^\& b, *({}^\& c) := {}^v({}^v b, m')\} \overset{(dr1)}{\rightsquigarrow}$$
$$\boxed{\{{}^v a := {}^\& b, {}^v c := {}^v({}^v b, m')\}}$$

5.5.4 Apply merged Updates on Term

5.5.4.1 Apply on simple program variable

Experiment 38

```
(a=b;a=c):a
```

$$\{{}^v a := {}^v b\}\{{}^v a := {}^v c\}{}^v a \overset{[21]}{\rightsquigarrow}$$
$$\{\underbrace{{}^v a}_{X_1} := \underbrace{{}^v b}_{y_1}, \underbrace{{}^v a}_{X_2} := \underbrace{{}^v c}_{y_2}\}_2 \underbrace{{}^v a}_{{}^v Z} \overset{uv}{\rightsquigarrow}$$

$$\text{if}\,\&\underbrace{{}^v a}_{X_2} \doteq U\&\underbrace{{}^v a}_{{}^v Z}\ \text{then}\ \underbrace{{}^v c}_{y_2}\ \text{else}$$
$$\text{if}\,\&\underbrace{{}^v a}_{X_2} \sqsubset^* U\&\underbrace{{}^v a}_{{}^v Z}\ \text{then}\ (U_{2-1}(\underbrace{{}^v a}_{{}^v Z})) \lhd \langle x_{[\dots]} := U_2({}^v Z, x_{[\dots]})\rangle\ \text{else}$$
$$\text{if}\,\&\underbrace{{}^v a}_{X_2} \sqsupset^* U\&\underbrace{{}^v a}_{{}^v Z}\ \text{then}\ {}^v(U \underbrace{a}_{Z})$$

else $U_{2-1}(\underbrace{{}^v a}_{{}^v Z})$ fi fi fi

$\boxed{\& {}^v a \overset{(\mathrm{Rv1})}{\rightsquigarrow} {}^{\&} a}$

$\boxed{U \& {}^v a \overset{(\mathrm{Rv1})}{\rightsquigarrow} U\, {}^{\&} a \overset{(\mathrm{ur})}{\rightsquigarrow} {}^{\&} U a \overset{(\mathrm{ua})}{\rightsquigarrow} {}^{\&} a}$

if ${}^{\&} a \doteq {}^{\&} a$ then ${}^v c$ else
if ${}^{\&} a \sqsubset^* {}^{\&} a$ then $(U_1({}^v a)) \lhd \langle x_{[\ldots]} := U_2{}^v({}^v Z, x_{[\ldots]})\rangle$ else
if ${}^{\&} a \sqsupset^* {}^{\&} a$ then ${}^v(Ua)$
else $U_1({}^v a)$ fi fi fi $\overset{(\mathrm{subcal})}{\rightsquigarrow}$

$\boxed{{}^{\&} a \doteq {}^{\&} a \overset{(\mathrm{eq})}{\rightsquigarrow} \mathit{true}}$

if *true* then ${}^v c$ else ... fi $\overset{(\mathrm{if})}{\rightsquigarrow}$

$\boxed{{}^v c}$

Experiment 39

```
(a=b;c=a):a
```

$\{{}^v a := {}^v b\}\{{}^v c := {}^v a\}\, {}^v a \overset{[22]}{\rightsquigarrow}$
$\{\underbrace{{}^v a}_{X_1} := \underbrace{{}^v b}_{y_1}, \underbrace{{}^v c}_{X_2} := \underbrace{{}^v b}_{y_2}\}_2 \underbrace{{}^v a}_{{}^v Z} \overset{\mathrm{uv}}{\rightsquigarrow}$

---

if $\& \underbrace{{}^v c}_{X_2} \doteq U \& \underbrace{{}^v a}_{{}^v Z}$ then $\underbrace{{}^v b}_{y_2}$ else
if $\& \underbrace{{}^v c}_{X_2} \sqsubset^* U \& \underbrace{{}^v a}_{{}^v Z}$ then $(U_{2-1}(\underbrace{{}^v a}_{{}^v Z})) \lhd \langle x_{[\ldots]} := U_2{}^v({}^v Z, x_{[\ldots]})\rangle$ else
if $\& \underbrace{{}^v c}_{X_2} \sqsupset^* U \& \underbrace{{}^v a}_{{}^v Z}$ then ${}^v(U \underbrace{a}_{Z})$
else $U_{2-1}(\underbrace{{}^v a}_{{}^v Z})$ fi fi fi

$\boxed{\& {}^v c \overset{(\mathrm{Rv1})}{\rightsquigarrow} {}^{\&} c}$

$\boxed{U \& {}^v a \overset{(\mathrm{Rv1})}{\rightsquigarrow} U\, {}^{\&} a \overset{(\mathrm{ur})}{\rightsquigarrow} {}^{\&} U a \overset{(\mathrm{ua})}{\rightsquigarrow} {}^{\&} a}$

if ${}^{\&} c \doteq {}^{\&} a$ then ${}^v b$ else
if ${}^{\&} c \sqsubset^* {}^{\&} a$ then $(U_1({}^v a)) \lhd \langle x_{[\ldots]} := U_2{}^v({}^v Z, x_{[\ldots]})\rangle$ else
if ${}^{\&} c \sqsupset^* {}^{\&} a$ then ${}^v(Ua)$
else $U_1({}^v a)$ fi fi fi $\overset{(\mathrm{subcal})}{\rightsquigarrow}$

$\boxed{{}^{\&} c \doteq {}^{\&} a \overset{(\mathrm{eq})}{\rightsquigarrow} \mathit{false}}$

$\boxed{{}^{\&} c \sqsubset^* {}^{\&} a \overset{(\mathrm{ss})}{\rightsquigarrow} \mathit{false}}$

$\boxed{{}^{\&} c \sqsupset^* {}^{\&} a \overset{(\mathrm{ss})}{\rightsquigarrow} \mathit{false}}$

if *false* then ${}^v b$ else

if *false* then $(U_1(^va)) \lhd \langle x_{[...]} := U_2{}^v(^vZ, x_{[...]}) \rangle$ else
if *false* then $^v(Ua)$
else $U_1(^va)$ fi fi fi $\overset{\text{(if)}}{\rightsquigarrow}$

Note: $U_1(^va) = \{\ \underbrace{^va}_{X_1} := \underbrace{^vb}_{y_1}\ ,\ \underbrace{^vc}_{X_2} := \underbrace{^va}_{y_2}\ \}_1\ \underbrace{^va}_{^vZ}$

if & $\underbrace{^va}_{X_1} \doteq U\&\ \underbrace{^va}_{^vZ}$ then $\underbrace{^vb}_{y_1}$ else

if & $\underbrace{^va}_{X_1} \sqsubset^* U\&\ \underbrace{^va}_{^vZ}$ then $(U_{1-1}(\underbrace{^va}_{^vZ})) \lhd \langle x_{[...]} := U_2{}^v(^vZ, x_{[...]}) \rangle$ else

if & $\underbrace{^va}_{X_1} \sqsupset^* U\&\ \underbrace{^va}_{^vZ}$ then $^v(U\underbrace{a}_{Z})$

else $U_{1-1}(\underbrace{^va}_{^vZ})$ fi fi fi $\overset{\text{(subcal)}}{\rightsquigarrow}$

$\boxed{\&^va \overset{\text{(Rv1)}}{\rightsquigarrow} {}^\&a}$

$\boxed{U\&^va \overset{\text{(Rv1)}}{\rightsquigarrow} U\ {}^\&a \overset{\text{(ur)}}{\rightsquigarrow} {}^\&Ua \overset{\text{(ua)}}{\rightsquigarrow} {}^\&a}$

if ${}^\&a \doteq {}^\&a$ then ^vb else
if ${}^\&a \sqsubset^* {}^\&a$ then $(U_0(^va)) \lhd \langle x_{[...]} := U_2{}^v(^vZ, x_{[...]}) \rangle$ else
if ${}^\&a \sqsupset^* {}^\&a$ then $^v(Ua)$
else $U_0(^va)$ fi fi fi

$\boxed{{}^\&a \doteq {}^\&a \overset{\text{(eq)}}{\rightsquigarrow} true}$
if *true* then ^vb else ... fi $\overset{\text{(if)}}{\rightsquigarrow}$
$\boxed{^vb}$

Experiment 40

(a=b;c=a):c

$\{^va := {}^vb\}\{^vc := {}^va\}\ ^vc \overset{[22]}{\rightsquigarrow}$
$\{\ \underbrace{^va}_{X_1} := \underbrace{^vb}_{y_1}\ ,\ \underbrace{^vc}_{X_2} := \underbrace{^vb}_{y_2}\ \}_2\ \underbrace{^vc}_{^vZ}\ \overset{\text{(uv)}}{\rightsquigarrow}$

---

if & $\underbrace{^vc}_{X_2} \doteq U\&\ \underbrace{^vc}_{^vZ}$ then $\underbrace{^vb}_{y_2}$ else

if & $\underbrace{^vc}_{X_2} \sqsubset^* U\&\ \underbrace{^vc}_{^vZ}$ then $(U_{2-1}(\underbrace{^vc}_{^vZ})) \lhd \langle x_{[...]} := U_2{}^v(^vZ, x_{[...]}) \rangle$ else

if & $\underbrace{^vc}_{X_2} \sqsupset^* U\&\ \underbrace{^vc}_{^vZ}$ then $^v(U\underbrace{c}_{Z})$

else $U_{2-1}(\underbrace{^vc}_{^vZ})$ fi fi fi $\overset{\text{(subcal)}}{\rightsquigarrow}$

$\boxed{\&\,{}^vc \overset{(Rv1)}{\leadsto} {}^{\&}c}$

$\boxed{U\&\,{}^vc \overset{(Rv1)}{\leadsto} U\,{}^{\&}c \overset{(ur)}{\leadsto} {}^{\&}Uc \overset{(ua)}{\leadsto} {}^{\&}c}$

if ${}^{\&}c \doteq {}^{\&}c$ then ${}^vb$ else
if ${}^{\&}c \sqsubset^* {}^{\&}c$ then $(U_1({}^vc)) \lhd \langle x_{[\ldots]} := U_2{}^v({}^vZ, x_{[\ldots]})\rangle$ else
if ${}^{\&}c \sqsupset^* {}^{\&}c$ then ${}^v(Uc)$
else $U_1({}^vc)$ fi fi fi $\overset{(subcal)}{\leadsto}$

$\boxed{{}^{\&}c \doteq {}^{\&}c \overset{(eq)}{\leadsto} true}$

if *true* then ${}^vb$ else … fi $\overset{(if)}{\leadsto}$

$\boxed{{}^vb}$

Experiment 41

```
(a=b;a.m=c):a
```

$\{{}^va := {}^vb\}\{{}^v({}^va, m) := {}^vc\}\,{}^va \overset{[23]}{\leadsto}$

$\{\underbrace{{}^va}_{X_1} := \underbrace{{}^vb}_{y_1}, \underbrace{{}^v({}^va, m)}_{X_2} := \underbrace{{}^vc}_{y_2}\}_2 \underbrace{{}^va}_{{}^vZ} \overset{(uv)}{\leadsto}$

---

if $\&\underbrace{{}^v({}^va, m)}_{X_2} \doteq U\&\underbrace{{}^va}_{{}^vZ}$ then $\underbrace{{}^vc}_{y_2}$ else

if $\&\underbrace{{}^v({}^va, m)}_{X_2} \sqsubset^* U\&\underbrace{{}^va}_{{}^vZ}$ then $(U_{2-1}({}^vZ)) \lhd \langle x_{[\ldots]} := U_2{}^v(\underbrace{{}^va}_{{}^vZ}, x_{[\ldots]})\rangle$ else

if $\&X_2 \sqsupset^* U\&{}^vZ$ then ${}^v(U\,Z)$

else $U_{2-1}({}^vZ)$ fi fi fi $\overset{(subcal)}{\leadsto}$

$\&{}^v({}^va, m) \doteq U\&\,{}^va \overset{(Rv2)}{\leadsto}$ (with X_2 under $\&{}^v({}^va, m)$ and ${}^vZ$ under ${}^va$)

${}^{\&}({}^{\&}a, m) \doteq U\,{}^{\&}a \overset{(ur)}{\leadsto}$

${}^{\&}({}^{\&}a, m) \doteq {}^{\&}(Ua) \overset{(ua)}{\leadsto}$

${}^{\&}({}^{\&}a, m) \doteq {}^{\&}(a) \overset{(eq)}{\leadsto}$

false

$\&{}^v({}^va, m) \sqsubset^* U\&{}^va \overset{(Rv2)}{\leadsto}$

${}^{\&}({}^{\&}a, m) \sqsubset^* U\,{}^{\&}a \overset{(ur)}{\leadsto}$

${}^{\&}({}^{\&}a, m) \sqsubset^* {}^{\&}(Ua) \overset{(ua)}{\leadsto}$

${}^{\&}({}^{\&}a, m) \sqsubset^* {}^{\&}a \overset{(ss)}{\leadsto}$

true

if *false* then ${}^vc$ else

if *true* then $(U_1(\underbrace{{}^va}_{{}^vZ})) \lhd \langle x_{[\&X \sqsubseteq^* {}^{\&}(U\&{}^vZ, x)]} := U_2\ {}^v(\underbrace{{}^va}_{{}^vZ},$

$x_{[\&X \sqsubseteq^* {}^{\&}(U\&^{v}Z,x)]})\rangle$ else
if $\&X_1 \sqsupset^* U\&^{v}Z$ then ${}^{v}(UZ)$
else $U_{2-1}({}^{v}Z)$ fi fi fi $\overset{(\mathrm{if})}{\rightsquigarrow}$

$$(U_1({}^{v}a)) \lhd \langle x_{[\&\underbrace{{}^{v}({}^{v}a,m)}_{X_2} \sqsubseteq^* {}^{\&}(U\&\underbrace{{}^{v}a}_{{}^{v}Z},x)]} := U_1\ {}^{v}({}^{v}a,\ x_{[\&\underbrace{{}^{v}({}^{v}a,m)}_{X_2} \sqsubseteq^* {}^{\&}(U\&\underbrace{{}^{v}a}_{{}^{v}Z},x)]})\rangle \overset{(\mathrm{subcal})}{\rightsquigarrow}$$

$$[\&\underbrace{{}^{v}({}^{v}a,m)}_{X_2} \sqsubseteq^* {}^{\&}(U\&\underbrace{{}^{v}a}_{{}^{v}Z},x)] \overset{(\mathrm{Rv2})}{\rightsquigarrow}$$
$$[{}^{\&}({}^{\&}a,m) \sqsubseteq^* {}^{\&}(U^{\&}a,x)] \overset{(\mathrm{Rv1})}{\rightsquigarrow}$$
$$[{}^{\&}({}^{\&}a,m) \sqsubseteq^* {}^{\&}({}^{\&}a,x)] \overset{(\mathrm{eps})}{\rightsquigarrow}$$
$$x \doteq m$$
$\overset{(\mathrm{subst})}{\rightsquigarrow}$

$$(U_1({}^{v}a)) \lhd \langle m := U_2\,{}^{v}({}^{v}a,m)\rangle \overset{(\mathrm{subcal})}{\rightsquigarrow}$$

$$U_2\,{}^{v}({}^{v}a,m) = \{{}^{v}a := {}^{v}b,\ {}^{v}({}^{v}a,m) := {}^{v}c\}_2\,{}^{v}({}^{v}a,m) \overset{(\mathrm{subcal})}{\rightsquigarrow}$$
similar as $\{X := Y, X := Z\,{}^{v}c\}X \overset{[38]}{\rightsquigarrow} Z$ $\overset{(\mathrm{subst})}{\rightsquigarrow} {}^{v}c$
$\overset{(\mathrm{subst})}{\rightsquigarrow}$

$$(U_1({}^{v}a)) \lhd \langle m := {}^{v}c\rangle \overset{(\mathrm{subcal})}{\rightsquigarrow}$$

$$U_1({}^{v}a) = \{\underbrace{{}^{v}a}_{X_1} := \underbrace{{}^{v}b}_{y_1},\ \underbrace{{}^{v}({}^{v}a,m)}_{X_2} := \underbrace{{}^{v}a}_{y_2}\}_1\ \underbrace{{}^{v}a}_{{}^{v}Z} \overset{(\mathrm{uv})}{\rightsquigarrow}$$

if $\&\underbrace{{}^{v}a}_{X_1} \doteq U\&\underbrace{{}^{v}a}_{{}^{v}Z}$ then $\underbrace{{}^{v}b}_{y_1}$ else
if $\&\underbrace{{}^{v}a}_{X_1} \sqsubset^* U\&\underbrace{{}^{v}a}_{{}^{v}Z}$ then $(U_{1-1}(\underbrace{{}^{v}a}_{{}^{v}Z})) \lhd \langle x_{[\ldots]} := U_2\,{}^{v}({}^{v}Z, x_{[\ldots]})\rangle$ else
if $\&\underbrace{{}^{v}a}_{X_1} \sqsupset^* U\&\underbrace{{}^{v}a}_{{}^{v}Z}$ then ${}^{v}(U\underbrace{a}_{Z})$
else $U_{1-1}(\underbrace{{}^{v}a}_{{}^{v}Z})$ fi fi fi $\overset{(\mathrm{subcal})}{\rightsquigarrow}$

$$\&\,{}^{v}a \overset{(\mathrm{Rv1})}{\rightsquigarrow} {}^{\&}a$$

$$U\&\,{}^{v}a \overset{(\mathrm{Rv1})}{\rightsquigarrow} U\,{}^{\&}a \overset{(\mathrm{ur})}{\rightsquigarrow} {}^{\&}Ua \overset{(\mathrm{ua})}{\rightsquigarrow} {}^{\&}a$$

if ${}^{\&}a \doteq {}^{\&}a$ then ${}^{v}b$ else
if ${}^{\&}a \sqsubset^* {}^{\&}a$ then $(U_0({}^{v}a)) \lhd \langle x_{[\ldots]} := U_2\,{}^{v}({}^{v}Z, x_{[\ldots]})\rangle$ else
if ${}^{\&}a \sqsupset^* {}^{\&}a$ then ${}^{v}(Ua)$
else $U_0({}^{v}a)$ fi fi fi

$${}^{\&}a \doteq {}^{\&}a \overset{(\mathrm{eq})}{\rightsquigarrow} \mathit{true}$$

if *true* then ${}^{v}b$ else … fi $\overset{(\mathrm{if})}{\rightsquigarrow}$

${}^{v}b$

$\overset{\text{(subst)}}{\leadsto}$

$\boxed{{}^{v}b \lhd \langle m := {}^{v}c \rangle}$

Experiment 42

```
(a=b;c=a.m):c
```

$$\{{}^{v}a := {}^{v}b\}\{{}^{v}c := {}^{v}({}^{v}a, m)\}\, {}^{v}c \overset{[25]}{\leadsto}$$

$$\{\underbrace{{}^{v}a}_{X_1} := \underbrace{{}^{v}b}_{y_1}, \underbrace{{}^{v}c}_{X_2} := \underbrace{{}^{v}({}^{v}b, m')}_{y_2}\}_2 \underbrace{{}^{v}c}_{{}^{v}Z} \overset{\text{(uv)}}{\leadsto}$$

$$\text{if}\,\&\underbrace{{}^{v}c}_{X_2} \doteq U\&\underbrace{{}^{v}c}_{{}^{v}Z}\ \text{then}\, \underbrace{{}^{v}({}^{v}b, m')}_{y_2}\ \text{else}$$
$$\text{if}\,\&{}^{v}c \sqsubset^{*} U\&{}^{v}c\,\text{then}\,(U_{2-1}({}^{v}c)) \lhd \langle x_{[\ldots]} := U_2\,{}^{v}({}^{v}Z, x_{[\ldots]})\rangle\ \text{else}$$
$$\text{if}\,\&{}^{v}c \sqsupset^{*} U\&{}^{v}\text{cthen}\,{}^{v}(Uc)$$
$$\text{else}\ U_{2-1}({}^{v}c)\ \text{fi fi fi}$$

$\boxed{\&\,{}^{v}c \overset{\text{(Rv1)}}{\leadsto} {}^{\&}c}$

$\boxed{U\&\,{}^{v}c \overset{\text{(Rv1)}}{\leadsto} U\,{}^{\&}c \overset{\text{(ur)}}{\leadsto} {}^{\&}Uc \overset{\text{(ua)}}{\leadsto} {}^{\&}c}$

$$\text{if}\ {}^{\&}c \doteq {}^{\&}c\,\text{then}\ {}^{v}b\,\text{else}$$
$$\text{if}\ {}^{\&}c \sqsubset^{*} {}^{\&}c\,\text{then}\,(U_1({}^{v}c)) \lhd \langle x_{[\ldots]} := U_2\,{}^{v}({}^{v}Z, x_{[\ldots]})\rangle\ \text{else}$$
$$\text{if}\ {}^{\&}c \sqsupset^{*} {}^{\&}c\,\text{then}\,{}^{v}(Uc)$$
$$\text{else}\ U_1({}^{v}c)\ \text{fi fi fi} \overset{\text{(subcal)}}{\leadsto}$$

$\boxed{{}^{\&}c \doteq {}^{\&}c \overset{\text{(eq)}}{\leadsto} \mathit{true}}$

$$\text{if}\ \mathit{true}\ \text{then}\,{}^{v}({}^{v}b, m')\ \text{else} \ldots \text{fi} \overset{\text{(if)}}{\leadsto}$$

$\boxed{{}^{v}({}^{v}b, m')}$

Experiment 43

```
(a.m=b;c=a):c
```

$$\{{}^{v}({}^{v}a, m) := {}^{v}b\}\{{}^{v}c := {}^{v}a\}\, {}^{v}c \overset{[26]}{\leadsto}$$

$$\{\underbrace{{}^{v}({}^{v}a, m)}_{X_1} := \underbrace{{}^{v}b}_{y_1}, \underbrace{{}^{v}c}_{X_2} := \underbrace{{}^{v}a \lhd \langle m := {}^{v}b\rangle}_{y_2}\}_2 \underbrace{{}^{v}c}_{{}^{v}Z} \overset{\text{(uv)}}{\leadsto}$$

$$\text{if}\,\&\underbrace{{}^{v}c}_{X_2} \doteq U\&\underbrace{{}^{v}c}_{{}^{v}Z}\ \text{then}\, \underbrace{{}^{v}a \lhd \langle m := {}^{v}b\rangle}_{y_2}\ \text{else}$$
$$\text{if}\,\&{}^{v}c \sqsubset^{*} U\&{}^{v}c\,\text{then}\,(U_{2-1}({}^{v}c)) \lhd \langle x_{[\ldots]} := U_2\,{}^{v}({}^{v}Z, x_{[\ldots]})\rangle\ \text{else}$$
$$\text{if}\,\&{}^{v}c \sqsupset^{*} U\&{}^{v}c\,\text{then}\,{}^{v}(Uc)$$
$$\text{else}\ U_{2-1}({}^{v}c)\ \text{fi fi fi}$$

$\boxed{\&\,{}^{v}c \overset{\text{(Rv1)}}{\leadsto} {}^{\&}c}$

$\boxed{U\&{}^{v}c \overset{(\mathrm{Rv1})}{\rightsquigarrow} U\,{}^{\&}c \overset{(\mathrm{ur})}{\rightsquigarrow} {}^{\&}Uc \overset{(\mathrm{ua})}{\rightsquigarrow} {}^{\&}c}$

if ${}^{\&}c \doteq {}^{\&}c$ then ${}^{v}a \lhd \langle m := {}^{v}b\rangle$ else
if ${}^{\&}c \sqsubset^{*} {}^{\&}c$ then $(U_1({}^{v}c)) \lhd \langle x_{[\ldots]} := U_2{}^{v}({}^{v}Z, x_{[\ldots]})\rangle$ else
if ${}^{\&}c \sqsupset^{*} {}^{\&}c$ then ${}^{v}(Uc)$
else $U_1({}^{v}c)$ fi fi fi $\overset{(\mathrm{subcal})}{\rightsquigarrow}$

$\boxed{{}^{\&}c \doteq {}^{\&}c \overset{(\mathrm{eq})}{\rightsquigarrow} \mathit{true}}$

if true then ${}^{v}a \lhd \langle m := {}^{v}b\rangle$ else ... fi $\overset{(\mathrm{if})}{\rightsquigarrow}$

$\boxed{{}^{v}a \lhd \langle m := {}^{v}b\rangle}$

Experiment 44

```
(a=&b;c=*a):c
```

$\{{}^{v}a := \&{}^{v}b\}\{{}^{v}c := *({}^{v}a)\}\,{}^{v}c \overset{[34]}{\rightsquigarrow}$
$\{{}^{v}a := {}^{\&}b, {}^{v}c := {}^{v}b\}\,{}^{v}c \overset{(\mathrm{subcal})}{\rightsquigarrow}$

Similar as for $\boxed{\{X := Y, Z := Y\}\, Z \overset{[40]}{\rightsquigarrow} Y}$

$\boxed{{}^{v}b}$

Experiment 45

$(a.m = b; c = a) : a$

$\{{}^{v}({}^{v}a, m) := {}^{v}b\}\{{}^{v}c := {}^{v}a\}\,{}^{v}a \overset{[26]}{\rightsquigarrow}$
$\{\underbrace{{}^{v}({}^{v}a, m)}_{X_1} := \underbrace{{}^{v}b}_{y_1}, \underbrace{{}^{v}c}_{X_2} := \underbrace{{}^{v}a \lhd \langle m := {}^{v}b\rangle}_{y_2}\}_2\, \underbrace{{}^{v}a}_{{}^{v}Z} \overset{(\mathrm{uv})}{\rightsquigarrow}$

---

if $\&\underbrace{{}^{v}c}_{X_2} \doteq U\&\underbrace{{}^{v}a}_{{}^{v}Z}$ then $\underbrace{{}^{v}a \lhd \langle m := {}^{v}b\rangle}_{y_2}$ else
if $\&\underbrace{{}^{v}c}_{X_2} \sqsubset^{*} U\&\underbrace{{}^{v}a}_{{}^{v}Z}$ then $(U_{2-1}(\underbrace{{}^{v}a}_{{}^{v}Z})) \lhd \langle x_{[\ldots]} := U_2{}^{v}({}^{v}Z, x_{[\ldots]})\rangle$ else
if $\&\underbrace{{}^{v}c}_{X_2} \sqsupset^{*} U\&\underbrace{{}^{v}a}_{{}^{v}Z}$ then ${}^{v}(U\underbrace{a}_{Z})$
else $U_{2-1}(\underbrace{{}^{v}a}_{{}^{v}Z})$ fi fi fi $\overset{(\mathrm{subcal})}{\rightsquigarrow}$

$\boxed{\&{}^{v}c \overset{(\mathrm{Rv1})}{\rightsquigarrow} {}^{\&}c}$

$\boxed{U\&{}^{v}a \overset{(\mathrm{Rv1})}{\rightsquigarrow} U\,{}^{\&}a \overset{(\mathrm{ur})}{\rightsquigarrow} {}^{\&}Ua \overset{(\mathrm{ua})}{\rightsquigarrow} {}^{\&}a}$

if ${}^{\&}c \doteq {}^{\&}a$ then ${}^{v}a \lhd \langle m := {}^{v}b\rangle$ else
if ${}^{\&}c \sqsubset^{*} {}^{\&}a$ then $(U_1({}^{v}a)) \lhd \langle x_{[\ldots]} := U_2{}^{v}({}^{v}Z, x_{[\ldots]})\rangle$ else
if ${}^{\&}c \sqsupset^{*} {}^{\&}a$ then ${}^{v}(Ua)$

else $U_1({}^v a)$ fi fi fi $\overset{\text{(subcal)}}{\rightsquigarrow}$

${}^{\&}c \doteq {}^{\&}a \overset{\text{(eq)}}{\rightsquigarrow} \mathit{false}$

${}^{\&}c \sqsubset^* {}^{\&}a \overset{\text{(ss)}}{\rightsquigarrow} \mathit{false}$

${}^{\&}c \sqsupset^* {}^{\&}a \overset{\text{(ss)}}{\rightsquigarrow} \mathit{false}$

if *false* then ${}^v b$ else
if *false* then $(U_1({}^v a)) \triangleleft \langle x_{[\ldots]} := U_2\,{}^v({}^v Z, x_{[\ldots]})\rangle$ else
if *false* then ${}^v(Ua)$
else $U_1({}^v a)$ fi fi fi $\overset{\text{(if)}}{\rightsquigarrow}$

$$U_1({}^v a) = \{\underbrace{{}^v({}^v a, m)}_{X_1} := \underbrace{{}^v b}_{y_1}, {}^v c := {}^v a \triangleleft \langle m := {}^v b\rangle\}_1 \underbrace{{}^v a}_{{}^v Z} \overset{\text{(uv)}}{\rightsquigarrow}$$

---

if $\& \underbrace{{}^v({}^v a, m)}_{X_1} \doteq U\& \underbrace{{}^v a}_{{}^v Z}$ then $\underbrace{{}^v b}_{y_1}$ else
if $\&\underbrace{{}^v({}^v a, m)}_{X_1} \sqsubset^* U\& \underbrace{{}^v a}_{{}^v Z}$ then $(U_{1-1}(\underbrace{{}^v a}_{{}^v Z})) \triangleleft \langle x_{[\ldots]} := U_1\,{}^v(\underbrace{{}^v a}_{{}^v Z}, x_{[\ldots]})\rangle$ else
if $\& X_1 \sqsupset^* U\&{}^v Z$ then ${}^v(U Z)$
else $U_{1-1}({}^v Z)$ fi fi fi $\overset{\text{(subcal)}}{\rightsquigarrow}$

$\&{}^v(\underbrace{{}^v a, m)}_{X_1} \doteq U\& \underbrace{{}^v a}_{{}^v Z} \overset{\text{(Rv2)}}{\rightsquigarrow}$
${}^{\&}({}^{\&}a, m) \doteq U{}^{\&}a \overset{\text{(ur)}}{\rightsquigarrow}$
${}^{\&}({}^{\&}a, m) \doteq {}^{\&}(Ua) \overset{\text{(ua)}}{\rightsquigarrow}$
${}^{\&}({}^{\&}a, m) \doteq {}^{\&}(a) \overset{\text{(eq)}}{\rightsquigarrow}$
false

$\&{}^v({}^v a, m) \sqsubset^* U\&{}^v a \overset{\text{(Rv2)}}{\rightsquigarrow}$
${}^{\&}({}^{\&}a, m) \sqsubset^* U\,{}^{\&}a \overset{\text{(ur)}}{\rightsquigarrow}$
${}^{\&}({}^{\&}a, m) \sqsubset^* {}^{\&}(Ua) \overset{\text{(ua)}}{\rightsquigarrow}$
${}^{\&}({}^{\&}a, m) \sqsubset^* {}^{\&}a \overset{\text{(ss)}}{\rightsquigarrow}$
true

if *false* then ${}^v b$ else
if *true* then $(U_0(\underbrace{{}^v a}_{{}^v Z})) \triangleleft \langle x_{[\& X \sqsubseteq^* {}^{\&}(U\&{}^v Z, x)]} := U_1\;{}^v(\underbrace{{}^v a}_{{}^v Z},$
$x_{[\& X \sqsubseteq^* {}^{\&}(U\&{}^v Z, x)]})\rangle$ else
if $\& X_1 \sqsupset^* U\&{}^v Z$ then ${}^v(U Z)$
else $U_{1-1}({}^v Z)$ fi fi fi $\overset{\text{(if)}}{\rightsquigarrow}$

$$(U_0({}^va)) \lhd \langle x_{[\&\underbrace{{}^v({}^va,m)}_{X_1} \sqsubseteq^* {}^\&(U\& \underbrace{{}^va}_{{}^vZ},x)]} := U_0{}^v({}^va, x_{[\&\underbrace{{}^v({}^va,m)}_{X_1} \sqsubseteq^* {}^\&(U\& \underbrace{{}^va}_{{}^vZ},x)]})\rangle$$

$$[\&\underbrace{{}^v({}^va,m)}_{X_1} \sqsubseteq^* {}^\&(U\& \underbrace{{}^va}_{{}^vZ},x)] \overset{(Rv2)}{\rightsquigarrow}$$
$$[{}^\&({}^\&a,m) \sqsubseteq^* {}^\&(U^\&a,x)] \overset{(ur)}{\rightsquigarrow}$$
$$[{}^\&({}^\&a,m) \sqsubseteq^* {}^\&({}^\&a,x)] \overset{(eps)}{\rightsquigarrow}$$
$$x \doteq m$$
$$\overset{(subst)}{\rightsquigarrow}$$

$$(U_0({}^va)) \lhd \langle m := U_1{}^v({}^va,m)\rangle \overset{(subcal)}{\rightsquigarrow}$$

$$U_1{}^v({}^va,m) = \{{}^v({}^va,m) := {}^vb, {}^vc := {}^va \lhd \langle m := {}^vb\rangle\}_1{}^v({}^va,m) \overset{(subcal)}{\rightsquigarrow}$$
similar as for $\{X := Y, Z := Y\}_1 X \overset{[39]}{\rightsquigarrow} Y$ $\overset{(subst)}{\rightsquigarrow}$
$${}^vb$$
$$\overset{(subst)}{\rightsquigarrow}$$

$$(U_0({}^va)) \lhd \langle m := {}^vb\rangle \overset{(subcal)}{\rightsquigarrow}$$

$$U_0({}^va) \overset{(u0)}{\rightsquigarrow}$$
$${}^*(U\&({}^va)) \overset{(Rv1)}{\rightsquigarrow}$$
$${}^*(U^\&a) \overset{(ur)}{\rightsquigarrow}$$
$${}^*({}^\&Ua) \overset{(ua)}{\rightsquigarrow}$$
$${}^*({}^\&a) \overset{(dr1)}{\rightsquigarrow}$$
$${}^va$$
$$\overset{(subst)}{\rightsquigarrow}$$

$${}^va \lhd \langle m := {}^vb\rangle$$

5.5.4.2 Apply Update on Sub-Structure

Experiment 46

```
(a=b;a=c):a.m
```

$$\{{}^va := {}^vb\}\{{}^va := {}^vc\}\ {}^v({}^va,m) \overset{[21]}{\rightsquigarrow}$$
$$\{\underbrace{{}^va}_{X_1} := \underbrace{{}^vb}_{y_1}, \underbrace{{}^va}_{X_2} := \underbrace{{}^vc}_{y_2}\}_2\ \underbrace{{}^v({}^va,m)}_{{}^vZ} \overset{(uu)}{\rightsquigarrow}$$

$$\text{if}\ \&\underbrace{{}^va}_{X_2} \doteq U\&\underbrace{{}^v({}^va,m)}_{{}^vZ}\ \text{then}\ \underbrace{{}^vc}_{y_2}\ \text{else}$$
$$\text{if}\ \&\underbrace{{}^va}_{X_2} \sqsubset^* U\&\underbrace{{}^v({}^va,m)}_{{}^vZ}\ \text{then}\ (U_{2-1}(\underbrace{{}^v({}^va,m)}_{{}^vZ})) \lhd \langle x_{[\ldots]} := U_2{}^v({}^vZ, x_{[\ldots]})\rangle\ \text{else}$$
$$\text{if}\ \&\underbrace{{}^va}_{X_2} \sqsupset^* U\&\underbrace{{}^v({}^va,m)}_{{}^vZ}\text{then}\ {}^v(U\ \underbrace{({}^va,m)}_{Z})$$
$$\text{else}\ U_{2-1}(\underbrace{{}^v({}^va,m)}_{{}^vZ})\ \text{fi fi fi} \overset{(subcal)}{\rightsquigarrow}$$

$\boxed{\& \, {}^v a \overset{(\mathrm{Rv1})}{\rightsquigarrow} {}^\& a}$

$\boxed{U \& \, {}^v({}^v a, m) \overset{(\mathrm{Rv2})}{\rightsquigarrow} U \, {}^\&(\& \, {}^v a, m) \overset{(\mathrm{ur})}{\rightsquigarrow} {}^\&(U \, {}^\& a, Um) \overset{(\mathrm{ua})}{\rightsquigarrow} {}^\&({}^\& a, m')} \overset{(\mathrm{subst})}{\rightsquigarrow}$

if ${}^\& a \doteq {}^\&({}^\& a, m')$ then ${}^v c$ else
if ${}^\& a \sqsubset^* {}^\&({}^\& a, m')$ then $(U_1({}^v a)) \lhd \langle x_{[\ldots]} := U_2 \, {}^v({}^v Z, x_{[\ldots]})\rangle$ else
if ${}^\& a \sqsupset^* {}^\&({}^\& a, m')$ then ${}^v(U({}^v a, m))$
else $U_1({}^v a)$ fi fi fi $\overset{(\mathrm{subcal})}{\rightsquigarrow}$

$\boxed{{}^\& a \doteq {}^\&({}^\& a, m') \overset{(\mathrm{eq})}{\rightsquigarrow} \mathit{false}}$

$\boxed{{}^\& a \sqsubset^* {}^\&({}^\& a, m') \overset{(\mathrm{ss})}{\rightsquigarrow} \mathit{false}}$

$\boxed{{}^\& a \sqsupset^* {}^\&({}^\& a, m') \overset{(\mathrm{ss})}{\rightsquigarrow} \mathit{true}}$

if *false* then ${}^v c$ else
if *false* then $(U_1({}^v a)) \lhd \langle x_{[\ldots]} := U_2 \, {}^v({}^v Z, x_{[\ldots]})\rangle$ else
if *true* then ${}^v(U({}^v a, m))$
else $U_1({}^v a)$ fi fi fi $\overset{(\mathrm{if})}{\rightsquigarrow}$

${}^v(U({}^v a, m)) \overset{(\mathrm{uf})}{\rightsquigarrow}$

${}^v(U \, {}^v a, Um) \overset{(\mathrm{subcal})}{\rightsquigarrow}$

$\boxed{U \, {}^v a = \{{}^v a := {}^v b, {}^v a := {}^v c\}_2 \, {}^v a \overset{[38]}{\rightsquigarrow} {}^v c} \overset{(\mathrm{subst})}{\rightsquigarrow}$

$\boxed{{}^v({}^v c, m')}$

Experiment 47

```
(a=b;c=a):a.m
```

$\{{}^v a := {}^v b\}\{{}^v c := {}^v a\} \, {}^v({}^v a, m) \overset{[22]}{\rightsquigarrow}$

$\{ \underbrace{{}^v a}_{X_1} := \underbrace{{}^v b}_{y_1}, \underbrace{{}^v c}_{X_2} := \underbrace{{}^v b}_{y_2} \}_2 \underbrace{{}^v({}^v a, m)}_{{}^v Z} \overset{(\mathrm{uv})}{\rightsquigarrow}$

---

if $\& \underbrace{{}^v c}_{X_2} \doteq U \& \underbrace{{}^v({}^v b, m)}_{{}^v Z}$ then $\underbrace{{}^v a}_{y_2}$ else

if $\& \underbrace{{}^v c}_{X_2} \sqsubset^* U \& \underbrace{{}^v({}^v b, m)}_{{}^v Z}$ then $(U_{2-1}(\underbrace{{}^v({}^v a, m)}_{{}^v Z})) \lhd \langle x_{[\ldots]} := U_2 \, {}^v({}^v Z, x_{[\ldots]})\rangle$ else

if $\& \underbrace{{}^v c}_{X_2} \sqsupset^* U \& \underbrace{{}^v({}^v b, m)}_{{}^v Z}$ then ${}^v(U \underbrace{({}^v a, m)}_{Z})$

else $U_{2-1}(\underbrace{{}^v({}^v a, m)}_{{}^v Z})$ fi fi fi $\overset{(\mathrm{subcal})}{\rightsquigarrow}$

$\boxed{\& \, {}^v c \overset{(\mathrm{Rv1})}{\rightsquigarrow} {}^\& c}$

$\boxed{U\&\,{}^{v}({}^{v}b,m) \overset{(\mathrm{Rv2})}{\rightsquigarrow} U\,{}^{\&}(\&\,{}^{v}b,m) \overset{(\mathrm{ur})}{\rightsquigarrow} {}^{\&}(U\,{}^{\&}b,Um) \overset{(\mathrm{ua})}{\rightsquigarrow} {}^{\&}({}^{\&}b,m')} \overset{(\mathrm{subst})}{\rightsquigarrow}$
if ${}^{\&}c \doteq {}^{\&}({}^{\&}b,m')$ then ${}^{v}a$ else
if ${}^{\&}c \sqsubset^{*} {}^{\&}({}^{\&}b,m')$ then $(U_1({}^{v}({}^{v}a,m))) \lhd \langle x_{[\ldots]} := U_2\,{}^{v}({}^{v}Z, x_{[\ldots]})\rangle$ else
if ${}^{\&}c \sqsupset^{*} {}^{\&}({}^{\&}b,m')$ then ${}^{v}(U\,({}^{v}a,m))$
else $U_1({}^{v}({}^{v}a,m))$ fi fi fi $\overset{(\mathrm{subcal})}{\rightsquigarrow}$

$\boxed{{}^{\&}c \doteq {}^{\&}({}^{\&}b,m') \overset{(\mathrm{eq})}{\rightsquigarrow} \mathit{false}}$

$\boxed{{}^{\&}c \sqsubset^{*} {}^{\&}({}^{\&}b,m') \overset{(\mathrm{ss})}{\rightsquigarrow} \mathit{false}}$

$\boxed{{}^{\&}c \sqsupset^{*} {}^{\&}({}^{\&}b,m') \overset{(\mathrm{ss})}{\rightsquigarrow} \mathit{false}}$

if *false* then ${}^{v}a$ else
if *false* then $(U_1({}^{v}({}^{v}a,m))) \lhd \langle x_{[\ldots]} := U_2\,{}^{v}({}^{v}Z, x_{[\ldots]})\rangle$ else
if *false* then ${}^{v}(U\,({}^{v}a,m))$
else $U_1({}^{v}({}^{v}a,m))$ fi fi fi $\overset{(\mathrm{if})}{\rightsquigarrow}$

$$U_1({}^{v}a) = \{\underbrace{{}^{v}a}_{X_1} := \underbrace{{}^{v}b}_{y_1},\ \underbrace{{}^{v}c}_{X_2} := \underbrace{{}^{v}b}_{y_2}\}_1\ \underbrace{{}^{v}({}^{v}a,m)}_{{}^{v}Z} \overset{(\mathrm{uv})}{\rightsquigarrow}$$

---

if $\&\,\underbrace{{}^{v}a}_{X_1} \doteq U\&\underbrace{{}^{v}({}^{v}a,m)}_{{}^{v}Z}$ then $\underbrace{{}^{v}b}_{y_1}$ else

if $\&\,\underbrace{{}^{v}a}_{X_1} \sqsubset^{*} U\&\underbrace{{}^{v}({}^{v}a,m)}_{{}^{v}Z}$ then $(U_{1-1}(\underbrace{({}^{v}({}^{v}a,m))}_{{}^{v}Z})) \lhd \langle x_{[\ldots]} := U_2\,{}^{v}({}^{v}Z,$ $x_{[\ldots]})\rangle$ else

if $\&\,\underbrace{{}^{v}a}_{X_1} \sqsupset^{*} U\&\underbrace{{}^{v}({}^{v}a,m)}_{{}^{v}Z}$ then ${}^{v}(U\,\underbrace{({}^{v}a,m)}_{Z})$

else $U_{1-1}(\underbrace{{}^{v}({}^{v}a,m)}_{{}^{v}Z})$ fi fi fi $\overset{(\mathrm{subcal})}{\rightsquigarrow}$

$\boxed{\&\,{}^{v}a \overset{(\mathrm{Rv})}{\rightsquigarrow} {}^{\&}a}$

$\boxed{U\&\,{}^{v}({}^{v}a,m) \rightsquigarrow \text{see box above} \rightsquigarrow {}^{\&}({}^{\&}a,m')} \overset{(\mathrm{subst})}{\rightsquigarrow}$
if ${}^{\&}a \doteq {}^{\&}({}^{\&}a,m')$ then ${}^{v}b$ else
if ${}^{\&}a \sqsubset^{*} {}^{\&}({}^{\&}a,m')$ then $(U_0\,{}^{v}({}^{v}a,m)) \lhd \langle x_{[\ldots]} := U_2\,{}^{v}({}^{v}Z, x_{[\ldots]})\rangle$ else
if ${}^{\&}a \sqsupset^{*} {}^{\&}({}^{\&}a,m')$ then ${}^{v}(U\,({}^{v}a,m))$
else $U_1({}^{v}({}^{v}a,m))$ fi fi fi $\overset{(\mathrm{subcal})}{\rightsquigarrow}$

$\boxed{{}^{\&}a \doteq {}^{\&}({}^{\&}a,m') \overset{(\mathrm{eq})}{\rightsquigarrow} \mathit{false}}$

$\boxed{{}^{\&}a \sqsubset^{*} {}^{\&}({}^{\&}a,m') \overset{(\mathrm{ss})}{\rightsquigarrow} \mathit{false}}$

$\boxed{{}^{\&}a \sqsupset^{*} {}^{\&}({}^{\&}a,m') \overset{(\mathrm{ss})}{\rightsquigarrow} \mathit{true}} \overset{(\mathrm{subst})}{\rightsquigarrow}$

if *false* then ${}^{v}b$ else

if *false* then $(U_0\,{}^v({}^va,m)) \lhd \langle x_{[\ldots]} := U_2\,{}^v({}^vZ, x_{[\ldots]})\rangle$ else
if *true* then ${}^v(U\,({}^va,m))$
else $U_1({}^v({}^va,m))$ fi fi fi $\overset{(\text{if})}{\leadsto}$

${}^v(U\,({}^va,m)) \overset{(\text{uf})}{\leadsto}$
${}^v(U\,{}^va, Um) \overset{(\text{subcal})}{\leadsto}$
$\boxed{U\,{}^va \leadsto \text{see box above } {}^vb} \overset{(\text{subst})}{\leadsto}$
$\boxed{{}^v({}^vb,m')}$

Experiment 48

```
(a=b;a.m=c):a.m
```

$\{{}^va := {}^vb\}\{{}^v({}^va,m) := {}^vc\}\,{}^v({}^va,m) \overset{[23]}{\leadsto}$
$\{{}^va := {}^vb, {}^v({}^va,m) := {}^vc\}_2\,{}^v({}^va,m) \overset{(\text{subcal})}{\leadsto}$
$\boxed{\text{This corresponds to}\{X := Y, X := Z\}_2\,X \overset{[38]}{\leadsto} Z}$
$\boxed{{}^vc}$

Experiment 49

```
(a.m=b;a=c):a.m
```

$\{{}^v({}^va,m) := {}^vb\}\{{}^va := {}^vc\}\,{}^v({}^va,m) \overset{[24]}{\leadsto}$
$\{\underbrace{{}^v({}^va,m)}_{X_1} := \underbrace{{}^vb}_{y_1}, \underbrace{{}^va}_{X_2} := \underbrace{{}^vc}_{y_2}\}_2\,\underbrace{{}^v({}^va,m)}_{{}^vZ} \overset{(\text{uv})}{\leadsto}$

---

if $\&\underbrace{{}^va}_{X_2} \doteq U\&\underbrace{{}^v({}^va,m)}_{{}^vZ}$ then $\underbrace{{}^vc}_{y_2}$ else
if $\&\underbrace{{}^va}_{X_2} \sqsubset^* U\&\underbrace{{}^v({}^va,m)}_{{}^vZ}$ then $(U_{2-1}(\underbrace{{}^v({}^va,m)}_{{}^vZ})) \lhd \langle x_{[\ldots]} := U_2\,{}^v({}^vZ, x_{[\ldots]})\rangle$ else
if $\&\underbrace{{}^va}_{X_2} \sqsupset^* U\&\underbrace{{}^v({}^va,m)}_{{}^vZ}$ then ${}^v(U\,\underbrace{({}^va,m)}_{Z})$
else $U_{2-1}(\underbrace{{}^v({}^va,m)}_{{}^vZ})$ fi fi fi $\overset{(\text{subcal})}{\leadsto}$

$\boxed{\&\,{}^va \overset{(\text{Rv1})}{\leadsto} {}^\&a}$
$\boxed{U\&\,{}^v({}^va,m) \overset{(\text{Rv2})}{\leadsto} U\,{}^\&(\&\,{}^va,m) \overset{(\text{Rv1})}{\leadsto} {}^\&(U\,{}^\&a, Um) \overset{(\text{ur})}{\leadsto} {}^\&({}^\&a,m')} \overset{(\text{subst})}{\leadsto}$
if ${}^\&a \doteq {}^\&({}^\&a,m')$ then ${}^vc$ else
if ${}^\&a \sqsubset^* {}^\&({}^\&a,m')$ then $(U_1({}^va)) \lhd \langle x_{[\ldots]} := U_2\,{}^v({}^vZ, x_{[\ldots]})\rangle$ else
if ${}^\&a \sqsupset^* {}^\&({}^\&a,m')$ then ${}^v(U\,({}^va,m))$

else $U_1({}^va)$ fi fi $\overset{\text{(subcal)}}{\leadsto}$

$\boxed{{}^\&a \doteq {}^\&({}^\&a, m') \overset{\text{(eq)}}{\leadsto} \mathit{false}}$

$\boxed{{}^\&a \sqsubset^* {}^\&({}^\&a, m') \overset{\text{(ss)}}{\leadsto} \mathit{false}}$

$\boxed{{}^\&a \sqsupset^* {}^\&({}^\&a, m') \overset{\text{(ss)}}{\leadsto} \mathit{true}}$ $\overset{\text{(subst)}}{\leadsto}$

if false then ${}^vc$ else

if false then $(U_1({}^va)) \lhd \langle x_{[\ldots]} := U_2{}^v({}^vZ, x_{[\ldots]})\rangle$ else

if true then ${}^v(U({}^va, m))$

else $U_1({}^va)$ fi fi $\overset{\text{(if)}}{\leadsto}$

${}^v(U({}^va, m)) \overset{\text{(uf)}}{\leadsto}$

${}^v(U{}^va, Um) \overset{\text{(subcal)}}{\leadsto}$

$\boxed{U{}^va = \{{}^va := {}^vb, {}^va := {}^vc\}_2{}^va \overset{[38]}{\leadsto} {}^vc}$ $\overset{\text{(subst)}}{\leadsto}$

$\boxed{{}^v({}^vc, m')}$

Experiment 50

```
(a.m=b;c=a):c.m
```

$\{{}^v({}^va, m) := {}^vb\}\{{}^vc := {}^va\}\,{}^v({}^vc, m) \overset{[26]}{\leadsto}$

$\{\underbrace{{}^v({}^va, m)}_{X_1} := \underbrace{{}^vb}_{y_1}, \underbrace{{}^vc}_{X_2} := \underbrace{{}^va \lhd \langle m := {}^vb\rangle}_{y_2}\}_2\,\underbrace{{}^v({}^vc, m)}_{{}^vZ} \overset{\text{(uv)}}{\leadsto}$

---

if $\&\underbrace{{}^vc}_{X_2} \doteq U\&\underbrace{{}^v({}^vc, m)}_{{}^vZ}$ then $\underbrace{{}^va \lhd \langle m := {}^vb\rangle}_{y_2}$ else

if $\&{}^vc \sqsubset^* U\&{}^v({}^vc, m)$ then $(U_{2-1}({}^v({}^vc, m))) \lhd \langle x_{[\ldots]} := U_2{}^v({}^vZ, x_{[\ldots]})\rangle$ else

if $\&{}^vc \sqsupset^* U\&{}^v({}^vc, m)$ then ${}^v(U({}^vc, m))$

else $U_{2-1}({}^v({}^vc, m))$ fi fi $\overset{\text{(subcal)}}{\leadsto}$

$\boxed{\&{}^vc \overset{\text{(Rv1)}}{\leadsto} {}^\&c}$

$U\&{}^v({}^vc, m) \overset{\text{(Rv2)}}{\leadsto}$
$U{}^\&(\&{}^vc, m) \overset{\text{(ur)}}{\leadsto}$
${}^\&(U{}^\&c, Um) \overset{\text{(ur)}}{\leadsto}$ $\overset{\text{(subst)}}{\leadsto}$
${}^\&({}^\&Uc, m') \overset{\text{(ua)}}{\leadsto}$
${}^\&({}^\&c, m')$

if ${}^\&c \doteq {}^\&({}^\&c, m')$ then ${}^va \lhd \langle m := {}^vb\rangle$ else

if ${}^\&c \sqsubset^* {}^\&({}^\&c, m')$ then $(U_1({}^v({}^vc, m))) \lhd \langle x_{[\ldots]} := U_2{}^v({}^vZ, x_{[\ldots]})\rangle$ else

if ${}^\&c \sqsupset^* {}^\&({}^\&c, m')$ then ${}^v(U({}^vc, m))$

$\text{else } U_1({}^v({}^vc, m)) \text{ fi fi fi} \overset{(\text{subcal})}{\leadsto}$

$\boxed{{}^{\&}c \doteq {}^{\&}({}^{\&}c, m') \overset{(\text{eq})}{\leadsto} \mathit{false}}$

$\boxed{{}^{\&}c \sqsubset^* {}^{\&}({}^{\&}c, m') \overset{(\text{ss})}{\leadsto} \mathit{false}}$

$\boxed{{}^{\&}c \sqsupset^* {}^{\&}({}^{\&}c, m') \overset{(\text{ss})}{\leadsto} \mathit{true}} \overset{(\text{subst})}{\leadsto}$

$\text{if } \mathit{false} \text{ then } {}^va \lhd \langle m := {}^vb \rangle \text{ else}$

$\text{if } \mathit{false} \text{ then } (U_1({}^v({}^vc, m))) \lhd \langle x_{[\ldots]} := U_2{}^v({}^vZ, x_{[\ldots]}) \rangle \text{ else}$

$\text{if } \mathit{true} \text{ then } {}^v(U\,({}^vc, m))$

$\text{else } U_1({}^v({}^vc, m)) \text{ fi fi fi} \overset{(\text{if})}{\leadsto}$

${}^v(U\,({}^vc, m)) \overset{(\text{uf})}{\leadsto}$

${}^v(U\,{}^vc, Um)) \overset{(\text{subcal})}{\leadsto}$

$\boxed{\begin{array}{l} U\,{}^vc = \{{}^v({}^va, m) := {}^vb, {}^vc := {}^va \lhd \langle m := {}^vb \rangle\}_2\, {}^vc \overset{(\text{subcal})}{\leadsto} \\ \boxed{\text{similar to } \{X := Y, Z := Y\} Z \overset{[40]}{\leadsto} Y} \overset{(\text{subst})}{\leadsto} {}^va \lhd \langle m := {}^vb \rangle \end{array}} \overset{(\text{subst})}{\leadsto}$

${}^v({}^va \lhd \langle m := {}^vb \rangle, m')) \overset{(\text{us})}{\leadsto}$

$\text{if } m \doteq m' \text{ then } {}^vb \text{ else } {}^v({}^va, m') \text{ fi} \overset{(\text{subcal})}{\leadsto}$

$\boxed{\text{in the experiments holds } m \doteq Um \leadsto m \doteq m \leadsto \mathit{true}} \overset{(\text{subst})}{\leadsto}$

$\text{if } \mathit{true} \text{ then } {}^vb \text{ else } {}^v({}^va, Um) \text{ fi} \overset{(\text{if})}{\leadsto}$

$\boxed{{}^vb}$

Experiment 51

```
(a.m=b;c=a):c.w
```

$\{{}^v({}^va, m) := {}^vb\}\{{}^vc := {}^va\}\, {}^v({}^vc, w) \overset{[26]}{\leadsto}$

$\{\underbrace{{}^v({}^va, m)}_{X_1} := \underbrace{{}^vb}_{y_1}, \underbrace{{}^vc}_{X_2} := \underbrace{{}^va \lhd \langle m := {}^vb \rangle}_{y_2}\}_2\, \underbrace{{}^v({}^vc, w)}_{{}^vZ} \overset{(\text{subcal})}{\leadsto}$

Similar as for `(a.m=b;c=a):c.m` except for the end $\leadsto$

$\vdots$

${}^v(U\,({}^vc, w)) \overset{(\text{uf})}{\leadsto}$

${}^v(U\,{}^vc, Uw)) \overset{(\text{subcal})}{\leadsto}$

$\boxed{\begin{array}{l} U\,{}^vc = \{{}^v({}^va, m) := {}^vb, {}^vc := {}^va \lhd \langle m := {}^vb \rangle\}_2\, {}^vc \overset{(\text{subcal})}{\leadsto} \\ \boxed{\text{similar to } \{X := Y, Z := Y\} Z \overset{[40]}{\leadsto} Y} \overset{(\text{subst})}{\leadsto} {}^va \lhd \langle m := {}^vb \rangle \end{array}} \overset{(\text{subst})}{\leadsto}$

${}^v({}^va \lhd \langle m := {}^vb \rangle, w)) \overset{(\text{us})}{\leadsto}$

$\text{if } m \doteq Uw \text{ then } {}^vb \text{ else } {}^v({}^va, w) \text{ fi} \overset{(\text{subcal})}{\leadsto}$

$\boxed{m \doteq Uw \rightsquigarrow \text{“}w\text{” is not updated} \rightsquigarrow m \doteq w \overset{(eq)}{\rightsquigarrow} \mathit{false}} \overset{(subst)}{\rightsquigarrow}$

if *false* then $^v b$ else $^v(^v a, Uw)$ fi $\overset{(if)}{\rightsquigarrow}$

$\boxed{^v(^v a, w)}$

Experiment 52

```
(a=&b;c=*a):c.m
```

$\{^v a := \&^v b\}\{^v c := {}^*(^v a)\}^v(^v c, m) \overset{[34]}{\rightsquigarrow}$

$\{^v a := {}^\& b, {}^v c := {}^v b\}\ {}^v(^v c, m) \overset{(subcal)}{\rightsquigarrow}$

$\boxed{\text{Similar as for } \{X := Y, X := Z\}_2\ {}^v(X, m) \overset{[47]}{\rightsquigarrow} {}^v(Z, m')} \overset{(subst)}{\rightsquigarrow}$

$\boxed{^v(^v b, m')}$

5.5.4.3 Apply Update on dereferenced Variable

Experiment 53

```
(a=b;c=a):*c
```

$\{^v a := {}^v b\}\{^v c := {}^v a\}\ {}^*(^v c) \overset{[22]}{\rightsquigarrow}$

$\{^v a := {}^v b, {}^v c := {}^v a\}\ {}^*(^v c) \overset{(ud)}{\rightsquigarrow}$

$\overset{*}{\{^v a := {}^v b, {}^v c := {}^v a\}}|\{^v a := {}^v b, {}^v c := {}^v a\}^v c \overset{(subcal)}{\rightsquigarrow}$

$\boxed{\{^v a := {}^v b, {}^v c := {}^v a\}^v c \overset{[40]}{\rightsquigarrow} {}^v b} \overset{(subst)}{\rightsquigarrow}$

$\boxed{\overset{*}{\{^v a := {}^v b, {}^v c := {}^v a\}}|\ {}^v b}$

Experiment 54

```
(a=c;b=&a):*b
```

$\{^v a := {}^v c\}\{^v b := \&^v a\}\ {}^*(^v b) \overset{[27]}{\rightsquigarrow}$

$\{^v a := {}^v c, {}^v b := {}^\& a\}\ {}^*(^v b) \overset{(ud)}{\rightsquigarrow}$

$\overset{*}{\{^v a := {}^v c, {}^v b := {}^\& a\}}|\{^v a := {}^v c, {}^v b := {}^\& a\}^v b \overset{(subcal)}{\rightsquigarrow}$

$\boxed{\begin{array}{l} \{^v a := {}^v c, {}^v b := {}^\& a\}^v b \overset{(subcal)}{\rightsquigarrow} \\ \boxed{\text{similar to } \{X := Y, Z := Y\} Z \overset{[40]}{\rightsquigarrow} Y} \overset{(subst)}{\rightsquigarrow} \\ {}^\& a \end{array}} \overset{(subst)}{\rightsquigarrow}$

$\overset{*}{\{^v a := {}^v c, {}^v b := {}^\& a\}}|\ {}^\& a \overset{(udr)}{\rightsquigarrow}$

$\{^v a := {}^v c, {}^v b := {}^\& a\}({}^*({}^\& a)) \overset{(dr1)}{\rightsquigarrow}$

$\{^v a := {}^v c, {}^v b := {}^\& a\}^v a \overset{(subcal)}{\rightsquigarrow}$

similar to $\{X := Y, Z := Y\} X \overset{[39]}{\rightsquigarrow} Y$ $\overset{(subst)}{\rightsquigarrow}$

${}^{v}c$

Experiment 55

```
(a.m=c;b=&a):*b
```

$\{{}^{v}({}^{v}a, m) := {}^{v}c\}\{{}^{v}b := \&{}^{v}a\} *({}^{v}b) \overset{[28]}{\rightsquigarrow}$

$\{{}^{v}({}^{v}a, m) := {}^{v}c, {}^{v}b := {}^{\&}a\} *({}^{v}b) \overset{(ud)}{\rightsquigarrow}$

$\overset{*}{\{}_{{}^{v}({}^{v}a,m) := {}^{v}c, {}^{v}b := {}^{\&}a\}} | \{{}^{v}({}^{v}a, m) := {}^{v}c, {}^{v}b := {}^{\&}a\}{}^{v}b \overset{(subcal)}{\rightsquigarrow}$

$\{{}^{v}({}^{v}a, m) := {}^{v}c, {}^{v}b := {}^{\&}a\}{}^{v}b \overset{(subcal)}{\rightsquigarrow}$

similar to $\{X := Y, Z := Y\} Z \overset{[40]}{\rightsquigarrow} Y$ $\overset{(subst)}{\rightsquigarrow}$

${}^{\&}a$ $\overset{(subst)}{\rightsquigarrow}$

$\overset{*}{\{}_{{}^{v}({}^{v}a,m) := {}^{v}c, {}^{v}b := {}^{\&}a\}} | {}^{\&}a \overset{(udr)}{\rightsquigarrow}$

$\{{}^{v}({}^{v}a, m) := {}^{v}c, {}^{v}b := {}^{\&}a\}(*({}^{\&}a)) \overset{(dr1)}{\rightsquigarrow}$

$\{{}^{v}({}^{v}a, m) := {}^{v}c, {}^{v}b := {}^{\&}a\}{}^{v}a \overset{(subcal)}{\rightsquigarrow}$

similar as for $\{{}^{v}(X, m) := Y, Z := X\}_2 Z \overset{[43]}{\rightsquigarrow} X \lhd \langle m := Y\rangle$ $\overset{(subst)}{\rightsquigarrow}$

${}^{v}a \lhd \langle m := {}^{v}c\rangle$

Experiment 56

```
(a=&b;b=c):*a
```

$\{{}^{v}a := \&{}^{v}b; {}^{v}b := {}^{v}c\} *({}^{v}a) \overset{[31]}{\rightsquigarrow}$

$\{{}^{v}a := {}^{\&}b, {}^{v}b := {}^{v}c\}*({}^{v}a) \overset{(ud)}{\rightsquigarrow}$

$\overset{*}{\{}_{{}^{v}a := {}^{\&}b, {}^{v}b := {}^{v}c\}} | \{{}^{v}a := {}^{\&}b, {}^{v}b := {}^{v}c\}{}^{v}a \overset{(subcal)}{\rightsquigarrow}$

$\{{}^{v}a := {}^{\&}b, {}^{v}b := {}^{v}c\}{}^{v}a \overset{(subcal)}{\rightsquigarrow}$

similar to $\{X := Y, Z := Y\} X \overset{[39]}{\rightsquigarrow} Y$ $\overset{(subst)}{\rightsquigarrow}$

${}^{\&}b$ $\overset{(subst)}{\rightsquigarrow}$

$\overset{*}{\{}_{{}^{v}a := {}^{\&}b, {}^{v}b := {}^{v}c\}} | {}^{\&}b \overset{(udr)}{\rightsquigarrow}$

$\{{}^{v}a := {}^{\&}b, {}^{v}b := {}^{v}c\}*({}^{\&}b) \overset{(dr1)}{\rightsquigarrow}$

$\{{}^{v}a := {}^{\&}b, {}^{v}b := {}^{v}c\}{}^{v}b \overset{(subcal)}{\rightsquigarrow}$

similar to $\{X := Y, X := Z\} X \overset{[38]}{\rightsquigarrow} Z$ $\overset{(subst)}{\rightsquigarrow}$

${}^{v}c$

Experiment 57

`(a=&b;b.m=c):*a`

$\{{}^va := \&{}^vb;\ {}^v({}^vb,m) := {}^vc\}\ {}^*({}^va) \overset{[32]}{\leadsto}$ see above

$\{{}^va := {}^{\&}b,\ {}^v({}^vb,m) := {}^vc\}^*({}^va) \overset{(ud)}{\leadsto}$

$\overset{*}{\{{}^va := {}^{\&}b,\ {}^v({}^vb,m) := {}^vc\}}|\{{}^va := {}^{\&}b,\ {}^v({}^vb,m) := {}^vc\}{}^va \overset{(subcal)}{\leadsto}$

$\{{}^va := {}^{\&}b,\ {}^v({}^vb,m) := {}^vc\}{}^va \overset{(subcal)}{\leadsto}$
similar as for $\{X := Y, Z := Y\}X \overset{[39]}{\leadsto} Y$ $\overset{(subst)}{\leadsto}$
${}^{\&}b$ $\overset{(subst)}{\leadsto}$

$\overset{*}{\{{}^va := {}^{\&}b,\ {}^v({}^vb,m) := {}^vc\}}|{}^{\&}b \overset{(udr)}{\leadsto}$

$\{{}^va := {}^{\&}b,\ {}^v({}^vb,m) := {}^vc\}^*({}^{\&}b) \overset{(dr1)}{\leadsto}$

$\{{}^va := {}^{\&}b,\ {}^v({}^vb,m) := {}^vc\}{}^vb \overset{(subcal)}{\leadsto}$

Similar as to $\{X := Y,\ {}^v(X,m) := Z\}_2 X \overset{[41]}{\leadsto} Y \lhd \langle m := Z\rangle$
or to $\{{}^v({}^va,m) := {}^vb\}\ {}^va \overset{[6]}{\leadsto} {}^va \lhd \langle m := {}^vb\rangle$ $\overset{(subst)}{\leadsto}$

${}^vb \lhd \langle m := {}^vc\rangle$

Experiment 58

`(a=&b;c=a):*c`

$\{{}^va := \&{}^vb\}\{{}^vc := {}^va\}\ {}^*({}^vc) \overset{[33]}{\leadsto}$

$\{{}^va := {}^{\&}b, {}^vc := {}^{\&}b\}^*({}^vc) \overset{(ud)}{\leadsto}$

$\overset{*}{\{{}^va := {}^{\&}b, {}^vc := {}^{\&}b\}}|\{{}^va := {}^{\&}b, {}^vc := {}^{\&}b\}{}^vc \overset{(subcal)}{\leadsto}$

$\{{}^va := {}^{\&}b, {}^vc := {}^{\&}b\}{}^vc \overset{(subcal)}{\leadsto}$
similar as for $\{X := Y, Z := Y\}X \overset{[39]}{\leadsto} Y$ $\overset{(subst)}{\leadsto}$
${}^{\&}b$

$\overset{*}{\{{}^va := {}^{\&}b, {}^vc := {}^{\&}b\}}|{}^{\&}b \overset{(udr)}{\leadsto}$

$\{{}^va := {}^{\&}b, {}^vc := {}^{\&}b\}({}^*({}^{\&}b)) \overset{(dr1)}{\leadsto}$

$\{{}^va := {}^{\&}b, {}^vc := {}^{\&}b\}{}^vb \overset{(uv)}{\leadsto}$ ...no updates to ${}^vb$

${}^vb$

Experiment 59

`(a=&b;*a=c):*a`

$\{{}^va := \&{}^vb\}\{\ {}^*({}^va) := {}^vc\}\ {}^*({}^va) \overset{[35]}{\leadsto}$

$\{{}^va := {}^{\&}b, {}^vb := {}^vc\}^*({}^va) \overset{[56]}{\leadsto}$

$\boxed{{}^{v}c}$

Experiment 60

```
(a=&b;(*a).m=c):*a
```

$\{{}^{v}a{:=}\,{}^{\&}b\}\{{}^{v}({}^{*}({}^{v}a),m):={}^{v}c\}\,{}^{*}({}^{v}a)\overset{[36]}{\rightsquigarrow}$

$\{{}^{v}a{:=}\,{}^{\&}b,\ {}^{v}({}^{v}b,m'):={}^{v}c\}\,{}^{*}({}^{v}a)\overset{[57]}{\rightsquigarrow}$

$\boxed{{}^{v}b\lhd\langle m':={}^{v}c\rangle}$

5.5.4.4 Apply Update on dereferenced Sub-Structure

Experiment 61

```
(a=b;c=a):(*c).m
```

$\{{}^{v}a{:=}\,{}^{v}b\}\{{}^{v}c{:=}\,{}^{v}a\}\,{}^{v}({}^{*}({}^{v}c),m)\overset{[22]}{\rightsquigarrow}$

$\{\underbrace{{}^{v}a}_{X_1}:=\underbrace{{}^{v}b}_{y_1},\underbrace{{}^{v}c}_{X_2}:=\underbrace{{}^{v}a}_{y_2}\}_2\,\underbrace{{}^{v}({}^{*}({}^{v}c),m)}_{{}^{v}Z}\overset{(\mathrm{uv})}{\rightsquigarrow}$

$\mathrm{if}\,\&\underbrace{{}^{v}c}_{X_2}\doteq U\&\underbrace{{}^{v}({}^{*}({}^{v}c),m)}_{{}^{v}Z}\,\mathrm{then}\,\underbrace{{}^{v}a}_{y_2}\,\mathrm{else}$

$\mathrm{if}\,\&\underbrace{{}^{v}c}_{X_2}\sqsubset^{*}U\&\underbrace{{}^{v}({}^{*}({}^{v}c),m)}_{{}^{v}Z}\,\mathrm{then}\,(U_{2-1}(\underbrace{{}^{v}({}^{*}({}^{v}c),m)}_{{}^{v}Z}))\lhd\langle x_{[\ldots]}:=U_2\,{}^{v}({}^{v}Z,$

$x_{[\ldots]})\rangle$

$\mathrm{else\,if}\,\&\underbrace{{}^{v}c}_{X_2}\sqsupset^{*}U\&\underbrace{{}^{v}({}^{*}({}^{v}c),m)}_{{}^{v}Z}\mathrm{then}\,{}^{v}(U\,\underbrace{({}^{*}({}^{v}c),m)}_{Z})$

$\mathrm{else}\,U_{2-1}(\underbrace{{}^{v}({}^{*}({}^{v}c),m)}_{{}^{v}Z})\,\mathrm{fi\,fi\,fi}\overset{(\mathrm{subcal})}{\rightsquigarrow}$

$\boxed{\&\,{}^{v}c\overset{(\mathrm{Rv1})}{\rightsquigarrow}{}^{\&}c}$

$U\&\,{}^{v}({}^{*}({}^{v}c),m)\overset{(\mathrm{Rv2})}{\rightsquigarrow}$ $U\,{}^{\&}(\&{}^{*}({}^{v}c),m)\overset{(\mathrm{Rd})}{\rightsquigarrow}$ $U\,{}^{\&}({}^{v}c,m)\overset{(\mathrm{ur})}{\rightsquigarrow}$ ${}^{\&}(U{}^{v}c,Um)\overset{(\mathrm{subcal})}{\rightsquigarrow}$ $U\,{}^{v}c=\{{}^{v}a{:=}\,{}^{v}b,{}^{v}c{:=}\,{}^{v}a\}\,{}^{v}c\overset{(\mathrm{subcal})}{\rightsquigarrow}$ similar to $\{X:=Y,Z:=Y\}Z\overset{[40]}{\rightsquigarrow}Y$ $\overset{(\mathrm{subst})}{\rightsquigarrow}$ ${}^{v}a$ ${}^{\&}({}^{v}a,m')$	$\overset{(\mathrm{subst})}{\rightsquigarrow}$

$\mathrm{if}\ {}^{\&}c\doteq{}^{\&}({}^{v}a,m')\ \mathrm{then}\ {}^{v}a\,\mathrm{else}$

$$\text{if } {}^{\&}c \sqsubset^* {}^{\&}({}^{v}a, m') \text{ then } (U_1({}^{v}({}^{*}({}^{v}c), m))) \lhd$$
$$\langle x_{[\underbrace{\& \; {}^{v}c}_{X_2} \sqsubseteq^* {}^{\&}({}^{\&}(\& \overset{*}{U} | {}^{v}a, m'), x)]} := U_2(\underbrace{{}^{v}({}^{*}({}^{v}c), m)}_{{}^{v}Z}, x_{[\underbrace{\& \; {}^{v}c}_{X_2} \sqsubseteq^* {}^{\&}({}^{\&}(\& \overset{*}{U} | {}^{v}a, m'), x)]})\rangle$$
$$\text{else if } {}^{\&}c \sqsupset^* {}^{\&}({}^{v}a, m') \text{ then } {}^{v}(\underbrace{U\,{}^{*}({}^{v}c), Um}_{Z})$$
$$\text{else } U_1({}^{v}({}^{*}({}^{v}c), m)) \text{ fi fi fi } \overset{(\text{subcal})}{\rightsquigarrow}$$

Since the conditions ${}^{\&}c \doteq {}^{\&}({}^{v}a, m')$, ${}^{\&}c \sqsubset^* {}^{\&}({}^{v}a, m')$, and ${}^{\&}c \sqsupset^* {}^{\&}({}^{v}a, m')$ cannot be decided at this point so that further expansion of the then/else parts can be delayed

$U^*({}^{v}c) \overset{(\text{ud})}{\rightsquigarrow} \overset{*}{U} \| U\,{}^{v}c \overset{(\text{subcal})}{\rightsquigarrow}$
$U\,{}^{v}c = \{{}^{v}a := {}^{v}b, {}^{v}c := {}^{v}a\}_2\, {}^{v}c \rightsquigarrow$ see box above $\rightsquigarrow {}^{v}a$ $\overset{(\text{subst})}{\rightsquigarrow}$
$\overset{*}{U} \| {}^{v}a$

$\overset{(\text{subst})}{\rightsquigarrow}$

if ${}^{\&}c \doteq {}^{\&}({}^{v}a, m')$ then ${}^{v}a$ else
if ${}^{\&}c \sqsubset^* {}^{\&}({}^{v}a, m')$ then $(U_1({}^{v}({}^{*}({}^{v}c), m))) \lhd$
$\langle x_{[\& {}^{v}c \sqsubseteq^* {}^{\&}({}^{\&}(\& \overset{*}{U} \| {}^{v}a, m'), x)]} := U_2({}^{v}({}^{*}({}^{v}c), m), x_{[\& {}^{v}c \sqsubseteq^* {}^{\&}({}^{\&}(\& \overset{*}{U} \| {}^{v}a, m'), x)]})\rangle$
else if ${}^{\&}c \sqsupset^* {}^{\&}({}^{v}a, m')$ then ${}^{v}(\overset{*}{U} \| {}^{v}a, m')$
else $U_1({}^{v}({}^{*}({}^{v}c), m))$ fi fi fi

Experiment 62

```
(a=c;b=&a):(*b).m
```

$$\{{}^{v}a := {}^{v}c\}\{{}^{v}b := \&{}^{v}a\}\; {}^{v}({}^{*}({}^{v}b), m) \overset{[27]}{\rightsquigarrow}$$
$$\{\underbrace{{}^{v}a}_{X_1} := \underbrace{{}^{v}c}_{y_1}, \underbrace{{}^{v}b}_{X_2} := \underbrace{{}^{\&}a}_{y_2}\}_2\; \underbrace{{}^{v}({}^{*}({}^{v}b), m)}_{{}^{v}Z} \overset{(\text{uv})}{\rightsquigarrow}$$

$$\text{if } \& \underbrace{{}^{v}b}_{X_2} \doteq U\&\underbrace{{}^{v}({}^{*}({}^{v}b), m)}_{{}^{v}Z} \text{ then } \underbrace{{}^{\&}a}_{y_2} \text{ else}$$
$$\text{if } \& \underbrace{{}^{v}b}_{X_2} \sqsubset^* U\&\underbrace{{}^{v}({}^{*}({}^{v}b), m)}_{{}^{v}Z} \text{ then } (U_{2-1}(\underbrace{{}^{v}({}^{*}({}^{v}b), m)}_{{}^{v}Z})) \lhd \langle x_{[\ldots]} := U_2\, {}^{v}({}^{v}Z,$$
$$x_{[\ldots]})\rangle \text{ else}$$
$$\text{if } \& \underbrace{{}^{v}b}_{X_2} \sqsupset^* U\&\underbrace{{}^{v}({}^{*}({}^{v}b), m)}_{{}^{v}Z} \text{ then } {}^{v}(U\,Z)$$
$$\text{else } U_{2-1}(\underbrace{{}^{v}({}^{*}({}^{v}b), m)}_{{}^{v}Z}) \text{ fi fi fi } \overset{(\text{subcal})}{\rightsquigarrow}$$

$\&\,{}^{v}b \overset{(\text{Rv1})}{\rightsquigarrow} {}^{\&}b$

$$U\,\&\,{}^{v}(^{*}(^{v}b), m) \overset{(\mathrm{Rv2})}{\rightsquigarrow}$$
$$U\,{}^{\&}(\&^{*}(^{v}b), m) \overset{(\mathrm{Rd})}{\rightsquigarrow}$$
$$U\,{}^{\&}(^{v}b, m) \overset{(\mathrm{ur})}{\rightsquigarrow}$$
$$^{\&}(U\,{}^{v}b, U\,m) \overset{(\mathrm{subcal})}{\rightsquigarrow} \qquad \overset{(\mathrm{subst})}{\rightsquigarrow}$$
$$U\,{}^{v}b = \{\,{}^{v}a := {}^{v}c, {}^{v}b := {}^{\&}a\}\,{}^{v}b \overset{(\mathrm{subcal})}{\rightsquigarrow}$$
$$\boxed{\text{similar to } \{X := Y, Z := Y\}\,Z \overset{[40]}{\rightsquigarrow} Y} \overset{(\mathrm{subst})}{\rightsquigarrow} \quad \overset{(\mathrm{subst})}{\rightsquigarrow}$$
$$^{\&}a$$
$$^{\&}(^{\&}a, m')$$

$$\text{if } {}^{\&}b \doteq {}^{\&}(^{\&}a, m') \text{ then } {}^{v}a \text{ else}$$
$$\text{if } {}^{\&}b \sqsubset^{*} {}^{\&}(^{\&}a, m') \text{ then } (U_1(^{v}(^{*}(^{v}b), m))) \lhd \langle x_{[\ldots]} := U_2\,{}^{v}(^{v}Z, x_{[\ldots]})\rangle \text{ else}$$
$$\text{if } {}^{\&}b \sqsupset^{*} {}^{\&}(^{\&}a, m') \text{ then } {}^{v}(U\,Z)$$
$$\text{else } U_1(^{v}(^{*}(^{v}b), m)) \text{ fi fi fi} \overset{(\mathrm{subcal})}{\rightsquigarrow}$$

$$\boxed{{}^{\&}b \doteq {}^{\&}(^{\&}c, m') \overset{(\mathrm{eq})}{\rightsquigarrow} \mathit{false}}$$
$$\boxed{{}^{\&}b \sqsubset^{*} {}^{\&}(^{\&}c, m') \overset{(\mathrm{ss})}{\rightsquigarrow} \mathit{false}}$$
$$\boxed{{}^{\&}b \sqsupset^{*} {}^{\&}(^{\&}c, m') \overset{(\mathrm{ss})}{\rightsquigarrow} \mathit{false}} \overset{(\mathrm{subst})}{\rightsquigarrow}$$

$$\text{if } \mathit{false} \text{ then } {}^{v}a \text{ else}$$
$$\text{if } \mathit{false} \text{ then } (U_1(^{v}(^{*}(^{v}b), m))) \lhd \langle x_{[\ldots]} := U_2\,{}^{v}(^{v}Z, x_{[\ldots]})\rangle \text{ else}$$
$$\text{if } \mathit{false} \text{ then } {}^{v}(U\,Z)$$
$$\text{else } U_1(^{v}(^{*}(^{v}b), m)) \text{ fi fi fi} \overset{(\mathrm{if})}{\rightsquigarrow}$$

$$U_1(^{v}(^{*}(^{v}b), m)) =$$
$$\{\underbrace{{}^{v}a}_{X_1} := \underbrace{{}^{v}c}_{y_1}, \underbrace{{}^{v}b}_{X_2} := \underbrace{{}^{\&}a}_{y_2}\}_1\, \underbrace{{}^{v}(^{*}(^{v}b), m)}_{{}^{v}Z} \overset{(\mathrm{uv})}{\rightsquigarrow}$$

$$\text{if}\,\&\underbrace{{}^{v}a}_{X_1} \doteq U\&\underbrace{{}^{v}(^{*}(^{v}b), m)}_{{}^{v}Z} \text{ then } \underbrace{{}^{v}c}_{y_1} \text{ else}$$
$$\text{if}\,\&\underbrace{{}^{v}a}_{X_1} \sqsubset^{*} U\&\underbrace{{}^{v}(^{*}(^{v}b), m)}_{{}^{v}Z} \text{ then } (U_{2-1}(^{v}Z)) \lhd \langle x_{[\ldots]} := U_2\,{}^{v}(^{v}Z, x_{[\ldots]})\rangle \text{ else}$$
$$\text{if}\,\&\underbrace{{}^{v}a}_{X_1} \sqsupset^{*} U\&\underbrace{{}^{v}(^{*}(^{v}b), m)}_{{}^{v}Z} \text{ then } {}^{v}(U\,\underbrace{(^{*}(^{v}b), m)}_{Z})$$
$$\text{else } U_{2-1}(^{v}Z) \text{ fi fi fi} \overset{(\mathrm{subcal})}{\rightsquigarrow}$$

$$\boxed{\&\,{}^{v}a \overset{(\mathrm{Rv1})}{\rightsquigarrow} {}^{\&}a}$$
$$\boxed{U\,\&\,{}^{v}(^{*}(^{v}b), m) \rightsquigarrow \text{see box above}} \overset{(\mathrm{subst})}{\rightsquigarrow}$$
$$^{\&}(^{\&}a, m')$$

$\text{if}\,{}^{\&}a \doteq {}^{\&}({}^{\&}a, m')\,\text{then}\,{}^{v}c\,\text{else}$
$\text{if}\,{}^{\&}a \sqsubset^{*} {}^{\&}({}^{\&}a, m')\,\text{then}\,(U_{2-1}({}^{v}({}^{*}({}^{v}b), m))) \lhd \langle x_{[...]} := U_2\,{}^{v}({}^{v}Z, x_{[...]})\rangle\,\text{else}$
$\text{if}\,{}^{\&}a \sqsupset^{*} {}^{\&}({}^{\&}a, m')\,\text{then}\,{}^{v}(U\,({}^{*}({}^{v}b), m))$
$\text{else}\,U_0({}^{v}Z)\,\text{fi fi fi} \overset{(\text{subcal})}{\leadsto}$

$\boxed{{}^{\&}a \doteq {}^{\&}({}^{\&}a, m') \overset{(\text{eq})}{\leadsto} \textit{false}}$

$\boxed{{}^{\&}a \sqsubset^{*} {}^{\&}({}^{\&}a, m') \overset{(\text{ss})}{\leadsto} \textit{false}}$

$\boxed{{}^{\&}a \sqsupset^{*} {}^{\&}({}^{\&}a, m') \overset{(\text{ss})}{\leadsto} \textit{true}} \overset{(\text{subst})}{\leadsto}$

$\text{if}\,\textit{false}\,\text{then}\,{}^{v}c\,\text{else}$
$\text{if}\,\textit{false}\,\text{then}\,(U_{2-1}({}^{v}({}^{*}({}^{v}b), m))) \lhd \langle x_{[...]} := U_2\,{}^{v}({}^{v}Z, x_{[...]})\rangle\,\text{else}$
$\text{if}\,\textit{false}\,\text{then}\,{}^{v}(U\,({}^{*}({}^{v}b), m))$
$\text{else}\,U_0({}^{v}Z)\,\text{fi fi fi} \overset{(\text{if})}{\leadsto}$

${}^{v}(U\,({}^{*}({}^{v}b), m)) \overset{(\text{uf})}{\leadsto}$

${}^{v}(U^{*}({}^{v}b), Um)) \overset{(\text{subcal})}{\leadsto}$

$U^{*}({}^{v}b) = \{{}^{v}a := {}^{v}c, {}^{v}b := {}^{\&}a\}^{*}({}^{v}b) \overset{(\text{ud})}{\leadsto}$

${}^{*}_{\{{}^{v}a := {}^{v}c, {}^{v}b := {}^{\&}a\}}|\{{}^{v}a := {}^{v}c, {}^{v}b := {}^{\&}a\}{}^{v}b \overset{(\text{subcal})}{\leadsto}$

$U\,{}^{v}b = \{{}^{v}a := {}^{v}c, {}^{v}b := {}^{\&}a\}\,{}^{v}b \overset{(\text{subcal})}{\leadsto}$

$\boxed{\text{similar to } \{X := Y, Z := Y\}Z \overset{[40]}{\leadsto} Y} \overset{(\text{subst})}{\leadsto}$ $\overset{(\text{subst})}{\leadsto}$

${}^{\&}a$ $\overset{(\text{subst})}{\leadsto}$

${}^{*}_{\{{}^{v}a := {}^{v}c, {}^{v}b := {}^{\&}a\}}|{}^{\&}a \overset{(\text{udr})}{\leadsto}$

$\{{}^{v}a := {}^{v}c, {}^{v}b := {}^{\&}a\}\,{}^{*}({}^{\&}a) \overset{(\text{dr1})}{\leadsto}$

$\{{}^{v}a := {}^{v}c, {}^{v}b := {}^{\&}a\}\,{}^{v}a \overset{(\text{subcal})}{\leadsto}$

$\boxed{\text{similar as for } \{X := Y, Z := Y\}X \overset{[39]}{\leadsto} Y} \overset{(\text{subst})}{\leadsto}$

${}^{v}c$

$\boxed{{}^{v}({}^{v}c, m')}$

Experiment 63

```
(a.m=c;b=&a):(*b).m
```

$\{{}^{v}({}^{v}a, m) := {}^{v}c\}\{{}^{v}b := \&{}^{v}a\}\,{}^{v}({}^{*}({}^{v}b), m) \overset{[28]}{\leadsto}$

$\{\underbrace{{}^{v}({}^{v}a, m)}_{X_1} := \underbrace{{}^{v}c}_{y_1}, \underbrace{{}^{v}b}_{X_2} := \underbrace{{}^{\&}a}_{y_2}\}_2\,\underbrace{{}^{v}({}^{*}({}^{v}b), m)}_{{}^{v}Z} \overset{(\text{uv})}{\leadsto}$

$\text{if}\,\&\underbrace{{}^{v}b}_{X_2} \doteq U\&\underbrace{{}^{v}({}^{*}({}^{v}b), m)}_{{}^{v}Z}\,\text{then}\,\underbrace{{}^{\&}a}_{y_2}\,\text{else}$

$$\text{if } \underbrace{\&\ {}^{v}b}_{X_2} \sqsubset^{*} U\&^{v}\underbrace{(\,{}^{*}({}^{v}b), m)}_{{}^{v}Z} \text{ then } (U_{2-1}(\underbrace{{}^{v}(\,{}^{*}({}^{v}b), m)}_{{}^{v}Z})) \lhd \langle x_{[\ldots]} := U_2\,{}^{v}(\,{}^{v}Z,$$

$$x_{[\ldots]})\rangle \text{ else}$$

$$\text{if } \underbrace{\&\ {}^{v}b}_{X_2} \sqsupset^{*} U\&^{v}\underbrace{(\,{}^{*}({}^{v}b), m)}_{{}^{v}Z} \text{then } {}^{v}(U\,Z)$$

$$\text{else } U_{2-1}(\underbrace{{}^{v}({}^{*}({}^{v}b), m)}_{{}^{v}Z}) \text{ fi fi} \overset{\text{(subcal)}}{\rightsquigarrow}$$

$$\boxed{\&\,{}^{v}b \overset{\text{(Rv1)}}{\rightsquigarrow} {}^{\&}b}$$

$$U\&\,{}^{v}({}^{*}({}^{v}b), m) \overset{\text{(Rv2)}}{\rightsquigarrow}$$
$$U\,{}^{\&}(\&^{*}({}^{v}b), m) \overset{\text{(Rd)}}{\rightsquigarrow}$$
$$U\,{}^{\&}({}^{v}b, m) \overset{\text{(ur)}}{\rightsquigarrow}$$
$${}^{\&}(U\,{}^{v}b, U\,m) \overset{\text{(subcal)}}{\rightsquigarrow}$$
$$U\,{}^{v}b = \{\,{}^{v}({}^{v}a, m) := {}^{v}c, {}^{v}b := {}^{\&}a\}\,{}^{v}b \overset{\text{(subcal)}}{\rightsquigarrow}$$
$$\boxed{\text{similar to } \{X := Y, Z := Y\}Z \overset{[40]}{\rightsquigarrow} Y} \overset{\text{(subst)}}{\rightsquigarrow}$$
$${}^{\&}a \quad \overset{\text{(subst)}}{\rightsquigarrow}$$
$${}^{\&}({}^{\&}a, m') \quad \overset{\text{(subst)}}{\rightsquigarrow}$$

$$\text{if } {}^{\&}b \doteq {}^{\&}({}^{\&}a, m') \text{ then } {}^{v}a \text{ else}$$
$$\text{if } {}^{\&}b \sqsubset^{*} {}^{\&}({}^{\&}a, m') \text{ then } (U_1({}^{v}(\,{}^{*}({}^{v}b), m))) \lhd \langle x_{[\ldots]} := U_2\,{}^{v}(\,{}^{v}Z, x_{[\ldots]})\rangle \text{ else}$$
$$\text{if } {}^{\&}b \sqsupset^{*} {}^{\&}({}^{\&}a, m') \text{ then } {}^{v}(U\,Z)$$
$$\text{else } U_1({}^{v}({}^{*}({}^{v}b), m)) \text{ fi fi fi} \overset{\text{(subcal)}}{\rightsquigarrow}$$

$$\boxed{{}^{\&}b \doteq {}^{\&}({}^{\&}a, m') \overset{\text{(eq)}}{\rightsquigarrow} \mathit{false}}$$
$$\boxed{{}^{\&}b \sqsubset^{*} {}^{\&}({}^{\&}a, m') \overset{\text{(ss)}}{\rightsquigarrow} \mathit{false}}$$
$$\boxed{{}^{\&}b \sqsupset^{*} {}^{\&}({}^{\&}a, m') \overset{\text{(ss)}}{\rightsquigarrow} \mathit{false}} \overset{\text{(subst)}}{\rightsquigarrow}$$

$$\text{if } \mathit{false} \text{ then } {}^{v}a \text{ else}$$
$$\text{if } \mathit{false} \text{ then } (U_1({}^{v}(\,{}^{*}({}^{v}b), m))) \lhd \langle x_{[\ldots]} := U_2\,{}^{v}(\,{}^{v}Z, x_{[\ldots]})\rangle \text{ else}$$
$$\text{if } \mathit{false} \text{ then } {}^{v}(U\,Z)$$
$$\text{else } U_1({}^{v}({}^{*}({}^{v}b), m)) \text{ fi fi fi} \overset{\text{(if)}}{\rightsquigarrow}$$

$$U_1({}^{v}({}^{*}({}^{v}b), m)) =$$
$$\{\underbrace{{}^{v}({}^{v}a, m)}_{X_1} := \underbrace{{}^{v}c}_{y_1}, {}^{v}b := {}^{\&}a\}_1\, \underbrace{{}^{v}(\,{}^{*}({}^{v}b), m)}_{{}^{v}Z} \overset{\text{(uv)}}{\rightsquigarrow}$$

$$\text{if } \&\underbrace{{}^{v}({}^{v}a, m)}_{X_1} \doteq U\&^{v}\underbrace{(\,{}^{*}({}^{v}b), m)}_{{}^{v}Z} \text{ then } \underbrace{{}^{v}c}_{y_1} \text{ else}$$

$$\text{if } \&\underbrace{{}^{v}({}^{v}a, m)}_{X_1} \sqsubset^{*} U\&^{v}\underbrace{(\,{}^{*}({}^{v}b), m)}_{{}^{v}Z} \text{ then } (U_{1-1}(\underbrace{{}^{v}(\,{}^{*}({}^{v}b), m)}_{{}^{v}Z})) \lhd$$

$$\langle x_{[\ldots]} := U_2\,{}^v({}^vZ, x_{[\ldots]})\rangle \text{ else}$$

$$\text{if } \underbrace{\&^v({}^va,m)}_{X_1} \sqsupset^* U\&^v\underbrace{({}^*({}^vb),m)}_{{}^vZ} \text{ then } {}^v(U\,Z)$$

$$\text{else } U_{1-1}(\underbrace{{}^v({}^*({}^vb),m)}_{{}^vZ}) \text{ fi fi} \overset{\text{(subcal)}}{\leadsto}$$

$$\boxed{\&\,{}^v({}^va,m) \overset{\text{(Rv2)}}{\leadsto} {}^\&(\&\,{}^va,m) \overset{\text{(Rv1)}}{\leadsto} {}^\&({}^\&a,m)}$$

$$\boxed{U\&\,{}^v({}^*({}^vb),m) \leadsto \text{see box above} \quad {}^\&({}^\&a,m')}$$

$$\text{if } {}^\&a \doteq {}^\&({}^\&a,m') \text{ then } {}^vc \text{ else}$$
$$\text{if } {}^\&a \sqsubset^* {}^\&({}^\&a,m') \text{ then } (U_{2-1}({}^v({}^*({}^vb),m))) \lhd \langle x_{[\ldots]} := U_2\,{}^v({}^vZ, x_{[\ldots]})\rangle \text{ else}$$
$$\text{if } {}^\&a \sqsupset^* {}^\&({}^\&a,m') \text{ then } {}^v(U\,\underbrace{({}^*({}^vb),m)}_{Z})$$
$$\text{else } U_0({}^v({}^*({}^vb),m)) \text{ fi fi} \overset{\text{(subcal)}}{\leadsto}$$

$$\boxed{{}^\&a \doteq {}^\&({}^\&a,m') \overset{\text{(eq)}}{\leadsto} \mathit{false}}$$

$$\boxed{{}^\&a \sqsubset^* {}^\&({}^\&a,m') \overset{\text{(ss)}}{\leadsto} \mathit{false}}$$

$$\boxed{{}^\&a \sqsupset^* {}^\&({}^\&a,m') \overset{\text{(ss)}}{\leadsto} \mathit{true}}$$

$$\text{if } \mathit{false} \text{ then } {}^vc \text{ else}$$
$$\text{if } \mathit{false} \text{ then } (U_{2-1}({}^v({}^*({}^vb),m))) \lhd \langle x_{[\ldots]} := U_2\,{}^v({}^vZ, x_{[\ldots]})\rangle \text{ else}$$
$$\text{if } \mathit{true} \text{ then } {}^v(U\,({}^*({}^vb),m))$$
$$\text{else } U_0({}^v({}^*({}^vb),m)) \text{ fi fi} \overset{\text{(if)}}{\leadsto}$$

$${}^v(U({}^*({}^vb),m)) \overset{\text{(uf)}}{\leadsto}$$
$${}^v(U{}^*({}^vb),Um) \overset{\text{(subcal)}}{\leadsto}$$

$$\boxed{\begin{array}{l}
U{}^*({}^vb) \overset{\text{(ud)}}{\leadsto} \overset{*}{U}|U{}^vb \overset{\text{(subcal)}}{\leadsto} \\
\boxed{\begin{array}{l} U\,{}^vb = \{{}^va := {}^vc, {}^vb := {}^\&a\}_2\,{}^vb \overset{\text{(subcal)}}{\leadsto} \\ \boxed{\text{similar to } \{X := Y, Z := Y\}Z \overset{[40]}{\leadsto} Y} \overset{\text{(subst)}}{\leadsto} \\ {}^\&a \end{array}} \overset{\text{(subst)}}{\leadsto} \\
\overset{*}{U}|{}^\&a \overset{\text{(udr)}}{\leadsto} \\
U({}^*({}^\&a)) \overset{\text{(dr1)}}{\leadsto} \\
\{{}^v({}^va,m) := {}^vc, {}^vb := {}^\&a\}_2\,{}^va \overset{\text{(subcal)}}{\leadsto} \\
\boxed{\text{similarly as for } \{{}^v(X,m) := Y, Z := X \lhd \langle m := Y\rangle\}_2\, X \overset{[45]}{\leadsto} X \lhd \langle m := Y\rangle} \\
{}^va \lhd \langle m' := {}^vc\rangle
\end{array}}$$

$$\overset{\text{(subst)}}{\leadsto}$$

$$^{v}(^{v}a \lhd \langle m' := {}^{v}c\rangle, Um) \overset{(vs)}{\leadsto}$$
$$\text{if } m' \doteq Um \text{ then } {}^{v}c \text{ else } {}^{v}(^{v}a, Um) \text{ fi} \leadsto$$
$$\text{if } m' \doteq m' \text{ then } {}^{v}c \text{ else } {}^{v}(^{v}a, m') \text{ fi} \overset{(eq)(if)}{\leadsto}$$
$$\boxed{{}^{v}c}$$

Experiment 64

```
(a=&b;b=c):(*a).m
```

$$\{^{v}a := \&^{v}b\}\{^{v}b := {}^{v}c\}\, {}^{v}(^{*}(^{v}a), m) \overset{[31]}{\leadsto}$$
$$\{^{v}a := {}^{\&}b, \underbrace{^{v}b}_{X_2} := \underbrace{^{v}c}_{y_2}\}_2\, {}^{v}(^{*}(^{v}a), m) \overset{(uv)}{\leadsto}$$

$$\text{if } \& \underbrace{^{v}b}_{X_2} \doteq U\&\underbrace{^{v}(^{*}(^{v}a), m)}_{^{v}Z} \text{ then } \underbrace{^{v}c}_{y_2} \text{ else}$$
$$\text{if } \& \underbrace{^{v}b}_{X_2} \sqsubset^{*} U\&\underbrace{^{v}(^{*}(^{v}a), m)}_{^{v}Z} \text{ then } (U_{2-1}(^{v}Z)) \lhd \langle x_{[\ldots]} := U_2\, {}^{v}(^{v}Z, x_{[\ldots]})\rangle \text{ else}$$
$$\text{if } \& \underbrace{^{v}b}_{X_2} \sqsupset^{*} U\&\underbrace{^{v}(^{*}(^{v}a), m)}_{^{v}Z} \text{ then } {}^{v}(U\, \underbrace{(^{*}(^{v}a), m)}_{Z})$$
$$\text{else } U_{2-1}(^{v}Z) \text{ fi fi fi} \overset{(subcal)}{\leadsto}$$

$$\boxed{\&\, ^{v}b \overset{(Rv1)}{\leadsto} {}^{\&}b}$$

$$U\,\&\, ^{v}(^{*}(^{v}a), m) \overset{(Rv2)}{\leadsto}$$
$$U\, ^{\&}(\&^{*}(^{v}a), m) \overset{(Rd)}{\leadsto}$$
$$U\, ^{\&}(^{v}a, m) \overset{(ur)}{\leadsto}$$
$$^{\&}(U^{v}a, Um) \overset{(subcal)}{\leadsto}$$
$$U\, ^{v}a = \{^{v}a := {}^{\&}b, {}^{v}b := {}^{v}c\}_2\, {}^{v}a \overset{(subcal)}{\leadsto}$$
$$\boxed{\text{similar as for } \{X := Y, Z := Y\}X \overset{[39]}{\leadsto} Y} \overset{(subst)}{\leadsto}$$
$$^{\&}b \overset{(subst)}{\leadsto}$$
$$^{\&}(^{\&}b, m') \overset{(subst)}{\leadsto}$$

$$\text{if } {}^{\&}b \doteq {}^{\&}(^{\&}b, m') \text{ then } {}^{v}c \text{ else}$$
$$\text{if } {}^{\&}b \sqsubset^{*} {}^{\&}(^{\&}b, m') \text{ then } (U_1(^{v}(^{*}(^{v}a), m))) \lhd \langle x_{[\ldots]} := U_2\, {}^{v}(^{v}Z, x_{[\ldots]})\rangle \text{ else}$$
$$\text{if } {}^{\&}b \sqsupset^{*} {}^{\&}(^{\&}b, m') \text{ then } {}^{v}(U\, \underbrace{(^{*}(^{v}a), m)}_{Z})$$
$$\text{else } U_1(^{v}Z) \text{ fi fi fi} \overset{(subcal)}{\leadsto}$$

$$\boxed{^{\&}b \doteq {}^{\&}(^{\&}b, m') \overset{(eq)}{\leadsto} \mathit{false}}$$
$$\boxed{^{\&}b \sqsubset^{*} {}^{\&}(^{\&}b, m') \overset{(ss)}{\leadsto} \mathit{false}}$$
$$\boxed{^{\&}b \sqsupset^{*} {}^{\&}(^{\&}b, m') \overset{(ss)}{\leadsto} \mathit{true}}$$

if *false* then ${}^{v}c$ else
if *false* then $(U_1({}^{v}({}^{*}({}^{v}a), m))) \lhd \langle x_{[...]} := U_2\, {}^{v}({}^{v}Z, x_{[...]})\rangle$ else
if *true* then ${}^{v}(U\,({}^{*}({}^{v}a), m))$
else $U_1({}^{v}Z)$ fi fi fi $\overset{(if)}{\rightsquigarrow}$

${}^{v}(U\,({}^{*}({}^{v}a), m)) \overset{(uf)}{\rightsquigarrow}$
${}^{v}(U\,{}^{*}({}^{v}a), Um) \rightsquigarrow$
${}^{v}(U\,{}^{*}({}^{v}a), m')) \overset{(subcal)}{\rightsquigarrow}$

$U\,{}^{*}({}^{v}a) = \{{}^{v}a := {}^{\&}b, {}^{v}b := {}^{v}c\}\; {}^{*}({}^{v}a) \overset{(ud)}{\rightsquigarrow}$
$\overset{*}{}_{\{{}^{v}a := {}^{\&}b,\, {}^{v}b := {}^{v}c\}}|\{{}^{v}a := {}^{\&}b, {}^{v}b := {}^{v}c\}{}^{v}a \overset{(subcal)}{\rightsquigarrow}$
$\{{}^{v}a := {}^{\&}b, {}^{v}b := {}^{v}c\}{}^{v}a \overset{(subcal)}{\rightsquigarrow}$
similar as for $\{X := Y, Z := Y\}X \overset{[39]}{\rightsquigarrow} Y$ $\overset{(subst)}{\rightsquigarrow}$ $\overset{(subst)}{\rightsquigarrow}$
${}^{\&}b$ $\overset{(subst)}{\rightsquigarrow}$
$\overset{*}{}_{\{{}^{v}a := {}^{\&}b,\, {}^{v}b := {}^{v}c\}}|{}^{\&}b \overset{(udr)}{\rightsquigarrow}$
$\{{}^{v}a := {}^{\&}b, {}^{v}b := {}^{v}c\}\; {}^{*}({}^{\&}b) \overset{(dr)}{\rightsquigarrow}$
$\{{}^{v}a := {}^{\&}b, {}^{v}b := {}^{v}c\}\; {}^{v}b \overset{(subcal)}{\rightsquigarrow}$
similar as for $\{X := Y, X := Z\}X \overset{[38]}{\rightsquigarrow} Z$ $\overset{(subst)}{\rightsquigarrow}$
${}^{v}c$

${}^{v}({}^{v}c, m')$

Experiment 65

```
(a=&b;b.m=c):(*a).m
```

$\{{}^{v}a := \&{}^{v}b\}\{\,{}^{v}({}^{v}b, m) := {}^{v}c\}\; {}^{v}({}^{*}({}^{v}a), m) \overset{[32]}{\rightsquigarrow}$
$\{{}^{v}a := {}^{\&}b, \underbrace{{}^{v}({}^{v}b, m)}_{X_2} := \underbrace{{}^{v}c}_{y_2}\}_2 \underbrace{{}^{v}({}^{*}({}^{v}a), m)}_{{}^{v}Z} \overset{(uv)}{\rightsquigarrow}$

---

if $\&\underbrace{{}^{v}({}^{v}b, m)}_{X_2} \doteq U\&\underbrace{{}^{v}({}^{*}({}^{v}a), m)}_{{}^{v}Z}$ then $\underbrace{{}^{v}c}_{y_2}$ else
if $\&\underbrace{{}^{v}({}^{v}b, m)}_{X_2} \sqsubset^{*} U\&\underbrace{{}^{v}({}^{*}({}^{v}a), m)}_{{}^{v}Z}$ then $(U_{2-1}(\underbrace{{}^{v}({}^{*}({}^{v}a), m)}_{{}^{v}Z})) \lhd$
$\langle x_{[...]} := U_2\, {}^{v}({}^{v}Z, x_{[...]})\rangle$ else
if $\&\underbrace{{}^{v}({}^{v}b, m)}_{X_2} \sqsupset^{*} U\&\underbrace{{}^{v}({}^{*}({}^{v}a), m)}_{{}^{v}Z}$ then ${}^{v}(U\,\underbrace{({}^{*}({}^{v}a), m)}_{Z})$
else $U_{2-1}({}^{v}Z)$ fi fi fi $\overset{(subcal)}{\rightsquigarrow}$

$\&\,{}^{v}({}^{v}b, m) \overset{(Rv2)}{\rightsquigarrow} {}^{\&}(\&{}^{v}b, m) \overset{(Rv1)}{\rightsquigarrow} {}^{\&}({}^{\&}b, m)$

$U\,\&\,{}^{v}({}^{*}({}^{v}a), m) \overset{(\mathrm{Rv2})}{\leadsto}$

$U\,{}^{\&}(\&^{*}({}^{v}a), m) \overset{(\mathrm{Rd})}{\leadsto}$

$U\,{}^{\&}({}^{v}a, m) \overset{(\mathrm{ur})}{\leadsto}$

${}^{\&}(U{}^{v}a, Um) \overset{(\mathrm{subcal})}{\leadsto}$ $\overset{(\mathrm{subst})}{\leadsto}$

$U{}^{v}a = \{{}^{v}a := {}^{\&}b, {}^{v}({}^{v}b, m) := {}^{v}c\}\, {}^{v}a \overset{(\mathrm{subcal})}{\leadsto}$

similar as for $\{X := Y, Z := Y\}\, X \overset{[39]}{\leadsto} Y$ $\overset{(\mathrm{subst})}{\leadsto}$ $\overset{(\mathrm{subst})}{\leadsto}$

${}^{\&}b$

${}^{\&}({}^{\&}b, m')$

if ${}^{\&}b \doteq {}^{\&}({}^{\&}b, m')$ then ${}^{v}c$ else
if ${}^{\&}b \sqsubset^{*} {}^{\&}({}^{\&}b, m')$ then $(U_1({}^{v}({}^{*}({}^{v}a), m))) \lhd \langle x_{[\ldots]} := U_2\, {}^{v}({}^{v}Z, x_{[\ldots]})\rangle$ else
if ${}^{\&}b \sqsupset^{*} {}^{\&}({}^{\&}b, m')$ then ${}^{v}(U({}^{*}({}^{v}a), m))$
else $U_1({}^{v}({}^{*}({}^{v}a), m))$ fi fi fi $\overset{(\mathrm{subcal})}{\leadsto}$

${}^{\&}b \doteq {}^{\&}({}^{\&}b, m') \overset{(\mathrm{eq})}{\leadsto} \mathit{false}$

${}^{\&}b \sqsubset^{*} {}^{\&}({}^{\&}b, m') \overset{(\mathrm{ss})}{\leadsto} \mathit{false}$

${}^{\&}b \sqsupset^{*} {}^{\&}({}^{\&}b, m') \overset{(\mathrm{ss})}{\leadsto} \mathit{true}$

$\overset{(\mathrm{subst})}{\leadsto}$

if *false* then ${}^{v}c$ else
if *false* then $(U_1({}^{v}({}^{*}({}^{v}a), m))) \lhd \langle x_{[\ldots]} := U_2\, {}^{v}({}^{v}Z, x_{[\ldots]})\rangle$ else
if *true* then ${}^{v}(U({}^{*}({}^{v}a), m))$
else $U_1({}^{v}Z)$ fi fi fi $\overset{(\mathrm{if})}{\leadsto}$

${}^{v}(U\,{}^{*}({}^{v}a), Um) \overset{(\mathrm{subcal})}{\leadsto}$

$U\,{}^{*}({}^{v}a) \overset{(\mathrm{ud})}{\leadsto}$

$\overset{*}{U}|U\,{}^{v}a \overset{(\mathrm{subcal})}{\leadsto}$

$U\,{}^{v}a \overset{(\mathrm{subcal})}{\leadsto}$ see box above

${}^{\&}b$

$\overset{*}{U}|{}^{\&}b \overset{(\mathrm{udr})}{\leadsto}$

$U({}^{*}({}^{\&}b)) \overset{(\mathrm{dr1})}{\leadsto}$

$U{}^{v}b = \{{}^{v}a := {}^{\&}b, {}^{v}({}^{v}b, m) := {}^{v}c\}\, {}^{v}b \overset{(\mathrm{subcal})}{\leadsto}$

similar as for $\{X := Y, {}^{v}(X, m) := Z\}_2\, X \overset{[41]}{\leadsto} Y \lhd \langle m := Z\rangle$

${}^{v}b \lhd \langle m := {}^{v}c\rangle$

${}^{v}({}^{v}b \lhd \langle m := {}^{v}c\rangle, m) \overset{(\mathrm{us})}{\leadsto}$

if $m \doteq m$ then ${}^{v}c$ else ${}^{v}({}^{v}b, m)$ fi $\overset{(\mathrm{eq})(\mathrm{if})}{\leadsto}$

$\boxed{{}^{v}C}$

Chapter 6

CDL

6.0.5 Notation

The notations and definitions of chapter 5 take effect in this chapter. Moreover, the occurences of program variables in updates, formulas and terms are subject to conversion as described in section 5.2 and defined in def. 5.8.

6.1 Syntax

We use the syntax as it is described up to this point from the previous chapters and make further extensions to complete the syntax definition of CDL.

Definition 6.1. (Extension of the signature Σ) *The signature Σ defined by def. 3.4 and extended by definitions 4.16, 4.17,5.7, and 5.9 is extended by the following rigid function and predicate symbols for the build-in types* $\mathrm{TYP}_{\mathrm{el}}^{C0}$ *of C0:*

- *For the remaing C0 operators* `<<`, `>>`, `&`, `|`, `^`, `~`, `&&`, `||`, `!`, `<`, `>`, `==` *we add the function symbols* $\overline{\texttt{<<}}_T$, $\overline{\texttt{>>}}_T$, $\overline{\texttt{\&}}_T$, $\overline{\texttt{|}}_T$, $\overline{\texttt{\^{}}}_T$, $\overline{\texttt{\~{}}}_T$, $\overline{\texttt{\&\&}}_T$, $\overline{\texttt{||}}_T$, $\overline{\texttt{!}}_T$, $\overline{\texttt{<}}_T$, $\overline{\texttt{>}}_T$, $\overline{\texttt{==}}_T$
- *isdef is an unary predicate.*

Definition 6.2. (Extension of Terms and Formulas) *The sets Trm and Fml as defined in def. 3.4 and 3.5 and extended by def. 4.2, 4.3, 6.2, and 5.10 are inductively extended by using the extended signature of definition 6.1.*

6.2 Semantic

Definition 6.3. (Rule schema form) *A* rule schema form *(short* form*) is an abstraction of a set of rule schemata.*

Definition 6.4. (Soundness of a rule schema form) *A rule schema form is sound if all rule schemata represented by the rule schema form are sound.*

6.2.1 Operators

The semantic of pointer operators is defined in section 5.4.2. The semantic of the operators for arithmetical types is defined in section 4.3. It remains to define the semantic of operators for build-in integral types and the functions introduced in definition 6.1. Through the definition of the semantics of the functions, the semantics of the operators are defined indirectly by conversion of the operators to functions.

Since the evaluation of operators does not change the state[6.1], we simplify the notation by writing f^I instead of $\mathrm{val}_I(s,\ f)$. Note that the types of possible terms/expressions are restricted according to the signatures defined in section 2.4.2 and definition 4.19.

In the following a and b are elements of the universe. The definitions of the functions produce overspecifications of the actual operators; the extent in which operators are used is limited by the definition of their signatures in section 4.3.2 and 2.4.

6.2.1.1 Arithmetic operators

- $CPlus_T{}^I(a,b) = \begin{cases} a +^I b \text{ , if } in_T{}^I(a +^I \mathtt{b}) = true \\ overflow_T{}^I(a +^I b), \text{ otherwise} \end{cases}$

- $CMinus_T{}^I(a,b) = \begin{cases} \mathtt{a} -^I \mathtt{b} \text{ , if } in_T{}^I(\mathtt{a} -^I \mathtt{b}) \doteq true \\ overflow_T{}^I(a -^I \mathtt{b}), \text{ otherwise} \end{cases}$

- $CMul_T{}^I(a,b) = \begin{cases} a *^I b \text{ , if } in_T{}^I(a *^I b) = true \\ \text{undefined, otherwise} \end{cases}$

- $CUMinus_T^I(a) = \begin{cases} a & \text{if } a = -2^{n-1} \\ -a & \text{otherwise} \end{cases}$

  where n is the number of bits associated with type T

- The definition of the semantics of division is missing in [14].

The result "undefined" is subject to the invocation of the method `overflow`(x,y,'op') as defined in definition 4.28.

6.2.1.2 Type conversion

An extension of the semantic of type casts for the arithmetical integral types is not given in [36]. However, it results from definition 4.28.

6.1. Any possible state changes caused by undefined behavior are moved to the semantic definition of statements.

We define the semantics of the three conversion functions in the following way:

- $\overline{\texttt{unsigned}}^I(a) = a \; mod \; 2^{32} = overflow_{\texttt{unsigned int}}(a)$
- For $T \neq \texttt{unsigend}$:
  $\overline{\mathrm{T}}^I(a) = \begin{cases} \text{a if } in_T{}^I(\text{a}) = true \\ \text{undefined otherwise} \end{cases}$

6.2.1.3 Comparison operators

- $a \overline{>}_T^I b = \begin{cases} true & \text{if } a > b \\ false & \text{otherwise} \end{cases}$
- $a \overline{<}_T^I b = \begin{cases} true & \text{if } a < b \\ false & \text{otherwise} \end{cases}$
- $a \overline{==}_T^I b = \begin{cases} true & \text{if } a = b \\ false & \text{otherwise} \end{cases}$

6.2.1.4 Logical Operators

For boolean values a and b we define the following operator semantics:

- $a \overline{||}_T^I b = \begin{cases} true & \text{if } a = true \text{ or } b = true \\ false & \text{otherwise} \end{cases}$
- $a \overline{\&\&}_T^I b = \begin{cases} true & \text{if } a = true \text{ and } b = true \\ false & \text{otherwise} \end{cases}$
- $\overline{!}_{\mathrm{T}}{}^I a = \begin{cases} true & \text{if } a = false \\ false & \text{otherwise} \end{cases}$

6.2.1.5 Bit-wise operators

With the help of the functions to_bv_t and $from\_bv_t$, which are defined in def. 2.2, we define the following bitwise operators for integer types T with bit-width n:

- $a \overline{\&}_T^I b = from\_bv_T(bvand(to\_bv_T(a), to\_bv_T(b)))$
- $a \overline{|}_T^I b = from\_bv_T(bvor(to\_bv_T(a), to\_bv_T(b)))$
- $a \overline{\hat{}}_T^I b = from\_bv_T(bvxor(to\_bv_T(a), to\_bv_T(b)))$
- $\overline{\sim}_T^I a = from\_bv_T(bvneg(to\_bv_T(a)))$
- $a \overline{<<}_T^I b = from\_bv_T(bvshl(to\_bv_T(a), b))$
- $a \overline{>>}_{\mathrm{T}}{}^I b = from\_bv_T(bvshr(to\_bv_T(a), b))$

The functions $bvand$, $bvor$, $bvneg$, $bvshl$, and $bvshr$ have the *obvious* meaning. The notation $x[i]$ denotes the i-th bit of the bit vector. For all $i \in \{0, ..., n-1\}$:

- $bvand(a[n-1], b[n-1])[i] = \begin{cases} 1 \text{ if } a[i] = 1 \text{ and } b[i] = 1 \\ 0 \text{ otherwise} \end{cases}$

- $bvor(a[n-1], b[n-1])[i] = \begin{cases} 1 \text{ if } a[i]=1 \text{ or } b[i]=1 \\ 0 \text{ otherwise} \end{cases}$

- $bvxor(a[n-1], b[n-1])[i] = \begin{cases} 1 \text{ if } a[i] \neq b[i] \\ 0 \text{ otherwise} \end{cases}$

- $bvneg(a[n-1])[i] = \begin{cases} 1 \text{ if } a[i]=0 \\ 0 \text{ otherwise} \end{cases}$

- $bvshl(a[n-1], b)[i] = \begin{cases} a[i-b] \text{ if } b \geqslant 0 \text{ and } i \geqslant b \\ 0 \quad\quad \text{ if } b \geqslant 0 \text{ and } i < b \\ \text{undefined if } b < 0 \end{cases}$

- $bvshl(a[n-1], b)[i] = \begin{cases} a[i+b] \text{ if } b \geqslant 0 \text{ and } i < n-b \\ 0 \quad\quad \text{ if } b \geqslant 0 \text{ and } i \geqslant n-b \\ \text{undefined if } b < 0 \end{cases}$

An alternative definition of the semantic of bit operators can be given using structural updates. For instance, a shift operation can be defined as:

$$\mathtt{a}\overline{\mathtt{<<}}_T\mathtt{b} \doteq 0 \lhd \langle \mathrm{bit}_T(0) := \mathtt{a}.\mathrm{bit}_T(0+\mathtt{b})\rangle \ldots \lhd \langle \mathrm{bit}_T(n) := \mathtt{a}.\mathrm{bit}_T(n+\mathtt{b})\rangle$$

where a and b are subject to conversion (to dual representation) and n is the number of bits associated with the type T and $\mathrm{bit}_T(x) \in \mathrm{ACC}$. Thus, a calculus for bit operation could be immediately derived from definitions of this kind. This motivates further to introduce *quantified structural updates* so that a bit-shift operation could be defined using only one quantified structural update. Other bit operators can be defined in a similar way.

In the specification of C0 the predicate *valid* is defined which determins in which cases expressions are defined or not. We prefere to use the predicate symbol *isdef* for this purpose. The predicate is important for the semantic of statements and its definition is given as follows (expressions are subject to conversion).

Definition 6.5. **(*isdef*)** *The predicate isdef is defined by*

- *isdef*(c) $\equiv$ *true* , *if* c *is a program constant (or literal)*
- *isdef*(x) $\equiv$ *true* , *if* x *is a simple program variable*
  (static properties like in [14] *are not checked)*
- *isdef*(a $\circ$ b) $\equiv$ *isdef*(a) $\wedge$ *isdef*(b) $\wedge$ a $\circ$ b $\neq$ `overflow`$(a, b, \prime\circ\prime)$
  where $\circ$ *is a C0 operator*
- *isdef*(a[e]) $\equiv$ *isdef*(a) $\wedge$ *isdef*(e) $\wedge$ e $< n \wedge$ e $\geqslant 0$ [6.2]
  where the type of a[e] *is* $T[n]$ *with* $T \in \mathrm{TYP}^{C0}$
- *isdef*(a.m) $\equiv$ *isdef*(a)
- *isdef*(*e) $\equiv$ *isdef*(e) $\wedge$ e $\neq 0$

6.2. *The condition that negative indices may not be accessed is not specified in [14] but in [25].*

- $isdef(\texttt{\&e}) \equiv isdef(\texttt{e})$
  (static properties like in [14] are not checked)
- $isdef(t) \equiv true$ *for all other terms*

Remark 6.6. This definition is also a definition of calculus rules for the simplification of the argument of *isdef*, i.e., the left-hand side of the equivalence relation is replaced by the right-hand side.

We simplify the semantic of C0 in the case that we do not model the memory of the abstract machine. For the executable machine of C0 a precise memory model is specified in which the memory has a finite size. In our model a null pointer does not exist, but according to the C0 specification, a null pointer can be introduced as the result of the `new` statement if no memory can be allocated.

In the case $\texttt{a} \circ \texttt{b}$ the constraint $\texttt{a} \circ \texttt{b} \neq \texttt{overflow}(a, b, '\circ')$ is not part of the original semantic definition of C0. However, this is the way how we import the ideas from section 4.3 in order to take effect in the semantic definition of C0.

6.2.2 Semantic of statements 1

In the follwing we assume that compound expressions `rexpr` and `lexpr` are converted to terms.

6.2.2.1 Definition

The semantic of C0 statements specified in [14] states, among others, that if an expression cannot be evaluated ($isdef(e) = false$), then an error flag is set and the program does not terminate. If the program does not terminate, then an error flag has no meaning in our definition of dynamic logic. The reason for this is that if the diamond operator is used, then the formula composed of the diamond operator is false, and if the box operator is used the respective formula is true. Therefore we present the semantic of C0 statements by defining the accessibility relation $\rho()$ ignoring the notion of an error flag.

Definition 6.7. (Statement semantic "valid termination")

1. $\rho_l(\texttt{stmt stmt\_list}) :=$ [6.3]
   $\{(s,t) : s\,\rho_l(\texttt{stmt})u,\ u\rho_l(\texttt{stmt\_list})t$ *for any* $u\}$
2. $s\rho_l(\texttt{if(rexpr) compound\_stmt}_1\ \texttt{else compound\_stmt}_2))t :\Leftrightarrow$ [6.4]

6.3. In C0 there is no abrupt termination of block statements.

6.4. The case for `if(rexpr) compound_stmt)` without an `else`-part is analogous.

$\text{val}_l(s, \textit{isdef}(\texttt{rexpr})) = \textit{true and}$

- $\text{val}_l(s, \texttt{rexpr}) = \textit{true and } s\rho_l(\texttt{compound\_stmt}_1)t, \textit{ or}$
- $\text{val}_l(s, \texttt{rexpr}) = \textit{false and } s\rho_l(\texttt{compound\_stmt}_2)t$

3. $s\rho_l(\texttt{while(rexpr) compound\_stmt})t :\Leftrightarrow$ [6.9]
there is $n \in \mathbb{N}, s = s_0, s_1, \ldots, s_n = t \in S$ *with*

- *for each* $0 \leqslant i < n \; s_i\rho_l(\texttt{compound\_stmt})s_{i+1}$
- *for each* $0 \leqslant i < n$
  - $\text{val}_l(s_i, \textit{isdef}(\texttt{rexpr})) = \textit{true and}$
  - $\text{val}_l(s_i, \texttt{rexpr}) = \textit{true}$
- $\text{val}_l(s_n, \textit{isdef}(\texttt{rexpr})) = \textit{true and}$
  $\text{val}_l(s_n, \texttt{rexpr}) = \textit{false}$

4. $s\rho_l(\texttt{lexpr=rexpr})t :\Leftrightarrow$ [6.5]

- $\text{val}_l(s, \textit{isdef}(\texttt{lexpr})) = \textit{true}$
- $\text{val}_l(s, \textit{isdef}(\texttt{rexpr})) = \textit{true}$
- $t = s \lessdot \text{val}_l(s, \{\texttt{lexpr} := \texttt{rexpr}\})$

5. $\rho_l(\texttt{lexpr=ID(rexpr}_1\texttt{, ..., rexpr}_n\texttt{)})t$ *is defined to be the smallest relation*

$$\rho_l(\texttt{identifier}_1\texttt{'=rexpr}_1\texttt{;}\ldots\texttt{identifier}_n\texttt{'=rexpr}_n\texttt{;}$$
$$\texttt{stmt\_list}'$$
$$\texttt{lexpr=rexpr'}_{RET})$$

where for $1 \leqslant i \leqslant n$ $\texttt{identifier}_i\texttt{'}$ *are fresh instances of the formal parameters* $\texttt{identifier}_i$ *of the function declaration,* `stmt_list return` $\texttt{rexpr}_{\texttt{RET}}$ *is the method body, and* $\texttt{stmt\_list}'$ *and* $\texttt{rexpr'}_{RET}$ *are obtained from* `stmt_list` *and* $\texttt{rexpr}_{RET}$ *respectively by replacing occurences of* $\texttt{identifier}_i$ *by* $\texttt{identifier}_i\texttt{'}$. *In order ensure well-defined semantics in case of arbitrary recursion, the forming of the fixed-point is necessary.*[6.5]

6. $s\rho_l(\texttt{lexpr= new T})t{:}\Leftrightarrow$
$\text{val}_l(s, \textit{isdef}(\texttt{lexpr})) = \textit{true and}$
$t = s \lessdot \text{val}_l(s, \{\texttt{lexpr} := \text{obj}_{\text{T}}(\textit{next}_{\text{T}}), \textit{next}_{\text{T}} := \textit{next}_{\text{T}} + 1\})$

Note that the update $\{\texttt{lexpr} := \texttt{rexpr}\}$ is a deep copy update; the semantic of deep copy updates is defined in section 5.4.2. In this way, we export the semantic definition to section 5.4.2.

6.5. Notice `lexpr` *and* `rexpr` *are subject to conversion.*

6.2.2.2 Rules and soundness

The rule schema for handling of assignments for the diamond operator is

$$\frac{\vdash isdef(\texttt{a}) \land isdef(\texttt{b}) \land \{\texttt{a} := \texttt{b}\} \langle\!\{\pi\omega\}\!\rangle \phi}{\vdash \langle\!\{\pi\ \texttt{a:=b}\ \omega\}\!\rangle \phi} \tag{6.1}$$

and the rule schema for handling of the assignments for the box operator is

$$\frac{\vdash (isdef(\texttt{a}) \land isdef(\texttt{b})) \rightarrow \{\texttt{a} := \texttt{b}\} [\![\pi\omega]\!] \phi}{\vdash [\![\pi\ \texttt{a:=b}\ \omega]\!] \phi} \tag{6.2}$$

are sound wrt. $\models_l$

In the following we will abstract a little bit from this rule. We represent the expressions which are subject to evaluation in first place (in this case `a` and `b`) by e. For the original modality $\langle\!\{\pi\ \texttt{a:=b}\ \omega\}\!\rangle$ we write $\langle\!\{\alpha(e)\}\!\rangle$ and $\langle\!\{\beta(e)\}\!\rangle$ for the (compound) modality $\{\texttt{a} := \texttt{b}\} \langle\!\{\pi\omega\}\!\rangle$ which is generally speaking obtained after one step of symbolic program execution. In this way, we describe a rule schema form which represents a set of rules of this form. By using this form, rule schemata for handling the `new` statement and `if` statement can be constructed similarly and their soundness can be proven analogically. The rule schema form representing rule schema 6.1 is:

$$\frac{\vdash isdef(e) \land \langle\!\{\beta(e)\}\!\rangle \phi}{\vdash \langle\!\{\alpha(e)\}\!\rangle \phi} \tag{6.3}$$

and for rule schema 6.2 the rule schema form is:

$$\frac{\vdash isdef(e) \rightarrow [\![\beta(e)]\!] \phi}{\vdash [\![\alpha(e)]\!] \phi} \tag{6.4}$$

We prove the soundness of rule schema form 6.4 with respect to $\models_l$. This means we have to show that

$$isdef(e) \rightarrow [\![\beta(e)]\!] \phi \models_l [\![\alpha(e)]\!] \phi$$

By definition 3.15 this means

$$\models \{isdef(e) \rightarrow [\![\beta(e)]\!] \phi\} \rhd [\![\alpha(e)]\!] \phi$$

which means more explicitly that we claim the following statement to be correct.

$$\textbf{All}\, l\ \textbf{All}\, s\, (l, s \models isdef(e) \rightarrow [\![\beta(e)]\!] \phi \textbf{ implies } l, s \models [\![\alpha(e)]\!] \phi)$$

By definition 3.14 this is equivalent to

$$\textbf{All}\, l\ \textbf{All}\, s\ \ (\mathrm{val}_l(s, \mathrm{Cl}_\forall\, isdef(e) \rightarrow [\![\beta(e)]\!] \phi) = true\ \textbf{implies}$$
$$\mathrm{val}_l(s, \mathrm{Cl}_\forall [\![\alpha(e)]\!] \phi) = true)$$

We will now transform the left side of the meta implication and ommit writing "**All** l **All** s" for a moment:

$$\mathrm{val}_l(s, \mathrm{Cl}_\forall\, isdef(e) \rightarrow \{\!\!\{\beta(e)\}\!\!\}\phi) = true$$

The universal quantification of eventual free variables is now implicitly assumed.

$$\mathrm{val}_l(s, isdef(e) \rightarrow \{\!\!\{\beta(e)\}\!\!\}\phi) = true$$

According to definition 3.13 this is the same as the statement:

$$\mathrm{val}_l(s, isdef(e))) = true\ \textbf{implies}\ \mathrm{val}_l(s, \{\!\!\{\beta(e)\}\!\!\}\phi) = true$$

We look now at the right side of the implication

$\mathrm{val}_l(s, \{\!\!\{\beta(e)\}\!\!\}\phi) = true$
By definition 3.13:
$\textbf{All}\ t(s\rho(\beta(e))t\ \textbf{implies}\ \mathrm{val}_l(t, \phi) = true)$

and replace the right side of the implication:

$$\mathrm{val}_l(s, isdef(e)) = true\ \textbf{implies}\ \textbf{All}\ t(s\rho(\beta(e))t\ \textbf{implies}\ \mathrm{val}_l(t, \phi) = true$$

In the following we express the statement differently but without change of meaning:

$$\mathrm{val}_l(s, isdef(e)) = false\ \textbf{or}\ \textbf{All}\ t(s\rho(\beta(e))t\ \textbf{implies}\ \mathrm{val}_l(t, \phi) = true$$

$$\textbf{All}\ t(\mathrm{val}_l(s, isdef(e)) = false\ \textbf{or}\ s\rho(\beta(e))t\ \textbf{implies}\ \mathrm{val}_l(t, \phi) = true$$

$$\textbf{All}\ t(\ (\mathrm{val}_l(s, isdef(e)) = false\ \textbf{or}\ (s\rho(\beta(e))t\ \textbf{implies}\ \mathrm{val}_l(t, \phi) = true)\ \ )$$

$$\textbf{All}\ t(\ (\mathrm{val}_l(s, isdef(e)) = false\ \textbf{or}\ (\textbf{not}\ s\rho(\beta(e))t\ \textbf{or}\ \mathrm{val}_l(t, \phi) = true)\ )$$

$$\textbf{All}\ t\Big(\ (\underbrace{\textbf{not}(\mathrm{val}_l(s, isdef(e)) = true)\ \textbf{OR}\ \textbf{not}\ (s\rho(\beta(e))t)}\ \textbf{OR}\ \mathrm{val}_l(t, \phi) = true)\ \Big)$$

$$\textbf{All}\ t(\ (\textbf{not}(\mathrm{val}_l(s, isdef(e))) = true\ \textbf{and}\ s\rho(\beta(e))t))\ \textbf{or}\ \mathrm{val}_l(t, \phi) = true)\ )$$

$$\textbf{All}\ t(\ \mathrm{val}_l(s, isdef(e)) = true\ \textbf{and}\ s\rho(\beta(e))t)\ \textbf{implies}\ \mathrm{val}_l(t, \phi) = true\ \ )$$

We replace the left side of the implication as follows.

$(\mathrm{val}_l(s, isdef(e))) = true\ \textbf{and}\ s\rho(\beta(e))t)$
this is the semantic definition of
$s\rho(\alpha(e))t)$

$$\textbf{All}\ t(\ \ s\rho(\alpha(e))t\ \textbf{implies}\ \mathrm{val}_l(t, \phi) = true\ \ )$$

According to definition 3.13 ,this is equivalent to

$$\textbf{All}\, t(\ \text{val}_l(t, [\![\alpha(e)]\!]\phi) = \mathit{true}\ )$$

We have proven that

$$\begin{aligned} \textbf{All}\, l\ \textbf{All}\, s\ \ & (\text{val}_l(s, \mathit{isdef}(e) \rightarrow [\![\beta(e)]\!]\phi) = \mathit{true} \\ & \textbf{implies} \\ & \text{val}_l(s, [\![\alpha(e)]\!]\phi) = \mathit{true}) \end{aligned}$$

and therefore we have proven the soundness of the assignment rule for the box operator. ■

The proof for the rule schema form for the diamond operator can be done analogically. We will not dwell on this because we only want to discuss the *design* of the semantic definition of C0 and the verification calculus.

6.2.2.3 Discussion

The rule schema form 6.4 can be further simplified to:

$$\frac{\mathit{isdef}(e) \vdash [\![\beta(e)]\!]\phi}{\vdash [\![\alpha(e)]\!]\phi}$$

The rule schema form 6.3 for the diamond operator can be simplified to:

$$\frac{\begin{array}{c}\vdash \mathit{isdef}(e) \\ \vdash \langle\!\{\beta(e)\}\!\rangle\phi\end{array}}{\vdash \langle\!\{\alpha(e)\}\!\rangle\phi}$$

The aspect of the semantic of C0 that a program does not terminate in case of an "*error*", can be used to express that all evaluated expressions are defined by using the diamond operator. However, broadly speaking, the strength of the diamond operator is the weakness of the box operator. When using the box operator, invalid expressions lead automatically to successful proofs —of course, this is not what we want. The box operator is important because it is used for the invariant rule; the invariant rule ensures only partial correctness. It is a very important alternative to induction; the latter can ensure total correctness.

One approach is therefore to replace some rule schemata by *stronger* rule schemata that do not allow to derive the partial correctness of programs just because some expression is not valid — and thus the program does not terminate. In other words, some valid formulas which are correct according to the semantic definition of C0 are then intentionally not derivable by the calculus. Thus, the calculus is not complete.[6.6]

In the first step we replace rule schemata of the form:

$$\frac{isdef(e) \vdash \{\!\{\beta(e)\}\!\}\phi}{\vdash \{\!\{\alpha(e)\}\!\}\phi}$$

by the stronger rules:

$$\frac{\vdash \{\!\{\beta(e)\}\!\}\phi}{\vdash \{\!\{\alpha(e)\}\!\}\phi}$$

In this form the correctness of non-terminating programs due to the evaluation of invalid expressions can no longer be proven. The possibility to prove the partial correctness of non-terminating programs due to infinite loops remains unchanged. However, if we even want to ensure that the evaluation of expressions is defined, we restrict the provability only to those formulas with defined expressions in programs by adding an additional proof obligation to the rule:

$$\frac{\begin{array}{c}\vdash isdef(e)\\ \vdash \{\!\{\beta(e)\}\!\}\phi\end{array}}{\vdash \{\!\{\alpha(e)\}\!\}\phi}$$

This approach of fixing the provability of the program specification is somewhat strange. The problem is not in the calculus but in the semantic of C0. Clearly, the semantic of C0 that a program does not terminate if an expression cannot be evaluated is not suitable when used with dynamic logic. We therefore modify the semantic definition of C0 such that in case an expression cannot be evaluated, an *error flag* is set and the program *terminates*. Technically speaking, in case the current state has the error flag set, the semantic of all statements is that the statements perform no action and leave the state unchanged — the implicit "program counter" does change in contrast to the original C0 semantic because statements are executed.

6.2.3 Semantic of statements 2

6.2.3.1 Definition

Definition 6.8. (Error flag) *If* s *is a state then* $s.\mathrm{err}$ *is the error flag of the state. If* $s.\mathrm{err} = 0$ *the error flag is not set, otherwise the error flag is set.*

In order for the error flag to take effect in the validity of formulas, we modify the definitions of the satisfaction relation and consequence relation as they are given in definitions 3.14 and 3.15 respectively.

6.6. That full completeness is not possible is clear due to integer arithmetic. The calculus is, however, not complete modulo integer arithmetic.

Definition 6.9. (Satisfaction Relation "error flag") *For a state w of an interpretation l and a formula $\phi \in \mathrm{Fml}$ we define the satisfaction relation $\models$ as*

$$l, s \models \phi \ :\Leftrightarrow \ s.\mathrm{err} = 0 \text{ and } \mathrm{val}_l(s, \mathrm{Cl}_\forall \phi) = \mathit{true}$$

where $\mathrm{Cl}_\forall \phi := \forall x_1 ... \forall x_n \phi$ *is the* universal closure *of the formula* ϕ*with the free variables* $\{x_1, ..., x_n\}$.

Definition 6.10. (Consequence Relation "error flag") *The* consequence relation *is defined as in definition 3.15 except that the satisfaction relation as it is defined in def.6.9 is used in the definition.*

Furthermore, we modify the semantic of the *isdef* predicate in the following definition.

Definition 6.11. (*isdef* "error flag") *We augment the definition of the valuation of the predicate isdef as follows:*

$$\begin{aligned} \mathrm{val}_l(s, \mathit{isdef}(e)) = \mathit{true} \ :\Leftrightarrow \ & s.\mathrm{err} = 0 \ \textbf{\textit{and}} \\ & \textit{according to definition 6.5:} \\ & \quad \mathrm{val}_l(s, \mathit{isdef}(e)) = \mathit{true} \end{aligned}$$

Within this context we give a new definition of the semantic of C0 statements so that in case an expression cannot be evaluated the error flag is set and the program terminates.

Definition 6.12. (Statement semantic "error flag")

1. $s\rho_l($ `stmt stmt_list`$)t :\Leftrightarrow$
   if $\mathrm{val}_l(s, \mathit{isdef}(1)) = \mathit{true}$ *then* [6.7]
   $(s, t) \in \{(s, t) : s\rho_l(\texttt{stmt})u, u\rho_l(\texttt{stmt\_list})t \textit{ for any } u\}$
   otherwise
   $t = s$ *with* $t.\mathrm{err} = 1$

2. $s\rho_l($`if(rexpr) compound_stmt`$_1$ *`else`* `compound_stmt`$_2$*)* $)t :\Leftrightarrow$ [6.8]
   if $\mathrm{val}_l(s, \mathit{isdef}(\texttt{rexpr})) = \mathit{true}$ *then*

   - $\mathrm{val}_l(s, \texttt{rexpr}) = \mathit{true}$ *and* $s\rho_l(\texttt{compound\_stmt}_1)t$*, or*
   - $\mathrm{val}_l(s, \texttt{rexpr}) = \mathit{false}$ *and* $s\rho_l(\texttt{compound\_stmt}_2)t$

   otherwise

6.7. $\mathrm{val}_l(s, \mathit{isdef}(1)) = \mathit{true}$ *is just another way to ensure* $s.\mathrm{err} = 0$ *according to def. 6.11*

6.8. *The case for* `if(rexpr) compound_stmt`*)* *without an* `else`*-part is analogous.*

$t = s$ *with* $t.\text{err} = 1$

3. $s\rho_l($`while(rexpr) compound_stmt`$)t :\Leftrightarrow$ [6.5]
   there is $n \in \mathbb{N}, s = s_0, s_1, \ldots, s_n = t \in S$ *with*

   - *for each* $0 \leqslant i < n$ $s_i\rho_l($`compound_stmt`$)s_{i+1}$
   - *for each* $0 \leqslant i < n$
     - $\text{val}_l(s_i, \textit{isdef}(\texttt{rexpr})) = \textit{true}$ *and*
     - $\text{val}_l(s_i, \texttt{rexpr}) = \textit{true}$
   - $\text{val}_l(s_n, \textit{isdef}(\texttt{rexpr})) = \textit{true}$ *and*
     $\text{val}_l(s_n, \texttt{rexpr}) = \textit{false}$

   otherwise
   $t = s_i$ *with* $t.\text{err} = 1$ *for the smallest* $0 \leqslant i \leqslant n$ *where* $\text{val}_l(s_i, \textit{isdef}(\texttt{rexpr})) = \textit{false}$

4. $s\rho_l($`lexpr=rexpr`$)t :\Leftrightarrow$ [6.9]
   if $\text{val}_l(s, \textit{isdef}(\texttt{lexpr})) = \textit{true}$ *and* $\text{val}_l(s, \textit{isdef}(\texttt{rexpr})) = \textit{true}$ *then*
   $t = s \lessdot \text{val}_l(s, \{\texttt{lexpr} := \texttt{rexpr}\})$
   otherwise
   $t = s$ *with* $t.\text{err} = 1$

5. $\rho_l($`lexpr=ID(rexpr`$_1$`, ..., rexpr`$_n$`)`$)t$ *is like in definition 6.7 to be the smallest relation* R *satisfying the equation*

$$R = \rho_l(\texttt{identifier}_1\texttt{'=rexpr}_1\texttt{;}\ldots\texttt{identifier}_n\texttt{'=rexpr}_n\texttt{;}\ \texttt{stmt\_list}'\ \texttt{lexpr=rexpr'}_{RET})$$

   where for $1 \leqslant i \leqslant n$ `identifier`$_i$`'` *are fresh instances of the formal parameters* `identifier`$_i$ *of the function declaration,* `stmt_list return rexpr`$_{\text{RET}}$ *is the method body, and* `stmt_list'` *and* `rexpr'`$_{RET}$ *are obtained from* `stmt_list` *and* `rexpr`$_{RET}$ *respectively by replacing occurences of* `identifier`$_i$ *by* `identifier`$_i$`'`*. In order ensure a well-defined semantics in case of arbitrary recursion, the forming of the fixed-point is necessary.*[6.9]

6. $s\rho_l($`lexpr= new T`$)t{:}\Leftrightarrow$
   if $\text{val}_l(s, \textit{isdef}(\texttt{lexpr})) = \textit{true}$ *then*
   $t = s \lessdot \text{val}_l(s, \{\texttt{lexpr} := \text{obj}_{\text{T}}(\textit{next}_{\text{T}}), \textit{next}_{\text{T}} := \textit{next}_{\text{T}} + 1\})$
   otherwise
   $t = s$ *with* $t.\text{err} = 1$

6.9. *Notice* `lexpr` *and* `rexpr` *are subject to conversion.*

6.2.3.2 Rules and soundness

Given this semantics we define the assignment rule schema for the box operator as we *wanted* it to be in the previous section.

$$\frac{\begin{array}{c}\vdash isdef(\mathtt{a}) \wedge isdef(\mathtt{b}) \\ \vdash \{\mathtt{a} := \mathtt{b}\}[\![\pi\omega]\!]\phi\end{array}}{\vdash [\![\pi\ \mathtt{a:=b}\,\omega]\!]\phi}$$

We abstract from this rule schema by the rule schema form

$$\frac{\begin{array}{c}\vdash isdef(e) \\ \vdash [\![\beta(e)]\!]\phi\end{array}}{\vdash [\![\alpha(e)]\!]\phi} \tag{6.5}$$

In order to show that the rule schema form 6.5 is sound wrt. $\models_l$ according to definition 6.10 we have to prove that

$$\{isdef(e), [\![\beta(e)]\!]\phi\} \models_l [\![\alpha(e)]\!]\phi$$

According to definition 6.10 this is the same as the statement

$$\models \{isdef(e), [\![\beta(e)]\!]\phi\} \rhd [\![\alpha(e)]\!]\phi$$

or as the statement

$$\textbf{All}\, l\; \textbf{All}\, s\, (l, s \models isdef(e) \wedge [\![\beta(e)]\!]\phi \textbf{ implies } l, s \models [\![\alpha(e)]\!]\phi)$$

By definition 6.9 the statement is the same as

$$\begin{array}{ll}\textbf{All}\, l\; \textbf{All}\, s & (s.\mathrm{err} = 0 \textbf{ and } \mathrm{val}_l(s, \mathrm{Cl}_\forall\, isdef(e) \wedge [\![\beta(e)]\!]\phi) = true \\ & \textbf{implies} \\ & s.\mathrm{err} = 0 \textbf{ and } \mathrm{val}_l(s, \mathrm{Cl}_\forall [\![\alpha(e)]\!]\phi) = true)\end{array}$$

We will now transform the left side of the meta implication, and omit writing "**All** l **All** s". For all states $s \in S^l$ we have to distinguish two cases

If $s.\mathrm{err} \neq 0$ then the premiss that $s.\mathrm{err} = 0$ **and** $\mathrm{val}_l(s,\ \mathrm{Cl}_\forall\ isdef(e) \wedge [\![\beta(e)]\!]\phi) = true$ is a contradiction so that according to the definition of the abbreviation "**implies**", we make no statement about the conclusion $s.\mathrm{err} = 0$ **and** $\mathrm{val}_l(s, \mathrm{Cl}_\forall [\![\alpha(e)]\!]\phi) = true)$.

Otherwise, if $s.\mathrm{err} = 0$ we omit repeatedly writing that we assume that $s.\mathrm{err} = 0$ and simplify the notation of the previous statement to:

$$\mathrm{val}_l(s, \mathrm{Cl}_\forall\, isdef(e) \wedge [\![\beta(e)]\!]\phi) = true \textbf{ implies } \mathrm{val}_l(s, \mathrm{Cl}_\forall [\![\alpha(e)]\!]\phi) = true$$

For notational simplification the universal quantification of free variables is now implicitly assumed for both sides of the previous implication statement.

$$\mathrm{val}_l(s,\ isdef(e) \wedge [\![\beta(e)]\!]\phi) = true \textbf{ implies } \mathrm{val}_l(s, [\![\alpha(e)]\!]\phi) = true$$

In the following boxes we expand the statement of both sides of the compound statement where we frequently use definition 3.13

$\mathrm{val}_l(s,\ \mathit{isdef}(e) \wedge [\{\beta(e)\}]\phi) = \mathit{true}$
$\mathrm{val}_l(s,\ \mathit{isdef}(e)) = \mathit{true}$ **and** $\mathrm{val}_l(s,\ [\{\beta(e)\}]\phi) = \mathit{true}$

$\mathrm{val}_l(s, [\{\alpha(e)\}]\phi) = \mathit{true}$
All $t\ s\rho_l(\alpha(e))t$ **implies** $\mathrm{val}_l(s, \phi) = \mathit{true}$

$s\rho_l(\alpha(e))t$
if $\mathrm{val}_l(s, \mathit{isdef}(e)) = \mathit{true}$ **then**
$s\rho_l(\beta(e))t$
otherwise
$t = s$ with $t.\mathrm{err} = 1$
This definition can be written in other words as:
$\mathrm{val}_l(s, \mathit{isdef}(e)) = \mathit{true}$ **implies** $s\rho_l(\beta(e))t$
and
$\mathrm{val}_l(s, \mathit{isdef}(e)) = \mathit{false}$ **implies** $t = s$ with $t.\mathrm{err} = 1$

Consequently, our claim is that:

$$\mathrm{val}_l(s,\ \mathit{isdef}(e)) = \mathit{true} \textbf{ and } \mathrm{val}_l(s,\ [\{\beta(e)\}]\phi) = \mathit{true}$$
$$\textbf{IMPLIES}$$
$$\textbf{All}\, t \begin{pmatrix} \mathrm{val}_l(s, \mathit{isdef}(e)) = \mathit{true} \textbf{ implies } s\rho_l(\beta(e))t \\ \textbf{and} \\ \mathrm{val}_l(s, \mathit{isdef}(e)) = \mathit{false} \textbf{ implies } t = s \text{ with } t.\mathrm{err} = 1 \end{pmatrix}$$
$$\textbf{implies } \mathrm{val}_l(s, \phi) = \mathit{true}$$

Two cases have to be considered. If $\mathrm{val}_l(s,\ \mathit{isdef}(e)) = \mathit{false}$, then we don't satisfy the premise that $\mathrm{val}_l(s,\ \mathit{isdef}(e)) = \mathit{true}$ **and** $\mathrm{val}_l(s,\ [\{\beta(e)\}]\phi) = \mathit{true}$. Thus, we make no statement about the truth of the conclusion.

The other case is that $\mathrm{val}_l(s,\ \mathit{isdef}(e)) = \mathit{true}$. If we keep this situation in mind, then the statement can be abbreviated. The statement

$$\mathrm{val}_l(s,\ \mathit{isdef}(e)) = \mathit{true} \textbf{ and } \mathrm{val}_l(s,\ [\{\beta(e)\}]\phi) = \mathit{true}$$

abbreviates to

$$\mathrm{val}_l(s,\ [\{\beta(e)\}]\phi) = \mathit{true}$$

the statement

$$\mathrm{val}_l(s, \mathit{isdef}(e)) = \mathit{true} \textbf{ implies } s\rho_l(\beta(e))t$$

abbreviates to

$$s\rho_l(\beta(e))t$$

and the statement

$$\mathrm{val}_l(s, \mathit{isdef}(e)) = \mathit{false} \textbf{ implies } t = s \text{ with } t.\mathrm{err} = 1$$

is *vacuously* true. Our claim is therefore under the consideration of $\text{val}_l(s, \mathit{isdef}(e)) = \mathit{true}$ that

$$\text{val}_l(s,\ \{\!\![\beta(e)]\!\!\}\phi) = \mathit{true}$$
$$\textbf{IMPLIES}$$
$$\textbf{All}\, t\ (s\rho_l(\beta(e))t\ )\ \textbf{implies}\, \text{val}_l(s, \phi) = \mathit{true}$$

Since the statement **All** t $(s\rho_l(\beta(e))t\ )$ **implies** $\text{val}_l(s,\ \phi) = \mathit{true}$ is the definition of $\text{val}_l(s,\ \{\!\![\beta(e)]\!\!\}\phi) = \mathit{true}$ we claim in other words that

$$\text{val}_l(s,\ \{\!\![\beta(e)]\!\!\}\phi) = \mathit{true}\ \textbf{IMPLIES}\ \text{val}_l(s,\ \{\!\![\beta(e)]\!\!\}\phi) = \mathit{true}$$

which is of course true and therefore the proof is complete. ■

A proof for the anlogous rule schema form for the diamond operator can be done in a similar way. A proof for the invariant rule needs some special considerations including an induction proof. The semantic and the calculus for this part of C0 is similar to that of parts of ODL and DLJ except that it has been extended by the notion of the error flag. Since the soundness of the ODL and DLJ calculus is proven in [33] and partially in [36] respectively, we have proven the "relative" soundness of the rule schema form 6.5 with *respect* to the extension of semantic and calculus of ODL by the error flag. This means that we assume that the rule

$$\frac{\vdash \{\!\![\beta(e)]\!\!\}\phi}{\vdash \{\!\![\alpha(e)]\!\!\}\phi}$$

is correct wrt. a similar semantic but without the notion of the error-flag as it is the case in ODL. We claim that rule schema that meat the form 6.6 are sound as well. Because of the soundness of the form 6.5 wrt. to $\models_l$ we conclude from lemma 3.30 and lemma 3.31 that the rule schema form

$$\frac{\begin{array}{c}\Gamma \vdash \mu\, \mathit{isdef}(e), \Delta \\ \Gamma \vdash \mu\, \{\!\![\beta(e)]\!\!\}\phi, \Delta\end{array}}{\Gamma \vdash \mu\, \{\!\![\alpha(e)]\!\!\}\phi, \Delta} \tag{6.6}$$

is sound wrt. the soundness of the "respective parts" of the calculi in ODL and DLJ.

However, the definition of a rule schema form and the instantiation of a rule schema form to build a rule schema are not formalized here. The proof of the soundness of the statement is therefore informal in this respect. For this reason our statement of the soundness of the rules that meet the rule schema form 6.6 does not go to the extent that we allow no doubt concerning the correctness of our statement. We therefore omit giving our statement in form of a theorem.

Chapter 7

Adaption of Program Rules from KeY Calculi for CDL

Remark: Program rules are symbolic program execution rules and program transformation rules.

7.1 Notation

In the following *lexpr* and *rexpr* are schema variables for `lexpressions` and `rexpressions` respectively. The *slhs* and *srhs* schema variables denote simple left-hand side expressions and simple right-hand side expressions obtained from `lexpressions` and `rexpressions` respectively by the application of the simplification rules as they are presented below. The schema variable *expr* denotes `lexpressions` and `rexpressions`. The symbols Γ and Δ stand for sets of formulas and μ represents a deep copy update. All updates are uniquely either deep copy updates or KeY updates, where the later are subject to immediate unfolding upon creation (this is for simplification of the rules but see section 5.3).

The symbols π and ω denote the program context like it is the case in the calculi for JavaCardDL and DLJ. We use the approach of KeY where sequent rules operate on the first active statement. This approach and the program context is not necessary for the handling of C0 because all *blocks* in C0 are exited by the end of the block. However, in MISRA C loops can be terminated by a `break` statement which requires this approach of in KeY. Therefore we use this approach for the case that the rules are further reused for a calculus for handling of MISRA C.

7.2 Included rules

The calculus of CDL consists of the rules introduced in the previous chapters and rules that are presented in this chapter. The following tables give an overview of the rules from the other chapters.

Rule ID	Rule Category	Section	Page
(R1)...(R12)	propositional rules	3.3	42
(R13)...(R20)	first-order rules	3.3	42
(R35) and (R36)	rewrite rule application	3.3	43
lemma 3.30 and 3.31	generalization	3.3	43
(R46) and (R47)	generalization	3.3	44
(R37) and (R38)	conditional term	4.2.4	55
(R1.1.0)...(R1.1.5)	operator conversion	4.3.5	65
def. 5.8	program variable conversion	5.2.6	77
dr1, dr2, dR	dereferenciation	5.2.6	76
Rd, Rv1, Rv2	referenciation	5.2.6	76
def. 6.5	*isdef*	6.2.1	136

Table 7.1. Included Rules

If deep copy updates are used then the rules of the following table must be included.

Rule ID	Rule Category	Section	Page
Rs	referenciation	5.4.3	83
uu, uv, u0, ur, uRr, ud ud2, udr, uud, us, ue ua, uf, uF	update application	5.4.3	84
vs, co	program variable rules	5.4.3	84
eps, eq, ss, if, subst	utility rules	5.4.3	85

Table 7.2. Deep Copy Update Rules

Otherwise, if deep copy updates are not used but KeY updates with unfolding instead, then the rules of the following table must be included.

Rule ID	Rule Category	Section	Page
(R27)...(R34)	term rewrite rules	4.2.4	55
(RQuan)	quantified update	4.2.4	56
(R48)...(R50)	derived inference rules	4.2.4	56
	unfolding	5.3	77

Table 7.3. KeY Update Rules

Additionally we include the following derived rules from [33].

(R51) conditional term known

$$\frac{e \vdash \phi(s)}{e \vdash \phi(\text{if } e \text{ then } s \text{ else } t \text{ fi})}$$

(R52) conditional term known

$$\frac{\vdash e, \phi(t)}{\vdash e, \phi(\text{if } e \text{ then } s \text{ else } t \text{ fi})}$$

(R53) conditional reconcile

$$\text{if } \chi \text{ then } s \text{ else } \phi(\text{if } \chi \text{ then } s' \text{ else } t \text{ fi}) \text{ fi} \leadsto$$
$$\text{if } \chi \text{ then } s \text{ else } \phi(t) \text{ fi}$$

(R54) `new` identity

$$\frac{}{n \neq m \vdash \text{obj}_C(n) \neq \text{obj}_C(m)}$$

(R55) modus ponens

$$\frac{}{\phi, \phi \rightarrow \psi \vdash \psi}$$

Table 7.4 Derived Inference Rules

7.3 Statements

Rule 2.0 *assignment-statement*
Purpose Symbolic execution of an assignment statement.
Remark The rule for the box operator $\{\!\!\{.\}\!\!\}$ is analogous.

$$\frac{\begin{array}{c}\Gamma \vdash \mu\, isdef(\texttt{slhs}), \Delta \\ \Gamma \vdash \mu\, isdef(\texttt{srhs}), \Delta \\ \Gamma \vdash \mu\, \{\texttt{slhs} := \texttt{srhs}\}\langle\!\{\pi\ \omega\}\!\rangle\phi, \Delta\end{array}}{\Gamma \vdash \mu\, \langle\!\{\pi\, \texttt{slhs = srhs;}\ \omega\}\!\rangle\phi, \Delta}$$

Description This rule symbolically executes an assignment statement. The symbolic execution results in a deep copy update attached to the formula that contained the assignment statement before. This means, after the symbolic execution of the assignment, the formula is evaluated in a state where `slhs` has the value `srhs` and the assignment disappears from the program.

Rule 2.1 *if-simplification*

Purpose This rule simplifies the condition expression of the if statement.

Remark The rule for the box operator $[\!\{.\}\!]$ is analogous.

$$\frac{\Gamma \vdash \mu \langle\!\{\pi\, \texttt{x=rexpr; if(x)}\ p\ \texttt{else}\ q\ \omega\}\!\rangle\Delta}{\Gamma \vdash \mu \langle\!\{\pi\, \texttt{if(rexpr)}\ p\ \texttt{else}\ q\ \omega\}\!\rangle\Delta}$$

Description `x` is a new program variable of type `bool`.

Rule 2.2 *if-Execution*

Purpose This rule symbolically executes the if statement.

Remark The rule for the box operator $[\!\{.\}\!]$ is analogous.

$$\frac{\begin{array}{c}\Gamma \vdash \mu\, isdef(\texttt{slhs})\,\Delta \\ \Gamma\ \mu\,\texttt{slhs} \doteq \texttt{true} \vdash \mu\, \langle\!\{\pi p \omega\}\!\rangle\Delta \\ \Gamma,\ \mu\,\texttt{slhs} \doteq \texttt{false} \vdash \mu\, \langle\!\{\pi q \omega\}\!\rangle\Delta\end{array}}{\Gamma \vdash \mu\, \langle\!\{\pi\, \texttt{if(slhs)}\ p\ \texttt{else}\ q\ \omega\}\!\rangle\phi}$$

Description Two proof obligations are created for possible program executions depending on whether $\texttt{slhs} \doteq \texttt{true}$ or $\texttt{slhs} \doteq \texttt{false}$. Additionally, the definedness of the conditional expression has to be ensured.

Rule 2.3 *unwind-while*

Purpose Unwind the while loop once. This is important for induction on the number of iterations of the loop.

$$\frac{\Gamma \vdash \mu\, \langle\!\{\pi\, \texttt{if(rexpr)\{}p\ \texttt{while(rexpr)\{}p\texttt{\}\}}\,\omega\}\!\rangle\Delta}{\Gamma \vdash \mu\, \langle\!\{\pi\, \texttt{while(rexpr)\{}p\texttt{\}}\, w\}\!\rangle\Delta}$$

Description p and q are compound statements. This rule transforms the program into an equivalent program. Since there is no abrupt completion of the loop body in C0 no labels have to be introduced in contrast to the calculus of JavaCardDL.

Rule 2.4 *loop-invariant*

Purpose Proof partial correctness of loops

Remark This rule is only sound wrt. $\models_g$

$$\frac{\Gamma \vdash \mu p, \Delta \qquad p, \texttt{rexpr} \vdash [\alpha]p \qquad p, \neg\texttt{rexpr} \vdash A}{\Gamma \vdash \mu[\texttt{while(rexpr)\{}\alpha\texttt{\}}]A, \Delta}$$

Description The invariant rule is an alternative to loop induction. This rule is sound with respect to $\models_g$ but not with respect to $\models_l$ therefore no context can be propagated to the proof obligations.

This rule is however only sound with respect to the C0 semantic definition 6.7 but not to the definition 6.12. This is because in the second case the definedness of the expression e is not checked. We haven't investigated how to insert the $isdef(e)$ formula into this rule schema but we suppose that the following rule schema is correct wrt. the semantics of definition 6.12:

$$\frac{\begin{array}{c}\vdash isdef(\texttt{rexpr}) \\ p, \texttt{rexpr}, isdef(\texttt{rexpr}) \vdash [\alpha] isdef(\texttt{rexpr}) \\ \Gamma \vdash \mu p, \Delta \\ p, \texttt{rexpr} \vdash [\alpha]p \\ p, \neg\texttt{rexpr} \vdash A\end{array}}{\Gamma \vdash \mu[\texttt{while(rexpr)\{}\alpha\texttt{\}}]A, \Delta}$$

Rule 2.5 *function-call*

Purpose This rule symbolically executes a function call.

Remark The rule for the box operator $[\![.]\!]$ is analogous.

$$\frac{\begin{array}{c}\Gamma \vdash \langle\!\langle \pi\texttt{lexpr}_1\texttt{=rexpr}_1, \ldots, \texttt{lexpr}_n\texttt{=rexpr}_n\texttt{;} \\ \texttt{statement\_list'}\omega \rangle\!\rangle \Delta\end{array}}{\Gamma \vdash \mu\langle\!\langle \pi\, \texttt{ID (rexpr}_1, \ldots, \texttt{rexpr}_n\texttt{)}\ \omega \rangle\!\rangle \Delta}$$

Description *ID* is the name of a function. $\texttt{lexpr}_1, ..., \texttt{lexpr}_n$ are are new instances of the formal parameters of the function declaration. `statement_list'` is the body of the function with all program variables declared in the body replaced by new instance of the program variables. All occurrences of the formal parameters in the original `statement_list` are replaced by $\texttt{lexpr}_1, ...,$ $\texttt{lexpr}_n$ respectively. An occurrence of a `return` statement at the end of `statement_list'` is removed.

Rule 2.6 *function-call-and-value-return*

Purpose This rule symbolically executes a function call and handles the return statement.

Remark The rule for the box operator $[\![.]\!]$ is analogous.

$$\frac{\begin{array}{l}\Gamma \vdash \langle\!\langle \pi\, \texttt{lexpr}_1\texttt{=}\texttt{rexpr}_1, ..., \texttt{lexpr}_n\texttt{=}\texttt{rexpr}_n\texttt{;} \\ \qquad\qquad \texttt{statement\_list'} \\ \qquad\qquad \texttt{lexpr=rexpr}_{\text{RET}}\texttt{'}\,\omega \rangle\!\rangle, \Delta\end{array}}{\Gamma \vdash \mu\langle\!\langle \pi\; \texttt{lexpr=}\mathit{ID}\texttt{(rexpr}_1, ..., \texttt{rexpr}_n\texttt{)}\;\; \omega\rangle\!\rangle\Delta}$$

Description *ID* is the name of a function. $\texttt{lexpr}_1, ..., \texttt{lexpr}_n$ are are new instances of the formal parameters of the function declaration. `statement_list'` is the body of the function with all program variables declared in the body replaced by new instance of the program variables. All occurrences of the formal parameters in the original `statement_list` are replaced by $\texttt{lexpr}_1, ...,$ $\texttt{lexpr}_n$ respectively.

$\texttt{rexpr}_{\text{RET}}$ is the original expression in the return statement of the body. $\texttt{rexpr}_{\text{RET}}$' is obtained from $\texttt{rexpr}_{\text{RET}}$ by replacing occurrences of local variables and formal parameters by $\texttt{lexpr}_1, ..., \texttt{lexpr}_n$ respectively.

Rule 2.7 *dynamic-creation*

Purpose Symbolic execution of the dynamic creation statement

Remark The rule for the box operator $[\![.]\!]$ is analogous.

Remark Note that $next_T$ is an abbreviation for ${}^{v}next_T$ as defined in def. 5.10.

$$\frac{\begin{array}{c}\Gamma \vdash \mu\, isdef(\texttt{slhs}), \Delta \\ \Gamma \vdash \mu \{\texttt{slhs} := obj_T(next_T), next_T := next_T + 1\} \langle\!\{\pi\ \ \omega\}\!\rangle \phi, \Delta\end{array}}{\Gamma \vdash \mu\, \langle\!\{\pi\, \texttt{slhs = new T;}\, \omega\}\!\rangle \phi, \Delta}$$

Description This rule creates a new object by assigning the program variable **`slhs`** the address of the new object represented by the term $obj_T(next_T)$ and increments for this type the non-rigid counter $next_{\mathrm{T}}$. Next time an object of this type is created its address will be represented by $obj_T(next_T + 1)$ relative to this one.

7.4 Derived Rules from DLJ

The included rules and the statement rules presented above constitute a complete calculus modulo integer arithmetic. The rules handle all elements of the logic part and all elements of the program part.

In this section we present rule schemata as they are defined similarly in [36]. We claim that the rule schemata and rewrite rules presented so far subsume the rules of DLJ, i.e., the rules schemata presented below are derived rule schemata of our calculus. They have been adapted (and corrected) to CDL and are presented here because they compose many rule applications yielding important "short-cut" rules. Furthermore they integrate concepts which are given in separate parts of the thesis. We reuse most of the descriptions from [36] and adapt them for our purposes. The enumeration of the rules is kept the in the same way as the rules of the source document are enumerated.

As an example we prove that the rule (R.6.4.2) is a derived rule of our calculus.

7.4.1 Derivation of Rule 6.4.2

The original rule 6.4.2 is

1. $\Gamma \vdash \mu\, isdef(\texttt{slhs})\,, \Delta$
2. $\Gamma \vdash \mu\, isdef(\texttt{srhs}_1)\,, \Delta$
3. $\Gamma \vdash \mu\, isdef(\texttt{srhs}_2)\,, \Delta$
4. $\Gamma \vdash \mu \neg \texttt{srhs}_2 \doteq 0$
5. $\Gamma\, \mu\, in_{T_1}(\texttt{srhs}_1), \mu\, in_{T_2}(\texttt{srhs}_2), \mu\, in_T(\texttt{srhs}_1\, \texttt{logOp}\, \texttt{srhs}_2 \vdash$
   $\mu\, \{\texttt{slhs} := \texttt{srhs}_1\, \texttt{logOp}\, \texttt{srhs}_2\} \langle\!\{\pi\ \ \omega\}\!\rangle \phi\ , \Delta$
6. $\Gamma\, \mu\, in_{T_1}(\texttt{srhs}_1), \mu\, in_{T_2}(\texttt{srhs}_2), \mu \neg in_T(\texttt{srhs}_1\, \texttt{logOp}\, \texttt{srhs}_2 \vdash$
   $\mu\, \langle\!\{\pi\ \texttt{slhs = overflow(srhs}_1\texttt{,srhs}_2\texttt{,'op')}\ \omega\}\!\rangle \phi\ , \Delta$
7. $\Gamma\, \mu \neg (in_{T_1}(\texttt{srhs}_1) \wedge in_{T_2}(\texttt{srhs}_2)) \vdash$
   $\mu\, \{\texttt{slhs} := \texttt{srhs}_1\, \texttt{logOp}\, \texttt{srhs}_2\} \langle\!\{\pi\ \ \omega\}\!\rangle \phi\, , \Delta$

$$\Gamma \vdash \mu\, \langle\!\{\pi\, \texttt{slhs = srhs}_1\ \texttt{op}\ \texttt{srhs}_2\texttt{;}\, \omega\}\!\rangle \phi\, , \Delta$$

for simple expressions $\texttt{srhs}_1$ and $\texttt{srhs}_2$ of arithmetical type. $\texttt{op}$ is one of the C0 operators +,-,*,/ and $\texttt{logOp}$ is the corresponding logical function $+, -, *, /$ on $\mathbb{Z}$. We prove that the rule 6.4.2 is a derived rule of our calculus. The following is the schema of the proof.

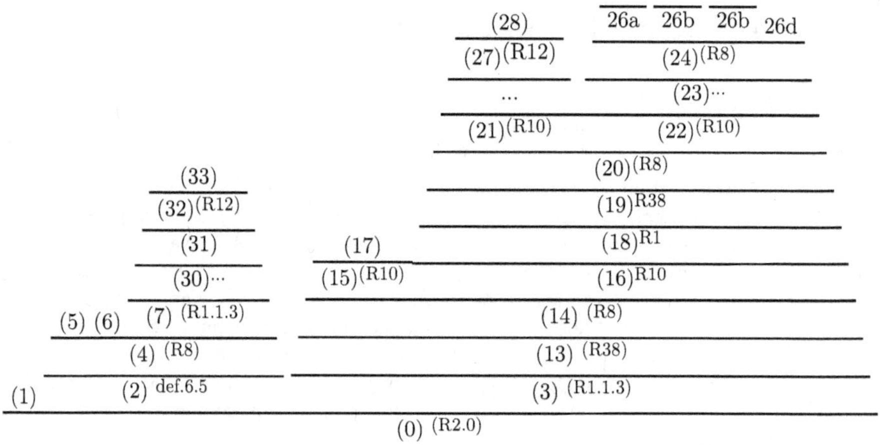

(0) $\vdash \langle\!\{\pi\, \texttt{slhs = srhs}_1\ \texttt{op}\ \texttt{srhs}_2\texttt{;}\, \omega\}\!\rangle \phi$

By assignment rule (R2.0)

(1) $\vdash isdef(\texttt{slhs})$

(2) $\vdash isdef(\texttt{srhs}_1\ \texttt{op}\ \texttt{srhs}_2)$

(3) $\vdash \{\texttt{slhs}{:=}\texttt{srhs}_1\ \texttt{op}\ \texttt{srhs}_2\} \langle\!\{\pi\ \ \omega\}\!\rangle \phi$

Regarding (2) we get from the rules of definition 6.5 (see the remark below the definition)

(4)

$\vdash isdef(\mathtt{srhs}_1) \wedge isdef(\mathtt{srhs}_2) \wedge \mathtt{srhs}_1\ op\ \mathtt{srhs}_2 \neq \mathtt{overflow}(\mathtt{srhs}_1, \mathtt{srhs}_2, \prime op \prime)$

By rule (R8) this is the conclusion of the premises:

(5) $\vdash isdef(\mathtt{srhs}_1)$

(6) $\vdash isdef(\mathtt{srhs}_2)$

(7) $\vdash \mathtt{srhs}_1\ op\ \mathtt{srhs}_2 \neq \mathtt{overflow}(\mathtt{srhs}_1, \mathtt{srhs}_2, \prime op \prime)$

We will return back to (7) later. Now we look at (3) again. By conversion from expressions to terms by (R1.1.3) we get from (3) the proof obligation:

(13)

$$\vdash \{\mathtt{slhs} := \left(\begin{array}{l} \text{if } in_T(X) \wedge in_T(Y) \wedge in_T(X\ \mathtt{logOp}\ Y) \text{ then} \\ \qquad X\ \mathtt{logOp}\ Y \\ \text{else if } \neg in_T(X) \vee \neg in_T(Y) \text{ then} \\ \qquad X\ \mathtt{logOp}\ Y \\ \text{else } \mathtt{overflow}(X, Y, \prime \circ \prime) \text{ fi fi} \end{array} \right) \} \langle\!\{\pi\ \omega\}\!\rangle \phi$$

Note we use the schema variables X and Y instead of $\mathtt{srhs}_1$ and $\mathtt{srhs}_2$ respectively for a shorter notation.

By (R38):

(14)

$\vdash in_T(X) \wedge in_T(Y) \wedge in_T(X\ \mathtt{logOp}\ Y) \rightarrow \{\mathtt{slhs} := X\ \mathtt{logOp}\ Y\} \langle\!\{\pi\ \omega\}\!\rangle \phi$

$\bigwedge$

$\neg(in_T(X) \wedge in_T(Y) \wedge in_T(X\ \mathtt{logOp}\ Y)) \rightarrow$

$\{\mathtt{slhs} := \text{if } \neg in_T(X) \vee \neg in_T(Y) \text{ then } X\ \mathtt{logOp}\ Y \text{ else } \mathtt{overflow}(X, Y, \prime \circ \prime) \text{ fi}\} \langle\!\{\pi\ \omega\}\!\rangle \phi$

By (R8):

(15)

$\vdash in_T(X) \wedge in_T(Y) \wedge in_T(X\ \mathtt{logOp}\ Y) \rightarrow \{\mathtt{slhs} := X\ \mathtt{logOp}\ Y\} \langle\!\{\pi\ \omega\}\!\rangle \phi$

and

(16)

$\vdash \neg(in_T(X) \wedge in_T(Y) \wedge in_T(X\ \mathtt{logOp}\ Y)) \rightarrow$

$\{\mathtt{slhs} := \text{if } \neg in_T(X) \vee \neg in_T(Y) \text{ then } X\ \mathtt{logOp}\ Y \text{ else } \mathtt{overflow}(X, Y, \prime \circ \prime) \text{ fi}\} \langle\!\{\pi\ \omega\}\!\rangle \phi$

(15) is transformed by rule (R10) to

(17) $in_T(X) \wedge in_T(Y) \wedge in_T(X\ \mathtt{logOp}\ Y) \vdash \{\mathtt{slhs} := X\ \mathtt{logOp}\ Y\} \langle\!\{\pi\ \omega\}\!\rangle \phi$

(16) yields by rule (R10) from

(18)

$\neg(in_T(X) \wedge in_T(Y) \wedge in_T(X\ \mathtt{logOp}\ Y)) \vdash$

$\{\mathtt{slhs} := \text{if } \neg in_T(X) \vee \neg in_T(Y) \text{ then } X\ \mathtt{logOp}\ Y \text{ else } \mathtt{overflow}(X, Y, \prime \circ \prime) \text{ fi}\} \langle\!\{\pi\ \omega\}\!\rangle \phi$

from which we obtain by rule (R1)

(19)

$\vdash in_T(X) \wedge in_T(Y) \wedge in_T(X\, \texttt{logOp}\, Y),$

$\{\texttt{slhs}{:=}\text{if } \neg in_T(X) \vee \neg in_T(Y) \text{ then } X\ \texttt{logOp}\ Y \text{ else } \texttt{overflow}(X, Y, \prime \circ \prime)\ \text{fi}\}\langle\!\langle \pi\ \omega \rangle\!\rangle \phi$

By rule (38):

(20)

$\vdash in_T(X) \wedge in_T(Y) \wedge in_T(X\, \texttt{logOp}\, Y),$

$(\neg in_T(X) \vee \neg in_T(Y)) \rightarrow \{\texttt{slhs}{:=}X\, \texttt{logOp}\, Y\}\langle\!\langle \pi\ \omega \rangle\!\rangle \phi$

$\bigwedge$

$\neg(\neg in_T(X) \vee \neg in_T(Y)) \rightarrow \{\texttt{slhs}{:=}\texttt{overflow}(X, Y, \prime \circ \prime)\}\langle\!\langle \pi\ \omega \rangle\!\rangle \phi$

By (R8)

(21)

$\vdash in_T(X) \wedge in_T(Y) \wedge in_T(X\, \texttt{logOp}\, Y),$

$(\neg in_T(X) \vee \neg in_T(Y)) \rightarrow \{\texttt{slhs}{:=}X\, \texttt{logOp}\, Y\}\langle\!\langle \pi\ \omega \rangle\!\rangle \phi$

and

(22)

$\vdash in_T(X) \wedge in_T(Y) \wedge in_T(X\, \texttt{logOp}\, Y),$

$\neg(\neg in_T(X) \vee \neg in_T(Y)) \rightarrow \{\texttt{slhs}{:=}\texttt{overflow}(X, Y, \prime \circ \prime)\}\langle\!\langle \pi\ \omega \rangle\!\rangle \phi$

Then from (22) we get by rule (R10)

(23)

$\neg(\neg in_T(X) \vee \neg in_T(Y)) \vdash$

$in_T(X) \wedge in_T(Y) \wedge in_T(X\, \texttt{logOp}\, Y), \{\texttt{slhs}{:=}\texttt{overflow}(X, Y, \prime \circ \prime)\}\langle\!\langle \pi\ \omega \rangle\!\rangle \phi$

here we cheat a little bit to make the proof shorter and write $(in_T(X) \wedge in_T(Y))$ instead of $\neg(\neg in_T(X) \vee \neg in_T(Y))$. The formulas are equivalent but there is no explicit rule for this conversion. Thus we get:

(24)

$in_T(X) \wedge in_T(Y) \vdash$

$in_T(X) \wedge in_T(Y) \wedge in_T(X\, \texttt{logOp}\, Y), \{\texttt{slhs}{:=}\texttt{overflow}(X, Y, \prime \circ \prime)\}\langle\!\langle \pi\ \omega \rangle\!\rangle \phi$

By (R8)

(26a)

$in_T(X), in_T(Y) \vdash in_T(X), \{\texttt{slhs}{:=}\texttt{overflow}(X, Y, \prime \circ \prime)\}\langle\!\langle \pi\ \omega \rangle\!\rangle \phi$

which is closed due to $in_T(X) \vdash in_T(X)$

(26b)

$in_T(X), in_T(Y) \vdash in_T(Y), \{\texttt{slhs}{:=}\texttt{overflow}(X, Y, \prime \circ \prime)\}\langle\!\langle \pi\ \omega \rangle\!\rangle \phi$

which is closed due to $in_T(Y) \vdash in_T(Y)$

(26c)
$in_T(X), in_T(Y) \vdash in_T(X\, \texttt{logOp}\, Y), \{\texttt{slhs}:=\texttt{overflow}(X, Y, \prime\circ\prime)\}\langle\!\{\pi\ \omega\}\!\rangle\phi$
which is equivalent to
(26d)
$in_T(X), in_T(Y), \neg in_T(X\, \texttt{logOp}\, Y) \vdash \{\texttt{slhs}:=\texttt{overflow}(X, Y, \prime\circ\prime)\}\langle\!\{\pi\ \omega\}\!\rangle\phi$
We return back to (21):
$\vdash in_T(X) \wedge in_T(Y) \wedge in_T(X\, \texttt{logOp}\, Y),$
$(\neg in_T(X) \vee \neg in_T(Y)) \rightarrow \{\texttt{slhs}:=X\, \texttt{logOp}\, Y\}\langle\!\{\pi\ \omega\}\!\rangle\phi$
which is a consequence by rule (R10) from:
$(\neg in_T(X) \vee \neg in_T(Y)) \vdash$
$in_T(X) \wedge in_T(Y) \wedge in_T(X\, \texttt{logOp}\, Y), \{\texttt{slhs}:=X\, \texttt{logOp}\, Y\}\langle\!\{\pi\ \omega\}\!\rangle\phi$
Again we cheat a little bit and write $\neg(in_T(X) \wedge in_T(Y))$ instead of $(\neg in_T(X) \vee \neg in_T(Y))$ which is however an equivalent formula.
(27)
$\neg(in_T(X) \wedge in_T(Y)) \vdash$
$in_T(X) \wedge in_T(Y) \wedge in_T(X\, \texttt{logOp}\, Y), \{\texttt{slhs}:=X\, \texttt{logOp}\, Y\}\langle\!\{\pi\ \omega\}\!\rangle\phi$
By due to rule (R12) we write
(28)
$\neg(in_T(X) \wedge in_T(Y)) \vdash \{\texttt{slhs}:=X\, \texttt{logOp}\, Y\}\langle\!\{\pi\ \omega\}\!\rangle\phi$
Now we return back to (7):
(7) $\vdash \mathit{srhs}_1\ \mathit{op}\ \mathit{srhs}_2 \neq \texttt{overflow}(\mathit{srhs}_1, \mathit{srhs}_2, \prime op\prime)$
By rule (R1.1.3) we get:
(30)

$$\vdash \left(\begin{array}{l} \text{if } in_T(X) \wedge in_T(Y) \wedge in_T(X\, \texttt{logOp}\, Y) \text{ then} \\ \qquad\qquad X\, \texttt{logOp}\, Y \\ \text{else if} \neg in_T(X) \vee \neg in_T(Y) \text{ then} \\ \qquad\qquad X\, \texttt{logOp}\, Y \\ \text{else } \texttt{overflow}(X, Y, \prime\circ\prime) \text{ fi fi} \end{array}\right) \neq \texttt{overflow}(\mathit{srhs}_1, \mathit{srhs}_2, \prime op\prime)$$

Again we write X and Y instead of srhs_1 and srhs_2 respectively for a shorter notation. We get a little bit "sloppy" here an skip the application of many rules. Since

$$X\, \texttt{logOp}\, Y \neq \texttt{overflow}(X, Y, \prime op\prime) \equiv \mathit{true}$$

the only "interesting" case is where the if-cascade of (30) has the value $\texttt{overflow}(X, Y, \prime op\prime)$. In this case the succedent is *false* and we have to *falsify* the premiss (any formula of the antecedent). When we look at the sequent (26d):

$in_T(X), in_T(Y), \neg in_T(X\,\mathtt{logOp}\,Y) \vdash \{\mathtt{slhs} := \mathtt{overflow}(X, Y, \prime o \prime)\}\langle\!\{\pi\ \omega\}\!\rangle\phi$

and compare it with the sequent (7) or (30) then we can assume that we obtain the proof obligation:

(31)

$in_T(X), in_T(Y), \neg in_T(X\,\mathtt{logOp}\,Y) \vdash \mathtt{overflow}(X, Y, \prime op \prime) \neq \mathtt{overflow}(X, Y, \prime op \prime)$

which is the same as:

(32)

$in_T(X), in_T(Y), \neg in_T(X\,\mathtt{logOp}\,Y) \vdash \mathit{false}$

By rule (R12) we get finally:

(33)

$in_T(X), in_T(Y), \neg in_T(X\,\mathtt{logOp}\,Y) \vdash$

Thus the proof obligation (26d) can be left out, because it is subsumed by the proof obligation (33). And this is exactly what is the description of premiss six of rule 6.4.2 says, namely that the formula in the succedent of the sequent (26d) can be left out. In DLJ the reason is that the method `overflow` is unspecified. We obtain the same effect for the proof by plugging it into the definition of the predicate *isdef*.

We have ignored one detail however. It is possible that $X\,\mathtt{logOp}\,Y \doteq \mathtt{overflow}(X, Y, \prime op \prime)$. This is the case if `logOp` is the division function and the divisor is zero. In this case the result is undefined and definition 4.28 takes its effect, which states that the result is `overflow(X,Y,'/')`. Thus the definition of the predicate *isdef* is prepared to handle the value of `overflow`, which may be caused by division by zero, but a rule is missing which generates this value. This can be simply integrated into another rule of the form of rule (R1.1.3) that is specialized for division. Providing this rule the inference of sequent (7) generates additionally the proof obligation

(34)

$$\vdash \neg \mathtt{srhs}_2 \doteq 0$$

Thus we end up with the proof obligations[7.1]:

(1) $\vdash \mathit{isdef}(\mathtt{slhs})$

(5) $\vdash \mathit{isdef}(\mathtt{srhs}_1)$

(6) $\vdash \mathit{isdef}(\mathtt{srhs}_2)$

(34) $\vdash \neg \mathtt{srhs}_2 \doteq 0$

(17) $in_T(X) \wedge in_T(Y) \wedge in_T(X\,\mathtt{logOp}\,Y) \vdash \{\mathtt{slhs} := X\ \mathtt{logOp}\ Y\}\langle\!\{\pi\ \omega\}\!\rangle\phi$

7.1. *context free inference* and *contextual lifting* lemmas are applied implicitly.

(33) $in_T(X), in_T(Y), \neg in_T(X\,\texttt{logOp}\,Y) \vdash$

(28) $\neg(in_T(X) \wedge in_T(Y)) \vdash \{\texttt{slhs}:=X\,\texttt{logOp}\,Y\}\langle\!\{\pi\ \omega\}\!\rangle\phi$

These proof obligations are exactly the same as the proof obligations obtained from rule (R 6.4.2).[7.2] Therefore we have proven that (R 6.4.2) is a derived rule of our calculus. ■

7.4.2 Rules for Simplifying Compound Expressions

The simplification rules for compound expressions seem to be not necessary in case of C0 and MISRA C because expressions in C0 and MISRA C are free of side effects.[7.3] However, due to the refinement of integral data types to arithmetical types, constrains have to be added for sub-expressions. In order for the rules which add constrains to be applicable, the expressions have to be reduced to contain at most one operator. In JavaCardDL the simplification of expressions has additionally the purpose to handle side effects in expressions.

Rule 6.3.1 *parentheses-elimination*

Purpose Elimination or redundant parentheses.

Remark The rule for the box operator $[\!\{.\}\!]$ is analogous.

$$\frac{\Gamma \vdash \mu\ \langle\!\{\pi\texttt{lexpr=rexpr;}\omega\}\!\rangle\phi\,,\Delta}{\Gamma \vdash \mu\ \langle\!\{\pi\texttt{lexpr=(rexpr);}\omega\}\!\rangle\phi\,,\Delta}$$

Description This rule transforms a statement containing pair of redundant parentheses into a semantically equivalent statement without the redundant parenthesis.

Rule 6.3.2 *array-access-simplification*

Purpose Simplification of a non-simple array access.

Requirements At least one of $\texttt{rexpr}_1 \ldots \texttt{rexpr}_n$ must not be a $\texttt{srhs}$.

Remark The rule for the box operator $[\!\{.\}\!]$ is analogous.

$$\frac{\begin{array}{c}\Gamma \vdash \mu\ isdef(\texttt{slhs}),\Delta \\ \Gamma \vdash \mu\ \langle\!\{\pi\ \texttt{b=a;x}_1\texttt{=rexpr}_1\texttt{;}\ldots\texttt{x}_n\texttt{=rexpr}_n\texttt{;} \\ \qquad\qquad \texttt{lexpr=b[x}_1\texttt{]}\ldots\texttt{[x}_n\texttt{];}\ \omega\}\!\rangle\phi\,,\Delta\end{array}}{\Gamma \vdash \mu\ \langle\!\{\pi\ \texttt{lexpr=a[rexpr}_1\texttt{]}\ldots\texttt{[rexpr}_n\texttt{];}\ \omega\}\!\rangle\phi\,,\Delta}$$

7.2. Under consideration of the description of (R 6.4.2) about the premiss number six.

7.3. In MISRA C expressions have to evaluate to the same value under any order of evaluation the standard permits and the standard does not specify the order of evaluation of operands.

Description

- a is a *rexpr* of an array type
- *b* is a new simple program variable of the type of a.
- x_i is a new simple program variable of the type of $expr_i$.

This rule transforms a non-simple array access into an implicit program variable which is an array access. This means, after the transformation, the array indices are simple expressions.

Rule 6.3.3 *left-hand-side-array-assignment-simplification*

Purpose Simplification of a non-simple left-hand side array access.

Requirements At least one of $rexpr_1, \ldots, rexpr_n$ must not be a *srhs*

Remark The rule for the box operator [{.}] is analogous.

$$\frac{\Gamma \vdash \mu \langle\!\{ \pi\ b\texttt{=a};x_1\texttt{=}rexpr_1;\ldots x_n\texttt{=}rexpr_n;\ b\texttt{[}x_1\texttt{]}\ldots\texttt{[}x_n\texttt{]} = rexpr;\omega \}\!\rangle \phi, \Delta}{\Gamma \vdash \mu \langle\!\{ \pi\ \texttt{a}\texttt{[}rexpr_1\texttt{]}\ldots\texttt{[}rexpr_n\texttt{]} = rexpr;\omega \}\!\rangle \phi, \Delta}$$

Description

- a is an lexpression of an array type
- *b* is a new simple program variable of the type of a.
- x_i is a new simple program variable of the type of $expr_i$.

This rule transforms a non-simple array access on the left-hand side of an assignment into a simple array access. This means, after the transformation, the array indices are *slhs* and the array access is a *slhs*.

Rule 6.3.6 *compound-binary-expression-simplification*

Purpose Simplification of a statement containing compound arithmetical expressions.

Requirements At least one of $rexpr_1, \ldots, rexpr_n$ must not be a *srhs*

Remark The rule for the box operator [{.}] is analogous.

$$\frac{\Gamma \vdash \mu\, isdef(lexpr), \Delta \qquad \Gamma \vdash \mu \langle\!\{ \pi\ y\texttt{=}lexpr_1;\ z\texttt{=}rexpr_2;\ lexpr\texttt{=}y\ op\ z;\ \omega \}\!\rangle \phi, \Delta}{\Gamma \vdash \mu \langle\!\{ \pi\ lexpr\texttt{=}rexpr_1\ op\ rexpr_2;\omega \}\!\rangle \phi, \Delta}$$

Description

- `op` is one of the binary arithmetical operators `*`, `/`, `%`, `+`, `-`, `<<`, `>>`, `&`, `|`, `^` or one of the comparison operators `<`, `>`, `<=`, `>=`, `==`, `!=`
- y is a new simple program variable of type of the expression $\texttt{rexpr}_1$.
- z is a new simple program variable of type of the expression $\texttt{rexpr}_2$.

This rule transforms a statement containing a compound binary expression into a semantically equivalent sequence of statements in which at first the compound expression are evaluated. The results of the evaluations are stored in new variables and finally, the binary operator is applied to the new variables.

The requirement, that at least one of both arguments has to be a compound expression, ensures that this rule is not applicable arbitrary often. Applying this rule more than one time does not contribute to further simplification of the program and might result in a loop when applying this rule automatically.

Rule 6.3.7 *compound-unary-expression-simplification*

Purpose Simplification of a statement containing compound unary operator applied.

Requirements `rexpr` is not a `slhs`.

Remark The rule for the box operator $[\!\{.\}\!]$ is analogous.

$$\frac{\begin{array}{c}\Gamma \vdash \mu\, isdef(\texttt{lexpr}), \Delta \\ \Gamma \vdash \mu \langle\!\{\pi\ \texttt{y=rexpr}_2\texttt{; lexpr= op y;}\ \omega\}\!\rangle \phi, \Delta\end{array}}{\Gamma \vdash \mu \langle\!\{\pi\ \texttt{lexpr = op rexpr}_2\texttt{;}\ \omega\}\!\rangle \phi, \Delta}$$

Description

- `op` is one of the unary arithmetical operators `-`, `~` or the unary boolean negation operator `!`.
- y is a new variable of type of the expression `rexpr`.

This rule transforms a statement containing an unary operator applied to a compound expression into a semantically equivalent sequence of statements in which at first the compound expression is evaluated. The result of this evaluations is stored in new program variables and finally, the unary operator is applied to the new program variables.

As in Rule 6.4.6, the requirement, that the expression *rexpr* is not allowed to be a simple expression, ensures that this rule is not applicable arbitrary often.

7.4.3 Rules for Handling Simple Expressions

Rule 6.4.2 *arithmetical-binary-expression-execution-right*

Purpose Symbolic execution of a binary expression of an arithmetical type for the diamond operator.

Requirements The type of the expression $\texttt{srhs}_1\ op\ \texttt{srhs}_2$ has to be an arithmetical type.

1. $\Gamma \vdash \mu\, isdef(\texttt{slhs}), \Delta$
2. $\Gamma \vdash \mu\, isdef(\texttt{srhs}_1), \Delta$
3. $\Gamma \vdash \mu\, isdef(\texttt{srhs}_2), \Delta$
4. $\Gamma \vdash \mu \neg \texttt{srhs}_2 \doteq 0$
5. $\Gamma\ \mu\, in_{T_1}(\texttt{srhs}_1), \mu\, in_{T_2}(\texttt{srhs}_2), \mu\, in_T(\texttt{srhs}_1\, \texttt{logOp}\, \texttt{srhs}_2 \vdash$ $\mu\, \{\texttt{slhs} := \texttt{srhs}_1\, \texttt{logOp}\, \texttt{srhs}_2\} \langle\!\langle \pi\ \omega \rangle\!\rangle \phi\ , \Delta$
6. $\Gamma\ \mu\, in_{T_1}(\texttt{srhs}_1), \mu\, in_{T_2}(\texttt{srhs}_2), \mu \neg in_T(\texttt{srhs}_1\, \texttt{logOp}\, \texttt{srhs}_2 \vdash$ $\mu \langle\!\langle \pi\ \texttt{slhs = overflow(srhs}_1\texttt{,srhs}_2\texttt{,'op')}\ \omega \rangle\!\rangle \phi\ , \Delta$
7. $\Gamma\ \mu \neg (in_{T_1}(\texttt{srhs}_1) \wedge in_{T_2}(\texttt{srhs}_2)) \vdash$ $\mu\, \{\texttt{slhs} := \texttt{srhs}_1\, \texttt{logOp}\, \texttt{srhs}_2\} \langle\!\langle \pi\ \omega \rangle\!\rangle \phi\ , \Delta$

$$\overline{\Gamma \vdash \mu \langle\!\langle \pi\, \texttt{slhs = srhs}_1\ op\ \texttt{srhs}_2\texttt{;}\ \omega \rangle\!\rangle \phi\, , \Delta}$$

Description

- *op* is one of the binary operators `*`, `/`, `+`, `-`
- `logOp` is the corresponding logical function to the C0 operator *op*:
  - If *op* is `*`, then `logOp` is $*$.
  - If *op* is `/`, then `logOp` is $/$.
  - If *op* is `+`, then `logOp` is $+$.
  - If *op* is `-`, then `logOp` is $-$.
- T_1 is the type of $\texttt{srhs}_1$.
- T_2 is the type of $\texttt{srhs}_2$.
- T is the type of $\texttt{srhs}_1\ op\ \texttt{srhs}_2$.

This rule symbolically executes an assignment statement where the right-hand side is a binary expression of an arithmetical type.

The grey shaded premiss number four only applies if `op` is the division operator `/` , otherwise this premiss has to be ignored. It ensures that the divisor is not zero.

For the explanation of the premises of the rule, we assume that Γ holds and Δ not (otherwise the rule is applicable trivially).

Premiss number five states that, if the arguments are in valid range and the result is in valid range as well (and thus no overflow occurs), the arithmetical C0 operation is symbolically executed. This results in an update attached to the formula.

Premiss number six states that, if the arguments are in valid range but the result would be not, the result of the arithmetical C0 operation is the return value of the function invocation of `overflow`. Since we are using semantics S_{KeY}, we have no specification for the function `overflow` and thus, the formula $\langle\!\{\pi$ `slhs = overflow(srhs`$_1$`,srhs`$_2$`,'op')` $\omega\}\!\rangle\phi$ is unsatisfiable. Therefore, this formula could be left out without changing the semantics of the rule.

Premiss number seven is for the case that at least one argument is not in valid range. This can only happen in unreal states and thus, overflow is allowed since it does not affect the behavior of the program during the execution on the virtual machine execution C0 because unreal states are not reachable by the virtual machine.

An equivalent variant of this rule would be to replace the premises number five and seven with the single premiss

$$\Gamma\ \mu\ in_T(\mathtt{srhs}_1\ \mathtt{logOp}\ \mathtt{srhs}_2) \vdash$$
$$\mu\ \{\mathtt{slhs} := \mathtt{srhs}_1\ \mathtt{logOp}\ \mathtt{srhs}_2\} \langle\!\{\pi\ \ \omega\}\!\rangle \phi\ , \Delta$$

From the above sequent the other two sequents are derivable by applying cut and weekening rules.

Note, that `op` must be non of the bit operators because bit operators are not allowed to be applied to expressions of the arithmetical types.

Rule 6.4.3 *arithmetical-binary-expression-execution-left*

Purpose Symbolic execution of a binary expression of an arithmetical type for the box operator.

Requirements The type of the expression $\texttt{srhs}_1\ op\ \texttt{srhs}_2$ has to be an arithmetical type.

$$
\frac{
\begin{array}{l}
1.\ \Gamma \vdash \mu\, isdef(\texttt{slhs})\,, \Delta \\
2.\ \Gamma \vdash \mu\, isdef(\texttt{srhs}_1)\,, \Delta \\
3.\ \Gamma \vdash \mu\, isdef(\texttt{srhs}_2)\,, \Delta \\
4.\ \Gamma \vdash \mu \neg \texttt{srhs}_2 \doteq 0 \\
5.\ \Gamma\ \mu in_{T_1}(\texttt{srhs}_1), \mu\, in_{T_2}(\texttt{srhs}_2), \mu\, in_T(\texttt{srhs}_1\, \texttt{logOp}\, \texttt{srhs}_2 \vdash \\
\quad \mu\, \{\texttt{slhs} := \texttt{srhs}_1\, \texttt{logOp}\, \texttt{srhs}_2\} [\![\pi\ \omega]\!] \phi\ , \Delta \\
6.\ \Gamma\ \mu\, in_{T_1}(\texttt{srhs}_1), \mu\, in_{T_2}(\texttt{srhs}_2), \mu \neg in_T(\texttt{srhs}_1\, \texttt{logOp}\, \texttt{srhs}_2 \vdash \\
\quad \mu [\![\pi\ \texttt{slhs = overflow(srhs}_1\texttt{,srhs}_2\texttt{,'op')}\ \omega]\!] \phi\ , \Delta \\
7.\ \Gamma\ \mu \neg (in_{T_1}(\texttt{srhs}_1) \wedge in_{T_2}(\texttt{srhs}_2)) \vdash \\
\quad \mu\, \{\texttt{slhs} := \texttt{srhs}_1\, \texttt{logOp}\, \texttt{srhs}_2\} [\![\pi\ \omega]\!] \phi\, , \Delta
\end{array}
}{
\Gamma \vdash \mu [\![\pi\, \texttt{slhs = srhs}_1\ \texttt{op}\ \texttt{srhs}_2\texttt{;}\, \omega]\!] \phi\, , \Delta
}
$$

Description

- `op` is one of the binary operators `*`, `/`, `+`, `-`
- `logOp` is the corresponding logical function to the C0 operator `op`:
  - If `op` is `*`, then `logOp` is $*$.
  - If `op` is `/`, then `logOp` is $/$.
  - If `op` is `+`, then `logOp` is $+$.
  - If `op` is `-`, then `logOp` is $-$.
- T_1 is the type of $\texttt{srhs}_1$.
- T_2 is the type of $\texttt{srhs}_2$.
- T is the type of $\texttt{srhs}_1\ op\ \texttt{srhs}_2$.

This rule symbolically executes an assignment statement where the right-hand side is a binary expression of an arithmetical type.

For a description of the rule we refer to the description of rule 6.4.2 except for the difference that in contrast to Rule 6.4.2, the formula $\mu[\![\pi\ \texttt{slhs = overflow(srhs}_1\texttt{,srhs}_2\texttt{,'op')}\ \omega]\!]\phi$ is satisfiable in S_{KeY} if ϕ evaluates to *true* (in this case ϕ is even valid) and therefore may not be left out.

Rule 6.4.5 *built-in-binary-expression-execution*

Purpose Symbolic execution of a binary expression of a built-in type.

Requirements The type of the expression $\mathtt{srhs}_1\ \mathit{op}\ \mathtt{srhs}_2$ has to be a built-in type

Remark The rule for the box operator $[\![\{.\}]\!]$ is analogous.

$$\frac{\begin{array}{l} 1.\ \Gamma \vdash \mu\, \mathit{isdef}(\mathtt{slhs}), \Delta \\ 2.\ \Gamma \vdash \mu\, \mathit{isdef}(\mathtt{srhs}_1), \Delta \\ 3.\ \Gamma \vdash \mu\, \mathit{isdef}(\mathtt{srhs}_2), \Delta \\ 4.\ \Gamma \vdash \mu \neg \mathtt{srhs}_2 \doteq 0 \\ 5.\ \Gamma \vdash \mu\, \{\mathtt{slhs} := \mathtt{srhs}_1\, \mathtt{logOp}\, \mathtt{srhs}_2\} \langle\!\langle \{\pi\ \ \omega\} \rangle\!\rangle \phi, \Delta \end{array}}{\Gamma \vdash \mu\, [\![\{\pi\, \mathtt{slhs}\ =\ \mathtt{srhs}_1\ \mathit{op}\ \mathtt{srhs}_2; \omega\}]\!] \phi, \Delta}$$

Description

- *op* is one of the binary operators `*`, `/`, `+`, `-`, `<<`, `>>`, `&`, `|`, and `^`
- `logOp` is the corresponding logical function to the C0 operator *op*:
  - If *op* is `*`, then `logOp` is CMul_T.
  - If *op* is `/`, then `logOp` is CDiv_T.
  - If *op* is `+`, then `logOp` is CPlus_T.
  - If *op* is `-`, then `logOp` is CMinus_T.
  - If *op* is `<<`, then `logOp` is $\overline{\texttt{<<}}_T$.
  - If *op* is `>>`, then `logOp` is $\overline{\texttt{>>}}_T$.
  - If *op* is `&`, then `logOp` is $\overline{\texttt{\&}}_T$.
  - If *op* is `|`, then `logOp` is $\overline{\texttt{|}}_T$.
  - If *op* is `^`, then `logOp` is $\overline{\texttt{\^{}}}_T$.
- T_1 is the type of $\mathtt{srhs}_1$.
- T_2 is the type of $\mathtt{srhs}_2$.
- T is the type of $\mathtt{srhs}_1\ \mathit{op}\ \mathtt{srhs}_2$.

This rule symbolically executes an assignment statement where the right-hand side is a binary expression of a build-in type.

The grey shaded premiss number four only applied if *op* is the division operator `/`, otherwise this premiss has to be ignored. It ensures that the divisor is not zero.

7.4.4 Rules for Handling Unary Operators

Rule 6.5.1 *unary-plus*

Purpose Symbolic execution of the unary plus operator applied to a simple expression.

Remark The rule for the box operator $[\![.]\!]$ is analogous.

$$\frac{\begin{array}{l}1.\ \Gamma \vdash \mathit{isdef}(\texttt{slhs}),\Delta\\ 2.\ \Gamma \vdash \mathit{isdef}(\texttt{srhs}),\Delta\\ 3.\ \Gamma \vdash \mu\,\{\texttt{slhs} := \texttt{srhs}\}\langle\!\langle\pi\ \ \omega\rangle\!\rangle\phi,\Delta\end{array}}{\Gamma \vdash \mu\,\langle\!\langle\pi\ \texttt{slhs =+srhs;}\ \omega\rangle\!\rangle\phi,\Delta}$$

Description This rule symbolically executes the unary plus operator. This actually means just to remove the operator because the unary plus operator does not change the value of the argument and an unary plus expression has no side-effects.

In contrast to the unary minus operator, there is only one rule for the unary plus operator as well for the built-in types as for the arithmetical types since the unary plus operator cannot cause overflow.

Rule 6.5.2 *arithmetical-unary-minus*

Purpose Symbolic execution of the unary minus operator applied to a simple expression of an arithmetical type for the diamond operator.

Requirements The type of `srhs` has to be an arithmetical type.

Remark The rule for the box operator $[\![.]\!]$ is analogous.

$$\frac{\begin{array}{l}1.\ \Gamma \vdash \mu\,\mathit{isdef}(\texttt{slhs}),\Delta\\ 2.\ \Gamma \vdash \mu\,\mathit{isdef}(\texttt{srhs}),\Delta\\ 3.\ \Gamma,\ \mu\,\texttt{srhs} \doteq \mathrm{MIN\_}T \vdash\\ \quad \mu\,\langle\!\langle\pi\ \texttt{slhs = overflow(srhs,'-');}\omega\rangle\!\rangle\phi,\Delta\\ 4.\ \Gamma\ \mu\,\neg\texttt{srhs} \doteq \mathrm{MIN\_}T \vdash \mu\,\{\texttt{slhs} := -\,\texttt{srhs}\}\langle\!\langle\pi\ \ \omega\rangle\!\rangle\phi,\Delta\end{array}}{\Gamma \vdash \mu\,\langle\!\langle\pi\ \texttt{slhs =-srhs;}\ \omega\rangle\!\rangle\phi,\Delta}$$

Description

- T is the type of `srhs`,
- MIN_T is the minimum value of the corresponding built-in type of the arithmetical type T.

This rule symbolically executes the assignment of an unary minus expression of an arithmetical type.

To explain the premises, we assume that Γ holds and Δ not (otherwise the rule is applicable trivially).

The third premiss applies to the case that **srhs** is equal to the minimum value MIN_T of the corresponding built-in type of T. In this case. Thus, the result of the unary minus expression is the return value of the function invocation of `overflow`.

The forth premiss states that the result of the unary minus expression is the mathematical negation of the value of **srhs**, if **srhs** is different from MIN_T. In this case, in real states no overflow occurs. In unreal states overflow occurs but is allowed since unreal states are not reachable by the machine executing the C0 program.

Rule 6.5.4 *build-in-unary-minus*

Purpose Symbolic execution of the unary minus operator applied to a simple expression of a build-in type.

Requirements The type of **srhs** has to be a build-in type.

Remark The rule for the box operator $[\![.]\!]$ is analogous.

$$\frac{\begin{array}{l}1.\ \Gamma \vdash \mu\, isdef(\mathtt{slhs}), \Delta \\ 2.\ \Gamma \vdash \mu\, isdef(\mathtt{srhs}), \Delta \\ 3.\ \Gamma\, \mu\, \mathtt{srhs} \doteq \mathrm{MIN\_}T \vdash \mu\, \{\mathtt{slhs} := \mathtt{srhs}\}\langle\!\{\pi\ \omega\}\!\rangle\phi, \Delta \\ 4.\ \Gamma\, \mu \neg \mathtt{srhs} \doteq \mathrm{MIN\_}T \vdash \mu\, \{\mathtt{slhs} := -\,\mathtt{srhs}\}\langle\!\{\pi\ \omega\}\!\rangle\phi, \Delta\end{array}}{\Gamma \vdash \mu\, \langle\!\{\pi\ \mathtt{slhs\ =\text{-}srhs;}\ \omega\}\!\rangle\phi, \Delta}$$

Description

- T is the type of **srhs**,
- MIN_T is the minimum value of type T.

To explain the premises, we assume that Γ holds and Δ not (otherwise the rule is applicable trivially).

The third premiss applies to the case that **srhs** is equal to the minimum value MIN_T of type of T. In this case overflow occurs and the result value of the unary minus expression is the same as the value of **srhs**.

The fourth premiss states that the result of the unary minus expression is the mathematical negation of the value of `srhs`, if `srhs` is different from MIN_T, because in this case no overflow occurs.

Rule 6.5.4 *build-in-bitwise-complement*

Purpose Symbolic execution of the bitwise complement operator.

Requirements The type of `srhs` has to be a build-in type.

Remark The rule for the box operator $[\!\{.\}\!]$ is analogous.

$$\frac{\begin{array}{l} 1.\ \Gamma \vdash \mathit{isdef}(\texttt{slhs}), \Delta \\ 2.\ \Gamma \vdash \mathit{isdef}(\texttt{srhs}), \Delta \\ 3.\ \Gamma\, \texttt{srhs} \doteq \mathrm{MIN\_}T \vdash \mu\, \{\texttt{slhs} := \tilde{\ }_T(\texttt{srhs})\}\langle\!\{\pi\ \omega\}\!\rangle\phi, \Delta \end{array}}{\Gamma \vdash \mu\, \langle\!\{\pi\ \texttt{slhs =\~{}srhs;}\ \omega\}\!\rangle\phi, \Delta}$$

Description

- T is the type of `srhs`,
- MIN_T is the minimum value of type T.

This rule symbolically executes the bitwise complement operator applied to a simple expression of a built-in type. Not, that bit operators are not allowed to be applied to arithmetical types.

7.4.5 Rules for Handling Increment and Decrement Expressions

The following rules are not relevant for C0 but they are listed here because they are useful for a calculus for handling MISRA C. Note, that in MISRA C increment and decrement operators must not be mixed in expressions with other operators. Furthermore, note that in contrast to the other rules, the increment and decrement operators are applied to a simple left-hand side instead of a simple right-hand. The reason for that is that these operators are not allowed to be applied to literals for example (which are simple right-hand sides) because the argument of the operator must evaluate to a variable.

Rule 6.6.1 *prefix-increment-expression*

Purpose Transformation of a prefix increment expression into a MISRA C addition.

Remark The rule for the box operator $[\!\{.\}\!]$ is analogous.

$$\frac{\begin{array}{l}1.\ \Gamma \vdash \mu\, \mathit{isdef}(\texttt{slhs}), \Delta \\ 2.\ \Gamma \vdash \mu \langle\!\{\pi\ \texttt{slhs}_2\texttt{=(}T\texttt{)(slhs}_2\texttt{+1);slhs}_1\texttt{=slhs}_2\texttt{;}\ \omega\}\!\rangle \phi, \Delta\end{array}}{\Gamma \vdash \mu \langle\!\{\pi\ \texttt{slhs}_1\ \texttt{=++srhs}_2\texttt{;}\ \omega\}\!\rangle \phi, \Delta}$$

Description T is the type of $\texttt{slhs}_1$.

Rule 6.6.2 *prefix-decrement-expression*

Purpose Transformation of a prefix increment expression into a MISRA C subtraction.

Remark The rule for the box operator $[\!\{.\}\!]$ is analogous.

$$\frac{\begin{array}{l}1.\ \Gamma \vdash \mathit{isdef}(\texttt{slhs}), \Delta \\ 2.\ \Gamma \vdash \mu \langle\!\{\pi\ \texttt{slhs}_2\texttt{=(}T\texttt{)(slhs}_2\ \texttt{- 1);slhs}_1\texttt{=slhs}_2\texttt{;}\ \omega\}\!\rangle \phi, \Delta\end{array}}{\Gamma \vdash \mu \langle\!\{\pi\ \texttt{slhs}_1\ \texttt{=--srhs}_2\texttt{;}\ \omega\}\!\rangle \phi, \Delta}$$

Description T is the promoted type of $\texttt{slhs}_1$.

Rule 6.6.3 *prefix-increment-statement*

Purpose Transformation of a prefix increment statement into a MISRA C addition.

Remark The rule for the box operator $[\!\{.\}\!]$ is analogous.

$$\frac{\Gamma \vdash \mu \langle\!\{\pi\ \texttt{slhs=(}T\texttt{)(slhs+1);}\ \omega\}\!\rangle \phi, \Delta}{\Gamma \vdash \mu \langle\!\{\pi\ \texttt{++srhs;}\ \omega\}\!\rangle \phi, \Delta}$$

Description T is the promoted type of $\texttt{slhs}$.

Rule 6.6.4 *prefix-decrement-statement*

Purpose Transformation of a prefix decrement statement into a MISRA C subtraction.

Remark The rule for the box operator $[\!\{.\}\!]$ is analogous.

$$\frac{\Gamma \vdash \mu \langle\!\{\pi\ \texttt{slhs=(}T\texttt{)(slhs-1);}\ \omega\}\!\rangle \phi, \Delta}{\Gamma \vdash \mu \langle\!\{\pi\ \texttt{--srhs;}\ \omega\}\!\rangle \phi, \Delta}$$

Description T is the promoted type of $\texttt{slhs}$.

Rule 6.6.5 *postfix-increment-expression*

Purpose Transformation of a postfix increment expression into a MISRA C addition.

Remark The rule for the box operator $[\!\{.\}\!]$ is analogous.

$$\frac{\Gamma \vdash \mu \langle\!\{\pi\ \texttt{slhs}_1\texttt{=}\texttt{slhs}_2\texttt{;}\texttt{slhs}_2\texttt{=(}T\texttt{)(}\texttt{slhs}_2\texttt{+1);}\ \omega\}\!\rangle \phi, \Delta}{\Gamma \vdash \mu \langle\!\{\pi\ \texttt{slhs}_1\ \texttt{=}\ \texttt{srhs}_2\texttt{++;}\ \omega\}\!\rangle \phi, \Delta}$$

Description T is the promoted type of $\texttt{slhs}_1$.

Rule 6.6.6 *postfix-decrement-expression*

Purpose Transformation of a postfix decrement expression into a MISRA C addition.

Remark The rule for the box operator $[\![\{.\}]\!]$ is analogous.

$$\frac{\Gamma \vdash \mu \langle\!\{\pi\ \texttt{slhs}_1\texttt{=}\texttt{slhs}_2\texttt{;}\texttt{slhs}_2\texttt{=(}T\texttt{)(}\texttt{slhs}_2\texttt{-1);}\ \omega\}\!\rangle \phi, \Delta}{\Gamma \vdash \mu \langle\!\{\pi\ \texttt{slhs}_1\ \texttt{=}\ \texttt{srhs}_2\texttt{--;}\ \omega\}\!\rangle \phi, \Delta}$$

Description T is the promoted type of $\texttt{slhs}_1$.

Rule 6.6.7 *postfix-increment-statement*

Purpose Transformation of a postfix decrement statement into a MISRA C addition.

Remark The rule for the box operator $[\![\{.\}]\!]$ is analogous.

$$\frac{\Gamma \vdash \mu \langle\!\{\pi\ \texttt{slhs=(}T\texttt{)(slhs+1);}\ \omega\}\!\rangle \phi, \Delta}{\Gamma \vdash \mu \langle\!\{\pi\ \texttt{srhs++;}\ \omega\}\!\rangle \phi, \Delta}$$

Description T is the promoted type of $\texttt{slhs}$.

Rule 6.6.8 *postfix-decrement-statement*

Purpose Transformation of a postfix decrement statement into a MISRA C subtraction.

Remark The rule for the box operator $[\![\{.\}]\!]$ is analogous.

$$\frac{\Gamma \vdash \mu \langle\!\{\pi\ \texttt{slhs=(}T\texttt{)(slhs-1);}\ \omega\}\!\rangle \phi, \Delta}{\Gamma \vdash \mu \langle\!\{\pi\ \texttt{srhs--;}\ \omega\}\!\rangle \phi, \Delta}$$

Description T is the promoted type of $\texttt{slhs}$.

7.4.6 Rules for Handling Type Casts

Note, that casts from an arithmetical type to a built-in type are always "narrowing" casts which may cause the invocation of the function `overflow` if overflow occurs.

Rule 6.7.1 *cast-simplification*

Purpose Simplification of a cast operator applied to a non-simple expression.

Requirements `rexpr` must not be a `srhs`.

Remark The rule for the box operators is analogous. We use the same symbol T for the type and type cast operation.

$$\frac{\begin{array}{l} 1.\ \Gamma \vdash \mu\, isdef(\texttt{slhs}), \Delta \\ 2.\ \Gamma \vdash \mu \langle\!\{\pi\ \texttt{x=expr; slhs=T(x);}\ \omega\}\!\rangle \phi, \Delta \end{array}}{\Gamma \vdash \mu \langle\!\{\pi\ \texttt{slhs =T(rexpr);}\ \omega\}\!\rangle \phi, \Delta}$$

Description x is a new program variable of the type of the expression `rexpr`.

This rule simplifies an assignment statement containing a cast operator applied to a non-simple expression by transforming the assignment statement into two statements where at first the non-simple expression is evaluated and then assigned to a new variable. Finally, the cast operator is applied to this new variable.

Rule 6.7.2 *widening-(or-identity-)cast*

Purpose Symbolic execution of a widening or identity type cast.

Requirements For the type S of `srhs` holds that either S and the target type T of the cast operation are equal of $S \prec^* T$.

Remark The rule for the box operators is analogous. We use the same symbol T for the type and type cast operation.

$$\frac{\begin{array}{l} 1.\ \Gamma \vdash \mu\, isdef(\texttt{slhs}), \Delta \\ 2.\ \Gamma \vdash \mu\, isdef(\texttt{srhs}), \Delta \\ 3.\ \Gamma \vdash \mu \{\texttt{slhs} := \texttt{srhs}\} \langle\!\{\pi\ \omega\}\!\rangle \phi, \Delta \end{array}}{\Gamma \vdash \mu \langle\!\{\pi\ \texttt{slhs =T(srhs);}\ \omega\}\!\rangle \phi, \Delta}$$

Description T is the type cast operator type of the cast operation.

This rule symbolically executes a "widening" type cast. Basically, widening an identity type cast cannot cause overflow and thus, there is only one rule for built-in types and arithmetical types.

Rule 6.7.3 *built-in-types-narrowing-cast*

Purpose Symbolic execution of a narrowing cast from a built-in type to another built-in type.

Requirements For the type S of **srhs** and the target type T of the cast operation holds $S \prec^* T$.

Remark The rule for the box operators is analogous. We use the same symbol T for the type and type cast operation.

$$\frac{\begin{array}{l} 1.\ \Gamma \vdash \mu\, \mathit{isdef}(\mathtt{slhs})\,,\Delta \\ 2.\ \Gamma \vdash \mu\, \mathit{isdef}(\mathtt{srhs})\,,\Delta \\ 3.\ \Gamma \vdash \mu\,\{\mathtt{slhs} := \mathit{overflow}_T(\mathtt{srhs})\}\langle\!\{\pi\ \ \omega\}\!\rangle\phi\,,\Delta \end{array}}{\Gamma \vdash \mu\,\langle\!\{\pi\ \ \mathtt{slhs\ =T(srhs);}\ \ \omega\}\!\rangle\phi\,,\Delta}$$

Description T is the target type of the cast operation.

This rule symbolically executes a narrowing type cast from a built-in type to another built-in type.

Rule 6.7.4 *arithmetical-narrowing-cast*

Purpose Symbolic execution of a narrowing cast from an arithmetical type to another arithmetical type to a built-in type for the diamond operator.

Requirements

- The target type T of the cast operation has to be an arithmetical type.
- For the types S of **srhs** and T hold $T \prec^* S$.

Remark The rule for the box operator is similar; see description below. We use the same symbol T for the type and type cast operation.

$$\frac{\begin{array}{l} 1.\ \Gamma \vdash \mu\, \mathit{isdef}(\mathtt{slhs})\,,\Delta \\ 2.\ \Gamma \vdash \mu\, \mathit{isdef}(\mathtt{srhs})\,,\Delta \\ 3.\ \Gamma\, \mu\, \mathit{in}_S(\mathtt{srhs}),\, \mu\, \mathit{in}_T(\mathtt{srhs}) \vdash \\ \qquad \mu\,\{\mathtt{slhs} := \mathtt{srhs}\}\langle\!\{\pi\ \ \omega\}\!\rangle\phi\,,\Delta \\ 4.\ \Gamma\, \mu\, \mathit{in}_S(\mathtt{srhs}),\, \mu \neg \mathit{in}_T(\mathtt{srhs}) \vdash \\ \qquad \mu\,\langle\!\{\pi\ \ \mathtt{slhs=overflow(srhs,'cast(}T\mathtt{)')}\ \ \omega\}\!\rangle\phi\,,\Delta \\ 5.\ \Gamma\, \mu \neg \mathit{in}_S(\mathtt{srhs}) \vdash \mu\,\{\mathtt{slhs} := \mathtt{srhs}\}\langle\!\{\pi\ \ \omega\}\!\rangle\phi\,,\Delta \end{array}}{\Gamma \vdash \mu\,\langle\!\{\pi\ \ \mathtt{slhs\ =T(srhs);}\ \ \omega\}\!\rangle\phi\,,\Delta}$$

Description

- S is the type of **srhs**.
- T is the target type of the cast operation.

For the explanation of the premises of the rule, we assume that Γ holds and Δ not.

Premiss number three states that the cast can be symbolically executed if **`srhs`** is in valid range as well of its own type `S` as of the target type `T`, because in this case no overflow occurs.

Premiss number four states that, if **`srhs`** is in valid range of its own type `S` but not of the target type `T`, the result of the cast operation is the return value of the function invocation of `overflow`. Since we are using semantics S_{KeY}, we have no specification for the function `overflow` and thus, the formula is unsatisfiable for the diamond operator and it is satisfiable for the box operator.

Premiss number five applies to the case that **`srhs`** is not in valid range of its own type `S`. This can only happen in unreal states and thus, overflow is allowed since it does not affect the behavior of the C0 program during the exection on the virtual machine because unreal states are not reachable by the virtual machine.

7.4.7 Rules for Conditional Expression and Numeric Comparison Operators

... The rule for conditional expressions performs program transformations whereas expressions containing numeric comparison operators are symbolically executed.

Rule 6.8.2 *equality-comparison*

Purpose Symbolic execution of an equality comparison.

Remark The rule for the box operator $[\![\{.\}]\!]$ is analogous.

$$\frac{\begin{array}{l}1.\ \Gamma \vdash \mu\, \mathit{isdef}(\texttt{slhs}), \Delta \\ 2.\ \Gamma \vdash \mu\, \mathit{isdef}(\texttt{srhs}_1), \Delta \\ 3.\ \Gamma \vdash \mu\, \mathit{isdef}(\texttt{srhs}_2), \Delta \\ 4.\ \Gamma,\ \mu\, \texttt{srhs}_1 \doteq \texttt{srhs}_2 \vdash \mu\, \{\texttt{slhs} := \mathrm{true}\} \langle\!\langle\{\pi\ \ \omega\}\rangle\!\rangle \phi, \Delta \\ 5.\ \Gamma,\ \mu \neg \texttt{srhs}_1 \doteq \texttt{srhs}_2 \vdash \mu\, \{\texttt{slhs} := \mathrm{false}\} \langle\!\langle\{\pi\ \ \omega\}\rangle\!\rangle \phi, \Delta\end{array}}{\Gamma \vdash \mu\, \langle\!\langle\{\pi \texttt{slhs=srhs}_1\texttt{==srhs}_2\texttt{;}\omega\}\rangle\!\rangle \phi, \Delta}$$

Description This rule symbolically executes an equality comparison of two simple expressions.

Rule 6.8.3 *inequality-comparison*

Purpose Symbolic execution of an equality comparison.

Remark The rule for the box operator $[\{.\}]$ is analogous.

$$\frac{\begin{array}{l}1.\ \Gamma \vdash \mu\, isdef(\texttt{slhs})\,,\Delta\\ 2.\ \Gamma \vdash \mu\, isdef(\texttt{srhs}_1)\,,\Delta\\ 3.\ \Gamma \vdash \mu\, isdef(\texttt{srhs}_2)\,,\Delta\\ 4.\ \Gamma,\ \mu\,\texttt{srhs}_1 \doteq \texttt{srhs}_2 \vdash \mu\,\{\texttt{slhs} := \text{false}\}\langle\{\pi\ \ \omega\}\rangle\phi\,,\Delta\\ 5.\ \Gamma,\ \mu\neg\texttt{srhs}_1 \doteq \texttt{srhs}_2 \vdash \mu\,\{\texttt{slhs} := \text{true}\}\langle\{\pi\ \ \omega\}\rangle\phi\,,\Delta\end{array}}{\Gamma \vdash \mu\,\langle\{\pi\texttt{slhs=srhs}_1\texttt{!=srhs}_2\texttt{;}\omega\}\rangle\phi\,,\Delta}$$

Description This rule symbolically executes an inequality comparison of two simple expressions.

Rule 6.8.4 *numeric-comparison*

Purpose Symbolic execution of an equality comparison.

Remark The rule for the box operator $[\{.\}]$ is analogous.

$$\frac{\begin{array}{l}1.\ \Gamma \vdash \mu\, isdef(\texttt{slhs})\,,\Delta\\ 2.\ \Gamma \vdash \mu\, isdef(\texttt{srhs}_1)\,,\Delta\\ 3.\ \Gamma \vdash \mu\, isdef(\texttt{srhs}_2)\,,\Delta\\ 4.\ \Gamma,\ \mu\,\texttt{srhs}_1\,\texttt{logOp}\,\texttt{srhs}_2 \vdash \mu\,\{\texttt{slhs} := \text{true}\}\langle\{\pi\ \ \omega\}\rangle\phi\,,\Delta\\ 5.\ \Gamma,\ \mu\neg\texttt{srhs}_1\,\texttt{logOp}\,\texttt{srhs}_2 \vdash \mu\,\{\texttt{slhs} := \text{false}\}\langle\{\pi\ \ \omega\}\rangle\phi\,,\Delta\end{array}}{\Gamma \vdash \mu\,\langle\{\pi\texttt{slhs=srhs}_1\ \texttt{op}\ \texttt{srhs}_2\texttt{;}\omega\}\rangle\phi\,,\Delta}$$

Description

- `op` is one of the C0 comparison operators <, <=, >, and >=.
- `logOp` is the corresponding logical predicate to the C0 operator `op`:
  - If `op` is <, then `logOp` is $<$.
  - If `op` is <=, then `logOp` is $\leqslant$.
  - If `op` is >, then `logOp` is $>$.
  - If `op` is <=, then `logOp` is $\geqslant$.

This rule symbolically executes a numeric comparison of two simple expressions. Alternatively the functions $\overline{<}$, $\overline{<=}$, $\overline{>}$, and $\overline{>=}$ could be used to perform an evaluation in the update; this would require the use of a conditional term.

7.4.8 Rules for Handling Boolean Logical Operator

Rule 6.9.1 *binary-boolean-logical-operators*

Purpose Symbolic execution of expressions containing binary boolean logical operators.

Remark The rule for the box operator $[\![.]\!]$ is analogous.

$$\frac{\begin{array}{l} 1.\ \Gamma \vdash \mu\, isdef(\texttt{slhs}), \Delta \\ 2.\ \Gamma \vdash \mu\, isdef(\texttt{srhs}_1), \Delta \\ 3.\ \Gamma \vdash \mu\, isdef(\texttt{srhs}_2), \Delta \\ 4.\ \Gamma,\ \mu\, \texttt{srhs}_1\, \texttt{logOp}\, \texttt{srhs}_2 \vdash \mu\, \{\texttt{slhs} := \mathrm{true}\} \langle\!\{\pi\ \omega\}\!\rangle \phi, \Delta \\ 5.\ \Gamma,\ \mu \neg \texttt{srhs}_1\, \texttt{logOp}\, \texttt{srhs}_2 \vdash \mu\, \{\texttt{slhs} := \mathrm{false}\} \langle\!\{\pi\ \omega\}\!\rangle \phi, \Delta \end{array}}{\Gamma \vdash \mu\, \langle\!\{\pi \texttt{slhs=srhs}_1\ \texttt{op}\ \texttt{srhs}_2\texttt{;}\omega\}\!\rangle \phi, \Delta}$$

Description

- *op* is one of the boolean logical operators `&`, `|`.
- `logOp` is the corresponding logical connective for the logical C0 operator *op*:
  - If *op* is `&`, then `logOp` is $\wedge$.
  - If *op* is `|`, then `logOp` is $\vee$.

This rule symbolically executes a numeric comparison of two simple expressions. Alternatively the functions $\overline{\&}$, $\overline{|}$ could be used to perform an evaluation in the update; this would require the use of a conditional term.

Rule 6.9.2 *unary-boolean-logical-operators*

Purpose Symbolic execution of expressions containing binary boolean logical operators.

Remark The rule for the box operator $[\![.]\!]$ is analogous.

$$\frac{\begin{array}{l} 1.\ \Gamma \vdash \mu\, isdef(\texttt{slhs}), \Delta \\ 2.\ \Gamma \vdash \mu\, isdef(\texttt{srhs}), \Delta \\ 3.\ \Gamma,\ \texttt{srhs} \doteq \mathrm{false} \vdash \mu\, \{\texttt{slhs} := \mathit{true}\} \langle\!\{\pi\ \omega\}\!\rangle \phi, \Delta \\ 4.\ \Gamma,\ \neg\texttt{srhs} \doteq \mathrm{false} \vdash \mu\, \{\texttt{slhs} := \mathit{false}\} \langle\!\{\pi\ \omega\}\!\rangle \phi, \Delta \end{array}}{\Gamma \vdash \mu\, \langle\!\{\pi \texttt{slhs}\ =\ \texttt{op}\ \texttt{srhs}\ \texttt{;}\omega\}\!\rangle \phi, \Delta}$$

Description *op* is one of the boolean logical operators `^`, `!`.

Rule 6.9.3 *conditional-and-operator*

Purpose Transformation of an expression containing a conditional "and" operator.

Remark The rule for the box operator $[\![\{.\}]\!]$ is analogous.

$$\frac{\Gamma \vdash \langle\!\{\pi x\texttt{=true;if(!}srhs_1\texttt{)}x\texttt{=false; else } x\texttt{=}srhs_2\texttt{;}slhs\texttt{=}x\texttt{;}\omega\}\!\rangle\phi, \Delta}{\Gamma \vdash \mu\,\langle\!\{\pi slhs\texttt{=}srhs_1 \texttt{ \&\& } srhs_2\texttt{;}\omega\}\!\rangle\phi, \Delta}$$

Description x is a new simple program variable of type `bool`.

In C0 expressions are free of side effects and this rule can simplified. However, in ANSI C and MISRA C the second argument of a conditional "and" operator is only evaluated if the first argument evaluates to `true`.

Rule 6.9.4 *conditional-or-operator*

Purpose Transformation of an expression containing a conditional "or" operator.

Remark The rule for the box operator $[\![\{.\}]\!]$ is analogous.

$$\frac{\Gamma \vdash \langle\!\{\pi x\texttt{=false;if(!}srhs_1\texttt{)}x\texttt{=false; else } x\texttt{=}srhs_2\texttt{;}slhs\texttt{=}x\texttt{;}\omega\}\!\rangle\phi, \Delta}{\Gamma \vdash \mu\,\langle\!\{\pi slhs\texttt{=}srhs_1 \texttt{ || } srhs_2\texttt{;}\omega\}\!\rangle\phi, \Delta}$$

Description x is a new simple program variable of type `bool`.

In C0 expressions are free of side effects and this rule can simplified. However, in ANSI C and MISRA C the second argument of a conditional "and" operator is only evaluated if the first argument evaluates to `false`.

Chapter 8
Implementation

8.1 Overview

This chapter describes the implementation issues of a KeY-based prototype which implements the calculus described in the previous chapters. The prototype is an extension of the KeY prover with the internal version `0.1748`. The source code of the KeY prover is over 150,000 lines long and consists of hundreds of classes. A complete extension of the KeY prover for the support of C has been considered too much for the scope of the thesis. Since the KeY prover consists of several subsystems, the implementation of the prototype is bounded to consider only issues which are relevant for the implementation of the calculus. What is left out is an infrastructure for the support of the C language. The implemented calculus operates instead on the syntactical structures of JAVA CARD DL, but it treats the language semantically like CDL. In this way, the following tasks have been omitted: the implementation of a parser for C, the implementation of classes for representing C programs, services providing static informations of the program (like binding of variables and methods, and type informations), and a clean and safe integration of these parts into the KeY prover without the destruction of the ability to verify JAVA CARD programs. Especially the last issue seems to be very complicated — this is the reason why a version of the KeY prover for the verification of *Abstract State Machines (ASM)* has been implemented as a separate system.

The programming language with the syntax of JAVA CARD, and the semantic of C is called JAVAC. Yet a perfect mapping between C and JAVAC is not possible on the syntactical level and also on the source code level of the KeY system where classes represent JAVA CARD's type system because, C declarations with arbitrary pointer types cannot be feasibly mapped to declarations in JAVA CARD . Due to these restrictions of the prototype, the purpose of this implementation is not to provide a system intended to be used for the verification of C programs but rather for the investigation of the implementation issues which would also be important for a real world implementation of a KeY prover with full C support. This investigation consists of the documentation of the parts of the KeY prover, which are relevant for the implementation of the calculus, and a set of guidelines which describe how certain implementation tasks can be realized — the latter are given along the description of the implementation of the prototype. The tasks which have been carried out for the implementation of the prototype can be summarized by the following list:

1. Declaration of new function symbols, predicate symbols, and schema variables.
2. Definition of new taclets.
3. Declaration of special methods for JAVAC that are dedicated to represent operators of C not present in JAVA CARD.
4. Declaration of new sorts for schema variables.
5. Definition of new meta constructs for the logic part
   a) for the static evaluation of terms and predicates.
   b) for the construction of terms and formulas that cannot be expressed in the taclet language alone.
6. Definition of new meta constructs for transformations of programs in the modal operators

The first two tasks are accomplished in the file `JavaC.key`, which is loaded during the initialization process of the system. For the accomplishment of the third task, the class `JavaC` is declared in the file `JavaC.java`, which must be included as part of the program context in every JAVAC example file. The tasks 4 to 6 require the modification or the extension of methods and classes of the KeY system. The tasks 4 *and* 6 also require extensions in the parser files for the parsers *JavaCC* [2] and *AntLR* [1]. All in all these tasks require the programmer to have a good knowledge of a certain subset of the KeY system which will be presented before the description of the implementation of the prototype.

8.2 Notation

In order to simplify the notation, we will use the names of classes written in a `monospaced` font as nouns in the text in order to refer to objects of these classes. For example, the word '`Term`' refers to an object of the class `Term` and the word 'term' refers to a logical term. The monospaced font is also used for words and symbols which literally occur in the source code or in input files. Whether a word written in a monospaced font is a JAVA object should be clear from the context in which it is used.

If we refer to the intuitive meaning of objects of certain classes the name of the class is written in an *italic* font, e.g. '*Term*' stands for the intuitive meaning of a `Term` (an object of the class `Term`) which may represent a logical term, predicate, operator, etc. or for the syntactical representation of these concepts. In this way, we can say for instance the top-level symbol of 'the *Term*' is rigid, which means that the function symbol, predicate symbol, or logical operator is rigid. However, it would make no sense to say that the top-level symbol of 'the `Term`' or 'the class `Term`' is rigid because here we refer in the first case to an object and in the second case to a class. Similarly, as with words in monospaced font, italicized words refer not only to concepts which have an associated class with it, but the italicized font is also used to emphasize words like it has been done so far.

The UML2 diagrams[8.1] in this chapter show only certain subsets of objects, classes and relations between them in the KeY system. The selections show elements which are important for the implementation of the prototype or elements which are considered important to be known for the programmer of a real word KeY prover for C. In the class diagrams and object diagrams the distinction between composition, aggregation and association has been omitted because firstly, the appropriate choice can often be argued depending on the abstraction from technical details and secondly because the differences are not important for the implementation of the prototype. From a technical perspective a JAVA object cannot contain another object (except for arrays) — as it is the case for C structures which contain other structures — but only references to other objects. Therefore aggregation seems to be suitable. On the other hand, when regarding what certain objects of the prover represent, composition seems to be more suitable, like in the case of *Terms*, which are composed of symbols. Composition is selected here as the default choice because it is mostly better suitable when regarding the purpose of the classes from an intuitive perspective. It is also better than the use of associations because it is easier to read in which order objects have to be accessed.

Directory paths are assumed to be relative to the directory where the KeY system is installed. When we refer to a directory we usually also refer to the subdirectories of the directory if there are any.

According to JAVA CARD terminology, a class may 'extend' another class and 'implement' an interface. For both cases we say instead that the class is 'derived' from another class and 'derived' from an interface. When we refer to source code files with the ending '`.java`' we write 'java file' instead of 'JAVA CARD file' because 'JAVA CARD' is used in a broader sense; similarly we say 'java statement' instead of 'JAVA CARD statement' etc.

8.1. In contrast to UML1, UML2 allows classes and objects to be contained in one diagram.

The distinction between a function symbol, term, and function is not respected in some cases. Terms may consist of function symbols and variables, and a function is the denotational meaning of a function symbol. Such precise distinction would expand sentences and would lead to a badly readable text. For instance when we refer to a function f we *often* mean the term with the top-level function symbol f, but the intended meaning should be clear from the context.

According to the JAVA language specification variables have types and objects have classes, so that a type is a compile time property and a class a runtime property. Since we use the term 'type' in a broader sense we will refere to classes as types and to objects as having types.

8.3 `.key`-Files

The KeY prover takes primarily as input files with the ending `.key` which is why we call them `.key`-files. `.key`-files may have a reference to JAVA CARD files that are also loaded by the prover. The purpose of `.key`-files is two-fold. During the initialization process of the prover `.key`-files containing definitions of function symbols, predicate symbols, schema variables, and — most importantly — taclets are loaded. The other purpose of `.key`-files is to load and save proof obligations or finished proofs.

8.3.1 javaC.key

The implementation of the calculus requires the declaration of new functions, predicates, schema variables and taclets. We explain how to accomplish these tasks by using a portion of the file `javaC.key` as an example and at the same time document these parts of the implementation of the prototype — except for taclets. The full definitions of taclets are presented in section 8.5 where the definitions from *this* section are used. The file `javaC.key` can be found in the directories `/system/resources/de/uka/ilkd/key/proof/rules/` and `/system/binary/de/uka/ilkd/key/proof/rules/`. During the compilation of the KeY system the version in the first directory is copied to the second directory. When the KeY prover is started the file from the second directory is used! The following listings appear subsequently in the file `javaC.key`.

```
\include javaRules;
```

Reserved words in `.key`-files begin with '\'. '`\include`' is used to include declarations from other `.key`-files. In this way, the file `javaC.key` is included into the initialization process of the prover by inclusion into the file `standardRules.key`, which is automatically loaded by the prover.

The declarations of sorts, functions, predicates, and schema variables are embedded into the braces of the `.key`-file sections `\sorts{...}`, `\functions{...}`, `\predicates{...}`, and `\schemaVariables{...}` in place of the dots '...'. A definition begins often with a key word like `\generic` and/or sort informations. The definition of several items of the same kind and the same sort can be written as a comma-separated list as the next listing shows.

```
\sorts{ \generic G1, G2, G3; }
```

Sorts are the "types" of elements of the logic which are functions, predicates, and variables. *Types* are used as "types" of elements in programs like methods, classes, and variables. Therefore it is not possible to declare a function by using *Types* like class types. In order to allow elements from the program part to occur in the logic parts, the *Sorts* of the respective logic elements must be of a *generic Sort* as shown in the example above or of *Sort* `any`. These *Sorts* are compatible with *Types* from the program part.

```
\functions{
  \nonRigidVarySort int v(any);
  \nonRigid int cr(any);
  any objEnum(int);
  int adrof(any);
  \nonRigid int nextObj;
}
```

The definition of rigid functions starts with a *Sort* which is the "return"-*Sort* of the function, followed by the function name and — in case of non-constants — by a list with *Sorts* in parenthesis which are the *Sorts* of the acceptable arguments. In order to declare a non-rigid function, the declaration must start with the key-word '`\nonRigid`' or '`\nonRigidVarySort`'. The latter is not part of the original syntax of `.key`-files, but it is introduced for the prototype in order to declare functions which reflect the *Sort* (and *Type*) of their argument in a concrete term (see section 8.5.3). The function symbols `v`, `cr`, and `nextObj` represent the function symbols ^{v}, ^{c}, and the non-rigid constant next from CDL. Since they take program variables as arguments, the *Sort* of their parameter is `any`. The *Sort* `int` of the function `v` is not important because of the preceeding key-word '`\nonRigidVarySort`' in its declaration. The function `objEnum` is the object enumerator. In contrast to their CDL, versions `objEnum` and `nextObj` carry no type informations. `adrof` represents the reference operator in the logic part.

```
\predicates{
  subStruct(any,any);
  nonDynamic(any);
```

```
  isDynamic(any);
}
```

Predicates are defined similarly as functions except that no *Sort* occurs before their name. The predicate `subStruct` corresponds to the predicate $\sqsubseteq$ in CDL.

Schema variables may occur in the program part and in the logic part. Their definition starts with one of the key-words '`\modalOperator`', '`\program`', '`\programlist`', '`\formula`', '`\variables`', or '`\term`'. In case of schema variables which represent elements of the program a *ProgramSV-Sort* follows the key-word '`\program`'. In case of logical variables and terms, a *Sort* follows the key-words '`\variables`' and '`\term`' respectively.

```
\schemaVariables{
  \modalOperator { diamond, box }#allnormalass;
  \program Variable #loc, #var0, #var1, #var2, #var3 ;
  \program Type #t, #t2 ;
  \program NonSimpleExpression #nse, #nse0, #nse1, #nse2, #nv
;
  \programList Expression #elist, #elist1;
  \program MethodName #mn;
  \program JavaCadrOf #adrOf;
  \program JavaCderef #deref;
  \program JavaCsizeOf #sizeOf;
  \program JavaCalloc #alloc;
  \program JavaCdelete #delete;
  \formula post, inv, post1;
  \variables any quanVar;
  \term G1 t0,t1; \term any trm0, trm1, trm2;
}
```

Besides the *ProgramSVSorts* `Variable`, `Type`, `Expression`, `NonSimpleExpression`, and `MethodName`, there are more *ProgramSVSorts* in the full definition like `SimpleExpression`, `Literal`, `LeftHandSide`, and `StaticVariable`, to name a few. The program elements for which their respective program variables may stand can be mostly concluded from the names. The definitions of schema variables with these *ProgramSVSort* have been taken out from the `\schemaVariables` section to save space.

A complete list with all available *ProgramSVSorts* can be determined by looking at the class attributes of class `ProgramSVSort` which are of a derived type from `ProgramSVSort`; there are, however, too many *ProgramSVSorts* to be listed and explained here. For the implementation of the prototype the additional *ProgramSVSorts* `JavaCadrOf`, `JavaCderef`, `JavaCsizeOf`, `JavaCalloc`, and `JavaCdelete` are introduced. They have a similar purpose as the *ProgramSVSort* `MethodName` . Schema variables of the *ProgramSV-Sorts* whose name starts with `JavaC` match with method names which are declared in the class `JavaC.class`. More on this topic can be found in section 8.5.

Taclets are defined in a section starting with '`\rules(`*`ruleset`*`){`' and ending with '`}`' where *`ruleset`* specifies a category of the of rules in this section. A taclet definition starts with the name of the taclet followed by curly brackets in which some of the key words '`\assumes`', '`\find`', '`\sameUpdateLevel`', '`\varcond`', '`\replacewith`', '`\add`', '`\addrules`', '`\addprogvars`', '`\heuristics`', '`\noninteractive`', and '`\displayname`' are embedded with their arguments. The meaning of the key words should be clear from section 4.1.1, except for the last three key-words which specify only technical details. '`\heuristics`' specifies a set to which the rule belongs. When starting automatic proof search, the user may select which sets of rules shall be or shall not be used. Taclets with the key-word '`\noninteractive`' are applied only automatically and '`\displayname`' is used to specify the visible name of the taclet in the pop-up window showing possible taclet applications in the interactive mode. The argument of `\find`, `\replacewith`, and `\add` can be a sequent — the sequent symbol is '`==>`' and may have have a formula on each side — a formula, or a term. The KeY syntax of the most important formulas and terms is given in section 8.3.3.

The following listing shows the *rules* section of the file `javaC.key`. The actual content of the taclet definitions is replaced by the dots '. . .' and will be presented in section 8.5 except for the content of the rule `javaC_unfoldEquals`, which is short enough to be shown here.

```
\rules(programRules:Java){
  javaC_JC_alloc_toPrgSVSort_checked {...}; (section 8.5.7.3)
  javaC_JC_alloc_toPrgSVSort{...}; (section 8.5.7.3)
  javaC_subStruct {...}; (section 8.5.7.1)
  javaC_isDynamic {...}; (section 8.5.7.2)
  javaC_nonDynamic {...}; (section 8.5.7.2)
  javaC_AsignToUpd_PrgSVSort_PrgSVSort_checked
{...}; (section 8.5.7.5)
  javaC_delete_PrgSVSort_checked {...}; (section 8.5.7.4)
  javaC_delete_PrgSVSort_NotChecked {...}; (section 8.5.7.4)
  javaC_unfoldEquals_checked {...}; (section 8.5.7.5)
  javaC_unfoldEquals {
    \find ( t0 = t1)
    \replacewith( #unfoldEquals(t0,t1) )
    \heuristics (simplify)
    \displayname "JC_unfoldEquals"
  }; (section 8.5.4.5)
```

```
  javaC_AToU_PrgSVSort_PrgSVSort {...};(section 8.5.4.4)
  javaC_unfoldassignment_PrgSVSort_PrgSVSort {...};(section 8.5.4.2)
}
```

Taclets are *often* defined multiple times with similar names and with schema variables with different combinations of *ProgramSVSorts*. The set of taclets shown above is only a subset of taclets in the file `javaC.key`. The taclet names are schematic. The substring *PrgSVSort* must be seen a substitute for variations of certain *ProgramSVSorts*.

What can not be defined in the `.key`-files are meta constructs like `#unfoldEquals`, and new *ProgramSVSorts* like `JavaCadrOf` are shown above; these have to be implemented by classes and integrated into the system in order to be recognized by the parser of `.key`-files.

8.3.2 Problem Files

Another purpose of `.key`-files to store proof obligations, proof trees and proofs[8.2]. These `.key`-files are also called problem files. They are typically created from OCL constrains by the verification middle-ware of the KeY-system, but they can also be created manually using a text editor. The UML model with the relevant types and relations between them, which are important for the proof obligations, is represented by java files. Java files can be attached to the problem file using the key-word `\javaSource` followed by the name of a file or a directory in quotation marks[8.3]. Java files are loaded in order to establish the program context for proofs which is a set of all needed declarations. Classes of the Java API are loaded automatically when the KeY prover is started. However, examples with JAVAC source code must include the declarations from the file `javaC.java`, which is located in the directory `/system/proofExamples/javaC/code` (see section 8.5.1.3). Program variables used in the proof obligation can be declared in the section `\programVariables{...}` in place of the dots '...'[8.4]. The declarations have the same syntax as declarations in JAVA CARD. A proof obligation consists of a formula which is embedded in the section `\problem`. The syntax of formulas in KeY is given in the next section. The following listing is a problem file which is an example of a JAVAC proof obligation.

```
\javaSource "code/";

\programVariables {
```

8.2. A proof tree can be viewed as a set of proof obligations, and a proof is a proof tree where all proof obligations have been proven; the tree is closed by axioms.

8.3. Relative paths are allowed

8.4. Program variables which don't occur in the formula may also be declared in the program part by ordinary variable declarations.

```
    int i;
    int j;
    int l;
    int k;
}
\problem {
 \<{
    i=3;
    j=i;
    l=JavaC.adrOf(j);
    k=JavaC.deref(l);
  }\> v(k) = 3
}
```

8.3.3 Syntax of Terms and Formulas in KeY

For the understanding of taclets in the file `javaC.key`, which are presented in section 8.5, and in order to give the reader the ability to write own taclets or problem files we present here the syntactical notations of the most important logical elements. In addition, the functions and predicates defined in the file `javaC.key` are important syntactical elements in the context of the thesis, but they will not be listed here since they can be viewed in section 8.3.1.

In the following tables `Fml` and *Fml* are placeholder for formulas — in "KeY-syntax" and "text book notation" respectively — and `Trm` and *Trm* are placeholders for terms. `Trm` occurs in places where also schema variables may occur that are defined as `program expression` in the file `javaC.key`. However, the placeholder `Trm` is preferred here, because expressions are translated into terms by a mechanism called *TypeConterter* when they are moved from the program part to the logic part (see section 8.4.5).

KeY-syntax	**text book notation**
`\if(`*Fml*`)\then(`*Trm*`)\else(`*Trm*`)`	if *Fml* then *Trm* else *Trm* fi
`\ifEx x;(`*Fml*`)\then(`*Trm*`)\else(`*Trm*`)`	if $\exists x.$*Fml* then *Trm* else *Trm* fi
`\<` *JavaBlock* `>\` *Trm*	$\langle\!|$ *JavaBlock* $|\!\rangle$ *Trm*
`\[` *JavaBlock* `]\` *Trm*	$[\![$ *JavaBlock* $]\!]$ *Trm*
{*Trm*$_0$:=*Trm*$_0$, …, *Trm*$_n$:=*Trm*$_n$}*Trm*	{*Trm*$_0$:= *Trm*$_0$, ..., *Trm*$_0$:= *Trm*$_0$} *Trm*
`{\for x;\if(`*Fml*`)`*Trm*`:=`*Trm*`}`*Trm*	{for x; *Fml*; *Trm* := *Trm*} *Trm*
`add(`*Trm*`, `*Trm*`)`	*Trm* + *Trm*
`sub(`*Trm*`,`*Trm*`)`	*Trm* − *Trm*
`neg(`*Trm*`)`	− *Trm*
`mul(`*Trm*`,`*Trm*`)`	*Trm* ∗ *Trm*
`jdiv(`*Trm*`,`*Trm*`)`	*Trm*/*Trm*
`jmod(`*Trm*`,`*Trm*`)`	*Trm* mod *Trm*
`#adrOf(`*Trm*`)`	meta construct

Table 8.1 Syntax of terms and meta constructs generating terms.

KeY-syntax	**text book notation**
`true`	true
`false`	false
`!Fml`	$\neg Fml$
`Fml & Fml`	$Fml \wedge Fml$
`Fml | Fml`	$Fml \vee Fml$
`Fml -> Fml`	$Fml \rightarrow Fml$
`Fml <- Fml`	$Fml \leftarrow Fml$
`Fml <-> Fml`	$Fml \leftrightarrow Fml$
`Trm = Trm`	$Trm \doteq Trm$
`leq(Trm,Trm)`	$Trm < Trm$
`\forall x; Fml`	$\forall x.Fml$
`\exists x; Fml`	$\exists x.Fml$
`\< JavaBlock >\ Fml`	$\langle\{JavaBlock\}\rangle Fml$
`\[ JavaBlock ]\ Fml`	$[\{JavaBlock\}]Fml$
`{Trm_0:=Trm_0,...,Trm_n:=Trm_n}Fml`	$\langle Trm_0 := Trm_0, ..., Trm_0 := Trm_0\rangle Fml$
`{\for x;\if(Fml)Trm:=Trm}Fml`	$\{\text{for } x; Fml; Trm := Trm\}Fml$
`\modality{mod} JavaBlock' \endmodality(Fml)`	schematic modality
`#isDynamic(Trm)`	meta construct
`#subStruct(Trm,Trm)`	meta construct
`#nonDynamic(Trm)`	meta construct
`#unfoldEquals(Trm,Trm)`	meta construct
`#assignmentToUpdates(Trm,Trm,Fml)`	meta construct

Table 8.2 Syntax of formulas and meta constructs which create formulas.

The schematic modality is used to match with different kinds of modalities. `\modality{mod}` is matched with the opening brace and `\endmodality(Fml)` is matched with the closing brace and the following formula or term respectively. The modality name `mod` can be defined in a `.key`-file, e.g. the modality name `#allnormalas` is defined in `javaC.key` for matching with the diamond and box operators. A `JavaBlock'` is of the form `{.. statement ...}`, where '`{`' and '`}`' are the braces of the `JavaBlock'`, the dots '`..`' and '`...`' represent the schematic program context and `statement` is a java statement which is in focus of the taclet[8.5]. The `JavaBlock` is a statement block in the sense of ordinary JAVA CARD syntax, i.e. it consists of the braces '`{`' and '`}`' between which java statements may be embedded. The modal formulas in the `rules`-section of `.key`-files have therefore the form `\modality{mod}{..statement...}\endmodality(Fml)`, and the modal formulas in the `problem`-section have the form `\<{statements}\>Fml` or `\[{statements}\]Fml`.

The meta constructs must not be confused with the functions and predicates defined in the file `javaC.key`, which have very similar names. They are

8.5. According to [11] taclets operate only on the first active statement, but the implementation of the schematic program by the class `ContextStatementBlock` allows `statement` to consist of several java statements.

used for static evaluation of the respective functions and predicates. Since the meta constructs have been implemented by java classes — in contrast to the functions and predicates — they are explained in section 8.5. One meta construct not listed in the tables is `#jc-unfold`. It is a *ProgramMetaConstruct*, which means that it may occur within programs and create *ProgramElements* in contrast to the meta constructs of the tables creating *Terms* (see sections 8.4.2 and 8.4.4). The difference between the meta constructs is explained in section 8.4.8.

8.4 Classes of the KeY prover

This section explains concepts of the KeY prover which are necessary for the understanding of the implementation of the prototype described in section 8.5. In the following subsections, the explanations in a section refer to the diagrams of the section if not stated otherwise.

8.4.1 Main application classes

In this section we give an overview of the KeY prover as an application. Looking at the KeY prover this way, a programmer who is unfamiliar with the KeY system thinks in terms of windows, views, controllers, loading of files, and things he knows from the theoretical part of the previous chapters, like a program context, proof trees, proof obligations, sequents, and terms and formulas. Diagram 8.1 consists of four parts which can be divided imaginaly by a horizontal and vertical line with the class `Proof` in the middle.

The class `Main` is derived from class `JFrame` and represents the main window of the KeY prover. It consists of several classes derived from class `Component` of the JAVA CARD API for the views and buttons of the main window. When the program is started the file `standardRules.key` located in `/system/resources/de/uka/ilkd/key/proof/rules/` is loaded together with all `.key`-files included by this file. In this way, the file `javaC.key` is loaded, which is described in section 8.3.1. Problem-files, which are described in section 8.3.2, are represented by the class `ProofOblInput` and loaded by the `ProblemLoader`, which uses the `ProblemInitialiser` to create a `Proof`. A *Proof* may be closed or open and consist of one or more proof obligations. Several *Proofs* may be loaded in the the KeY prover and are stored by the `ProofAggregate`, but only one `Proof` is in focus of the program on which the class `InteractiveProver` operates.[8.6] What `Proof` is in focus is determined

8.6. A '*Proof*' is loaded which is here a problem file from which a `Proof` is created. The `Proof` is an object of class `Proof`. It would be wrong to say that a `Proof` is loaded because no object is loaded and it would be wrong to say that a proof is loaded, because *Proof* may *still* have an open proof obligation.

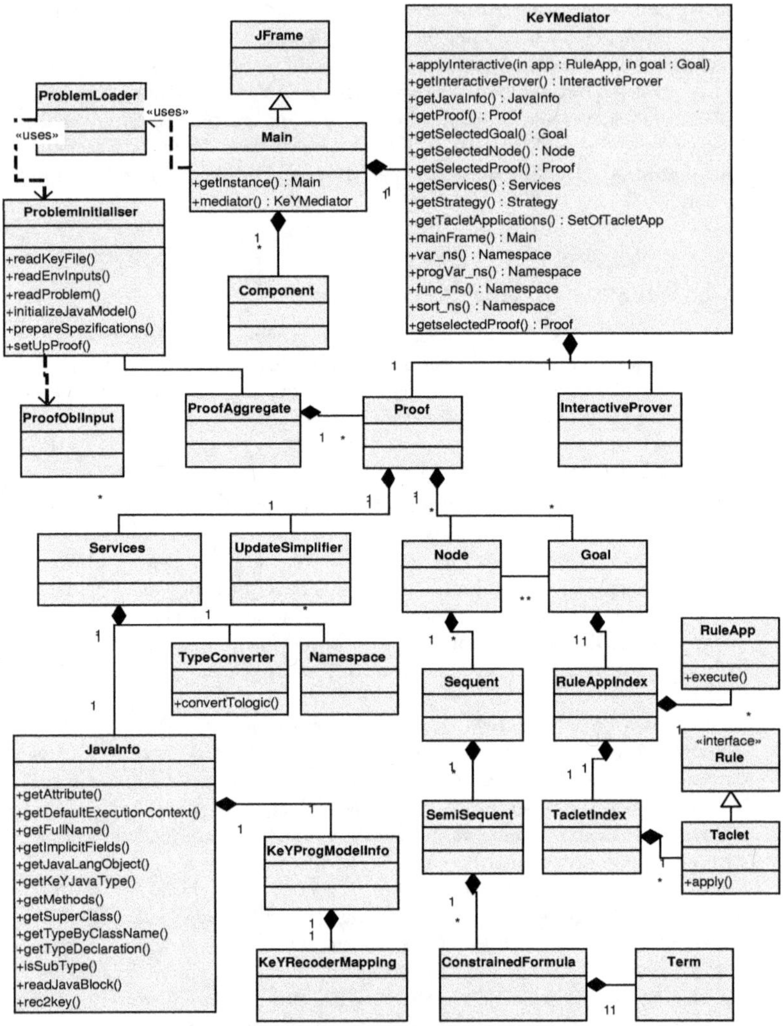

Diagram 8.1. Main application classes

by the method `getSelectedProof` of the `KeYMediator`. The `KeYMediator` can be viewed as very important class because it provides access to many informations associated with the currently selected `Proof`.[8.7] These informations can be accessed from any place of the KeY prover by obtaining the single instance of the class `Main` by its method `getInstance` and then the `KeYMediator` through the method `mediator`.

The *Proof* is the main subject on which the user of the KeY prover operates. The main components of the class `Proof` are shown in the lower half of the diagram. On the right side of the diagram the *visible* parts are shown. A *Proof* is a tree which consists of a *tree* of `Nodes`. A `Node` saves the *Rule* which has been applied on it. The semantic content of a *Node* is the `Sequent` which consists of two `SemiSequents` — the antecedent and the succedent. The visualization of a *Sequent* is done by the `SequentView`, which uses the class `LogicPrinter`. Leave-*Nodes* of the proof tree are either closed or open — if they are open, they are called proof obligations — and are represented by `Goals`. A *Goal* has other responsibilities then a *Node* because the user operates through the *InteractiveProver* on the open *Goals* by selecting a term, formula, or sequent and applying *Rules* on it. By clicking the right mouse button on one of these items a pop-up window opens, which shows a list with applicable *Rules* — mostly *Taclets*. This list is represented by the class `RuleAppIndex` where the items are `RuleApps`. A `Rule` like a `Taclet` represents a rule schema as defined in section 3.3. In contrast, the class `RuleApp` represents a rule which is an instantiated rule schema. The list is generated from a subset of the full list of all available *Taclets* represented by `TacletIndex`. When the user selects a *RuleApp* from the *RuleAppIndex* by a click on an item in the pop-up window, the method `execute` is invoked, which further invokes the method `apply` of a `Taclet`. The method `apply` of class `Taclet` applies a *Taclet* on the *Term* which is in focus. The application of a *Taclet* causes then — among others — the execution of meta constructs and the invocation of methods of the class `TypeConverter`. Only the last two issues are *therefore* of interest for the implementation of the prototype and are further discussed in the sections 8.4.8 and 8.4.5. The implementation of *Proofs*, *Taclets*, and their application is a part of the system which does not have to be changed. *Terms* are terms and formulas represented by the class `Term` which is further discussed in section 8.4.4. The class `Term` can be found in the bottom right corner of the diagram which shows how *Terms* are embedded in a *Node*.

The lower left part of the diagram shows parts of a *Proof* which are, loosely speaking, *not visible*. The `UpdateSimplifier` is used for the simplification of updates — more on this can be found in section 8.4.6. The most important parts of a `Services` object are `JavaInfo`, `TypeConverter`,

8.7. *Mediator* is the name of a design pattern. The *Mediator* defines an object that encapsulates how a set of objects interact. The *Mediator* promotes loose coupling by keeping objects from referring to each other explicitly, and it lets you vary their interaction independently [19].

and some instances of class `Namespace`. The `TypeConverter` is used when elements (like *ProgramVariables*) are moved from the program part to the logic part in order to convert them to *Terms*. The functions, predicates, sorts, and variables defined in `.key`-files — like the initialization files and problem files — can be accessed by `Namespaces`. Through the appropriate `Namespace`, an `Operator` representing a function symbol, predicate symbol, sort, or variable can be dynamically created by passing the name of the symbol to the method `lookup` of the respective `Namespace`. The `Operator` can then be further used to create a `Term` as described in section 8.4.4. This feature is used for the prototype implementation to create the function `v` *in which ProgramVariables* are embedded as arguments by the `TypeConverter` when moved to the logic part (see section 8.4.5). When a *Proof* is loaded the `ProblemInitialiser` also initializes a java model or program context which consists of the java classes specified after the key-word `\javaSource` of problem files (see section 8.3.2). The program context consists of the *static informations* of a program like declarations of classes and declarations of their members. These informations are obtained by the *Recoder*, which is an external JAVA compiler. The program elements of the parse tree of the *Recoder* are tranformed by the method `rec2key` of the class `JavaInfo` into *ProgramElements* defined in KeY. In a real world implementation of the KeY prover for C this part and the data structures representing the *ProgramElements* have to be implemented for C.

The program context is represented by the class `JavaInfo`. Thus, each `Proof` is associated with a `JavaInfo`, and several `Proofs` may share a `JavaInfo` if they may share the same program context.[8.8] `JavaInfo` provides many methods by which informations about classes, attributes, methods, types and relations between them can be obtained. For instance, the method `getAllAttributes` returns a list of possible runtime types of objects represented by the expression `x` in the expression `x.m` by passing the method `getAllAttributes`, the static type of `x` and and the name of the attribute `m`. That there may be several possible runtime types is due to sub-typing in java. When attributes are used in artificial program constructs introduced for the calculus of JAVA CARD DL or *exported* into the logic part, the ambiguity of the runtime type has to be resolved. Ambiguity is detected by the method `printInShortForm` of the class `LogicPrinter`. The method uses the method `getAllAttributes` by passing it the static type of an expression `x` and the name of an attribute `m` as described previously. In case of ambiguity the returned list by this method contains more than one element — which is the criterion to return *true*. The name and location of the dec-

8.8. When a problem file is loaded the KeY-prover asks the user whether an already existing environment should be used or whether a new environment should be created. This corresponds to the share or creation of a new `JavaInfo`.

laration of the method `printInShortForm` is motivated by its *primary* usage. In case of ambiguity the name of the attribute has to be extended by an '`@`' followed by the class name where the attribute is declared.

8.4.2 *SourceElements*

Objects that are instances of a derived class from the interface `SourceElement` represent syntactical elements of the program part. `SourceElement` classes are located in the directory `/system/de/uka/ilkd/key/java`. Diagram 8.2 shows only a subset of the classes derived from the interface `SourceElement` due to space limitations, and operations are omitted in general. In the upper part of the diagram very general classes and interfaces are shown which are very often used in declarations. The lower part of the diagram contains classes derived from the classes in the upper part in various combinations; however, all of them have the class `JavaNonTerminalProgramElement` in common. The lower part of the diagram is structured in columns.

These data types are immutable because their objects are shared between multiple *Nodes* of a *Proof* in order to save memory. The interface `SourceElement` is derived from the interface `SVSubstitute` so that schema variables can be declared in a `.key`-file which may be instantiated by *SourceElements* (see sections 8.3.1 and 8.4.3). The interface `SourceElement` declares the method `equalsModRenaming`, which should be used for comparing the syntactical equivalence of two *SourceElements*. The way how *SourceElements* are represented on the screen is determined by the method `prettyPrint`. The method `visit`, which is also declared in the interface `SourceElement`, is part of the well known visitor design pattern[8.9]. For instance, the meta construct implemented by the class `MethodBodyExpand` uses a visitor represented by class `ProgramVariableReplaceVisitor` in order to replace *ProgramVariables* from the declaration of a method by new *ProgramVariables*[8.10]. The interface `SourceElement` represents all syntactical entities which includes also *Comments*. Since *Comments* have no semantical value, the interface `ProgramElement` and the class `JavaProgramElement` are used more frequently in declarations[8.11].

8.9. The *Visitor* represents an operation to be performed on the elements of an object structure. *Visitors* lets you define a new operation without changing the classes of the elements on which it operates [19].

8.10. A method may be invoked multiple times because of recursion. This causes the creation of several versions of the program variables declared in the method body.

8.11. OCL constrains are encoded in comments when the KeY-tool is used for specification, but they have no meaning for the KeY prover because the OCL constrains are translated by the middleware into proof obligations in `.key`-files.

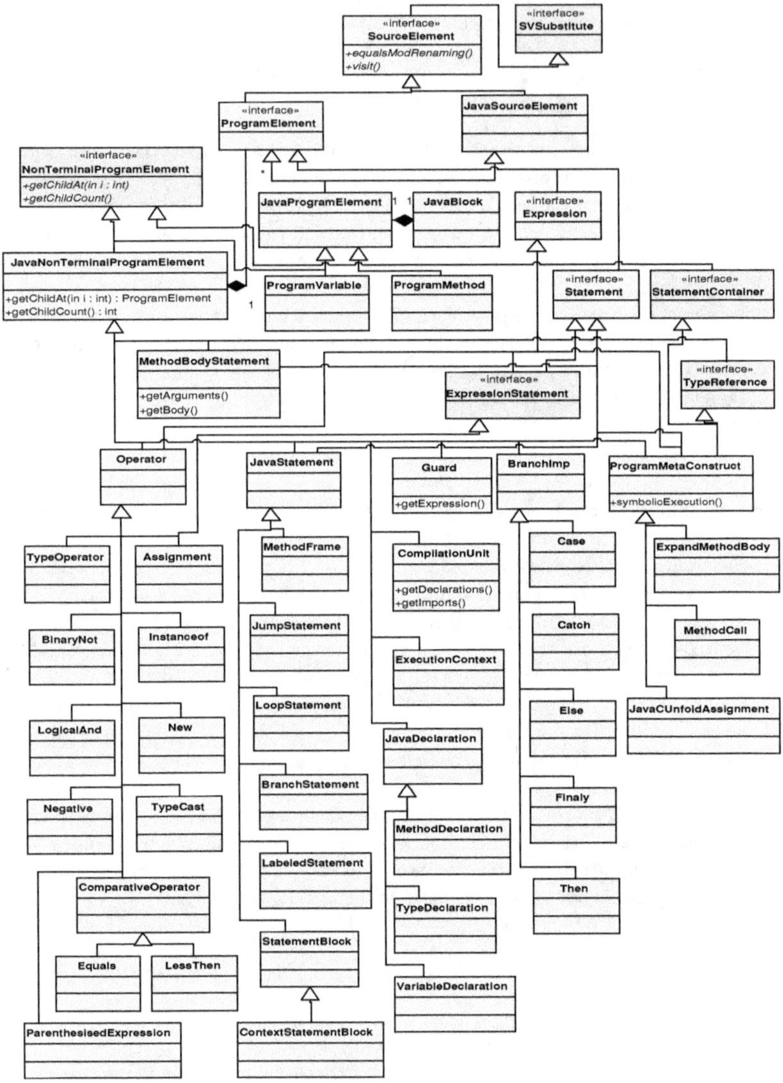

Diagram 8.2. Source elements

The classes and interfaces in the upper part of the diagram occur very often in declarations of methods. Furthermore, the names of these classes and interfaces are written in the thesis in italics in order to refer to the language constructs they represent and to further derived classes.[8.12] For these reasons it is worth taking a look at them. A `JavaBlock` is returned by the method `readJavaBlock` of the class `JavaInfo`, which provides a comfortable way to create *JavaProgramElements* from a *String* with JAVA CARD source code (see section 8.4.1). What is important in the context of the thesis is the *JavaProgramElement ProgramVariable*, which is further described in section 8.4.7. Almost all other important classes derived from class `JavaProgramElement` are also derived from the class `JavaNonTerminalProgramElement`, which represents all compound *ProgramElements*. The most important methods of the class are therefore `getChildCount` and `getChildAt`, which are used to access the `ProgramElements` contained in a `JavaNonTerminalProgramElement`. If we refer to the subelements of a *JavaNonTerminalProgramElement*, this means that we refer to the *ProgramElements*, which are represented by the `ProgramElements` retrieved by the method `getChildAt`.

The lower part of the diagram consist of classes which represent compound symbols. Thus, they are derived from the class `JavaNonTerminalProgramElement`. In the left column some classes are listed which are derived from the class `Operator`. The class `Operator` represents compound *Expressions* and is therefore derived from the Interface `Expression`. The class `Operator` must not be confused with the interface `Operator`. The latter is used to represent symbols of the logic part to which we also refer by the itlicized word '*Operators*' and which is further discussed in section 8.4.4. The same distinction applies to some of the derived classes from class `Operator` like `LogicalAnd`, `Equals`, and `LessThen` because there are similar classes on the logic side. The class `Assignment` is used by the implementation of the *ProgramMetaConstruct* `#jc-unfold` for generating a set of assignments (see section 8.5.4.2). Additionally, the derived class `CopyAssignment` is used, but it is not depicted in the diagram due to lack of space. The classes `TypeCast` and `ParenthesisedExpression` play a role in the modification of the *TypeConverter* (see sections 8.4.5 and 8.5.6.3).

The next column shows some classes derived from the class `JavaStatement`, which is again derived from the interface `Statement`. The class `ContextStatementBlock` on the very bottom of the diagram represents the schematic program which occurs in taclets — it represents a `JavaBlock'` as described in section 8.3.3. The class `MethodFrame` — in the upper part

8.12. This notation is described in section 8.2

of the column — represents a method body which is obtained from the substitution of a method call by its body. This substitution is performed by the meta construct *ExpandMethodBody*, which is represented by the class `ExpandMethodBody` and can be found in the very right column of the diagram[8.13].

All meta constructs which operate on the program part are derived from the class `ProgramMetaConstruct`. This class is derived from the class `JavaNonTerminalProgramElement`, and the interfaces `Expression`, `Statement`, `StatementContainer`, and `TypeReference`, from which follows that a *ProgramMetaConstruct* may occur at almost any place in a java program. The only class in this class diagram which is introduced for the implementation of the prototype is the *ProgramMetaConstruct* `JavaCUnfoldAssignment`, which implements the *ProgramMetaConstruct* `#jc-unfold`. More informations on meta constructs can be found in section 8.4.8.

In the middle of the lower part of the diagram the class `JavaDeclaration` can be seen, from which the classes `MethodDeclaration`, `TypeDeclaration`, and `VariableDeclaration` are derived. This class is important for unfolding, which is described in section 8.5.4. The classes mentioned in this paragraph are also contained in the diagram of the next section.

8.4.3 *Types* and *Sorts*

The diagram 8.3 contains in the left part classes derived from class `JavaProgramElement` which represent in the upper part *TypeCasts* and in the lower part *JavaDeclarations*. In the middle column the classes represent *Types*, and in the right column they represent *Sorts*. The classes which are *JavaDeclarations* and *Types* are located in the directory `/system/de/uka/ilkd/key/java`, and *Sort* classes can be found in the directory `/system/de/uka/ilkd/key/logic`. In the bottom right corner of the UML2-diagram an object diagram is contained with the objects `ANY`, `FORMULA`, `LOC_LIST`, and `NULL` of the type `Sort` or derived types of class `Sort`. These objects can be accessed through the attributes of the interface `Sort`[8.14]. The object `ANY` represents the *Sort* any in `.key`-files, and

8.13. C++ supports call by reference function invocation. An appropriate symbolical execution can be implemented by modifying the class `ExpandMethodBody` so that the formal parameters of a function are not replaced by new *ProgramVariables* but with the arguments.

8.14. In contrast to java UML does not allow the definition of initialized attributes in an interface.

the object FORMULA represents the *Sort* of formulas; objects representing schema variables declared with the key-word \formula (see section 8.3.1) have a reference to the Sorts. In the context of unfolding (see section 8.5.4), the *JavaDeclaration* classes FieldDeclaration and ClassDeclaration are important, which are derived from the classes VariableDeclaration and class TypeDeclaration respectively. The class TypeDeclaration is not only derived from class JavaDeclaration but also from the interface ClassType, which is an direct derivative of the interface Type.

Types and *Sorts* are analogous concepts as mentioned in section 8.3.1. Classes derived from the class Type represent the java types of *JavaProgramElements* (which they are associated with a type). A special class derived from the class Type is the class KeYJavaType, which contains a Type and a Sort. The Type and the Sort can be obtained by the methods getJavaType and getSort respectively. Classes derived from the interface Sort represent the "types" of *Terms* and *Operators* of the logic part (see next section). There is *sometimes* a direct correspondence between *Sorts* and *Types* like in the case of int. The class KeYJavaType provides, therefore, a connection between these two type systems for syntactical elements which may occur in the logic part and in the program part as it is the case for *ProgramVariables* and *AccessOps* (see section 8.4.7). A KeYJavaType can be obtained by the method getKeYJavaType of the TypeConverter (see 8.4.5) by passing it a Type as argument.

The class ProgramSVSort is derived from the interface Sort and is used for defining the *Sorts* of schema variables which substitute *JavaProgramElements*. This corresponds to task four of the overview section in this chapter. For the implementation of the prototype the *ProgramSVSorts* JavaCadrOf, JavaCderef, JavaCsizeOf, JavaCalloc, and JavaCdelete have been introduced into the KeY prover (see section 8.3.1). The introduction of a new *ProgramSVSort* does not require any changes to the parsers used for loading .key-files. A *ProgramSVSort* is integrated into the system by extending the class ProgramSVSort by a new class attribute which has itself a type derived from class ProgramSVSort. The declaration of the attribute requires the modifiers public static final. The class type of the attribute which is derived from the class ProgramSVSort must implement a constructor and the method canStandFor. The constructor must call the constructor of class ProgramSVSort and pass it the *Name* of the *Sort* it represents. The semantic of the *Sort* is implemented by the method canStandFor which takes either a ProgramElement or a Term (see section 8.4.4) as argument and decides whether it belongs to the *Sort*. In this way, the parser decides for which

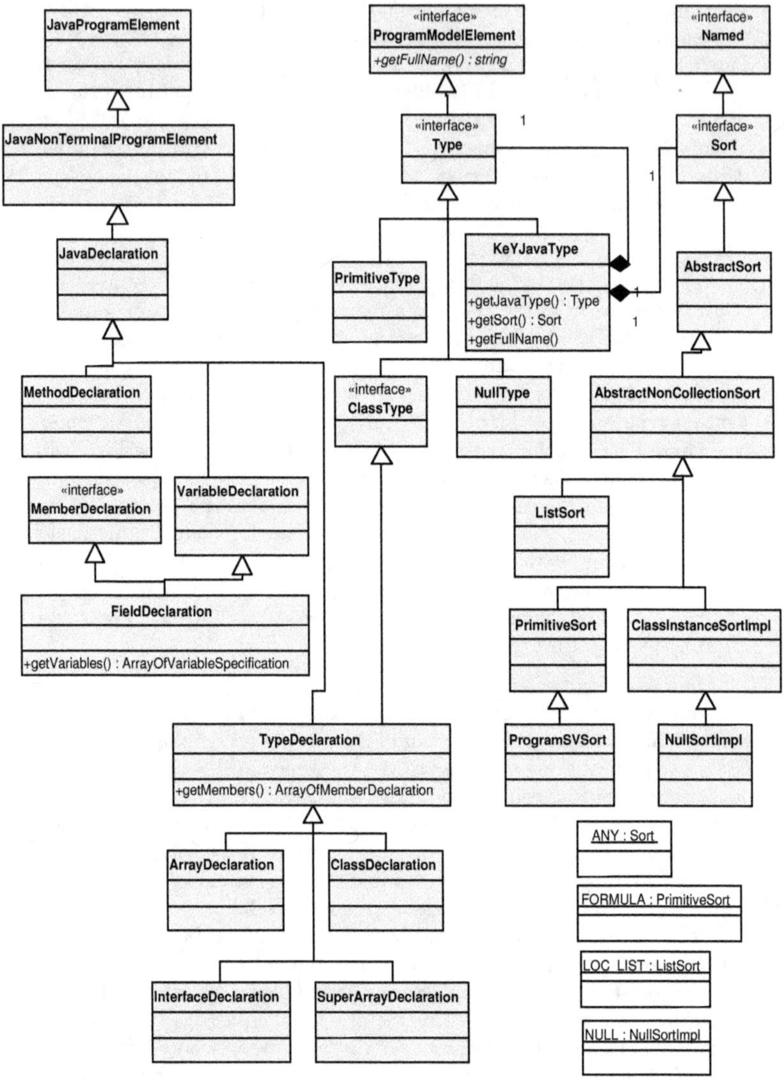

Diagram 8.3. Typecasts, Declarations, Types, and Sorts

SVSubstitutes a schema variable may stand — this is necessary in order to check whether a *Taclet* is applicable. Through the described extension of the class `ProgramSVSort`, the parser is automatically enabled to recognize the *ProgramSVSort* by using the reflection API.[8.15]

TypeCasts are represented by `TypeCasts`, which consist of a `TypeRef` and the *ProgramElement* which is type-casted. The `TypeRef` carries the type informations in a `KeYJavaType`, which can be accessed by the method `getKeYJavaType`.

What is also important to know is that a `KeYJavaType` and a `TypeDeclaration` can be obtained from the name of a class by the methods `getTypeByClassName` and `getTypeDeclaration` of the class `JavaInfo` respectively. It is *of course* required that the respective class declaration is loaded into the system (see section 8.3.2). The class `JavaInfo` is described in section 8.4.1.

8.4.4 *Terms* and *Operators*

The classes `Term` and the interface `Operator` represent syntactical elements of the logic part and are depicted in the class diagram 8.4. Almost all of the interfaces and classes of the diagram are defined in the directory `/system/de/uka/ilkd/key/logic`.[8.16] One must not mix up the interface `Operator` with the class `Operator` for representing compound *Expressions* in the program part (see section 8.4.2). The slanted version *Operator* refers to the syntactical elements which are represented by the interface `Operator`. It may represent symbols like function symbols, predicate symbols, quantors, logical connectives, program variables, and modal operators. The interface provides the most important properties of syntactical elements. It is derived from the interface `Named` and inherits therefore the method `name`. The methods with the self explaining meaning declared in the interface `Operator` are `arity`, `isRigid`, and `sort`. The method `match` is used for quantified updates and the method `validTopLevel` is used for checking the syntactical correctness of compound symbols respecting their sort and aritiy. The implementations of the methods `isRigid`, `sort`, and `validTopLevel` play important roles for the implementation of the prototype and are in some

8.15. Reflection is an Application Programming Interface (API) of JDK 1.1 for examining static informations like types and names of members in a class declaration at runtime. These informations are available from an object of the type `Class`, which can be retrieved from any object by the method `getClass` [24].

8.16. Except for elements which may occur in both, the logic part and the program part.

cases modified or overloaded by derived classes. Moreover, the latter two require some technical explanations, which will be given later in this section.

The lower half of the diagram 8.4 shows interfaces and classes derived from the interface `Operator`. The interface `Location` is used for updates. A *Location term* occurs at the same position as a location — but of course in a syntactical update. Since program variables, attributes, and arrays occur at the left side of elementary updates, the corresponding classes `ProgramVariable` and `AccessOp` and hence `ArrayOp` and `AttributeOp` are derived from the interface `Location`. These classes also represent *ProgramElements*. They belong to the logic part as well as to the program part and are therefore discussed in section 8.4.7. The class `AccessOp` is also derived from class `Op`.

The class `Op` represents junctors, modalities, quantifiers, the (compound) function symbol if...then...else...fi and the equality symbol by the classes `Junctor`, `Modality`, `Quantifier`, `IfThenElse`, and `Equlity`. The *Operator* represented by the class `IfExThenElse` is a special case of the mentioned function symbol if...then...else...fi as described in section 8.3.3. It is represented by this additional class because of its frequent usage for quantified updates.

Other function and predicate symbols like the ones defined in `.key`-files are *both* represented by the class `Function`, which is derived from class `TermSymbol`. *Functions* are distinguished into *RigidFunctions* and *NonRigidFunctions* by the derived classes `RigidFunction` and `NonRigidFunction` of class `Function`. In the original implementation of the KeY prover the class `NonRigidFunction` was not derived from the interface `Location`. This extension has been made because CDL requires updates on functions. The only class added for the implementation of the prototype is the class `NonRigidFunctionVarySort`. A *NonRigidFunctionVarySort* can be declared in a `.key`-file using the key-word `\nonRigidVarySort` (see section 8.3.1). Logical variables are represented by the class `LogicVariable`, which is also derived from the class `TermSymbol`.

Another class derived from the class `Op` is `AbstractMetaOperator`, which is also derived from the interface `MetaOperator`. This class represents meta constructs of the logic part in contrast to the class `ProgramMetaConstruct`, which is contained in the class diagram of section 8.4.2. These two classes are described in more detail in section 8.4.8. On the very right side of the diagram the interface `IUpdateOperator` is depicted, from which the class `QuanUpdateOperator` is derived. The class is not derived from the class `Op` or `Modality` as one might assume. What this class exactly represents is described in section 8.4.6. Finally, schema variables are represented by classes derived from the interface `SchemaVariable` like the classes `VariableSV` and `ProgramSV`. The class `ProgramSV` also may stand for *ProgramElements* because it is derived from the interface `ProgramConstruct`.

`Operators` are *singleton*, which means that two occurrences of *Operators* are represented by one object which is an instance of the interface `Operator`.[8.17] Two *Operators* with the same name but represented by two distinct objects, are different symbols for the KeY prover. Thus, a property of an *Operator* which may depend on the context of its occurrence cannot be simply encoded in the attribute of the singleton `Operator` because then the property would apply for all occurrences of the *Operator*. Instead, the property must be encoded in a method which is invoked with context informations. This is for instance the case for the methods `sort` and `validTopLevel` described below. The class `Op` contains `public static final` class attributes like `NOT`, `AND`, `OR`, `IMPL`, `EQUALS`, `ALL`, `EX`, `DIA`, `BOX` etc. which are statically initialized with objects representing common singleton *Ops*. In order to create another instance of a certain *Operator* like a *TermSymbol*, a `Namespace` has to be used (see section 8.4.1).[8.18] The class `Namespace` contains the method `lookup` which returns an `Operator` by passing it the *Name* of the desired *Operator*. For instance: `services.getNamespaces().functions().lookup(new Name("v"))`. The *Operator* has to be declared in a `.key`-file (see section 8.3.1).

The class `Term` represents logical terms and formulas, which are parts of *Sequents* (see section 8.4.1). A `Term` contains an instance of the interface `Operator`, which can be accessed by the method `op`. Since every `Term` contains one `Operator`, we refer to it by 'the `Operator` of the `Term`' or 'the *Operator* of the *Term*'. The second phrase refers to the top-level symbol of a term or formula. The class `Term` declares the methods `arity` and `isRigid`, which forward their invocation to the equally named methods of the `Operator` which is the `Operator` of the respective `Term`. If the arity of a *Term* is greater than zero then the `Term` represents a compound symbol and it contains sub-`Terms`. These sub-`Terms` can be accessed by the method `sub`. `Terms` can therefore be seen as the nodes of a tree template and the singleton `Operators` are the actual content. This concept is illustrated in diagram 8.5, where the names of the objects are equal to the syntactic elements they represent. The method `toString` creates a `String`, which represents

8.17. *Singleton* is a design pattern which ensures that a class only has one instance and provides as a global point of access to it [19].

8.18. Function and predicate symbols defined in `.key`-files are represented by the class `Function`, which is derived from class `TermSymbol`.

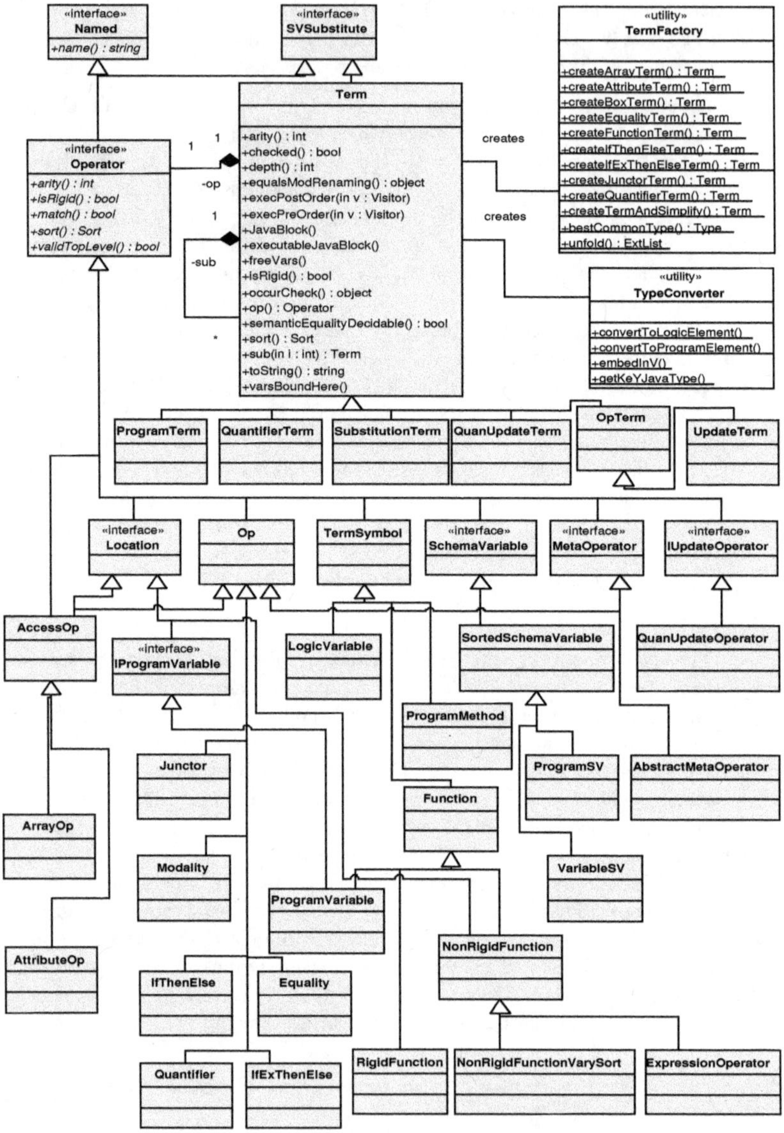

Diagram 8.4. Terms and Operators

a `Term` and its sub-`Terms` syntactically. This `String` can be used as a hash value to identify the corresponding *Term*.[8.19]

In order to create a `Term`, the methods of the class `TermFactory` have to be used.[8.20] The class contains a method for the creation of `Terms` with any kind of `Operator`. These methods ensure that no multiple `Operators` are created, representing the same *Operator*. An exception is when *TermSymbols* are created, e.g. *Functions*. In this case, a `TermSymbol` has to be created as described above and passed to the method `createFunctionTerm`. The `Operators` which do not represent *TermSymbols* are contained as `static final` class attributes in the class `Op`. When a `Term` is created the methods of the `TermFactory` ensure additionally that an appropriately derived class from the class `Term` is chosen depending on the `Operator`. If the `Operator` is a `Modality`, the created `Term` is a `ProgramTerm` which gives access to the *JavaBlock*[8.21] of the *Modality*[8.22]. If the `Operator` is a `Quantifier` or `QuanUpdateOperator`, the created `Terms` are instances of the classes `QuantifierTerm` and `QuanUpdateTerm` which have special implementations of the method `varsBoundHere`. The method `createJunctorTermAndSimplfy` creates a conjunction or disjunction of formulas and simplifies the resulting formula in case one of the formulas is the formula *true* or *false*.

When a `Term` is created the `Operator` and the `Sort` of the `Term` are saved in fields of the object.[8.23] The `Sort` of the `Term` is determined by the method `sort` of its `Operator` at the time of the creation of the `Term`. The previously mentioned context informations of the method `sort` of an `Operator` are the sub-`Terms` of the `Term` which is created. From this follows that the `Sort` of a `Term` has to be known at the time of its creation; but in one place in the implementation of the prototype this is not the case (see section 8.5.6.3). Similarly as the method `sort` the method `validTopLevel` of the `Operator` receives as input the contextual informations of the occurrence of the *Operator*, namely the `Term`, and checks whether the `Term` is constructed

8.19. A *Term* may be represented by two different `Terms` so that the `Term` reference is not a suitable hash value to identify a *Term*.

8.20. *Factory* is a design pattern which provides an interface for creating families of related or dependent objects without specifying their concrete classes [19].

8.21. The class `JavaBlock` is depicted in diagram 8.2.

8.22. It is not the `Modality` that contains the `JavaBlock` but the `Term` whose `Operator` is the `Modality` and which represents a *Term* beginning with a *Modality*.

8.23. Similarly as with '`Operator` of the `Term`', we refer with '`Sort` of the `Term`' to the `Sort` which is contained in the field `sort` of a `Term`.

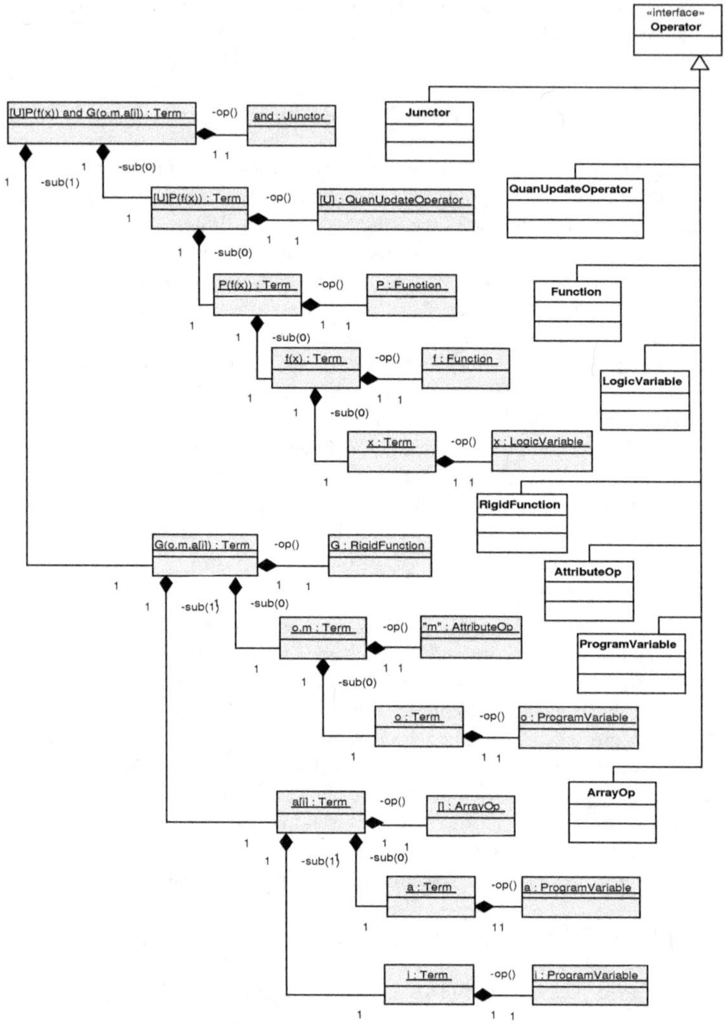

Diagram 8.5. Term example

appropriately.

`Terms` are also created by the *TypeConverter* and the *UpdateSimplifierTermFactory*, which are represented by the classes `TypeConverter` and `UpdateSimplifierTermFactory` respectively.[8.24] The *TypeConverter* is a utility which converts *ProgramElements* to *Terms* and establishes therefore a connection between the program part and the logic part. This concept is discussed in the next section. The methods `bestCommonType` and `unfold` of the class `TermFactory` have been added for the implementation of the prototype and are discussed in section 8.5.4. The class `UpdateSimplifierTermFactory` contains the method `createIfExCascade`, which creates a *chain* of *IfExThenElse* terms (see above) from a list by embedding them recursively in the *Else*-parts so that from the list

ifEx c_0 then t_0 else fi, ifEx c_1 then t_1 else fi, ..., ifEx c_n then t_n else fi

the term

ifEx c_0 then t_0 else ifEx c_1 then t_1 else ... ifEx c_n then t_n else *last* fi...fi fi

is created. The list is implemented by a class derived from the interface `IfExCascade`, which is declared in the `UpdateSimplifierTermFactory` (see section 8.4.6) and the last item embedded in the *Else*-part — denoted by *last* — is passed as the second parameter to the method.

8.4.5 Conversion from *ProgramElements* to *Terms*

When *Taclets* are applied on formulas or terms, which move *ProgramElements* from the program part to the logic part, a conversion of the *ProgramElements* to *Terms* has to take place, because all syntactical elements of the logic part are represented by *Terms* (see sections 8.4.2 and 8.4.4). This is where the *TypeConverter* comes into play. It is implemented by the class `TypeConverter` and depicted in the class diagram 8.4.[8.25] The class `TypeConverter` declares the method `convertToLogicElement`, which has if-cascades for the conversion of different kinds of *ProgramElements*. For the implementation of the prototype this method has been modified (see sections 8.5.3.4, 8.5.6.2, and 8.5.6.3). In cases where the object is an instance of the interface `ProgramInLogic` the conversion in the other direction can be done by using the method `convertToProgramElement` (see diagram 8.10). For

8.24. The classes cannot create `Terms`, but only their methods; for that reason the italic font is used.

8.25. The class `TypeConverter` is declared in the directory `/system/de/uka/ilkd/key/logic`.

the conversion of a *Type* into a *KeYJavaType* the method `getKeYJavaType` must be used which is also mentioned in section 8.4.3. The method `embedInV` is introduced for the prototype. It takes a `Term` as parameter and embeds the `Term` into another `Term` whose `Operator` represents the function symbol `v`. The usage of this method is explained in section 8.5.3.4.

Classes representing symbols which occur in the logic part and in the program part are subject to conversion by the *TypeConverter*. Examples for such symbols are *ProgramSVs*, *ProgramVariables*, *AttributeOps*, and *ArrayOps*. The later three are discussed in section 8.4.7.

8.4.6 Updates

Updates are represented in two ways. The lower part of the diagram 8.6 shows the representation of updates by the class `Update`.[8.26] `Updates` are created with the *UpdateFactory* by using the methods `elementaryUpdate`, `guard`, `parallel`, `quantify`, `sequential`, and `skip` of the class `UpdateFactory`.[8.27] An `Update` consists of a sequence of `AssignmentPairs` which can be accessed using the method `getAssignmentPair`.[8.28] An `AssignmentPair` consists in first place of two `Terms`. One `Term` — the *location* — is the left-hand side of an elementary update and the `Operator` of the `Term` must be derived from the interface `Location`. This `Term` can be accessed by the method `location`. The other `Term` — the *value* — can be accessed by the method `value` and is the right-hand side of an elementary update. Additionally an assignment may have a guard and bound variables which can be accessed by the methods `guard` and `boundVars`. Therefore an `AssignmentPair` represents a quantified update and an `Update` represents a set of them. This representation is very convenient, because it concentrates only on the update — the postponed term or formula is ignored — and treats an update as a sequence of quantified updates as described in [34]; but this is not the *real* representation of updates.

8.26. The class `Update` is declared in the directory `/system/de/uka/ilkd/key/rule/simplifier`.

8.27. The class `UpdateFactory` is declared in the directory `/system/de/uka/ilkd/key/logic`. *Factory* is a design pattern which provides an interface for creating families of related or dependent objects without specifying their concrete classes [19].

8.28. The class `AssignmentPair` is declared in the directory `/system/de/uka/ilkd/key/rule/simplifier`. The method `getAssignmentParis` returns a list of `AssignmentParis` where the passed `Location` may be aliased by `Locations` of the `AssignmentPairs`.

All elements of the logic part are represented by objects which are an instance of the class `Term` or the interface `Operator`. This applies also to update terms which consist of an update operator followed by a term or formula. Updates are represented by the class `QuanUpdateTerm` which is derived

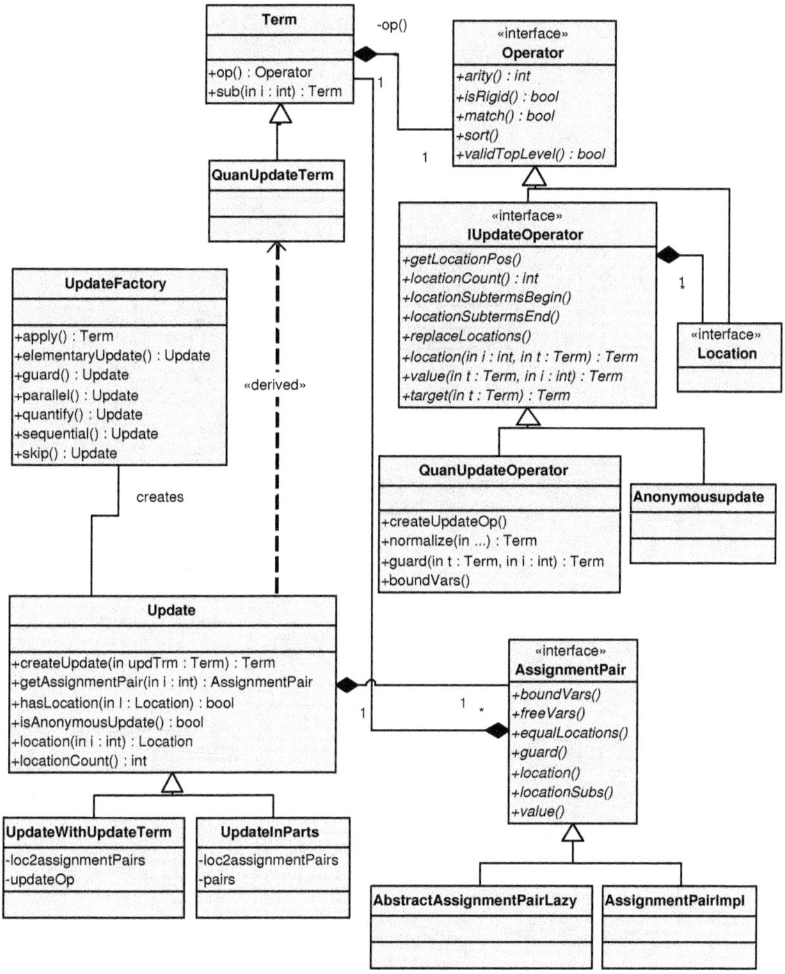

Diagram 8.6. Updates

from the class `Term`. The `Operator` of a `QuanUpdateTerm` is an instance of the interface `IUpdateOperator` and — in case of non-anonymous updates — also an instance of the class `QuanUpdateOperator`. *Terms* and *Operators* are described in section 8.4.4 in general, but the representation of *QuanUpdateTerms* with a *QuanUpdateOperator* is *a bit tricky* and deserves an example which is depicted by the diagram 8.7.

The *QuanUpdateTerm* $\{\text{for}\, x; \text{guard}; o.a := {}^{v}(f)\}$ is partially represented

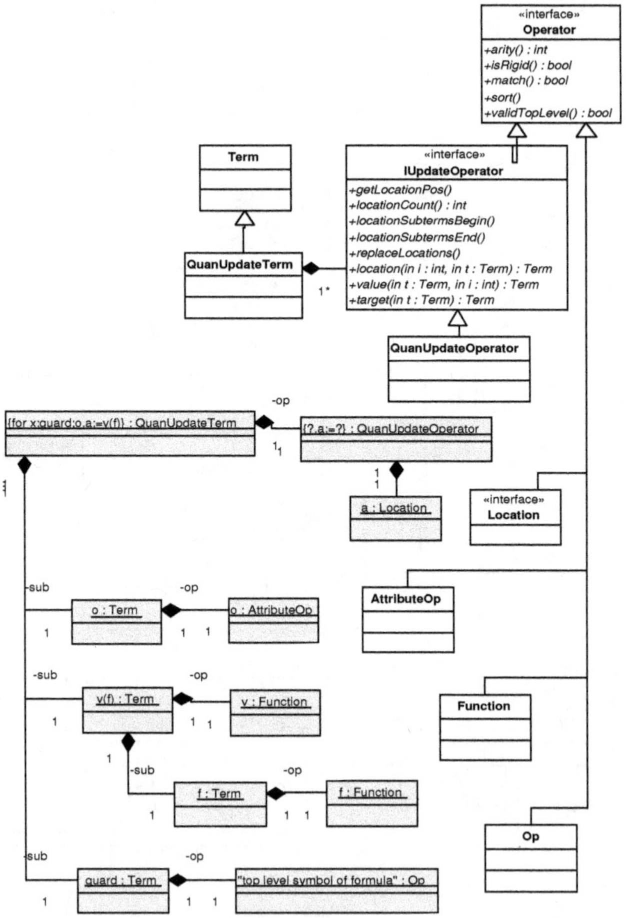

Diagram 8.7. Representation of a quantified update by a `Term`.

by a QuanUpdateTerm and a QuanUpdateOperator. The *Operator* contains the quantified variables and the top-level *Locations* of the *Terms* on the left-hand side of the elementary updates.[8.29] Here the quantified variable is x and the top-level *Location* of the *Term* on the left-hand side of the elementary update is a. Additionally the QuanUpdateOperator has an array of boolean values for each elementary update which indicate whether the elementary update has a guard. The other informations, the guard, o, and ${}^{v}(f)$, are contained in the sub-*Terms* of the *QuanUpdateTerm*. The Operator represents therefore a skeleton of a quantified update such that from the Locations contained in the QuanUpdateOperator its arity can be computed. Based on these informations contained in the QuanUpdateOperator of the QuanUpdateTerm the roles of the sub-*Terms* are defined so that the *location*, *value*, and the guard, of *AssignmentPairs* can be *reconstructed*. In order to make semantically equal updates unifiable the *implicit AssignmentPairs* of an IUpdateOperator are sorted by the method normalize. For instance the updates $\{a := x, b := y\}$ and $\{b := y, a := x\}$ cannot be unified, because they are syntactically different. Since a and b represent different *locations* the *AssignmentPairs* of the second update can be reordered to match the first update.

An Update can be created from a Term by using the method createUpdate of the class Update. The last sub-*Term* of a *QuanUpdateTerm* — not depicted in the object diagram 8.7 — is the term or formula which follows after the update.[8.30]

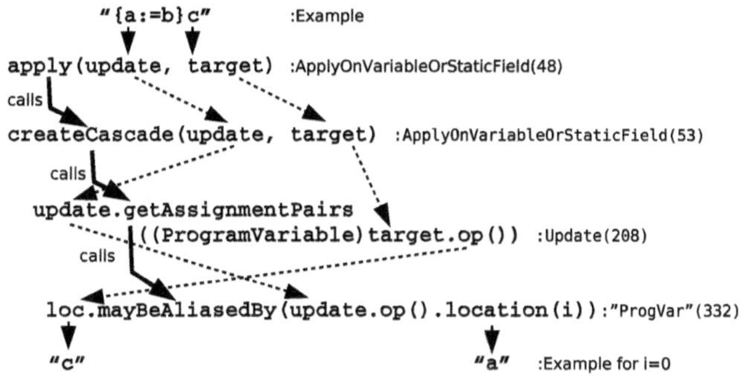

Figure 8.8 The method mayBeAliased

8.29. A *QuanUpdateTerm* may contain arbitrary many elementary updates.

8.30. It is recommended not to use the representation of updates by Terms and Operators for the creation or modification of updates, but rather the representation by the class Update and create updates using the *UpdateFactory*.

Operators which are also instances of the interface `Location` — this is the case for *ProgramVariables* and *AccessOps* (see section 8.4.7) — are allowed to be the top-level symbols of the terms on the left-hand side of elementary updates. They are required to be non-rigid and therefore the interface `Location` is derived from the interface `nonRigid`. The interface `Location` declares the method `mayBeAliasedBy` which is used for update simplification. Figure 8.8 shows a call tree and arrows indicating the flow of data which explains how this method is used. The method `apply` of class `AbstractUpdateRule` invokes the method `mayBeAliasedBy` of the interface `Location`. For a *Term* $\{a := b\}c$ where the update $\{a := b\}$ is applied by the method `apply` on the target c, the object for which the method `mayBeAliaseBy` is called, is the object which represents the target c and its argument is the *Location* of the update, i.e. in this case it is a. The method `mayBeAliasedBy` is also used by the method `getAssignmentPairs` described above.

For the simplification of updates, and terms and formulas with a preceeding update, the class `UpdateSimplifier` is responsible (see digram 8.9).[8.31] In order to simplify a *Term* or apply an *Update* on a *Term* the methods `simplify` and `apply` are used. Simplification is always the application of updates on certain syntactical elements like other updates, programs, formulas, terms,,, program variables etc. The actual simplification is performed by an *AbstractUpdateRule* for each of the cases.[8.32] Figure 8.9 shows a class diagram with classes which are derived from the class `AbstractUpdateRule`. The integration of the `AbstractUpdateRules` is accomplished in the constructor of the class `UpdateSimplifier` where a *ListOfIUpdateRule* is created with the `AbstractUpdateRules` which are considered for simplification when the methods `simplify` or `apply` are invoked. Therefore, the integration of a new *AbstractUpdateRule* into the system requires the extension of the *ListOfIUpdateRule*. The class `AbstractUpdateRule` is derived from the interface `IUpdateRule` from which the methods `isApplicable`, `apply`, and `matchingCondition` are inherited. Whether an *AbstractUpdateRules* is applicable on a syntactical element is determined by the method `isApplicable`. If the method returns `true` the application of the *Update* on the *target* is performed by the method `apply`.

If for a given *AttributeOp-Term* the method `getAssignmentPairs` delivers a list with more than one `AssignmentPairs` an if-cascade is created. The list is represented by a class derived from the interface

---

8.31. The class `UpdateSimplifier` is declared in the directory `/system/de/uka/ilkd/key/rule/simplifier`.

8.32. Classes derived from the interface `IUpdateRule` are declared in the directory `/system/de/uka/ilkd/key/rule`.

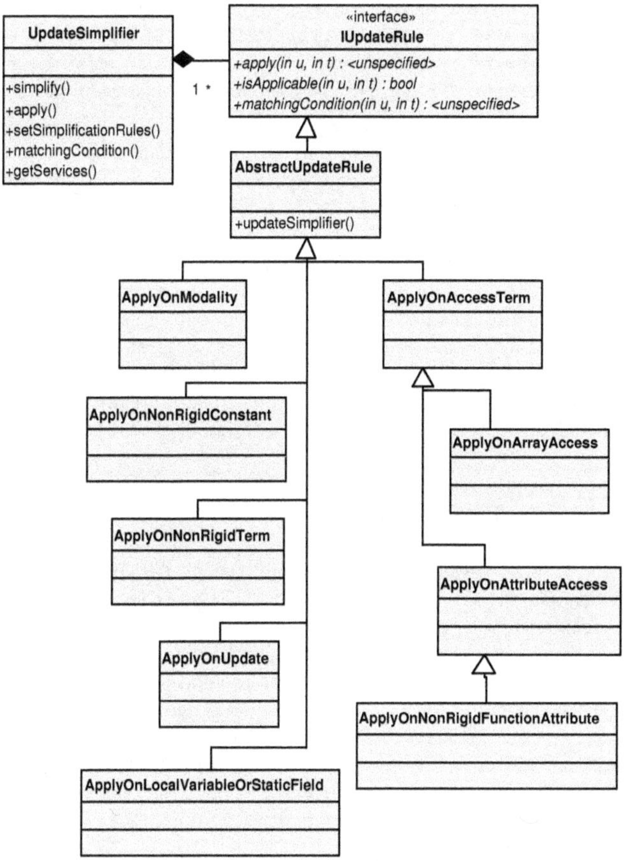

Diagram 8.9. Update Simplifier

IfExCascade. It contains the methods hasNext and next to iterate over items of the IfExCascade. An *IfExCascade* item consists of bound variables, a guard, and a term of the *Then*-part which can be accessed by the methods getMinmizedVars, getCondition, and getThenBranch. In other words an *IfExCascade* represents a list of *IfExThenElse-Terms*, but without the *Else*-parts. The IfExCascade for *AttributeOps* and *NonRigidFunctions* is created by the methods createCascade of the classes ApplyOnAttributeAccess and ApplyOnNonRigidFunctionAttribute respectively. The `IfExCascade` is passed to the method `createIfExCascade` of the class `UpdateSimplifierTermFactory` which is described in section 8.4.4. The terminating *Then-Term* — the second argument of the method `createIfExCascade` — is computed by the method `updateSubterms`.

The guard of an *IfExThenElse-Term* consists of one or more comparisons by equality predicates. In order to minimize the amount of user interaction during verification the method `compareObjects` of class `ApplyOnAccessTerm` tries to statically evaluate equalities and returns the formula *true*, *false*, or the unresolved equality. Conjunctions with *true* and *false* are simplified by the method `createJunctorTermAndSimplify` which is described in section 8.4.4. The method `matchingCondition` is also used for the computation of the guard. The `UpdateSimplifier` contains a list of `IUpdateRules` which is added by the method `setSimplificationRules` in the constructor of the `UpdateSimplifier`. Extensions for the prototype in this context are the method `getServices` of class `UpdateSimplifier` and the class `ApplyOnNonRigidFunctionAttribute` which are discussed in section 8.5.3.

8.4.7 Program variables

Figure 8.10 shows the class diagram of the classes `ProgramVariable`, `AttributeOp`, and `ArrayOp`.[8.33] The later two classes are derived from the class `AccessOp` and their syntactical counterparts are therefore called *AccessOps*. These classes represent symbols which occur in the program part as well as in the logic part and are therefore good examples of candidates for conversion by the *TypeConverter*. They are derived from the interface `Operator` (see section 8.4.4), to be able to occur in the logic part, and from the interface `SourceElement` (see section8.4.2) in order to occur in the program part. *ProgramVariables* and *AccessOps* may occur on the left-hand side of elementary updates and are therefore derived from the interface `Location`.

Because of the common concepts of *ProgramVariables* and *AccessOps* we will subsequently call them program variables.[8.34] Furthermore we distinguish between program variables in the logic part and program variables in the program part. Program variables in the logic part represent pointers and are rigid. Their value is stored by the non-rigid function `v` which takes the program variable as argument. Program variables in the program part represent the value that they contain so that they correspond to terms with the top-level function symbol `v`.

8.33. These classes are declared in the directory `/system/de/uka/ilkd/key/logic`.

8.34. Newly defined words are usually emphasized, but the italic font has a special meaning in this chapter which could lead to confusion here.

The name of a program variable can be determined by the method `name` inherited from the interface `Named` and it can be compared with other program variables using the method `equalsModRenaming`. The class `ProgramVariable` declares additionally the following three methods. The method `isStatic` returns true if the *ProgramVariable* is declared as static and the method `isImplicit` return true if the name of the *ProgramVariable* starts with a ‘<’. Implicit *ProgramVariables* are additional object fields of class `Object` which are used for storing informations about dynamic creation and the initialization process of objects by the calculus for JAVA CARD DL. The name of these implicit fields start with ‘<’ and end with ‘>’. `isImplicit` returns `true` if the name of the *ProgramVariable* starts with ‘<’. If the *ProgramVariable* is declared in a class type the method `getContainedInKeYJavaType` returns this class type. This way ambiguousness between variables which are declared in distinct classes and have the same name can be resolved.

Sorts and *Types* of program variables can be determined by the methods `sort` and `getKeYJavaType` (see 8.4.3). The later is declared in the interface `IProgramVariable`, which is more frequently used in declarations than the class `ProgramVariable`. For instance, an *AttributeOp* can be viewed as a function which is *indexed* by an *IProgramVariable*. An `IProgramVariable` is, usually, also an instance of class `ProgramVariable`. Note, that in the diagram 8.5 the argument of the *AttributeOp* ‘m’ — *indexed* by the *IProgramVariable* `m` — is the *Term* ‘o’.

The method `mayBeAliasedBy` of the interface `Location` is changed in the implementation of the prototype, because in CDL two distinct *ProgramVariables* in the logic part are never aliased in contrast to JAVA CARD DL (see 8.4.6). And because of problems in porting the C type system to the Java type system, the implementation of the method `validTopLevel` in class `AttributeOp` is changed to allow *AttributeOps* to have an argument of sort `any` where a sort representing a java type is expected.

8.4.8 Meta Constructs

In the KeY system two kinds of meta operators are distinguished. Classes which are derived from the class `AbstractMetaOperator` implement meta operators which may occur in the logic part of formulas, but not in the program part. For the later case the class `ProgramMetaConstruct` is used. A class diagram containing the class `ProgramMetaConstruct` is depicted in section 8.4.2. A class diagram showing the class `AbstractMetaOperator` is

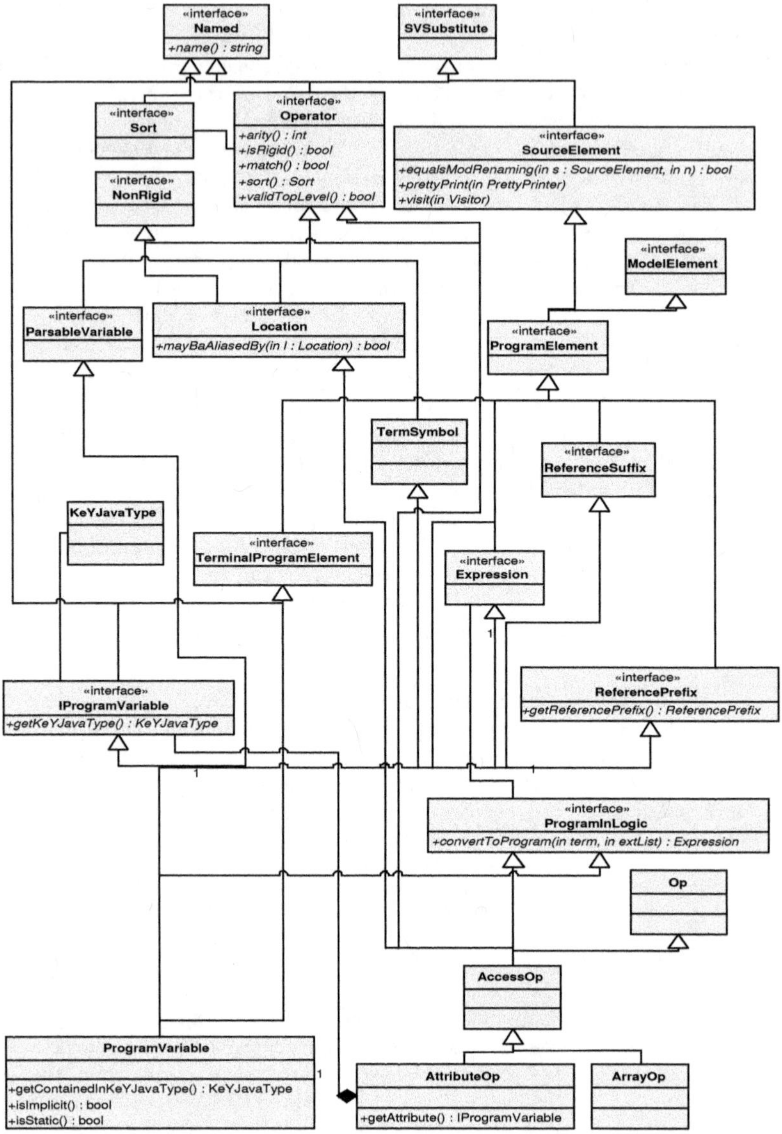

Diagram 8.10. Super classes and interfaces of program variables.

depicted in section 8.4.4 and additionally in this section, because the later contains the derived classes `AdrOf`, `IsDynamic`, `NonDynamic`, `SubStruct`, `MetaEmbedSubsInFunction`, `AssignmentToUpdates`, and `UnfoldEquals`, which have been introduced for the implementation of the prototype.

8.4.8.1 AbstractMetaOperator

The class `AbstractMetaOperator` implements the interface `MetaOperator`, which is again derived from the interface `Operator`. It is, therefore, used for the construction of *Terms* (see also section 8.4.4). These meta constructs may occur in formulas at positions which are dedicated for terms and formulas and may take terms and formulas as their arguments. It is, however, not possible to use meta construct which are represented by `AbstractMetaOperators` in the program part, because this would require the class to be derived from the class `ProgramElement`.

In order to extend the taclet language by a new meta operator for the logic part, no changes have to be made to the parser files. It suffices to extend the class `AbstractMetaOperator` with a new class attribute with the modifiers `final public static` which has a type derived from class `AbstractMetaOperator`. The KeY system extends the parser automatically with these meta constructs by using the reflection API.[8.35] The name of the meta construct, which actually occurs in the taclet definition of a `.key`-file, and its arity must be set by the constructor of the class `AbstractMetaOperator`. The first parameter of the constructor is of type `Name` and sets the name of the meta construct, which typically starts with the character '#', and the second parameter is of type `int` and sets the arity of the meta construct. When a new class is derived from class `AbstractMetaOperator`, the main task is to implement the method `calculate`, which is automatically invoked during taclet application. The signature of the method `calculate` is:

```
public Term calculate(Term t, SVInstantiations svi,
Services s)
```

This method is responsible for performing the syntactical substitution on the *Term* represented by `t`. The parameter `t` represents the whole occurrence of the meta construct together with its arguments. The `Operator` of the `Term` is, therefore, an instance of the current class, where this method is implemented. By accessing the sub-terms of `t`, the arguments of the occurrence of the meta construct can be accessed. The returned *Term* of this method

8.35. Reflections is an Application Programming Interface (API) for examining static informations like types and names of members in a class declaration at runtime.

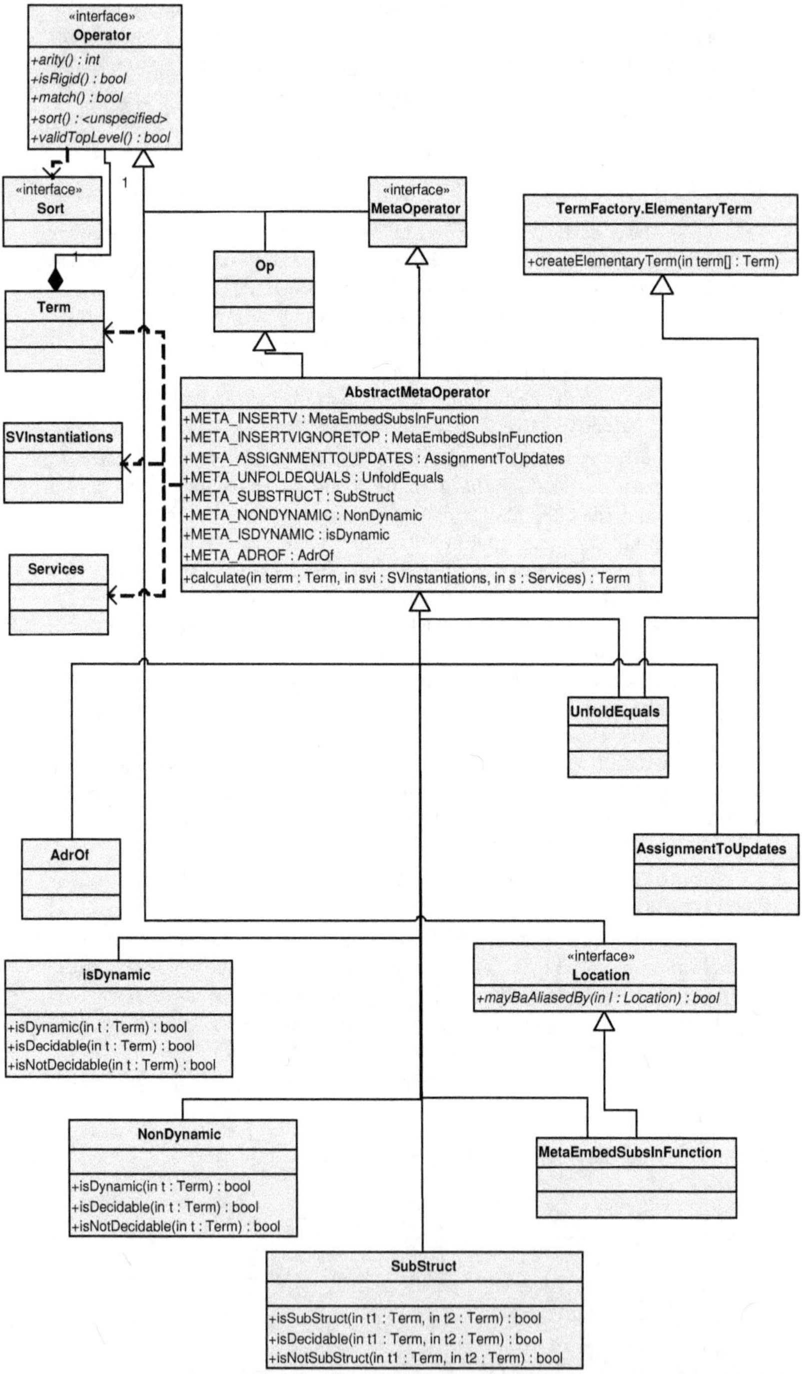
«interface»
Operator
+arity() : int
+isRigid() : bool
+match() : bool
+sort() : <unspecified>
+validTopLevel() : bool
«interface»
Sort
1
1
Term
SVInstantiations
Services
Op
«interface»
MetaOperator
TermFactory.ElementaryTerm
+createElementaryTerm(in term[] : Term)
AbstractMetaOperator
+META_INSERTV : MetaEmbedSubsInFunction
+META_INSERTVIGNORETOP : MetaEmbedSubsInFunction
+META_ASSIGNMENTTOUPDATES : AssignmentToUpdates
+META_UNFOLDEQUALS : UnfoldEquals
+META_SUBSTRUCT : SubStruct
+META_NONDYNAMIC : NonDynamic
+META_ISDYNAMIC : isDynamic
+META_ADROF : AdrOf
+calculate(in term : Term, in svi : SVInstantiations, in s : Services) : Term
UnfoldEquals
AdrOf
AssignmentToUpdates
isDynamic
+isDynamic(in t : Term) : bool
+isDecidable(in t : Term) : bool
+isNotDecidable(in t : Term) : bool
«interface»
Location
+mayBaAliasedBy(in l : Location) : bool
NonDynamic
+isDynamic(in t : Term) : bool
+isDecidable(in t : Term) : bool
+isNotDecidable(in t : Term) : bool
MetaEmbedSubsInFunction
SubStruct
+isSubStruct(in t1 : Term, in t2 : Term) : bool
+isDecidable(in t1 : Term, in t2 : Term) : bool
+isNotSubStruct(in t1 : Term, in t2 : Term) : bool

is then used to replace the occurrence of the meta construct. Note, that if a *ProgramElement* is passed to an *AbstractMetaOperator* as an argument, the *ProgramElement* is automatically converted into a *Term* by the *TypeConverter* before the method `calculate` is invoked (see section 8.4.5).

8.4.8.2 ProgramMetaConstruct

The class `ProgramMetaConstruct` is directly derived from the class `JavaNonTerminalProgramElement` and the interfaces `Expression`, `Statement`, `StatementContainer`, and `TypeReference`. A *ProgramMetaConstruct* may, therefore, occur in a program at positions where the respective *ProgramElements* occur — *ProgramElements* which are represented by the super class or at least one of the interface — and take *ProgramElements* as arguments.

A derived class from the class `ProgramMetaConstruct` must implement a constructor and the method `symbolicExecution`, which is invoked during *Taclet* application. The constructor must invoke the super constructor, which expects the name of the meta construct and a `ProgramElement` which represents the argument of the meta construct. The main issue of the implementation is of the method `symbolicExecution`, which has the signature:

```
public ProgramElement symbolicExecution(ProgramElement pe,
Services s, SVInstantiations svi)
```

The method plays the same role for *ProgramMetaConstructs* as the method `calculate` for *AbstractMetaOperators*. The main difference is that it takes a `ProgramElement` in place of a `Term` as argument. The `ProgramElement` represents the argument of the meta construct, but its actual content is determined by the further implementation tasks described below. The returned `ProgramElement` replaces the occurrence of the meta construct and must, thus, have an appropriate type and `Type`.

In contrast to *AbstractMetaOperators*, the integration of a new *ProgramMetaConstruct* into the taclet language requires the extension of the parser file `SchemaJavaParser.jj` which is located in the directory `/system/de/uka/ilkd/key/logic/parser` and the class `SchemaRecoder2KeY` located in the directory `/system/de/uka/ilkd/key/java`. Files with the ending '`.jj`' are parser files of the JAVACC parser generator [2]. In the scope of JAVACC, grammar rules are called productions. There are different kinds of productions, like BNF and regular expressions, and they may contain JAVA code. A production may, therefore, return a value. When a production is used in another production the returned value may be saved in a program variable by an ordinary assignment and used in the java block.

ProgramMetaConstructs are recognized by the production `KeYMetaConstructStatement`. In order to add a meta construct, the production must be extended with a regular expression production, for syntactic recognition of the *ProgramMetaConstruct*, followed by a java block. The regular expression production may use other productions for the recognition of arbitrary *ProgramElements* which are the arguments of the meta construct; for instance, `Expression()`, `StatementExpression()`, `Statement()`, etc. In the java block a `RKeYMetaConstruct` object must be created, initialized, and returned. The initialization is accomplished by setting the name of the *RKeYMetaConstruct* with the method `setName` and setting its content with the method `setChild`. The content consists of a `ProgramElement` constructed from the arguments of the meta construct.

The returned `RKeYMetaConstruct` is received by the method `convert` of the class `SchemaRecoder2KeY`. In order to make use of the new meta construct, this method must be extended by another if-cascade which checks the name of the `RKeYMetaConstruct`. In case of a match with the name of the new meta construct the `ProgramMetaConstruct` which implements the meta construct must be created and the content of the `RKeYMetaConstruct` passed as argument to its constructor, because this content is expected as argument of its super constructor as described above. The `ProgramMetaConstruct` must be returned by the method `convert`, which leads to the invocation of the method `symbolicExecution` of the respective `ProgramMetaConstruct`.

The only *ProgramMetaConstruct* introduced for the implementation of the prototype is represented by the class `JavaCUnfoldAssignment` and is further described in section 8.5.4.

8.5 Implementation of the Prototype

The prototype implements the calculus for CDL described in the previous chapters. Programs in the modalities comply with JAVA CARD syntax instead of C syntax for the reasons described in section 8.1. Language elements from C which find no correspondence in JAVA CARD are integrated into JAVAC by methods with dedicated method names and signatures. These methods are declared in the class `JavaC` which is described in section 8.5.1.3. A perfect mapping from C to JAVAC is, however, not possible, because of problems in porting the C type system to the JAVA CARD type system, as described in the next section. The other following sections describe how the parts of the calculus are integrated into the prototype, based on the background knowledge described in sections 8.3 and 8.4.

8.5.1 JavaC

8.5.1.1 Type system

For the realization of JavaC a mapping of the C type system to the Java Card type system is necessary. Types are used in declarations; they describe how program elements may be composed with each-other. Composition of program elements with not compatible types results in bad syntax, which implies that JavaC has to be type correct complying with Java Card syntax. A seeming solution is to allow only one type; for instance `int`. This way, all expressions could be arbitrarily composed. Elementary C types are, therefore, mapped to the Java type `int`. The actual size of a type in bytes is lost, so that, the MISRA C operator `sizeof` cannot be implemented with this approach. The operator `sizeof` is only important in MISRA C for the allocation of memory for *objects* and for pointer arithmetic like the iteration over elements of an array by their pointers.[8.36] In JavaC allocation is chosen to be treated like in C0[8.37], and pointer arithmetic is disallowed as it is the case in C0. Type informations are also important for detection of overflows and a correct treatment of bit-shift operators, and therefore, these capabilities have been taken out from the calculus.

What can not be ignored in the implementation — because this is a crucial difference between C and Java — is the treatment of assignments and comparisons between structures. The type of the *operands* must contain the information what the components of the structures are. An appropriate representative for structure types are classes, because they may consist of attributes, as it is similarly the case for structure types.[8.38] The same requirement applies to array types. A component-wise assignment or comparison between arrays is not implemented, because arrays are represented on the logic side as rigid functions, as it is the case for attributes of structures. Therefore, the theoretical concepts between structures and arrays of known

8.36. The iteration over elements of an array by their pointers is the only allowed form of pointer arithmetic in MISRA C.

8.37. There is a difference in allocation of memory, because the big step semantic of C0 assumes a limited amount of memory in contrast to the semantic of CDL.

8.38. The attributes of a structure are actually components of the structure, but the attributes of a Java object have only references to other objects.

size are the same and no additional knowledge about implementation issues would be gained from this extension of the prototype. Arrays in JAVAC are, therefore, only supported for explicit access of components by an index.

The major problem in mapping the type systems arises from pointer types, like a pointer to an `int`, pointer to a structure, or pointer to another pointer. The JAVA CARD type system does not have such an extension of primitive types and class types; this is, except for array chains of primitive type or class types, but a mapping of pointer types with arbitrary dereferenciation degrees to array types of varying dimensions is contra intuitive and would disallow the previously described usage of arrays. Sub-typing doesn't provide a suitable solution either, because this wouldn't work for primitive types and if primitive types would be omitted arithmetic operators couldn't be used. Yet, if a mapping of the type systems is possible, because in both systems extensions of a type (dereferenciation degree, sub-typing) can be defined which can be used for some homomorphic mapping, but an implementation would be very tricky, because this would require a generic creation of singleton derived classes. Short, in a real world application an infrastructure for C has to be implemented.

The current solution for JAVAC is that pointers to `int` are mapped to `int` and pointers to structures are mapped to the class `Object`. This approach has two negative consequences. The first is that the dereferenciation degree is lost and it is statically not decidable whether a JAVAC program is type correct with respect to its corresponding C program. At *runtime* dereferencing a variable of type `int`, which is assumed to hold a pointer, may result in actually dereferencing an integer. Secondly, if after dereferenciation of an `Object` the result is expected to be a structure, it is not known which structure it actually is. This makes component-wise assignments and comparisons impossible[8.39], because the components cannot be determined. An occurrence of the first problem can be recognized during verification, when a dereferenced symbol is substituted by an integer or an arithmetic expression.[8.40] The programmer has to take care of the second problem, by casting the class of a dereferenced `Object` into an appropriate class representing the correct C structure. This explains why pointers to structures are represented by `Objects` — the class `Object` can be casted to any other class according to JAVA CARD syntax.[8.41] An implementation of a parser for C0 and a C0 type system would resolve these problems.

8.39. A solution is provided by explicit type casts.

8.40. The dereferenced symbol of ^{v}s or `*s` is s, because in these terms s is the symbol which is dereferenced.

8.41. At runtime the type of an `Object` may not be casted to *any* other class type but only to super-types.

The function `v` has the sort `any`. The method `getType` of class `TermFactory` returns in this case a `Type` representing the class `Object`. The method `bestCommonType` returns the type of the left term if it can be determined, otherwise the type of the right term (see section 8.5.4.3).

8.5.1.2 Statements

Since statements in C0 are very similar to statements in JAVA CARD and no special treatment is required, a mapping of statements in C0 to statements in JAVAC is obvious. The syntax is the same except for possible *ReferencePrefixes* in front of method references, as it is the case for JAVAC operators described in the next section. Any constructs which are not supported in C0 are also not part of JAVAC like exceptions and jump statements.

8.5.1.3 Expressions

As it is the case for statements, expressions which are not supported in C0 are not part of JAVAC, e.g., exceptions and jump statements. Arithmetic operators are mapped to corresponding arithmetic operators in JAVA. Because of the lack of correct type informations[8.42] the size of the types of *ProgramVariables* is unknown, so that the recognition of overflow is ignored. For the same reason, operators which operate *semantically* on bits are not adapted for JAVAC except for the equality comparator.[8.43] Other operators, which have no correspondence in JAVA CARD, are integrated by methods with dedicated names and signatures. For instance the reference operator from C is represented in JAVAC by the method `adrOf` and the dereference operator is represented by the method `deref`. The methods are declared as `public static` methods of the class `JavaC`, which is declared in the file `javaC.java`.[8.44] Because of these modifiers in the declarations, no object variable has to be declared in the source code — the source code which is subject of verification — holding an instance of the class `JavaC`. A C expression like '`*a`' is represented as '`JavaC.adrOf(a)`' in JAVAC. The method bodies in the class `JavaC` are just dummy implementations. Without these dummy implementations, the methods would be abstract, which would disallow the *spontaneous* usage of the methods. The declared methods which represent the C0 operators `&`, `*`, `new`, and the MISRA C function `free` are `adrOf`, `deref`, `alloc`, and `delete` respectively and are called JAVAC operators or JAVAC methods.

8.42. due to the problems in mapping the C0 type system to the JAVA CARD type system

8.43. Technically speaking all operators operate on bits.

8.44. The file `javaC.java` is located in the directory `\system\poofExamples\javaC\code`

Other methods declared in class `JavaC` are either used for tests of the prototype or their special treatment is not implemented like in the case of `sizeOf`. The reason for the later is, firstly, that the C operator `sizeof` takes a type as argument. This would require a JAVA method to accept a type as argument with the described approach. Secondly, the implementation of the C type system is not considered as part of the prototype, and a mapping of the C type system to JAVA is not feasible as described in section 8.5.1.1. Before this problem was recognized, the method `alloc` was already in use in examples, by taking an arbitrary integer as argument instead of a value from the JAVAC operator `sizeOf`. Therefore, the semantic of the expression `JavaC.alloc(1)` is that it delivers an appropriate pointer as the C0 expression `new(`*`type`*`)` would do it for some type *`type`*. The type information can be ignored, because pointer arithmetic is not supported by KeY and no concrete memory representation is necessary.

Each method in this class is declared multiple times with varying signatures. The variations result from different combinations of the types `int` and `Object`. The reason for this is that the JAVAC operators may be used with variables of arbitrary types, like it is the case for the respective operators in C0. In JAVAC '`int`' represents an elementary type and structures are represented by classes which are all derived from the class `Object`.

8.5.1.4 Declarations

A mapping of C-specific declarations like type declarations by the key-word `typedef` or the declaration of external functions by the key-word `extern` are not implemented, because these issues belong to the parser and to classes representing static program structures, but not to the operational semantics which the calculus deals with. Declarations must comply with JAVA CARD syntax, which means in particular that methods which represent C functions must be declared in classes with the modifiers `public static final`. The same applies also to *ProgramVariables* and *AccessOps* which are declared globally in a C source file. Structure types are declared as classes as described in section 8.5.1.1 and *unions* and *enums* are not supported.

8.5.2 *ProgramSVSorts* for JavaC operators

In order to write specific taclets for the JAVAC operators, special *ProgramSVSort* are introduced, such that schema variables declared with this *ProgramSVSorts* match on the method names of the JAVAC operators. For this purposed the local class `SpecialMethodName` is declared in the class

ProgramSVSort, which is derived from class NameMatchingSort. The class NameMatchingSort is derived from class ProgramSVSort, as it is required for classes representing *ProgramSVSort* (see section 8.4.3). The constructor takes the name of the *ProgramSVSort* and the name of a method for which a schema variable of this sort may stand. The class ProgarmSVSort is extended by the following attribute declarations and initializers

```
public static final ProgramSVSort MN_ADDRESSOF =
   new SpecialMethodName(new Name("JavaCadrOf"), "adrOf");
public static final ProgramSVSort MN_DEREFERENCE =
   new SpecialMethodName(new Name("JavaCderef"), "deref");
public static final ProgramSVSort MN_SIZEOF =
   new SpecialMethodName(new Name("JavaCsizeOf"), "sizeOf");
public static final ProgramSVSort MN_ALLOC =
   new SpecialMethodName(new Name("JavaCalloc"), "alloc");
public static final ProgramSVSort MN_DELETE =
   new SpecialMethodName(new Name("JavaCdelete"), "delete");
```

The declarations of schema variables with the respective *ProgramSVSorts* is shown in section 8.3.1.

8.5.3 Moving *ProgramVariables* and *AccessOps* to the logic part

8.5.3.1 Modification of the classes ProgramVariable and AccessOp

In the class ProgramVariable the methods isRigid and mayBeAliasedBy are changed for the implementation of the prototype. The method isRigid returns true instead of false. In CDL program variables are non-rigid in the program part, but in the logic part the name of a program variable represents its *pointer*, which cannot be changed and is therefore rigid. The value of the program variable is stored in the non-rigid function v, which is *indexed* by the *pointer*. The same modification is done for the abstract class AccessOp, from which the method isRigid is inherited by the derived classes AttributeOp and ArrayOp. The class AttributeOp represents object fields and class attributes, and in case of JAVAC, attributes of structures. In JAVAC an *AttributeOp* is therefore a rigid function symbol for each attribute name; it represents the function symbol $^\bullet$. Leaving the return value of isRigid to be false would technically result in the creation of conditional terms, which the user would have to evaluate manually by applying taclets with a static decision procedure to determine whether two variables are distinct, or not.

The method `mayBeAliasedBy` is stricter than in its original form. Different program variables in the logic part — their pointer values of the *ProgramVariables* in the program part — are distinct. A *ProgramVariable* in the logic part may be aliased only by itself; therefore `this==loc` is returned. Since *ProgramVariables* in the logic part are rigid, they may not occur as *locations* in updates, so that the method could even return `false`.

8.5.3.2 Class `NonRigidFunctionVarySort`

The function `v` is represented by the class `NonRigidFunctionVarySort` which is derived from class `NonRigidFunction` (see section 8.4.4). The function is declared in the file `JavaC.key` as a function of *Sort* `int` (see section 8.3.1). This *Sort* is, however, unimportant, because the purpose of the function is to represent the value of a program variable from the program part and, hence, it must have the *Sort* of the program variable in the program part. The function `sort` of class `NonRigidFunctionVarySort` returns, therefore, the *Sort* of the term which is embedded in the term with this *Operator* as top-level symbol.[8.45] In other words the sort of `v(a)` is the sort of `a`. However, if `v(a)` represents a pointer which may be dereferenced once the term `v(v(a))` has still the sort of `v(a)`, which has again the sort of `a`. This is not the correct sort in general. But if the correct type information is not encoded in the sort of `v(v(a))` then unfolding in the logic part cannot be performed. The class `NonRigidFunctionVarySort` is, therefore, extended further as described in section 8.5.6.3.

In order to define a function in a `.key`-file to be represented by an object of class `NonRigidFunctionVarySort` the token `\nonRigidVarySort` must be used (see section 8.3.1). The file `lexer.g` is extended by the token `NONRIGIDVARYSORT`, which has the value `"\\nonRigidVarySort"`.[8.46] The integration of the class `NonRigidFunctionVarySort` into the system is done in the parser file `keyparser.g`. The token `NONRIGIDVARYSORT` is used in the rules `pred_decl` and `func_decl` for parsing predicate and function declarations.[8.47] When this token occurs in a `.key`-file a `NonRigidFunctionVarySort` is created analogously to the creation of `NonRigidFunction` in the rule definitions.

Files ending with '`.g`' are parser files of the tool AntLR [1]. The files `lexer.g` and `keyparser.g` are located in the directory `/system/de/uka/ilkd/key/logic/parser`.

8.45. Without referenciation and dereferenciation the sub-term is a program variable in the logic part

8.46. The backslash '\' is an escape character. An actual backslash occurring in the string is represented by two backslashes.

8.47. A grammar from which a parser is generated by AntLR [1] consists of rules. The rules may contain JAVA code.

8.5.3.3 Conversion by a meta construct

There are two possibilities how to handle the conversion of program variables of the program part to terms. The first possibility described here is by using a meta construct and the other solution is by using the *TypeConverter* described in the next section.

The meta construct which performs the conversion is implemented by the class `MetaEmbedSubsInFunction`, which is derived from the class `AbstractMetaOperator` and the interface `Location`. The class may be parameterized to represent different meta constructs like `#inservV` and `#insertVIgnoreTop`. The constructor takes the name of the meta construct, the name of a function symbol, and a boolean value, which controls the exact behavior of the meta construct. The possible behaviors are explained with the descriptions of the mentioned meta constructs.

The meta construct `#insertV` has the arity 1. It takes a *ProgramVariable* or *AccessOp* `x` and embeds it as argument of the function `v` yielding `v(x)`. In case of reference chains like `a.b.c` the result is `v(v(v(a).b).c)`. More generally the semantic of the meta construct can described by the following rewrite rule:

$$\texttt{\#insertV}(X) \quad \rightsquigarrow$$

$$\begin{cases} {}^{v}X\,,\text{for } X \in \textit{Program Variable} \\ {}^{v}(f(\texttt{\#insertV}(x_1),...,\texttt{\#insertV}(x_n)))\,,\text{for } X = f(x_1,...,x_n) \\ g(\texttt{\#insertV}(x_1),...,\texttt{\#insertV}(x_n))\,,\text{for } X = g(x_1,...,x_n) \end{cases}$$

where f is an *AccessOp* and g is not a program variable.

The meta construct is integrated into the system by an extension of the class `AbstractMetaOperator` with the attribute `META_INSERTV` (see section 8.4.8). The conversion by the meta construct was the first choice during the implementation of the prototype.[8.48] It turns out that the *TypeConverter* is more suitable for this task as it will become clear in the following sections, which is an important realization gained from the implementation of the prototype.

8.5.3.4 Conversion by the *TypeConverter*

The *TypeConverter* provides a *natural* place for the implementation of the conversion mechanism, which converts program variables of the program part to terms with the top-level function symbol `v`. The class `TypeConverter` is extended by the method `embedInV`. It takes a `Term` a argument and creates a new `Term` with the `Operator` `v` and the passed argument as the sub-`Term` of the new `Term`. In other words `embedInV(t)` returns `v(t)`.[8.49]

8.48. Because of a missing documentation the *TypeConverter* was not considered.

In order to convert ProgramVariables and AccessOps according to the mono representation (see section 5.2) of program variables the Terms created by the methods createAttributeTerm, createVariableTerm, and createArrayTerm in the methods convertReferencePrefix, convertVariableReference, and convertArrayReference are passed through the method embedInV before their further processing. The converting methods operate recursively on the structure of the expressions, so that for example, a *ReferencePrefix* of the form a.b.c is converted into the *Term* v(v(v(a).b).c), as the meta construct #insertV would do.

Furthermore, the *TypeConverter* is extended to map a *TypeCast* to the sort of the resulting *Term* with the operator *NonRigidFunctionVarySort*. This issue is, however, not described here but in section 8.5.6, because it deals with problems which arise with dereferenciation.

8.5.3.5 Taclets

Because of the two approaches of conversion of program variables, there are two sets of taclets. The set of taclets which works with conversion by a meta construct is contained in the file JavaC.key, but it is commented out to omit conflicts. One of the taclets is:

```
javaC_assign_var_var {
  \find (
    \modality{#allnormalass}
      {.. #var0 = #var1; ...}
    \endmodality(post)
  )
  \replacewith (
    {#insertV(#var0):= #insertV(#var1)}
       \modality{#allnormalass}
         {.. ...}
       \endmodality(post)
  )
  \displayname "JC_assign_var_var"
};
```

It matches on an assignment and creates an update while converting the left-hand side and right-hand side of update.

8.49. Where t and v(t) are just symbols which are represented by actual Terms.

A modification has been made to the class `ProgramVariableSort` which should be mentioned here. The class is derived from the class `LeftHandSideSort` and the schema variables declared with the respective *ProgramSVSorts* `variable` and `lefthandside` can be seen in section 8.3.1. The class `ProgramVariableSort` is modified so that a schema variable of this sort can stand for reference chains like `a.b.c`. This way they can be treated like *ProgramVariables* by the taclets. In other words the *ProgramVariableSort* represents now program variables and not only *ProgramVariables*. Program variables are *exported* to the logic part in some context like an assignment and, therefore, the associated taclets which make use of conversion are presented in the following sections.

8.5.3.6 Updates

The introduction of the class `NonRigidFunctionVarySort` and the modifications to the classes `ProgramVariable` and `AccessOp` requires an extension of classes related to the *UpdateSimplifier*. The class `NonRigidFunction` is *extended* by the interface `Location` in order to allow terms with the top level function symbols `cr` and `v` to occur on the left hand side of updates.[8.50] Consequently, the method `mayBeAliasedBy` (see section 8.4.6) is implemented and returns true if the parameter `loc` and `this` are equal, which ensures the equality of the *Operators*, because they are singleton (see section 8.4.4). Thus functions represented by the class `NonRigidFunctionVarySort` may also be used on the left-hand side of updates. For this reason the method `normalize` of the class `QuanUpdate` has to be extended. The treatment of `NonRigidFunctionVarySorts` by the method is implemented analogously to the implementation of the treatment of `AttributeOps`.

In order to extend the *UpdateSimplifier* to *handle NonRigidFunctionVarySorts* the class `ApplyOnNonRigidFunctionAttribute` is introduced. It represents an *AbstractUpdateRule* for the simplification of terms with the functions `v` or `cr`. The rule works analogously to the rule for update application on attributes in Java Card DL. Therefore, the class is derived from class `ApplyOnAttributeAccess`, as can be seen in the class diagram 8.9. The rule is integrated into the system by the extension of the `ListOfIUpdateRule` in the constructor of the class `UpdateSimplifier` (see section 8.4.6) with an `ApplyOnNonRigidFunctionAttribute`.

When the rule is considered for simplification the method `isApplicable` checks whether the top-level symbol of the target is `v` or `cr`. If the rule is applicable the method `apply` is invoked, which uses the method `createCascade` (see section 8.4.6). The method `createCascade` retrieves

8.50. *Terms* with the top-level function symbols `v` and `cr` are terms.

the *PropagationResult* $Uf_{\text{sub1}}, \ldots, Uf_{\text{subn}}$, the *Update* $\langle \ldots, f(x_k) := y_k, \ldots, f(x_m) := y_m, \ldots\rangle$, and the target *Term* $f(f_{\text{sub1}}, \ldots, f_{\text{subn}})$.[8.51] By using the method `getAssignmentPairs` the *AssignmentPairs* which may be aliased by the target are extracted from the update and an *IfExCascade* of the form ifEx $x_k = Uf_{\text{sub1}}$ then y_k, ..., ifEx $x_m = Uf_{\text{sub1}}$ then y_m is created. The equality predicates are created by the method `compareObjects` (see section 8.4.6) which is modified according to the semantic of the equality predicate in CDL. In the original form of the method `compareObjects` the equality between two *ProgramVariable-Terms* or *AttributeOp-Terms* cannot be decided, but in CDL they are rigid, so that, differently named *ProgramVariables* or *AccessOps* are distinct. The final if-cascade is created by the method `createIfExCascade` (see 8.4.4) from the created `IfExCascade` and a `Term` which is created by the method `updateSubterms`. The method `updateSubterms` returns a `Term` constructed from the `Operator` of the target and the mentioned `PropagationResult`, which yields $f(Uf_{\text{sub1}}, \ldots, Uf_{\text{subn}})$.

When updates are merged, locations are tested whether they are aliased, which may cause many trivial equations, because of the rigidity of program variables in the logic part. To reduce the amount of user interaction the invocation of the method `createTerm` in the method `apply` of class `ApplyOnRigidOperatorTerm` is replaced by the method `createTermAndSimplify` of the `TermFactory` which automatically performs some simplifications.

8.5.4 Unfolding

This section describes how unfolding of assignments and unfolding of comparison by the equality predicate is implemented. The unfolding of assignments can be performed by a *ProgramMetaConstruct* in the program part or by an *AbstractMetaOperator* in the logic part resulting in a set of updates. These two possibilities are also connected to the mechanism for converting program variables from the program part to the logic part (see section 8.5.3). The conversion of program variables by an *AbstractMetaOperator* requires, in cases where unfolding is necessary, a previous unfolding by a *ProgramMetaConstruct*. Unfolding by an *AbstractMetaOperator* may *accept* conversion of expressions from the program part either by another *AbstractMetaOperator* or by the *TypeConverter*; both of them cannot be used at once. The conversion by the *TypeConverter* and the unfolding by an *AbstractMetaOperator* are the preferred mechanisms. The mechanism for unfolding of assignments by an *AbstractMetaOperator* can be reused for the unfolding of a comparison

8.51. For the function symbols `v` and `cr` and for *AttributeOps* it is: $n = 1$.

by a predicate. Independently from the unfolding method, the *Types* of the operands must be known, in order to traverse over the attributes in the class declarations of the types and create appropriate *ReferencePrefix* chains for the operands of the elementary operations, e.g., assignment, update, comparison, etc. The procedure for traversing attributes in the class declarations is the same for any unfolding method and is therefore presented first.

8.5.4.1 Traversing attributes of *ClassDeclarations*

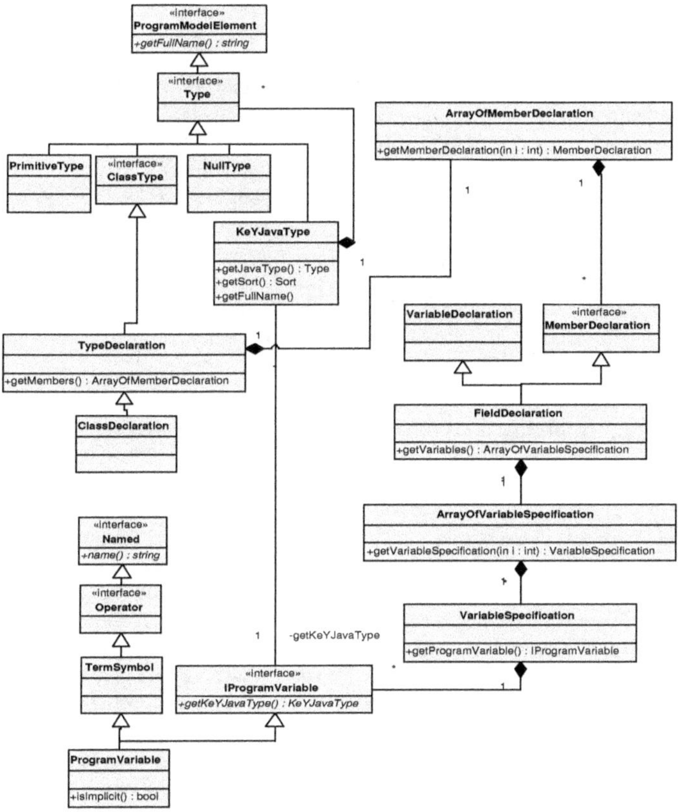

Diagram 8.12. Traversing attributes of class declarations

The procedure of traversing the attributes of class declarations works recursively. The necessary classes which have to be considered by the procedure are depicted by the class diagram 8.12. Given an `IProgramVariable` its `KeYJavaType` can be obtained by the method `getKeYJavaType`, from which the `Type` can be obtained (see section 8.4.3). The `Type` is checked whether it is a `PrimitiveType` or a `ClassType`. `PrimitiveTypes` represent elementary types, which are not subject to unfolding.[8.52] If possible the `ClassType` is converted into a `JavaDeclaration`, then into a `TypeDeclaration`, and finally it is checked whether it is a `ClassDeclaration`. In case the `Type` we've started with is a `ClassDeclaration` we access its members by the inherited method `getMembers`, which yields an `ArrayOfMemberDeclaration`. The elements of this class can be accessed by the method `getMemberDeclaration`. The returned `MemberDeclaration` may, however, be a declaration of a method. Therefore, only `MemberDeclarations` which are also `FieldDeclarations` are considered. Since the JAVA CARD syntax allows the declaration of several fields separated by semicolons after a type name, a `FieldDeclaration` consists of an `ArrayOfVariableSpecification`, which can be accessed by the method `getVariables`. The individual `VariableSpecifications` are accessed by the method `getVariableSpecification`, from where finally the sub-`IProgramVariable` can be accessed by the method `getProgramVariable`. The obtained `IProgramVariable` is usually an instance of the class `ProgramVariable` which declares the method `isImplicit`. Implicit program variables are not subject to unfolding and can be filtered out by checking whether the method `isImplicit` returns true (see section 8.4.7).

8.5.4.2 Unfolding assignments in the program part

Unfolding of an assignment between structure types into a sequence of assignments between elementary types in the program part is accomplished by the *ProgramMetaConstruct* `#jc-unfold` which takes two arguments — the left-hand side and the right-hand side of the assignment. The meta construct `#jc-unfold` is implemented by the class `JavaCUnfoldAssignment`, which is derived from class `ProgramMetaConstruct`. In order to make the parser recognize the meta construct, the file `SchemaJavaParser.jj` is extended. In this file the production `KeYMetaConstructStatement` (see section 8.4.8) is extended to recognize the token `#jc-unfold`, which is followed by two *Expressions* and create a `CopyAssignment` from these *Expressions*. The name '`#jc-unfold`' and the `CopyAssignment` are used to create a `RKeYMetaConstruct` which is returned and received by the

8.52. Basic types could be unfolded up to the bit level.

method convert of class SchemaRecoderToKeY. The method convert is, therefore, extended to recognize the *RKeYMetaConstruct* and create a JavaCUnfoldAssignment.

To create the assignments, the method symbolicExecution uses the method createElementaryAssignments, which takes two ProgramElements — left-hand side and right-hand side of the assignment — and traverses over the attributes declared in a *ClassDeclaration* of the ProgramElements, as it is described in the previous section. A ClassDeclaration is a Type which can be obtained from the method getType. The advantage of this method is that it makes use of *TypeCasts*. In case of a TypeCast, its implicit Type is obtained from the TypeRef which is contained in the TypeCast (see section 8.4.3). In order to allow the attachment of attributes to the ProgramElements, they are converted to ReferencePrefixes by the method toRefPrefix. When two reference chains are created the final assignment is created by the method createElementaryAssignment. At the end the assignments are put into a JavaBlock which is substituted for the meta construct. The taclet for unfolding assignments using this meta construct is defined by:

```
javaC_unfoldassignment_var_var {
  \find (
    \modality{#allnormalass}
      {.. #var0 = #var1; ...}
    \endmodality(post)
  )
  \replacewith (
    \modality{#allnormalass}
      {.. #jc-unfold (#var0 , #var1); ...}
    \endmodality(post)
  )
  \displayname "JC_unfoldassignment_var_var"
};
```

The preferred method of unfolding assignments is however by using an AbstractMetaOperator described in the following sections.

8.5.4.3 Unfolding of Terms

Two *AbstractMetaOperators* are implemented for unfolding, one for unfolding of assignments and one for unfolding of comparisons. Their common aspect, the actual unfolding, is implemented by the method unfold, by which the

TermFactory is extended. Additional extensions of the class TermFactory are the methods getType and bestCommonType and the local interface ElementaryTerm. The two methods are used only in this context and can be viewed as utility methods of the method unfold. The method bestCommonType tries to reduce the problem of loss of type informations. It takes two operands and determines their *Types* using the method getType. The Type of the first operand is taken as the common Type for unfolding if it can be determined, otherwise the Type of the second operand is used. This way unfolding can be performed even if the Type of the second operand is not correct or if the Type of the first operand is unknown[8.53].

The logical function objEnum declared in JavaC.key represents the object enumerator function obj_T: $\mathbb{N} \rightarrow \mathrm{Ptr}$, except that the type information T is not encoded. Therefore the "type" declaration of the function should be int → Object. The declaration of a function with this type is however disallowed by the syntax of .key-files, because classes are not allowed to occur in the type definition of logical functions. Instead one has to use the sort any or define a sort using the keyword \generic which may represent arbitrary classes (see section 8.3.1). The method getType takes care of this problem: by passing a Term of sort any to the method getType the returned *Type* represents the class Object.

The signature of the method unfold is:

```
public ExtList unfold(Term[] terms, ElementaryTerm
elemTerm, Type t1, Services serv)
```

The method generates an ExtList of Terms for each elementary type contained in the type represented by t1. For example if the represented type is a class with two fields of type integer — representing a C structure consisting of two integers — then two Terms are added into the ExtList, namely, one for each field. The method unfold is used by the calculate methods of the AbstractMetaOperator classes UnfoldEquals and AssignmentToUpdates. Placing the method in the class TermFactory seems reasonable, since it is used for Term creation as the majority of the other methods in this class. The disadvantage is that Services is not available in TermFactory, because the TermFactory is independent from the loaded program context. In order to traverse through all fields of the type (class) declaration represented by t1, type informations are necessary, but they have to be accessed through Services. For this reason an instance of the class Services has to be passed to unfold. Furthermore, Services is in this context also used to access the TypeConverter by the method Services.getTypeConverter.

8.53. The *Type was* unknown for the case of the *Sort* any. But at the current stage of the implementation this case doesn't occur.

Unfolding is associated with an "operation" like assignment, comparison, or a bit-wise operator. The operation is represented by the `Operator` of each of the generated `Terms` in the `ExtList`. In order to generalize the method `unfold` for arbitrary operations it is independent of the concrete `Operator`. For this purpose the interface `ElementaryTerm` is defined in the class `TermFactory` with the single abstract method `createElementaryTerm`. A class implementing `ElementaryTerm` determines the concrete `Operator` of the final `Terms` in the resulting `ExtList` of `unfold`. In order to allow `Operators` of arbitrary arity, the method `createElementaryTerm` takes an array of `Terms` as argument, which will be called operands. For instance in case of an assignment from one variable to another or the comparison between two variables the arity is two, but in case of an assignment of the result of a bit-wise operation between two variables to another variable, a compound operator of arity three has to be constructed. The reason for this is that `a=b|c;` has the semantic of $\mathtt{a.}x_1\mathtt{=b.}x_1\mathtt{|c.}x_1\mathtt{;}\ldots\ \mathtt{a.}x_n\mathtt{=b.}x_n\mathtt{|c.}x_n\mathtt{;}$ where $x_1 \ldots x_n$ stand for the attributes of the structure which is represented by `t1`.[8.54] Unfolding only `b|c` would result in $\mathtt{b.}x_1\mathtt{|c.}x_1\mathtt{;}\ldots\ \mathtt{b.}x_n\mathtt{|c.}x_n\mathtt{;}$ which is neither an expression nor a statement. The unfolding of bit-wise operations has not been implemented, because the unfolding of assignments and comparisons suffices to illustrate this concept.

The meta constructs invoking `unfold` operate on the logic part. Since in the logic part program variables represent pointers, the created reference chains must be embedded as arguments of the function `v` as the *Type-Converter* would do — in contrast to the meta construct `#jc-unfold`. The method `unfold` takes care of this embedding by invoking the method `embedInV` of class `TypeConverter` while going through the attributes of the `ClassDeclaration` of the passed `Type` as described above. An instance of class `TypeConverter` can be retrieved by using the method `getTypeConverter` of the class `Services`. The rewriting which is performed by the method `unfold` can be represented by the following rewrite rule:

$$\mathtt{unfold(\{a,b\},op_{=},T)} \rightsquigarrow \begin{cases} 1.\ \{\mathtt{unfold(\{}{}^{v}(\mathsf{a}.x_1),{}^{v}(\mathsf{b}.x_1)\mathtt{\}},\mathrm{op}_{=},\mathrm{T}_1\mathtt{)}, \\ \qquad\vdots \\ \quad ,\mathtt{unfold(\{}{}^{v}(\mathsf{a}.x_n),{}^{v}(\mathsf{b}.x_n)\mathtt{\}},\mathrm{op}_{=},\mathrm{T}_n\mathtt{)}\} \\ 2.\ \mathsf{a}=\mathsf{b} \end{cases}$$

1. T is a class, 2. T is a primitive type

where $x_1, \ldots, x_n$ are the field names of the class type represented by the `Type` `T` and $\mathrm{T}_1, \ldots, \mathrm{T}_n$ are the types of these fields. Note that `a` and `b` are assumed to be converted by the *TypeConverter*, i.e., without referenciation their top-level function symbol is ^{v}.

8.54. `a`, `b`, and `c` are assumed to be side-effect free expressions.

The methods `createElementaryAssignment` and `getType` of the class `JavaCUnfoldAssignment` play similar roles as the methods `createElementaryTerm` and `getType` of the class `TermFactory`, but they cannot be substituted for each-other, because the former operate on `ProgramElements` and the later on `Terms`.

8.5.4.4 Unfolding of assignments in the logic part

Unfolding of assignments in the logic part is accomplished by the *AbstractMetaOperator* `#assignmentToUpdates`, which is implemented by the class `AssignmentToUpdates`. Thus the class is derived from the class `AbstractMetaOperator`, but also from the interface `TermFactory.ElementaryTerm`. It takes three arguments, where the first two arguments are the left-hand side and the right-hand side of the assignment from which updates are created and the third argument is the formula which shall be nested in the update. Using the method `bestCommonType` a `Type` is determined from the first two arguments of the meta construct. This `Type` is used for unfolding by the method `unfold` of the `TermFactory` to produce elementary `Updates`. The creation of an elementary `Update` is done by the method `createElementaryTerm`, which is inherited from the interface `TermFactory.ElementaryTerm`. In order to make the method `unfold` use the method `createElementaryTerm` the `AssignmentToUpdates` object is passed to `unfold` as argument. Finally the created elementary `Updates` are merged into a parallel `Update` and a `Term` is constructed from this parallel `Update` and the third argument of the meta construct as target. The meta construct is integrated into the system by extending the class `AbstractMetaOperator` with the attribute `META_ASSIGNMENTTOUPDATES`, which is initialized with an `AssignmentToUpdates` object.

This meta operator is used by the rules with the name pattern `javaC_AsignToUpd_`*`SVSort`*`_`*`SVSort`* as exemplified by the following taclet definition:

```
javaC_AToU_var_var {
  \find (
    \modality{#allnormalass}
       {.. #var0 = #var1; ...}
    \endmodality(post)
  )
  \replacewith (
    #assignmentToUpdates(
        #var0,
        #var1,
        \modality{#allnormalass}{.. ...}\endmodality(post)
)
  )
```

```
    \displayname "JC_AssignToUpd_var_var"
};
```

8.5.4.5 Unfolding of comparisons

Unfolding of a comparison between two terms by the equality predicate into a conjunction of comparisons is performed by the meta construct `#unfoldEquals`. The meta construct is implemented by the class `UnfoldEquals`, which is derived from the class `AbstractMetaOperator` and implements the interface `TermFactory.ElementaryTerm` just like the meta construct `#assignmentToUpdates` described above. The meta construct takes two arguments which are the operators of the comparison. The unfolding is performed when the method `calculate` is invoked, which again uses the method `unfold` from the class `TermFactory`. As the second argument of `unfold`, which determines how the comparison terms between the sub-variables are constructed, `this` is passed. The implemented method `createElementaryTerm` creates an equality term using the method `createEqualityTerm`. The execution of the method `calculate` results in the rewrite rule:

$$
\begin{array}{l}
\texttt{\#unfoldEquals(v(a),v(b))} \rightsquigarrow \\
\quad \texttt{v(}.m_{i_k}\texttt{...v(}.m_{i_1}\texttt{(v(a)))...)} \;=\; \texttt{v(}.m_{i_k}\texttt{...v(}.m_{i_1}\texttt{(v(b)))...)} \;\; \texttt{\&} \\
\qquad\qquad\qquad\qquad \vdots \qquad\qquad\qquad\qquad \texttt{\&} \\
\quad \texttt{v(}.m_{j_k}\texttt{...v(}.m_{j_1}\texttt{(v(a)))...)} \;=\; \texttt{v(}.m_{j_k}\texttt{...v(}.m_{j_1}\texttt{(v(b)))...)}
\end{array}
$$

where `&` is the syntactical notation in the taclet language for the logical connective $\wedge$. The function symbols $.m_{i_1} \ldots .m_{i_k} \ldots .m_{j_1} \ldots .m_{j_k}$ stand for the object fields (*AttributeOps*) of the `Type` which is determined by the method `bestCommonType` with the parameters `v(a)` and `v(b)`. It is important to be aware of the fact that the passed program variables are in the logic part.[8.55] A comparison between program variables like `a=b` cannot be unfolded because in the logic part they are pointers. The method calculate tries, also, to evaluate the comparisons statically, which may result in a *large* conjunction of trivial formulas, namely true and false. In order to reduce the amount of user interaction the method `createJunctorTermAndSimplify` is used to create the conjunction, which automatically simplifies trivial conjunctions. The usefulness of this method becomes obvious by example `assignment5.key`. The meta construct is integrated into the system by extending the class `AbstractMetaOperator` with the attribute `META_UNFOLDEQUALS`, which is initialized with an `UnfoldEquals` object.

Unfolding of a comparison can be performed by using the taclet `javaC_unfoldEquals` which uses the described meta construct:

8.55. Therefore not the program variables are passed, but *terms* with the top-level function symbol v and the program variables as *sub-terms*.

```
javaC_unfoldEquals {
  \find ( t0 = t1)
  \replacewith( #unfoldEquals(t0,t1) )
  \displayname "JC_unfoldEquals"
};
```

8.5.5 Guidelines for the implementation of deep copy updates

From the descriptions of the concepts in KeY and the experience from the implementation of the prototype some required implementation tasks for structural updates can be concluded. The following list is not complete, but is a good starting point.

- Derive classes `DeepCopyUpdate` and `StructuralUpdate` from the class `Update`.
- The *UpdateFactory* must be extended for the creation of `DeepCopyUpdate` and `StructuralUpdates` from `AssignmentPairs`
- *AbstractUpdateRules* which use ordinary updates must be removed and replaced by rules for *DeepCopyUpdates* according to the calculus of structural updates in section ?. The simplification rules of both update types (KeY updates and deep copy updates) are not compatible.
- An *Operator* for the espilon term must be introduced.

8.5.6 Reference and dereference operators

In this section we describe two possible approaches of the implementation of the reference and dereference operators, according to the two approaches of converting of program variables to terms in section 8.5.3, which is either by using a meta construct or the *TypeConverter*. Furthermore, we address an issue relevant for unfolding, namely type informations. We describe a solution how the type informations of a dereferenced program variable from the program part can be made available in the logic part through the *Sort* of a *Term*.

8.5.6.1 Implementation by meta constructs

Following the approach of converting program variables to the logic part by a meta construct, the created term can be dereferenced by embedding it as argument of function `v`. This can be simply expressed in the taclet language by the following taclet definition:

```
javaC_var_deref_nse {
  \find (
    \modality{#allnormalass}
      {.. #var1 = #t.#deref(#nse2); ...}
    \endmodality(post)
  )
  \replacewith (
    {#insertV(#var1):=v(#insertV(#nse2))}
    \modality{#allnormalass}
      {.. ...}
    \endmodality(post)
  )
  \displayname "JC.var_deref_var"
};
```

For the schema variable `#deref` (defined in section 8.3.1), for matching with the JAVAC operator `JavaC.deref`, a new *ProgramSVSort* is introduced by extending the class `ProgramSVSort` with the attribute `MN_DEREFERENCE`, which is initialized with `new SpecialMethodName(new Name("JavaCderef"), "deref")`. Similarly for the schema variable `#adrOf` for matching with the JAVAC operator `JavaC.adrOf` the `ProgramSVSort`: `new SpecialMethodName(new Name("JavaCadrOf"), "adrOf");` is added. The JAVAC operator `JavaC.adrOf` is used for referenciation, which in contrast to dereferenciation, requires the removal of the top-most function `v` of the converted term. This can be done with the meta construct `#insertVIgnoreTop` which is represented by a `MetaEmbedSubsInFunction` object like the meta construct `#insertV` (see section 8.5.3), but the arguments in the initialization of the object differ from the arguments in the initialization of the object representing `#insertV`. This has the effect, that the top-most *Term* with the *Operator* `v` is not created. In other words when the meta construct is applied on a program variable `x` the result is `x` and for the program variable `a.b.c` the result is `v(v(a).b).c`. The taclet which handles referenciation using this meta construct is defined as follows:

```
javaC_var_adrOf_nse {
  \find (
    \modality{#allnormalass}
      {.. #var1 = #t.#adrOf(#nse1); ...}
    \endmodality(post)
  )
  \replacewith (
    {#insertV(#var1):=#insertVIgnoreTop(#nse1)}
```

```
    \modality{#allnormalass}
      {.. ...}
    \endmodality(post)
  )
  \displayname "JC.var_adrOf_nse"
};
```

Here, the drawback of the conversion by a meta construct becomes visible. The handling of the conversion and other issues like dereferenciation and referenciation must be both expressed in the taclets. Furthermore, individual rules must be written for different combinations of reference and dereference operators on the left-hand side and right-hand side of an assignment or there must exist rules which break-down assignments with complex reference and dereference expressions into assignments with simpler expressions. The main drawback is, however, that loss of type informations as described in section 8.5.6.3 cannot be *fixed* which makes this approach incompatible with unfolding.

It may be necessary reference (to obtain a pointer/reference to) a term in the logic part like it is done in the taclets `javaC_AsignToUpd_`*SVSort*`_`*SVSort*`_checked` and `javaC_unfoldEquals_checked` presented in section 8.5.7. In this case the meta construct `#insertVIgnoreTop` is useless, because no additional functions must be inserted into the term. The removal of the top-most function `v` can be performed by the meta operator `#adrOf` which is implemented by the class `AdrOf` derived from class `AbstractMetaOperator`.[8.56] The meta construct has arity one and is applied on *Terms* with the *Operator* `adrof`; the function `adrof` is defined in section 8.3.1. The argument of the function `adrof` is expected to be a *Term* with the *Operator* `v`. If `v` is not provided — for instance because it has been already removed like in the case `JavaC.adrOf(JavaC.adrOf(x))` — the *Term* on which the meta construct operates remains unchanged, i.e., the previous example would yield the *Term* `adrof(x)`.[8.57] The execution of this meta operator performs the following rewrite rule:

$$\texttt{\#adrOf(adrof(}X\texttt{))} \rightsquigarrow \begin{cases} x\,,\text{if } X = \texttt{v}(x) \\ \texttt{adrof}(X), \text{otherwise} \end{cases}$$

Note, the meta construct `#insertVIgnoreTop(`x`)` could also be realized by the construct `#adrOf(adrof(#insertV(`x`))`.

8.56. There is also a schema variable with the same name.

8.57. Assuming that the *TypeConverter* is used for conversion of the program variable `x`.

8.5.6.2 Implementation by the *TypeConverter*

Handling of the reference and dereference operators by the *TypeConverter* is the preferred solution. Interesting about this approach is that no additional taclets have to be written. The effect of the JAVAC operator `JavaC.adrOf` is computed in the method `convertToLogicElement`. The method retrieves a `MethodReference` and obtains the name of the represented *MethodReference* by the method `getMethodName` of the `MethodReference` (see section 8.4.2). In case the name equals 'adrOf', the argument of the `MethodReference` is obtained by the method `getArgumentAt` and converted by the method `convertToLogicElement`. The top-most `Term` with the *Operator* `v` is removed by returning only the sub-`Term` of the created `Term`.

The conversion of an expression with the top-level JAVAC operator `JavaC.deref` works analogously to the conversion of the JAVAC operator `JavaC.adrOf` in the method `convertToLogicElement`. The name of the *MethodReference* is checked to be equal with 'deref' and the argument retrieved by the method `getArgumentAt` is converted by the method `convertToLogicElement`. The returned `Term` is finally passed through the method `embedInV`.

8.5.6.3 Handling of type informations

Determining the type of the operands is tricky in presence of the dereference operator due to the inexistence of pointer types in the JAVA CARD type system. In JAVAC pointer types are represented by the JAVA type `Object`. If a pointer variable is dereferenced then no type informations are available for this expression, because the JAVAC operator `JavaC.deref` is of type `Object` or `int`, depending on which declaration of the method is chosen. The result of the dereferenced variable may have the type of another pointer, a compound type, or of a basic type, and has nothing to do with the type of `JavaC.deref`. The correct type information is, however, crucial for unfolding, because otherwise the attributes of the operands cannot be determined. For instance, when regarding only the program part, in the assignment `a=JavaC.deref(b)` the type of `JavaC.deref(b)` is `Object`, but the real type which would be expected in C is unknown. The strategy of the method `bestCommonType` fails in the case of the assignment `JavaC.deref(a)=JavaC.deref(b)`. The type of both operands is `Object` which represents a pointer, but the intended C type may be a structure. Regarding the logic part, the *TypeConverter* converts the expression `JavaC.deref(a)` into the *Term* `v(v(a))`, which has the same *Sort* as the sub-*Term* `a`. The expression `a` is, however, a pointer, because it is dereferenced, and it points to an object of some type, but the `Sort` of the *Term* `a` has as nothing to do with the *Sort* of the dereferenced object.

To provide the correct type informations for the whole unfolding procedure the left-hand side of the assignment must be type-casted. This explains why the class type `Object` has been chosen to represent pointer types; it can be casted to arbitrary class types representing different structures. The conversion of a `TypeCast` is implemented by the method `convertTypeCast` and requires a *trick*. The goal of the conversion is that the implicit type informations of the *TypeCast* of an expression — for instance `(structA)JavaC.deref(a)` — becomes the *Sort* of the *Term* which is created by conversion from the expression. First of all, the expression in the *TypeCast* must be converted — which yields the *Term* `v(v(a))` from the above example. In order to retrieve the *Sort* of the *TypeCast*, the `TypeRef` contained in the `TypeCast` is retrieved from which a `KeYJavaType` containing the `Sort` can be accessed by the method `getKeYJavaType` (see section 8.4.3).

Once the `Term` is created, it is, however, too late to change its `Sort`, because the `Sort` of a `Term` is set during the creation of the `Term` by using the method `sort` of the `Operator` of the `Term` as described in section 8.4.4. The idea is to extend the method `sort` of the class `NonRigidFunctionVarySort` — which represents the *Operator* `v` in this case — with a hash table which can be dynamically extended with individual *Sorts* for *Terms* with this *Operator*. The `String` retrieved by the method `toString` of the created `Term` is used as the key and the `Sort` implicitly contained in the *TypeCast* as a value of the hash table. In order to extend the hash table the class `NonRigidFucntionVarySort` is extended by the method `setSubTermDependentSort` which is invoked by the method `convertTypeCast` when the `Term` and the `Sort` are obtained. The method `sort` of the class is modified such that if the hash table contains an entry for the *Term*, it returns the saved `Sort`, otherwise the method `sort` returns the *Sort* of the first sub-*Term* as described in section 8.5.3. The trick is that after the `Term` is created and the hash table is extended with the sub-*Term* dependent *Sort* the *Term* is created *again*.[8.58] Both `Terms` represent the same *Term*, but since the hash table is extended with the *Term* and `Sort` from the *TypeCast* in the second case, the method `sort` of the `Operator` delivers the correct `Sort` during the creation of the second `Term`.

Because of the need for *TypeCasts* the method `convertReferencePrefix` is extended to remove *Parentheses* in *ParenthesisedExpressions* and to forward the conversion of `TypeCasts` by the method `convertTypeCast`. The reasons for this extension is that otherwise the *ReferencePrefix* `(expr).a` cannot be converted, which is however desired in JAVAC, because `expr` is often a *TypeCast* of a *ProgramVariable* or of a dereferenced expression.

8.58. It is not necessary to create the *whole* `Term` again. It suffices to create just a new top-level `Term` with the function symbols and the sub-`Terms` from the first `Term`.

The unconstraint construction of expressions with the function `v` and and *AttributeOps* requires some modifications of the KeY prover to avoid exceptions from the syntax checking mechanisms. Because of sub-typing the runtime type of a program variable may be a subtype of its static type. Therefore a field name attached to the program variables is mapped dynamically to a field declaration of the type of the object it contains. Consider the formula `v(a)=v((v(v(p)).m)` from example `allocdelete2.key`.[8.59] The *KeYJavaType* of the term `v(v(p))` is the *KeYJavaType* of `p`. Since `v(p)` is dereferenced it must represent a C pointer which is represented in JAVAC by the class `Object`. Since all classes are derived from the class `Object` the binding of the attribute name `m` to a field declaration is ambiguous in the term `v(v(p)).m` when considering what all the possible runtime objects of `v(v(p))` could be. On the other hand, when considering the static type of `v(v(p))`, an appropriate attribute with the name `m` cannot be created, because the class `Object` of the JAVA CARD API doesn't contain this attribute. Without modifications of the system, these two problems would cause exceptions during loading of `.key`-files and creation of `Terms` like `v(v(p)).m`.[8.60] Since sub-typing plays no role in JAVAC the parts which cause exceptions for the first problem can be modified. This amounts to modifications of the methods `getAllAttributes` of class `JavaInfo` and `printInShortForm` of class `LogicPrinter` (see section 8.4.1 for the description of the methods) and the parser file `keyparser.g`.[8.61] In order to solve the second problem the method `validTopLevel` of the class `AttributeOp` is modified to perform no checking but return always true (see section 8.4.4).

8.5.7 Dynamic creation and deletion

Taclets for handling dynamic creation and deletion require the function `cr`, which states whether the object embedded as its argument is created (`cr`=1) or not (`cr`=0) and the predicate `isDynamic`, by which the taclet prevents, in a semantic sense, to delete static object. Since the argument of the function `cr` must be of a pointer type, a reference operator in the logic part is needed, which is represented by the function `adrof`. In the presence of structures, additionally quantified updates and the predicate `subStruct` are needed. The needed function and predicate symbols are declared in section 8.3.1. In addition to the predicates, also meta constructs are needed for their static evaluation and are described first.

8.59. = is the equality predicate

8.60. The exception is *caught* by an exception handler which informs the user, but this doesn't make sense for JAVAC

8.61. The modifications are very technical and give no valuable insights of the system, but they have been mentioned for a more complete documentation.

8.5.7.1 SubStruct

The class `SubStruct` is derived from the class `AbstractMetaOperator` and it implements the meta construct `#subStruct` of arity one for the evaluation of the predicate `subStruct`. The class defines in addition to the method `calculate` the methods `isSubStruct`, `isNotSubStruct`, and `isDecidable`, which are the decision procedures for the formula $x \sqsubset y$. If `isSubStruct` returns true the formula is true. If it returns false it doesn't necessarily mean that the formula is false, it may mean that the decision procedure cannot decide the truth value. The static undecidabiltiy of the predicate `subStruct` is due to the missing type informations in the enconding of pointer types. The meta construct does not consider the tpyes of the arguments, but only their term structure. The same applies to `isNotSubStruct`. It returns true only if the formula $x \sqsubset y$ is known to be false — based on the structure of the terms `x` and `y`. The static decidability of the predicate can be decided itself by `isDecidable` which returns true if `isSubStruct` returns ture or `isNotSubStruct` returns true. The implementation of the method `isDecidable` does not used the method `isNotSubStruct`, but the other way round. The method `isNotSubStruct` returns true if `isSubStruct` returns false and `isDecidable` returns true, which is equivalent to the former definition. The method `isDecidable` uses for its task the method `semanticEqualityDecidable` by which the class `Term` is extended. The equality is statically not decidable in particular in the case if a dereferenciation is not yet evaluated, for instance, in the formula `v(v(a))=v(b)`. Therefore, the method `calculate` returns the *Terms* true, or false, or in case `isDecidable` returns false the *Term* `subStruct(`x`,`y`)` is returned in its original form.

The last result may cause *infinite* application of the taclet `javaC_subStruct`, which is defined below, without any effect.[8.62] This problem can be handled by extending predicates with a flag which is set if a static decision procedure has been applied on it, but a decision could not be made. The semantic of the predicate is independent of this flag, it controls only the applicability of rules in order to prevent infinite loops. This feature bears some problems, because the flag must influence unification, but not `equalsModRenaming` and other decision procedures. The question is whether the *Term* extended with the flag should be extended by another sub-*Term* or whether the class `Term` should be extended by an attribute representing the flag. The first solution would change the arity of the *Term* and have influence on the decision procedures, but it would fit nicely with the unification procedure. In the second case the unification procedure needs to be changed.

8.62. In the KeY-prover a limit can be set on the amount of rule applications.

A better approach of handling the static undecidability of the predicate is to evaluate the static decidability of the predicate *before* the application of a taclet containing this meta construct. An elegant solution to perform this check is to introduce a new *SVSort* which allows schema variables of this sort to match only formulas for which `isDecidable` returns true. The only drawback of this approach is a reduction of speed, since it is faster to check a flag than compute the decision procedure.

The described meta construct is integrated into the system by extending the class `AbstractMetaOperator` with the attribute `META_SUBSTRUCT` and the following taclet:

```
javaC_subStruct {
  \find ( subStruct(t0,tG2))
  \replacewith( #subStruct(subStruct(t0,tG2)) )
  \displayname "JC_subStruct"
};
```

8.5.7.2 isDynamic

A decision procedure for the predicate `isDynamic` is implemented by the method `isDynamic` of the class `IsDynamic`, which is derived from class `AbstractMetaOperator`. It represents the meta construct `#isDynamic`. This meta construct checks whether the *Operator* of the passed *Term* is `objEnum`, which is the characteristic of terms which represent dynamically created objects. Furthermore, in this class the methods `isNotDynamic` and `isDecidable` are defined. The concept of these procedures follows the concepts of the decision procedures for the predicate `subStruct` described above. The method `isDynamic` returns true only if it knows that the formula is a tautology and the method `isNotDynamic` returns true only if it knows that the formula is not satisfiable. If both methods return ture the method `isDecidable` returns true as well. Analogously to the meta construct `#isDynamic` the meta construct `#nonDynamic` is implemented by reusing the methods of class `IsDynamic`. The taclets for the application of the meta construct are defined as follows:

```
javaC_isDynamic {
  \find ( isDynamic(t0))
  \replacewith( #isDynamic(isDynamic(t0)) )
  \displayname "JC_isDynamic"
};
javaC_nonDynamic {
  \find ( nonDynamic(t0))
```

```
  \replacewith(#nonDynamic(nonDynamic(t0)))
  \displayname "JC_nonDynamic"
};
```

8.5.7.3 Dynamic creation

In order to match with the JAVAC operator `JavaC.alloc` the class `ProgramSVSort` is extended by the attribute `MN_ALLOC` which is initialized with the object `new SpecialMethodName(new Name("JavaCalloc"), "alloc");`. There are two taclets for handling the dynamic creation of objects.

```
javaC_JC_alloc_toNse{
  \find (
    \modality{#allnormalass}
      {.. #nse = #t.alloc(#expr1); ...}
    \endmodality(post)
  )
  \replacewith (
    {\for quanVar;
       \if(subStruct(quanVar,
                     objEnum(nextObj)))
          cr(quanVar):=1,
     #nse:=objEnum(nextObj),
     nextObj:=add(nextObj,1)
    }
    \modality{#allnormalass}
      {.. ...}
    \endmodality(post)
  )
  \displayname "JC_alloc"
};
```

```
javaC_JC_alloc_toNse_checked{
  \find (
    \modality{#allnormalass}
      {.. #nse= #t.alloc(#expr1); ...}
    \endmodality(post)
  )
  \replacewith (
    ( {\for quanVar;
         \if(subStruct(quanVar,
                       objEnum(nextObj)))
           cr(quanVar):=1,
      #nse:=objEnum(nextObj),
      nextObj:=add(nextObj,1)
      }
      \modality{#allnormalass}
        {.. ...}
      \endmodality(post)
    )
    &
    (cr(#adrOf(adrof(#var0)))=1
  \displayname "JC_alloc_checked"
};
```

The second version of the taclet ensures that the expression of the schema variable `#nse` denotes a location which is created.

8.5.7.4 Dynamic deletion

The `ProgramSVSort` for matching with the JavaC-operator `JavaC.delete` is represented by the object `new SpecialMethodName(new Name("JavaCdelete"), "delete");` by which the attribute `MN_DELETE` of the class `ProgramSVSort` is initialized. The taclets for handling of this JAVAC operator are defined as:

```
javaC_delete_nse_NotChecked{
  \find (
    \modality{#allnormalass}
      {.. #t.delete(#expr1); ...}
    \endmodality(post)
  )
  \replacewith (
    {\for quanVar;
       \if(subStruct(quanVar,#expr1))
         cr(quanVar):=0
    }
    \modality{#allnormalass}
      {.. ...}
    \endmodality(post)
  )
  \displayname "JC_delete_nse_NotChecked"
};
```

```
javaC_delete_nse_checked{
  \find (
    \modality{#allnormalass}
      {.. #t.delete(#expr1); ...}
    \endmodality(post)
  )
  \replacewith (
      ( {\for quanVar;
            \if(subStruct(quanVar,#expr1))
              cr(quanVar):=0
        }
        \modality{#allnormalass}
          {.. ...}
        \endmodality(post)
      )
    &
      #isDynamic(isDynamic(#expr1))
    &
      cr(#expr1)=1
  )
  \displayname "JC_delete_nse_checked"
};
```

8.5.7.5 Other related extensions

```
javaC_AsignToUpd_var_var_checked {
  \find (
    \modality{#allnormalass}
      {.. #var0 = #var1; ...}
    \endmodality(post)
  )
  \replacewith (
      #assignmentToUpdates(
        #var0,
        #var1,
        \modality{#allnormalass}
          {.. ...}
        \endmodality(post)
      )
    &
      (cr(#adrOf(adrof(#var0)))=1|nonDynamic(#adrOf(adrof(#var0))))
    &
      (cr(#adrOf(adrof(#var1)))=1|nonDynamic(#adrOf(adrof(#var1))))
  )
  \displayname "JC_AsignToUpd_var_var_checked"
};

javaC_unfoldEquals_checked {
  \find ( t0 = t1)
```

```
    \replacewith(
        #unfoldEquals(t0,t1)
      &
        (cr(#adrOf(adrof(t0)))=1|nonDynamic(#adrOf(adrof(t0))))
      &
        (cr(#adrOf(adrof(t1)))=1|nonDynamic(#adrOf(adrof(t1))))
    )
    \displayname "JC_unfoldEquals_checked"
};
```

- `Junctor.validTopLevel` is extended to allow a *Junctor* to have meta construct as operands. A conjunction between a formula and a meta construct occurs in the taclet `javaC_unfoldEquals_checked`
- The taclet `javaC_unfoldEquals_checked` uses the meta construct `#adrOf` implemented by class `AdrOf` and constructs a formula which contains the predicate `nonDynamic`. If possible the predicate `nonDynamic` can be statically evaluated by the method `isNotDynamic` of the class `IsDynamic` which represents the meta construct `#nonDynamic`. The evaluation can be performed, by applying the taclet `javaC_nonDynamic`.

8.6 Examples

The thesis has a CD attached to the cover with the implemented prototype[8.63]. The installation procedure is explained in the file "README" on the CD. This section describes only briefly how to use the examples. The examples don't give any insights into proof theory; their purpose is just to test the technical features described in this chapter.

When the KeY prover is started an example can be loaded through the menu item: File → Load. The examples are located in the directory "`Examples/JavaC/`" on the CD.

The following tables are a guide for using the examples. In the left column the syntactical elements are denoted on which a rule shall be applied. Which rule shall be applied is denoted in the right column of the tables. In order to apply a rule, first click on the respective syntactical element. Then a pop-up window shows up with a list of applicable rules. A click on a rule name causes rule application. The name of the rules introduced for the prototype start with the prefix "JC". Note, all rules of the version of the prover from which the prototype has been developed are still contained in the prover. Mixing the original assignment rules with the new rules leads to meaningless results.

8.63. The original thesis with the attached CD can be found in the library of the University of Koblenz-Landau.

Assignment1.key (conversion of pointer operators)

Target	Rule name
`i=3;`	JC_AssignToUpd_var_lit
`j=i;`	JC_AssignToUpd_var_var
`l=JavaC.adrOf(j);`	JC_AssignToUpd_var_nse
`k=JavaC.deref(l);`	JC_AssignToUpd_var_nse
`<{ }>`	empty_modality

Assignment2.key (propagation of updates)

Target	Rule name
`l=2;`	JC_AssignToUpd_var_lit
`i.c3b.b1=l;`	JC_AssignToUpd_var
`j.c3b.b2=i.c3b.b1;`	JC_AssignToUpd_nse_nse
`k=j.c3b.b2;`	JC_AssignToUpd_var_nse
`<{ }>`	empty_modality

Assignment3.key (propagation of updates)

Target	Rule name
`structC[] i;`	eliminate_variable_declaration
`structC[] j;`	eliminate_variable_declaration
`l=2;`	JC_AssignToUpd_var_lit
`k=l+x;`	JC_AssignToUpd_var_nse
`i[l].c2=k;`	JC_AssignToUpd_var
`j[l].c1=i[l].c2;`	JC_AssignToUpd_nse_nse
`x=j[l].c1;`	JC_AssignToUpd_var_nse
`<{ }>`	empty_modality

Assignment4.key (Pointer operators and structures)

Target	Rule name
`structC[] i;`	eliminate_variable_declaration
`structC[] j;`	eliminate_variable_declaration
`l=2;`	JC_AssignToUpd_var_lit
`j[l+i[1].c1].c2=JavaC.adrOf(l);`	JC_AssignToUpd_nse_nse
`x=JavaC.adrOf(i[l].c3b.b1);`	JC_AssignToUpd_var_nse
`i[l].c3b.b1=JavaC.deref(j[l+i[1].c1].c2);`	JC_AssignToUpd_nse_nse
`y=JavaC.deref(x);`	JC_AssignToUpd_var_nse
`<{ }>`	empty_modality

UnfoldEquals.key, UnfoldEquals2.key (Unfolding comparison)

Click on the sub-formulas of the proof obligation consisting of an equality predicate. Apply the rule JC_unfoldEquals to test unfolding.

Assignment5.key (Unfolding)

Target	Rule name
`b.c1=JavaC.adrOf(a);`	JC_AssignToUpd_nse_nse
`a=b;`	JC_AssignToUpd_var_var
`c=JavaC.deref(a.c1);`	JC_AssignToUpd_var_nse
`<{ }>`	empty_modality

The result of this proof tree remains in the proof obligation `v(c)=v(a)` (equality comparison). The unfolded updates could not be applied on this formula. For this reason it is necessary to unfold updates and comparisons in first place. Try this example again as follows:

Target	Rule name
`b.c1=JavaC.adrOf(a);`	JC_AssignToUpd_nse_nse
`a=b;`	JC_AssignToUpd_var_var
`c=JavaC.deref(a.c1);`	JC_AssignToUpd_var_nse
`v(c)=v(a);`	JC_UnfoldEquals
`<{ }>`	empty_modality

Assignment6.key (Unfolding)

Target	Rule name
`b.c1=JavaC.adrOf(a);`	JC_AssignToUpd_nse_nse
`a=b;`	JC_unfoldassignment_var_var
20 times	JC_AssignToUpd_nse_nse
`{}`	emptyBlock
`c=JavaC.deref(a.c1);`	JC_unfoldassignment_var_nse
20 times	JC_AssignToUpd_nse_nse
`{}`	emptyBlock
`v(c)=v(a);`	JC_UnfoldEquals
`<{ }>`	empty_modality

Assignment7.key (pointer operators in presence of structures)

Target	Rule name
`b.a1=JavaC.adrOf(x);`	JC_AssignToUpd_nse_nse
`a.a2=JavaC.adrOf(y);`	JC_AssignToUpd_nse_nse
`i=((structC)(JavaC.deref(a.a2))).c2;`	JC_AssignToUpd_var_nse
`((structC)(JavaC.deref(b.a1))).c2=i;`	JC_AssignToUpd_nse_var
`<{ }>`	empty_modality

TestPredicates.key (static evaluation)

Click on the formulas with the predicates `subStruct`, `nonDynamic`, and `isDynamic` and apply the rules JC_subStruct, JC_nonDynamic, and JC_isDynamic to test the static evaluation procedures.

Assignment1.key (conversion of pointer operators)

Target	Rule name
i=3;	JC_AssignToUpd_var_lit_checked
nonDynamic(i)	JC_nonDynamic
cr(i)=1|true	concrete_or_3
..& true	concrete_and_3

The rest is as above.

methodCall1.key (call by reference as it is the case for arrays in MISRA C)

Target	Rule name
j=1;	JC_AssignToUpd_var_lit
i=Main.identity(j)	method_call (click "apply" in the pop-up window)
int i_1;	eliminate_variable_declaration
int x#0=i;	variable_declaration
int x#0;	eliminate_variable_declaration
x=j;	JC_AssignToUpd_var_var
Main(i_1)::Main.identity(x);	method_body_expand
return x;	method_call_return
i_1=x;	JC_AssignToUpd_var_var
{}	method_call_empty
{}	empty_block
i=i_1	JC_AssignToUpd_var_var
k=Main.changeParamByRef(i,2);	method_call (click "apply" in the pop-up window)
int i_1;	eliminate_variable_declaration
int value#4=2;	variable_declaration
int value#4;	eliminate_variable_declaration
value=2;	JC_AssignToUpd_var_var
Notice, no instance of the first formal parameter is created.	
Main(i_1)::Main.changeP...	method_body_expand
int ii;	eliminate_variable_declaration
Notice that the program variable i is used within the method body instead of an instance of the formal parameter as it is the case for "value"	
i=value;	JC_AssignToUpd_var_var
ii=i;	JC_AssignToUpd_var_var
return ii;	method_call_return

i_1=ii;	JC_AssignToUpd_var_var
{}	method_call_empty
{}	empty_block
k=i_1	JC_AssignToUpd_var_var
<{ }>	empty_modality

alloc_delete.key (Allocation and deallocation of memory)

Note that allocation is present only in C0 and deallocation is neither in C0 nor in MISRA C present.

Target	Rule name
a.c6=JavaC.alloc(1);	JC_alloc (click "apply")
b=(structC)JavaC.deref(a.c6);	JC_AssignToUpd_var_nse
JavaC.delete(a.c6);	JC_delete_nse_checked(click "apply")
isDynamic(objEnum(nextObj))	JC_isDynamic
subStruct(objEnum(nextObj), objEnum(nextObj))	JC_subStruct
if(true) then(1) else (cr...	ifthenelse_true
1=1	equal_literals
true & true	concrete_and_3
...true	concrete_and_3
v(b)=v(v(v(a).c6))	JC_unfoldEquals
<{ }>	empty_modality

Chapter 9
Summary and Conclusions

We have defined a dynamic logic for C0 and reused concepts developed in the KeY project like updates and refined integral types. The C0 operators are overloaded for arithmetical types and definitions of syntax and semantic are adjusted in a modular fashion. The calculus for handling of refined integral types is realized by rewrite rules which convert expressions into terms instead by rule schemata that (i) handle assignment statements, (ii) check whether expressions are defined, and (iii) implement the actual refinement of integral types at the same time.

Furthermore special concepts have been integrated for handling features not present in JAVA CARD. The handling of the reference and dereference operators, by which program variables may be assigned values without occurring in assignments, can be handled by treating program variables like objects and their value as attributes. For this purpose a special representation of program variables as terms is required. Different representations have been investigated especially with respect to deep copy assignments.

Assignments between nested structures and arrays may create "relatively big" sets of updates. Our improvement of KeY updates is realized by deep copy updates which do not require explicit listing of assignments between substructures. The development of deep copy updates required most effort in the development of the thesis and has finally resulted in a general and powerful calculus with a complex semantic. A proof of the correct behavior of deep copy updates is complicated but 65 experiments which yield the desired results give support to believe that the calculus correctly implements deep copy assignments. Furthermore, deep copy updates can be useful when mixing arithmetical and bit-wise operators; however, this issue has not been investigated any further within this thesis.

The semantic of C0 has been formalized through the definition of the semantic of CDL according to the specification of C0 in [14] and analyzed with respect to proof theory. It turns out that the non-termination property in case of undefined expressions is not suitable when using dynamic logic. As an alternative approach the notion of an error flag is manifested in the definitions of semantic and in the calculus rules. This requires however a modification of the invariant rule. A constraint consisting of the predicate *isdef* must be integrated into the invariant rule but we haven't investigated this issue any further.

A full calculus (probably complete modulo integer arithmetic) for handling C0 with integer refinement, pointer operators, and deep copy updates has been developed by an incremental extension of the rule set throughout the thesis. The rules handle all syntactical elements of the logic part and the program part. The rules of DLJ in [36] are derived rules in our calculus. We have proven this for rule (R 6.4.2) which is the most complicated one.

Because of the variety of "concepts" presented in this thesis, the thesis documents several components of KeY and can be viewed as a reference manual. Especially documented is a portion of the implementation of the KeY system. Such a documentation is simply not available otherwise. It is however important for an implementor if the KeY system should be extended for another programming language. Through the implementation of a prototype experience has been gained and documented. The result of the investigation is that a parser for C has to be integrated into the system together with a subsystem for providing static informations about the program.

C0 is a small, simple, and precisely specified C-like language. Therefore, when it comes down to create a verification system for MISRA C many details have to be addressed.

One question is whether the task of verification should be to verify specified properties of programs assuming that the program is conforming to the MISRA C specification; or whether the task of verification should include or even focus on checking whether a program is MISRA C conforming. Issues that cannot be ensured statically in general are for instance the requirement that directly and indirectly recursive functions do not occur in a MISRA C program and that a pointer value must not be passed to an object which may exist longer than the object from which the pointer was obtained.

When developing a verification system for MISRA C a decision has to be made in what respect programs should be considered correct or not, which is due to the unspecified representation of integers:

- A verified program is correct for all MISRA C implementations
- The verification system can be instantiated for a certain platform
- The verification system is designed for the verification of MISRA C programs only for certain platforms.

When a decision is made concerning the mentioned issues, then the next step can be approached by formalizing the semantic of MISRA C as it is done for C0. CDL provides a basis which can be extended for the treatment of MISRA C.

Appendix A
List of modifications and extensions

The following list consists of directory paths and filenames which are either modified or added to the KeY-system. The names after the filenames are *mostly* names of classes, interfaces, methods, and attributes which are subject to modifications or are introduced for the implementation of the prototype. The numbers behind the names are the line numbers of declarations or modifications in the files.

- → `/system/poofExamples/javaC/code/JavaC.java`: `JavaC`
- → `/system/de/uka/ilkd/key/pp/LogicPrinter.java`: `printInShortForm`(2124)
- → `/system/de/uka/ilkd/key/logic/`
  - → `TermFactory.java`: `services`(70), `createAttributeTerm`(262), `createTermAndSimplify`(724), `ElementaryTerm`(1083), `getType`(1095), `bestCommonType`(1117), `unfold`(1161)
  - → `Term.java`: `semanticEqualityDecidable`(337)
  - → `op/`
    - → `AdrOf.java`: `AdrOf`, `calculate`(35)
    - → `UnfoldEquals.java`: `UnfoldEquals`(31), `calculate`(39), `createElementaryTerm`(80)
    - → `AbstractMetaOperator.java`: `MEAT_INSERTV`(40), `META_INSERTIGNORETOP`(43), `META_ASSIGNMENTTOUPDATES`(46), `META_UNFOLDEQUALS`(52), `META_SUBSTRUCT`(54), `META_ISSTATIC`(56), `META_ISDYNAMIC`(58), `META_ADROF`(60)
    - → `ProgramVariable.java`: `isRigid`(320), `mayBeAliasedBy`(333)
    - → `QuanUpdateOperator.java`: `normalize`(818)
    - → `SubStruct.java`: `SubStruct`(23), `calculate`(30), `isSubStruct`(57), `isDecidable`(83), `isNotSubStruct`(118)
    - → `TermSymbol.java`: `isRigid`(67)
    - → `AccessOp.java`: `isRigid`(28)
    - → `MetaEmbedSubsInFunction.java`: `MetaEmbedSubsInFunction`, `isRigid`(49), `validTopLevel`(61), `calculate`(73), `calculateRecursive`(112), `mayBeAliasedBy`(175), `match`(183)
    - → `Junctor.java`: `validTopLevel`(42)

  - → NonRigidFunction.java: import(18), implements Location(28), mayBeAliasedBy(34), sort(81)
  - → AttributeOp.java: validTopLevel(91)
  - → IsDynamic: isDynamic, calculate(32), isDynamic(53), isDecidable(66), isNotDynamic(78)
  - → NonRigidFunctionVarySort.java: NonRigidFunctionVarySort, setSubTermDependentSort(45), sort(60),
- → sort/ProgramSVSort.java: MN_ADDRESSOF(121), MN_DEREFERENCE(124), MN_SIZEOF(127), MN_ALLOC(130), MN_DELETE(133), MN_ADROFASSIGN(136), canStandFor(471), SpecialMethodName(1410), canStandFor(1417)
- → parser/
  - → lexer.g: NONRIGIDVARYSORT(135)
  - → keyparser.g: getAttribute(726), pred_decl(751, 785), func_decl(863)
  - → schemajava/SchemaJavaParser.jj: PrimaryExpression(2431, 2452), KeYMetaConstructStatement(3404)
- → rule/
  - → UpdateSimplifier.java: getServices(47), UpdateSimplifier(59)
- → rule/updatesimplifier/
  - → ApplyOnNonRigidFunctionAttribute.java: isApplicable(54), updateSubTerms(125), getCondition(186),
  - → ApplyOnAccessTerm.java: compareObjects(43),
  - → ApplyOnRigidOperatorTerm.java: apply(65),
- → rule/metaconstruct/
  - → AssignmentToUpdates.java: AssignmentToUpdates(32), calculate(48), createElementaryTerm(120)
  - → MethodCall.java: import(52), createParamAssignemts(366), getVariables(438)
  - → JavaCUnfoldAssignment: JavaCUnfoldAssignment(24), symbolicExecution(39), getType(61), createElementaryAssignment(86), toRefPrefix(90), createElementaryAssignments(106), dump(223)
- → java/
  - → TypeConverter.java: convertReferencePrefix(154, 177, 179), convertTypeCast(199), embedInV(234), convertVariableReference(256, 268, 271, 274), convertArrayReference(295), convertToLogicElement(381, 393),
  - → SchemaRecoder2KeY.java: convert(160)
  - → JavaInfo.java: getAllAttributes(842, 877)

→ /system/resources/de/uka/ilkd/key/proof/rules/javaC.key

Bibliography

[1] AntLR parser generator. `http://www.antlr.org` (accessed 15th August 2005).

[2] Java compiler compiler. `http://javacc.dev.java.net` (accessed 9th August 2005).

[3] Lambda calculus. `http://en.wikipedia.org/wiki/Lambda_calculus` (accessed June 2005).

[4] AHRENDT, W., BAAR, T., BECKERT, B., BUBEL, R., GIESE, M., HÄHNLE, R., MENZEL, W., MOSTOWSKI, W., ROTH, A., SCHLAGER, S., AND SCHMITT, P. H. The KeY tool. *Software and System Modeling 4*, 1 (2005), 32–54.

[5] AMERICAN NATIONAL STANDARDS INSTITUTE. *American National Standard for Programming Languages: C,ANSI X3.159-1989*, 1989. The draft is available at `http://rm-f.net/~orange/devel/specifications/c89-draft.html` (accessed 16th February 2006).

[6] AMERICAN NATIONAL STANDARDS INSTITUTE. *Rationale for American National Standard for Information Systems: Programming Language C*, 1989. Supplement to ANSI X3.159-1989. Available at `http://www2.informatik.uni-wuerzburg.de/staff/joscho/c/c89_rat.ps` and at `http://www-info2.informatik.uni-wuerzburg.de/staff/joscho/c/c89_rat.ps` (accessed 16th February 2006).

[7] AMERICAN NATIONAL STANDARDS INSTITUTE. *ANSI/ISO 9899-1990, American National Standard for Programming Languages: C*, 1990. Revision and redesignation of ANSI X3.159-1989.

[8] AMERICAN NATIONAL STANDARDS INSTITUTE. *Technical Corrignedum Number I to ANSI/ISO 9899-1990 American National Standard for Programming Languages: C*, 1994.

[9] AMERICAN NATIONAL STANDARDS INSTITUTE. *Rationale for International Stnadard, Programming Language, C*, April 2003. Available at `http://www.open-std.org/jtc1/sc22/wg14/www/docs/C99RationaleV5.10.pdf` (accessed 16th February 2006).

[10] ATTALI, I., AND JENSEN, T. P., Eds. *Java on Smart Cards: Programming and Security, First International Workshop, JavaCard 2000, Cannes, France, September 14, 2000, Revised Papers* (2001), vol. 2041 of *Lecture Notes in Computer Science*, Springer.

[11] BECKERT, B., GIESE, M., HABERMALZ, E., HÄHNLE, R., ROTH, A., RÜMMER, P., AND SCHLAGER, S. Taclets: A new paradigm for constructing interactive theorem provers. *RACSAM*, 8 (2004), 1–37.

[12] BECKERT, B., AND SCHLAGER, S. Software verification with integrated data type refinement for integer arithmetic. In *IFM* (2004), pp. 207–226.

[13] Blackburn, P., de Rijke, M., and Venema, Y. *Modal Logic*. Cambridge University Press, Cambridge, United Kingdom, 2004.

[14] C. Berg, M. Klein, D. Leinenbach, and W. J. Paul. Formal operational semantics of C0. Internal Technical Report 8, Universität des Saarlandes, May 2004. `http://www.verisoft.de` (accessed 23rd August 2005).

[15] C. Cook, E. Cohen, and T. Redmond. A formal denotational semantics for C. Internal technical report, Trusted Information Systems, 1994.

[16] Feather, C. D. W. *The Annotated Annotated C Standard*. `http://www.lysator.liu.se/c/schildt.html` accessed 14 Febuary 2006. Review of *The Annotated ANSI C Standard* by Herbert Schildt.

[17] Fitting, M., and Mendelsohn, R. L. *First-Order Modal Logic*, vol. 277 of *Synthese library*. Kluwer Accademic Publishers, 1999.

[18] Gabbay, D. M., Hogger, C., and Robinson, J. A. *Handbook of Logic in Aritificial Intelligence and Logic Programming*, vol. 1. Oxford University Press, London, 1993.

[19] Gamma, E., Helm, R., Johnson, R., and Vlissides, J. *Design Patterns*. Addison Wesley, Boston, USA, 1994.

[20] Gladisch, C. How c differs from java for symbolic program execution. In *Proceedings, C/C++ Verification Workshop, Oxford, United Kingdom* (July 2007), H. Tews, Ed. technical report ICIS-R07015 of the Radboud University Nijmegen.

[21] Glassborow, F. Book review c:the complete reference. `http://www.accu.informika.ru/bookreviews/public/reviews/` (accessed 16th Febuary 2006).

[22] Harel, D., Kozen, D., and Tiuryn, J. *Dynamic Logic*. The MIT Press, London, England, 2000.

[23] Henk, B. *The lambda calculus, its syntax and semantics*. North-Holland, 1984.

[24] Krüger, G. *Handbuch der Java Programmierung*, 4 ed. Addison Wesley, München, Germany, 2005.

[25] Leinenbach, D. Die sprache C0. Internal Technical Report 2, Universität des Saarlandes, June 2004. `http://www.verisoft.de` (accessed 23rd August 2005).

[26] MISRA Consortium, and McCall, G. *MISRA-C:2004*, 2nd ed. MIRA Limited, Nuneaton Warwickshire UK, 2004.

[27] Mostowski, W. *Formal Development of Safe and Secure Java Card Applets*. PhD thesis, Chalmers University of Technology, Göteborg, Sweden, 2005.

[28] Norrish, M. An abstract dynamic semantics for C. Internal technical report, Trusted Information Systems, October 1994.

[29] Norrish, M. Derivation of verification rules for C from operational definitions. In *Proceedings of the 9th International Conference on Theorem Proving in Higher Order Logics: TPHOLs96* (1996), J. Grundy, J. von Wright, and J. Harrison, Eds., no. 1, pp. 69–75.

[30] Object Modeling Groupe. Unified modelling language specification version 1.5, March 2003.

[31] Papaspyrou, N. *A Formal Semantics for the C Programming Language*. PhD thesis, National Technical University of Athens, Athens, Greece, 1998. `citeseer.ist.psu.edu/papaspyrou98formal.html`.

[32] PAPASPYROU, N. A case study in specifying the denotational semantics of C. Athens, Greece, 1999. `http://citeseer.ist.psu.edu/papaspyrou99case.html` (accessed 15th Febuary 2006).

[33] PLATZER, A. An object-oriented dynamic logic with updates. Master's thesis, University of Karlsruhe, Karlsruhe, Germany, September 2004.

[34] RÜMMER, P. A language for sequential, parallel and quantified updates of first-order structures. March 2005.

[35] SCHILDT, H. *C: The Complete Reference 4th Edition*, 4th ed. McGraw-Hill Osborne Media, January 2002.

[36] SCHLAGER, S. Handling of integer arithmetic in the verification of java programs. Master's thesis, University of Karlsruhe, Karlsruhe, Germany, May 2002.

[37] SEEBACH, P. *C:The Complete Nonsense*. `http://herd.plethora.net/~seebs/c/c_tcr.html` Accessed 14 Febuary 2006. Review of *C: The Complete Reference 4th Edition* by Herbert Schildt.

[38] STEPHAN, W. Verification of pointer programs in dynamic logic. Internal Technical Report 7, Universität des Saarlandes, December 2003. `http://www.verisoft.de` (accessed 23rd August 2005).

[39] STRECKER, M. Big step semantics for C0. Internal Technical Report 23, Universität des Saarlandes, March 2004. `http://www.verisoft.de` (accessed 23rd August 2005).

[40] SUN MICROSYSTEMS, INC., SANTA CLARA/CA, USA. Java card 2.2.1 platform specification, October 2003.

www.ingramcontent.com/pod-product-compliance
Lightning Source LLC
La Vergne TN
LVHW022304060326
832902LV00020B/3262